THE MAKING OF THE
STATE ENTERPRISE SYSTEM
IN MODERN CHINA

The Making of the State Enterprise System in Modern China

The Dynamics of Institutional Change

Morris L. Bian

HARVARD UNIVERSITY PRESS

Cambridge, Massachusetts, and London, England   2005

Library of Congress Cataloging-in-Publication Data

Bian, Morris L., 1961–
   The making of the state enterprise system in modern China : the dynamics of
institutional change / Morris L. Bian
      p. cm.
   Based on the author's thesis (doctoral—University of Washington) under the title: The
Sino-Japanese War and the shaping of a new institutional pattern of state enterprise in
China, 1935–1945. Both the scope of research and period covered have been expanded.
   Includes bibliographical references and index.
   ISBN 0–674–01717–X (alk. paper)
   1. Government business enterprises—China—History—20th century.
2. Danwei—History—20th century.   3. Industrial policy—China—History—20th century.
4. Industrial management—China—History—20th century.   5. Industrial
organization—China—History—20th century.   6. Ordnance—Manufacture—History—20th
century.   7. Steel industry and trade—China—History—20th century.   8. Iron industry
and trade—China—History—20th century.   I. Title.

HD4318.B53   2005
338.7'49'0951—dc22   2004059653

For Hui Chen

Contents

Acknowledgments

This book could not have been written without the assistance of many individuals and institutions at different stages of this intellectual journey. For my knowledge of history, I thank Howard Allen, David Bachman, Robin Zemin Ding, Kent Guy, Raymond Jonas, Kenneth Pyle, John Simon, William Turley, and Tianwei Wu. I owe special thanks to Kent Guy, William Kirby, and Kenneth Pyle for encouragement, support, guidance, and inspiration. For my knowledge of social science theories, I benefited tremendously from works by such scholars as Douglass North and Thomas Kuhn.

Many scholars, colleagues, and friends have provided a number of helpful comments and criticisms, among them are Stephen Averill, Jian Chen, Sherman Cochran, Joseph Esherick, Mark Frazier, Robert Gardella, Philip Huang, Elisabeth Köll, Lai Chi-Kong, and Edward McCord. I am grateful to them all. Parks Coble, Wayne Flynt, Kenneth Noe, and Andrea McElderry read drafts and provided valuable comments and suggestions.

Several institutions provided financial resources essential for research. My initial archival research was made possible by several fellowships from the University of Washington: the Rondeau Evans Dissertation Fellowship of the Department of History, the Chester Fritz Fellowship of the Henry Jackson School of International Studies, and the T. H. Kwoh Fellowship in Japanese Studies of the Henry Jackson School of International Studies. A Humanities Dissertation Fellowship from the University of Washington enabled me to complete the dissertation in the summer of 1998. Two Competitive Research Grants from Auburn University allowed me to conduct further research in Chinese archives in 1999 and 2002.

Equally indispensable for completing this study was access to archival and other materials granted by the following Chinese institutions: the Chongqing Municipal Archives, Library of Chinese Academy of Social Sciences, Shanghai Academy of Social Sciences, Sichuan Provincial Archives, Sichuan University Library, Second Historical Archives of China, and Yunnan Provincial Archives. Special thanks go to the directors and staff of the Chongqing Municipal Archives and the Second Historical Archives of China. I am also indebted to the following individuals for stimulating discussions as well as assistance: Chen Hongmin and Chen Jianping of the Center for Studying the History of Republican China at Nanjing University; Ling Yaolun of Sichuan University; Liu Fangjian of Southwestern University of Finance and Economics; Huang Liren, Lu Dayue, and Tang Runming of the Chongqing Municipal Archives; Lü Qisu of the Library of Chinese Academy of Social Sciences; Ma Zhendu of the Second Historical Archives of China; Wu Taichang of the Institute of Economics of the Chinese Academy of Social Sciences, Rong Weimu of the Institute of Modern History of the Chinese Academy of Social Sciences; Sun Zaiwei and Wang Weixing of the Jiangsu Academy of Social Sciences, and Zhou Zhenhua of the Shanghai Academy of Social Sciences.

I extend very special thanks to Parks Coble and William Kirby who reviewed my manuscript for Harvard University Press. At the Press, my sincere thanks to Kathleen McDermott for her interest in the project, her helpful suggestions along the way, and her timely responses to my queries. I am also indebted to Lewis Parker, editor at Westchester Book Services, for overseeing manuscript editing and production. Special thanks also go to Betty Pessagno for first-rate work in copyediting the manuscript. Finally, I gratefully acknowledge assistance from Christopher Mixon of Digital Resource Laboratory at Auburn University for enhancing images used in this book.

I gratefully acknowledge the support of Auburn University and especially my colleagues in the History Department who have either commented on aspects of my work or been supportive in other ways. Many personal friends and fellow students during my years in graduate school have also provided much needed moral support, among them are Harry Ammon, James Anderson, Jian Chen, Yingcong Dai, Renwei Huang Yi Li, Kan Liang, Robin McNeal, Steven Miles, Donglai Ren, Thomas Riley, Jennifer Rudolph, Steven Udry, Xu Wang, Heng You, and Qiang Zhai. My greatest debt, however, is to my wife, Hui Chen. This book would not have been possible without her support, companionship, and sacrifice.

Finally, I thank the Business History Conference for permission to reprint, in revised form, portions of an article, "The Sino-Japanese War and the Formation of the State Enterprise System in China: A Case Study of the Dadukou Iron and Steel Works, 1938–1945," which appeared in *Enterprise & Society* 3 (March 2002): 80–123. I also draw on reworked portions of "Building State Structure: Guomindang Institutional Rationalization during the Sino-Japanese War, 1937–1945," which appeared in *Modern China* 31, no. 1 (January 2005): 35–71. Material in this article is used here with permission from Sage Publications, Copyright © 2005.

Note on Romanization

In this work, the system generally used to romanize Chinese names is *pinyin*. In two cases, however, I have kept to traditional usage where it is firmly established; thus Sun Yatsen rather than Sun Zhongshan, and Chiang Kaishek rather than Jiang Jieshi.

The other Chinese mentioned in the text and Notes are given in *pinyin*. In cases where authors themselves used a different romanization, their names are given in *pinyin*, followed by their preferred form in parentheses.

THE MAKING OF THE
STATE ENTERPRISE SYSTEM
IN MODERN CHINA

Introduction

The fate of China's state-owned enterprise is uncertain at the dawn of the twenty-first century, but there is little doubt that the economic history of twentieth century China is to some extent the history of the rise, development, and decline of the state enterprise system. The term *state enterprise system* refers to the set of defining organizational and management characteristics of China's state-owned enterprise, which took shape during the Sino-Japanese War (1937–1945) and by the late 1950s had expanded to include the entire industrial sector. Not only does the state enterprise system form the core of China's economic system, but also it constitutes an integral part of China's state structure inasmuch as virtually all state-owned enterprises fall under the jurisdiction of the state economic bureaucracy. The defining characteristics of the state-owned enterprise include a bureaucratic governance structure, distinctive management and incentive mechanisms, and the provision of social services and welfare.[1]

These three defining characteristics manifest themselves in Chongqing Iron and Steel Corporation, a state-owned enterprise that ranked among the fifty largest industrial enterprises in China in 1994, with 49,625 employees and a capitalization of Ch$6 billion.[2] First, The Chongqing Iron and Steel Corporation is organized much like a formal administrative bureaucracy. Its top leaders included a general manager, a party secretary, and several deputy managers and deputy party secretaries. Under the top leaders were sixty-nine division-level units, which included twenty-three factories and collieries, fourteen subsidiary organizations, twenty-two administrative divisions and offices, and eight organizations of party, trade unions, and youth leagues. Many of these division-level units were not directly related to productive activities, but included party organizations, party-controlled trade unions, and communist youth leagues. They also contained a host of social service and welfare organizations, such as divisions of general affairs, hygiene, housing, and education.[3] All division heads were appointed officials with ranks and corresponding privileges.

Officials and managers of the Chongqing Iron and Steel Corporation often use ideological and psychological incentive mechanisms such as "emulation campaigns" to motivate employees to increase productivity. In 1994, it organized fifteen factories in an emulation campaign designed to attain the best targets in sixty-six categories of technology in order to raise production efficiency.[4] It also launched a campaign in technical training and emulation involving more than 12,300 employees in 153 types of work and procedures.[5] Even the Communist Youth League and the Association of Science and Technology undertook emulation campaigns.[6]

Finally, the Chongqing Iron and Steel Corporation provides comprehensive social services and welfare for its employees. As of 1994, a housing division provided 36,968 family housing units under its central administration in Chongqing.[7] The educational division operated seven kindergartens, eleven primary and secondary schools, one teachers' training college, and twelve school-run factories.[8] A large hospital and four outpatient clinics operated under the auspices of the hygiene division, with comprehensive medical facilities and more than 800 employees of its own.[9]

Competing Interpretations

When, how, and why did such an institutional pattern of state-owned enterprise take shape? Although studies of Chinese economic institutions abound, none explicitly addresses this question. This is due in part to the dominance and persistence of the view that China's basic economic system and its development strategy for the post–1949 period was a duplicate of the Stalinist model. As early as 1959, A. Doak Barnett wrote, "Although the Chinese Communists introduced significant innovations in their specific methods and timetable for socializing China's economy, they accepted with few, if any, major reservations the Soviet conception of rapid, forced industrialization, under state direction and control."[10] Less than a decade later, K. C. Yeh argued that the Communist development strategy almost completely duplicated the Soviet model. According to Yeh, the main features of the Soviet strategy included a steep rate of capital formation, overwhelming emphasis on industrial development, high priority of heavy industry in investment allocation, and preference for large plants and capital-intensive techniques.[11]

In a study published in 1971, Chu-yuan Cheng made the same argument about Communist development strategy.[12] As late as 1981, Cheng continued to assert that China's development strategy during the early 1950s was "almost a duplicate of the Stalinist model." In Cheng's view, Chinese leaders selected the Soviet model for three reasons. First, the Soviet model was the only one that was at once available, ideologically acceptable, and already tested in practice. Second, China anticipated Soviet aid. Finally, Communist leaders did not have a workable alternative of their own when they launched their industrialization program.[13]

Such an interpretation of China's development strategy finally found expression in the authoritative *Cambridge History of China* published in the early 1990s. According to Dwight H. Perkins, not only had the tools of planning and control over China's socialized economy been "borrowed wholesale" from the Soviet Union, but China's economic strategy emphasizing heavy industry was "virtually a carbon copy of Stalin's development strategy for Russia in the 1930s."[14] As late as 1999, Robert F. Dernberger continued to define the "adoption and implementation of the Soviet-type economy as China's economic system" as a major distinguishing feature of the period between 1952 and 1975.[15] Most recently, Louis Putterman and Xiao-yuan Dong reiterated the argument. In their view, "the role played by state industry in China's economic transformation between the 1950s and the late 1970s followed the pattern pioneered in the Soviet Union," although Mao Zedong attempted to achieve more rapid industrial growth "once the basic Soviet institutional model was in place."[16] Historians appear to have been satisfied with such an interpretation because there has been a general lack of interest in exploring the indigenous roots of China's economic system in the period before 1949.[17] When scholars do explore the indigenous roots of post–1949 institutions, such as the *danwei* (unit) system, they tend to focus on Communist institutions and practices.[18]

Since the early 1980s, scholars have offered different interpretations about when, how, and why the *danwei* system took shape. In the view of Gail Henderson and Myron Cohen, the *danwei* system emerged during the 1950s as part of the national plan to restrict the migration of rural residents into cities, to socialize industry and commerce, and to develop a rational system of job allocation and distribution of goods and services.[19] Others came to similar conclusions. Martin Whyte and William Parish argued that the distinctive features of the Chinese model of urbanism arose "not from a special Chinese historical and cultural tradition, but from changes introduced after 1949." Although they admitted that some large firms in pre–

1949 China provided housing and other amenities, they insisted that the "extensiveness of the resources provided to, and of the controls exercised over, employees by modern work units in China has no real parallel."[20]

Elizabeth Perry recently traced the origins of the *danwei* system to the government's labor policies in the early 1950s. According to Perry, it was the labor policies of that decade that institutionalized the *danwei* system. Nevertheless, Perry differed from earlier scholars in that she found a connection between the labor policies in the 1950s and the Communist labor movement from the 1920s through the 1940s. The officials in charge of labor policy were virtually all former leaders of the Communist labor movement. Perry argued that the *danwei* system thus should be understood "as the outcome of a heritage of protest—specifically labor conflict—rather than as the product of a simple Leninist imposition from above."[21]

In the first major monographic study of the *danwei* system, Zhou Yihu and Yang Xiaomin offered a comprehensive analysis of the structure, function, and evolution of the *danwei* system between 1949 and the 1990s. However, the authors did not look into the period before 1949 because they argued that the *danwei* system was "a product of building new state power" after 1949.[22]

Still, other scholars believed that the *danwei* system dates from the period before 1949. Lu Feng, for instance, traced the *danwei*'s origins to the period of revolutionary struggle of the Chinese Communist Party during the 1930s and 1940s. According to Lu, in its armed struggle against the Nationalist government, the Communist Party established its own government agencies, social service organizations, factories, and educational institutions in the base areas. They constituted the embryonic form of *danwei*. After its victory in 1949, Lu argued, the Communist Party began implementing social and political reorganization in order to realize socialist industrialization. In the process, the majority of Chinese people became members of political, military, economic, and cultural organizations, which took the form of *danwei*. Seen from such a perspective, *danwei* is the organizational by-product in China's drive toward socialist industrialization.[23] Later, Lu further developed this line of argument. He maintained that the *danwei* system had its origins in the Communist supply system of the revolutionary base areas and in the efforts made in the early 1950s to take over urban society by means of mobilization from below.[24]

Lü Xiaobo advanced a similar argument by focusing on the Communist free supply system and related practices of economic self-reliance that emerged in the Communist base areas. According to Lü, the Communist Party encouraged its administrative and military units to engage in production and permitted them to retain a portion of their revenues as collective assets. This development created a "small public," a realm that constitutes the "institutional foundation for units to pursue their own tangible interests." Lü concluded that "the economic and welfare functions of work units are rooted in the practices and institutions of the Yan'an era."[25]

In contrast to a rural, Communist explanation of the origins of the *danwei* system offered by Lu Feng and Lü Xiaobo, Yeh Wen-hsin searched for an "urban origin of the Communist *danwei*" by focusing on the Bank of China during the 1930s and 1940s. Yeh showed that the Bank of China built housing compounds for its employees, interconnected with gardens, pavilions, athletic fields, tennis and basketball courts, an auditorium, and classrooms. Yeh also demonstrated that at the heart of the banking organization was a "moralistic managing philosophy" that placed heavy emphasis on the character and behavior of employees. In Yeh's view, so much of an employee's daily life fell under the orchestration of corporate leadership that "most boundaries between the private and the public, the personal and the professional, were erased in this pervasive moralism." Yeh argued that the urban form of life in the Bank of China "bears a striking resemblance" to *danwei* in the post–1949 period: "although urban corporate communities may not have been the immediate and principal—institutional precursors of the socialist *danwei* in Communist cities, by the time the Communists moved into the city with their system of collective residential and work arrangements, a significant portion of Shanghai's middle-class urbanites had already been socialized by decades of comparable communal experience."[26]

Most recently, Mark W. Frazier presented the argument that "what we now called the *danwei* was not a single institution but was comprised of distinct institutions or rules and norms for how workers would be hired, organized, and compensated" or what he labeled "labor management institutions." For Frazier, "The *danwei* as it evolved in Chinese industry can be understood as a matrix of labor management institutions overlaid at different periods between the 1930s and the late 1950s. Economic and political crises of various sorts . . . mandated state intervention in the relationship between employers and workers. During such periods of crisis, state officials devised new institutions of labor management and workers and managers embedded these institutions within existing norms and rules."[27]

The Theoretical Framework

The works discussed above shed light on the significance of Soviet influence and the *danwei*'s possible origins in the Communist free supply system, in the heritage of labor protest, in the management practice of a major bank, and in the evolution of labor management institutions. Yet the arguments presented in these studies in the end are unable to explain the full range of possible origins of China's post–1949 state enterprise system and the *danwei* system. What we need is not simply another argument but a new theory, one that can account in a more satisfactory way for the endogenous and exogenous origins of China's state-owned enterprise and *danwei* systems. In sketching the outlines of just such a theory below, it is helpful first to address problems of the prevailing theory of institutional change, then offer an alternative theory that incorporates the insights of the New Institutional Economics and cognitive science, and finally describe how the new theory helps explain the formation of China's state enterprise system.

Many schools of thought in social sciences have contributed to our understanding of institutional change.[28] New Institutional Economics, in particular, has offered a dynamic framework for understanding institutional change, especially institutional change of a gradual and incremental nature. For example, based on his study of the economic history of Europe and the United States, Douglass C. North developed a theory of institutional change involving institutions and organizations. According to North, institutions are the humanly devised constraints that structure human interaction, whereas organizations are groups of individuals bound by some common purpose to achieve objectives. For North, "if institutions are the rules of the game, organizations and their entrepreneurs are the players."[29] Moreover, "institutions change, and fundamental changes in relative prices are the most important sources of that change. . . . [For] relative price changes alter the incentives of individuals in human interaction." In fact, according to North, not only do price changes constitute the causal forces for changes in institutions, "institutional change is typically incremental and is path-dependent."[30]

North's theory of institutional change provides a powerful explanation of the dynamics of gradual or incremental institutional change within a market-oriented economic system. Especially useful is the concept of "path dependence," which, as North defined it, refers to the "powerful influence of the past on the present and future."[31] For example, in explaining how the Northwest Ordnance "provided the basic framework dictating the pattern of expansion of the United States over the next century," North concluded that "Once a development path is set on a particular course, the network externalities, the learning process of organizations, and the historically derived subjective modeling of the issues reinforce the course."[32]

Despite these insights, critical questions remain. What do we mean by "institutions"? Must we distinguish between institutions and organizations? What causes institutional change? How should we define path dependence? Why is institutional change path-dependent? Can institutional change be path-independent? Why? How do we explain institutional change that is radical or revolutionary?[33]

Following North's example, most institutional economists define institutions as humanly devised systems and principles or the so-called rules of the game. Elias L. Khalil draws a sharp distinction between institutions and organizations. For him, "institutions are formal and informal social constraints," whereas "organizations are agents like households, firms, and states."[34] Eirik G. Furubotn and Rudolf Richter define "institutions" as "a set of formal and informal rules, including their enforcement arrangements."[35] By contrast, many economic historians define institutions as organizational establishments, such as the government, corporations, and religious organizations. Alfred D. Chandler Jr. uses the term *institutions* in the sense of modern business enterprise when he addresses the issue of decision making and institutional change in American business history.[36] Alan Booth, Joseph Melling, and Christoph Dartmann also define institutions as "organizations which pursue the collective interests of their members."[37]

In contrast to these definitions, the term *institutions* acquires a different meaning in this study. It refers not only to the humanly devised systems and principles that define and structure human action and interaction but also to the organizational establishments that embody these systems and principles. The humanly devised systems and principles and the organizational establishments can be viewed as complementary and inseparable: there are no humanly devised systems and principles without corresponding organizational establishments, and vice versa. When institutions change, both the humanly devised systems and principles and organizational establishments change.

Central to the understanding of institutional change is the theory of mental models. According to a leading authority in cognitive science, "human beings understand the world by constructing working models of it in their minds," models that are appropriately called mental models.[38] By definition, "a mental model is a representation that corresponds to a set of situations and that has a structure and content that captures what is common to these situations."[39] As such, "the structures of mental models are identical to the structures of the states of affairs, whether perceived or conceived, that the models represent."[40]

In fact, not only are mental models "the internal representations that individual cognitive systems create to interpret the external environment," but also they constitute ideologies when groups of individuals share these models.[41] As a form of knowledge, ideologies are both propositional and prescriptive.[42] As North puts it, ideologies "provide both an interpretation of the environment and a prescription as to how that environment should be ordered."[43]

There are important differences between mental models and ideologies.[44] *Mental models* are narrow in scope and function as they develop among individuals and inform and shape individual action. By contrast, *ideologies* are broad in scope and function as they develop among groups and inform and shape collective action. In order for mental models to become ideologies—the end product of the cognitive process—members of social groups must communicate, explain, and propagate their mental models through the medium of speech or writing. As Arthur Denzau and Douglass North put it, "Mental models are shared by communication, and communication allows the creation of ideologies and institutions."[45]

Because institutions as humanly devised systems and principles and organizational establishments are based on shared mental models or ideologies, institutional change results directly from the formation or revision of shared mental models or ideologies. Indirectly and fundamentally, however, institutional change results from alteration of human conditions within existing institutional environments.

The alteration of human conditions is the fundamental cause for institutional change. The nature of the alteration not only determines the nature of the formation or revision of mental models, but it ultimately determines the nature of institutional change. To understand the formation or revision of mental models and of institutional change, one must examine the alteration of human conditions.

The alteration of human conditions takes two basic forms: normal alteration and drastic alteration. "Normal" alteration refers to ordinary changes that typically show a regular and predictable pattern.[46] The normal alteration of human conditions underscores the necessity of institutional change by exposing the inadequacy of existing institutions; it requires human actors to respond by revising their existing mental models of institutional environments. Although normal alteration of human conditions causes revision of mental models, it only modifies existing mental models.[47] In turn, the modified mental models lead human actors to partially reorder their institutional environments, a move that eventually brings about gradual or incremental institutional change.

Taken together, the normal alteration of human conditions, the modification of mental models, and the partial reordering of institutional environments explain the dynamics of gradual or incremental institutional change. Precisely because the alteration of human conditions is normal, because mental models are modified but not replaced, because the reordering of institutional environments is partial, and because institutional change is local, members of a given society typically find that this pattern of change poses less of a threat to stability. This fact may contribute to their acceptance of gradual or incremental institutional change.

By contrast, drastic alteration of human conditions causes radical or revolutionary institutional change. "Drastic" alteration means extraordinary changes that typically show no regular or predicable pattern. Although signs or indications of such an alteration can be detected, drastic alteration of human conditions often comes as a shock or surprise. In addition, drastic alteration of human conditions underscores the necessity of institutional change by exposing the inadequacy of existing institutions or the absence of needed institutions. It forces human actors to respond by revising their existing mental models of institutional environments and by developing new ones. Finally, when a drastic alteration occurs, it does not simply modify existing mental models; rather, it transforms or replaces them.[48] In turn the transformed mental models or their replacements lead human actors to completely reorder their institutional environments, a move that eventually brings about radical or revolutionary institutional change.

Taken together, the drastic alteration of human conditions, the transformation or replacement of existing mental models, and the complete reordering of institutional environments explain the dynamics of radical or revolutionary institutional change. Precisely because the alteration of human conditions is drastic, because mental models are transformed or replaced, because the reordering of institutional environments is complete, and because institutional change is broad, members of a given society typically find that this pattern of change poses more of a threat to stability. This fact may contribute to their reluctance to accept radical or revolutionary institutional change.

Unlike normal alteration of human conditions, drastic alteration of human conditions often takes the form of a crisis, triggered by either an exogenous shock such as war or aggression, or an endogenous shock such as economic depression or civil war. An examination of crisis and its effects further illustrates the causal relationship between drastic alteration of human conditions and radical or revolutionary institutional change.

Many studies show that crisis profoundly influences the evolution of the human communities. Crisis underscores the necessity of institutional change by exposing the inadequacy of existing institutions or the absence of needed institutions, and it forces human actors to respond by transforming their existing mental models of institutional environments and by developing new mental models. In turn, the transformed mental models or the new mental models lead human actors to reorder their institutional environments by extending or expanding existing institutions or creating new ones. In other words, the transformed mental models or their replacements serve as a crucial link between crisis and radical or revolutionary institutional change. One could even argue that radical or revolutionary institutional change not only results from crisis but corresponds to it. The more severe and the more sustained a crisis, the more complete and thorough the alteration of mental models, and the more radical and revolutionary the outcome of institutional change. In short, crisis not only shapes radical or revolutionary institutional change but determines its timing and magnitude.

For instance, the economic crisis triggered by the Great Depression led to radical institutional changes in the United States. Central to these changes was a redefinition of the government's role in American life as a result of New Deal legislation. For decades to come, political debate would no longer focus on whether government should intervene to steer the economy and foster social justice, but rather on how and to what extent such intervention should take place.[49] At the same time, the development of this shared mental model led national leaders to create new government organizations and expand existing ones to oversee economic activities. Then again, during World War II, the war-triggered crisis led to radical institutional changes in many belligerent nations, such as the formation of the so-called welfare state. That crisis shapes radical or revolutionary change also finds expression in the development of science. As Thomas S. Kuhn shows, "a novel theory emerged only after a pronounced failure in the normal problem-solving activity. Furthermore . . . that breakdown and the proliferation of theories that is its sign occurred no more than a decade or two before the new theory's enunciation. The novel theory seems a direct response to crisis."[50]

Nevertheless, drastic alteration of human conditions does not define the nature and character of new institutions.[51] In order to understand the nature of the new institutional arrangement, we need to introduce the concept of resource endowments. The term *resource endowments* refers to the total means within a given geographical and ecological environment that are available for the development of human society. There are two types of resource endowments in the evolution of human civilization: initial resource endowments that date from the formative period of human civilization and generated resource endowments, which are derived from human action and interaction with initial resource endowments.[52]

Initial resource endowments may be considered primary resource endowments, and generated resource endowments, secondary resource endowments. Primary resource endowments are primary because their nature determines the basic socioeconomic orientation of a civilization. By contrast, secondary resource endowments are secondary in part because they are derived from human action and interaction with primary resource endowments. Secondary resource endowments are also often less enduring than primary resource endowments. Although mountains and rivers may not change much for thousands of years, politics and regimes have emerged, prospered, declined, and vanished throughout the same period of history.

Precisely because secondary resource endowments are derived from human action and interaction with primary resource endowments, secondary resource endowments constitute the immediate resource endowments for members of the human community. Secondary resource endowments take different forms, but prominent among them are institutional endowments, which refer to the totality of institutional resources available to human communities. As Harold Demsetz puts it, "as institutions emerge, mature, and are abandoned, each generation must include in its endowment the institutions it inherits from the past. In this sense, institutions become part of a more broadly defined set of endowments."[53] Obviously, institutional endowments differ between and among different human communities. Institutional endowments are also limited at any given point in time.

That institutional endowments are limited contributes to the formation of the characteristics of the two patterns of institutional change described above. Although scholars recognize that institutional change is often characterized by path dependence, they differ in how they define that term. For William Sewell, path dependence means that "what happened at an earlier point in time will affect the possible outcomes of a sequence of events occurring at a later point in time."[54] To James Mahoney, in contrast, "path dependence characterizes specifically those historical sequences in which contingent events set into motion institutional patterns or event chains that have deterministic properties."[55] In the view of Paul Pierson, path dependence refers to the "social processes that exhibit increasing returns," which means that "preceding steps in a particular direction induce further movement in the same direction" and that "the probability of further steps along the same path increases with each move down that path."[56] For the purposes of this study, the meaning of path dependence is restricted to the properties of existing institutional patterns or arrangements that confine and limit institutional change. Such a definition helps explain the persistence of existing forms or patterns of institutional arrangements.

Why is institutional change path-dependent? Again, scholarly explanations differ. For some, human actors rationally choose to reproduce existing institutions, which leads to path-dependent change, "because any potential benefits of transformation are outweighed by the costs."[57] For others, "institutional reproduction is explained specifically because of its functional consequences for a larger system within which the institution is embedded."[58] Although these are valid and plausible explanations, institutional change is path-dependent because of the constraints of limited institutional endowments. More often than not, gradual or incremental institutional change is characterized by path dependence.

When drastic alteration of human conditions occurs, it causes transformation or replacement of existing mental models. In turn, the transformed mental models or their replacements lead human actors to reorder or restructure their institutional environments. In the process, human actors overcome the limits of existing institutional endowments by extending and expanding existing institutions or creating new ones. In other words, institutional change is not only path-dependent but path-independent. Institutional change is path-independent because of the necessity of creating new resources in order to overcome the constraints of institutional endowments. If path dependence characterizes gradual or incremental institutional change, then path independence defines radical or revolutionary institutional change.[59]

The basic chain of logic applies to both patterns of institutional change: the alteration of human conditions exposes problems in existing institutional environments. The exposure requires human actors to revise their mental models. The revised mental model then leads human actors to reorder their institutional environments, a move that eventually brings about institutional change. Under both patterns, institutional change not only results from alteration of human conditions but corresponds to it.

In part because the same logic applies to both patterns of change, it is not always easy to distinguish gradual or incremental institutional change from radical or revolutionary institutional change. In addition, elements of new institutions or new institutional arrangements typically emerge before radical institutional change takes place. Finally, what seems to be radical or revolutionary institutional change within a given business enterprise, a given industry, or a given sector of the economy may appear to be gradual or incremental institutional change in a larger context. This theory presents the "ideal type" of two basic patterns of institutional change.

All the same, the differences between these two patterns are great enough to warrant an analytical distinction between them. First, the nature of change is different. One is radical or revolutionary, and the other is gradual or incremental: the first pattern represents transformation or replacement of existing institutions, whereas the second embodies modification of existing institutions. Unlike gradual or incremental institutional change, then, radical or revolutionary institutional change exerts the most profound impact on the evolution of human society. Second, and in part as a result of the first, the transformed institutions or their replacements are incompatible with preexisting institutions, although the new institutions often contain elements of existing ones.[60] Third, radical or revolutionary institutional change typically takes place in a relatively short temporal framework as a result of sudden and extraordinary changes caused by drastic alteration of human conditions. Finally, the evolution of human society tends to alternate between these two patterns of change: a period of gradual or incremental change is often followed by a period of radical or revolutionary change.[61]

The Argument

This theory provides an essential framework for understanding the formation of China's state enterprise system. This book presents the argument that the drastic alteration of human conditions triggered by Japan's invasion of China led to a sustained systemic crisis during the Sino-Japanese War (1937–1945).[62] The crisis underscored the necessity of institutional change by exposing the inadequacy of existing institutions and the absence of needed institutions, which forced the then ruling Nationalist Party elite to respond by transforming their existing mental models of institutional environments and by developing new ones. Their transformed mental models and new mental models led them to reorder and restructure the institutional environments through the creation of a new state enterprise system, which was characterized by a bureaucratic governance structure, distinctive management and incentive mechanisms, and the provision of social services and welfare. Although it is difficult to find evidence of a direct link between the crisis and the new institutional pattern of state-owned enterprise, there is ample evidence in the form of transformed mental models and new mental models to establish a causal relationship between them.

It was not crisis, however, that defined the nature of the state enterprise system; rather, it was the availability of endogenous and exogenous resources. The present book contends that China's existing institutional resources not only limited the choices of the Nationalist elite, but also led them to create new institutional resources and to appropriate institutional resources from the advanced industrial nations. In other words, a combination of limited institutional resources, endogenous creation, and exogenous appropriation of institutional resources explain the characteristics of the state enterprise system.

This argument will be substantiated and developed in much greater detail in the chapters that follow. Chapter 1 deals with the development of the ordnance industry, demonstrating how war-triggered crisis led to the formation of new mental models or revision of existing ones and the creation of new resources in state-owned ordnance industry after the Opium War (1839–1842). From the 1860s to the 1890s, the evolution of the ordnance industry revealed a pattern of crisis, mental model formation or revision, and expansion of state ownership and management of military enterprise, a pattern that repeated itself in resource expansion and centralization during the 1930s and 1940s. Moreover, the changes that occurred during these decades were path-dependent, as crisis strengthened the existing model of state ownership and management.

Crisis also motivated the expansion of heavy industries during the Sino-Japanese War, a topic that is explored in Chapter 2. This chapter shows that the sustained systemic crisis led to the creation, expansion, and centralization of resources in major state-owned heavy industries. The Japanese invasion of Manchuria gave rise to the National Defense Planning Commission and resource investigation. The deepening of the national crisis led to both the reorganization of the National Defense Planning Commission and its reorientation. Ultimately, the war-triggered sustained systemic crisis compelled the Nationalist elite to develop a new mental model, which in turn led them to undertake large-scale heavy industrial reconstruction. As was the case in the ordnance industry, the changes that occurred during these decades were path-dependent as crisis strengthened the existing model of state ownership and management.

Building on the foundation of Chapters 1 and 2, Chapter 3 examines the defining characteristics of state-owned enterprise by focusing on enterprise governance structures. This chapter presents the argument that path dependence also characterizes the evolution of enterprise governance structure. Although crisis caused resource creation, expansion, and centralization in the ordnance and heavy industries, it strengthened not only the existing model of state ownership and management but also the existing model of bureaucratic organization of enterprises within these industries due to the nature of China's institutional endowments. At the same time, as a result of the introduction of a modern educational system early in the twentieth century and the urgent need to develop national defense industries, a new class of technocrats replaced traditional bureaucrats in state-owned enterprise in these industries.

Chapter 4 describes the creation of enterprise management and incentive mechanisms. If the evolution and expansion of the bureaucratic governance structure were largely path-dependent because of the constraints of limited institutional endowments, the creation of enterprise management and incentive mechanisms was primarily path-independent because of these mechanisms' foreign origins and their ability to overcome the limits of existing institutional endowments. This chapter shows how the sustained systemic crisis caused the formation of new mental models and the revision of existing mental models among factory officials and managers. It also shows how their new and transformed mental models led them to introduce a new system of cost accounting and undertake a work emulation campaign.

Chapter 5 discusses the development of enterprise provision of social services and welfare. It presents the argument that the crisis of national social and economic life necessitated the development of institutions of social services and welfare. It demonstrates how the war-triggered crisis led directly to the formation of new mental models and the revision of existing mental models of factory officials and managers and indirectly to the development of social service and welfare institutions. As was the case with the creation of enterprise management and incentive mechanisms, path independence also characterizes the evolution of enterprise provision of social services and welfare.

Chapter 6 explains how state-owned enterprise came to be identified as *danwei*. As the Chinese state created, developed, and expanded industrial enterprises during the war, it also designated these enterprises as *danwei*. This chapter reveals that the *danwei* designation of state-owned enterprise originated in the Nationalist struggle to rationalize state institutions in response to the war-triggered sustained systemic crisis. As a result of this designation, the characteristics that state-owned enterprise developed also became the hallmarks of *danwei*.

Chapter 7 delineates the formation of the Nationalist ideology of the developmental state. It demonstrates that the war-triggered sustained systemic crisis that shaped the making of the state enterprise system also gave rise to an ideology of the developmental state. As a radically altered but shared mental model, this ideology provided an interpretation of China's institutional environment as well as a prescription of how to reorder that environment. Ultimately, this new mental model not only formed the ideological underpinnings of the state enterprise system but led directly to its formation.

The concluding chapter analyzes the dynamics that shaped the formation of China's state enterprise system and considers the implications of this study for understanding change and continuity in twentieth-century China and for developing theories of institutional change.

CHAPTER 1

Development of the Ordnance Industry

War, domestic rebellion, and economic depression all produce drastic alterations in human conditions. When these alterations occur, they often force human actors to respond by transforming their mental models of existing institutional environments and by developing new mental models. In turn, the transformed and new models lead human actors to reorder their institutional environments. In modern Chinese history, war-triggered crisis led to the formation of new mental models or the revision of existing ones and the creation of new resources in the state-owned ordnance industry. From the 1860s to the 1890s, the evolution of the ordnance industry revealed a pattern of crisis, mental model formation or revision, and expansion of state ownership and management of military enterprise, a pattern that repeated itself in resource expansion and centralization during the 1930s and 1940s. Moreover, the changes that occurred during these decades were path-dependent, as crises strengthened the existing model of state ownership and management.

The Ordnance Industry before 1928

The modern ordnance industry began in China during the 1860s. From the 1860s to the 1920s, the industry evolved in two discernible phases, the first being the period between 1860 and 1895, and the second between 1895 and 1925. To a large extent, crisis shaped developments in both phases.

The establishment of China's modern ordnance industry was a response to the domestic and foreign crises of the 1850s and 1860s. At the beginning of the 1850s, a peasant uprising, known as Taiping Rebellion (1851–1864), broke out in Guangxi province. By 1854 rebel forces had taken the city of Nanjing and threatened to topple the Qing dynasty. At the same time, the dynasty found itself fighting a Second Opium War (1856–1860) with Britain and France. It ended in the Anglo-French occupation of Beijing and the signing of new treaties in 1860. By that date, these "multiple crises" had caused China's governing elite to develop a new mental model, as "the notion that Chinese civilization would have to undergo fundamental changes to meet the foreign threats and domestic challenges . . . was gaining acceptance by a small number of influential Chinese leaders." Their new mental model led directly to their efforts at military modernization by establishing a modern ordnance industry.[1]

Over the next three decades, the Chinese ordnance industry took on several important characteristics. First, provincial government officials such as Zeng Guofan and Li Hongzhang, not the central government in Beijing, took the initiative in establishing ordnance bureaus and factories. Following the establishment of the first ordnance bureau in 1861, provincial authorities founded twenty-six ordnance bureaus and factories before the first Sino-Japanese War broke out in 1894.[2] The imperial government's role was confined to sanctioning and encouraging the establishment and operation of modern arsenals.[3] As in other key areas in modern industrial development, the Qing government made no comprehensive long-term plans for the ordnance industry.

Second, state ownership and management characterized the ordnance industry. In China, state control of vital resources dates from the Han dynasty, when the imperial government monopolized the production of salt and iron. As late as the eighteenth century, the Qing state continued to monopolize salt production and marketing.[4] Owing in part to the availability of limited institutional endowments of state ownership and management, government agencies completely owned and organized the three major arsenals—Jiangnan Arsenal, Jinling Arsenal, and Tianjin Arsenal. Beginning in the early 1880s, some government officials called for the establishment of ordnance factories by private entrepreneurs in response to the perceived failures of state-owned arsenals and the huge expenses incurred.[5] Their suggestions persuaded the imperial court to issue edicts ordering the encouragement and recruitment of merchants to establish ordnance bureaus and factories "in accordance with Western practice, with merchants being in charge and officials providing protection."[6] However, the idea of private ownership and management also met with fierce opposition from a number of government officials. In the words of one provincial governor, "although the accumulated abuses of government arsenals must be dealt with severely, official control of ordnance factories should never be allowed to slip away."[7] In the end, no privately owned ordnance factories were ever established.

Finally, two of the three major government arsenals—Jiangnan Arsenal and Tianjin Arsenal—were located in coastal areas. Both sites were selected for convenience in supplying ordnance and ammunition to pacification forces during the Taiping Rebellion. Furthermore, the treaty port locations facilitated the purchase of the imported raw materials and the hiring of foreign technicians essential to arsenal operations.[8] By the 1870s, however, provincial officials had realized the vulnerability of coastal arsenals to attack by foreign naval forces. In an 1874 memorial, Li Hongzhang suggested that new arsenals be established at inland sites on navigable waterways to reduce vulnerability while maintaining access to water transport.[9] Three years later, Wang Wenshao, governor of Hunan province, made a similar argument: "In recent years manufacturing bureaus have been established to produce arms and ammunition in Shanghai, Tianjin, and Nanjing. Certainly nothing is more urgent than the production of arms and ammunition for the purpose of self-strengthening. Nevertheless, although coastal areas should make necessary preparations, I believe that we should do something in the interior provinces. It is hard to predict what will happen to the manufacturing bureaus in the coastal areas if a military confrontation arises, but the interior provinces will certainly be in a position to offer assistance in case of emergency if manufacturing bureaus are also established in those provinces."[10]

Unfortunately their foresight was proved correct when the French destroyed the Fuzhou Arsenal and dockyard during the Sino-French War (1884–1885). China's defeat triggered renewed debate over the issue of location for government arsenals. Shortly after the war ended, Zhu Yixin, a junior compiler of Hanlin Academy, which was an institution in charge of drafting and editing imperial pronouncements and the compilation of officially sponsored historical works, submitted a memorial in which he suggested that new arsenals be established in Jiangxi and Hubei provinces to avoid repetition of the disaster that had occurred two months earlier.[11] Bian Baodi, governor-general of Hunan and Hubei provinces, seconded Zhu's suggestion.[12] Despite such warnings, no arsenal was actually established in Hubei until 1890, when Zhang Zhidong himself transferred from the post of governor-general of Guangdong and Guangxi provinces to that of Hunan and Hubei provinces and relocated the arsenal he had established in Guangdong province to Hubei province.[13]

The first Sino-Japanese War (1894–1895) marked the beginning of the

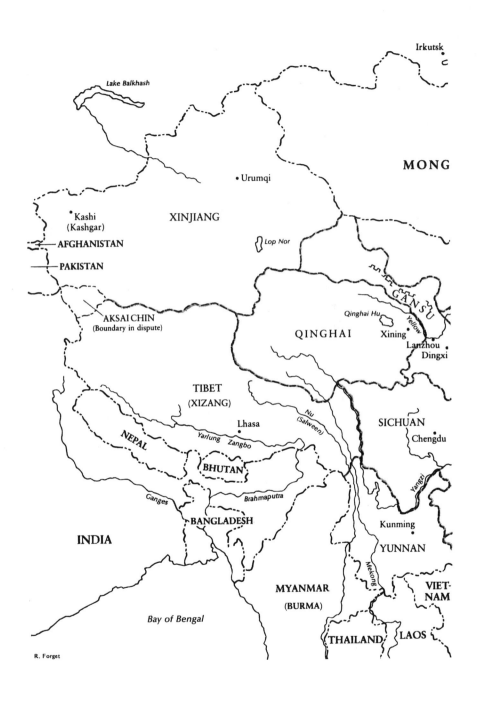

R. Forget

Administrative Regions of China. Reprinted by permission of the publisher from *China: A New History* by John King Fairbank and Merle Goldman, pp. 346–347, Cambridge, MA: The Belknap Press of Harvard University Press, Copyright © 1992, 1998 by the President and Fellows of Harvard College.

second phase of the modern Chinese ordnance industry. Although state ownership and management continued to characterize the ordnance industry, the war-triggered crisis led to several new developments after 1895. China's disastrous defeat prompted new efforts to establish and relocate ordnance bureaus and factories in China's interior after the war. As was the case with the Sino-French War a decade earlier, the Sino-Japanese War exposed the vulnerability of coastal arsenals and forced high-ranking officials to respond by revising their existing mental model to one that emphasized the interior as the ideal location for government arsenals. Their revised mental model in turn caused the imperial government to formulate a policy in favor of establishing and relocating arsenals in interior provinces.

The cognitive process of mental model revision is reflected in an 1895 memorial by Lin Shu, a member of the Hanlin Academy:

> All our shipyards and manufacturing bureaus are located in the coastal areas. Unfortunately, what we have devoted so much effort in building is also what our enemies have tried so hard to destroy. Once foreign threat becomes imminent, they are always the primary targets for attack, which often leaves them in shambles. What the French did to Fuzhou shipyard and what the Japanese did to Lushun shipyard are painful lessons for all of us. Both governor-general Shen Baozhen of Jiangsu, Jiangxi, and Anhui provinces and governor Ding Richang of Fujian province have suggested that manufacturing bureaus be established in interior provinces. Their suggestions are very valuable. I believe that we should order provincial governor-generals and governors to carefully examine the situations in the interior provinces and to relocate some of the shipyards and manufacturing bureaus to places where coal, iron and wood are readily available. The purpose is to avoid the concentration of all shipyards and manufacturing bureaus in the coastal areas, where they may expose themselves to dangerous situations.[14]

Others agreed. Zhang Zhidong, then governor-general of Hunan and Hubei provinces, wrote in July 1895, "We should establish ordnance bureaus and factories in all strategic locations, especially in the interior provinces. Only when we accomplish this could coastal areas and frontier regions receive assistance in case of a military emergency."[15] Two years later, Rong Lu, then head of the Ministry of War, also recommended the establishment of ordnance bureaus and factories in interior provinces such as Shanxi, Henan, Sichuan, and Hunan. Specifically, he suggested that

Jiangnan Arsenal "be relocated to Hunan province where it would have easy access to raw materials."[16] Ultimately, the written communications of high-ranking officials led them to develop a shared mental model, one that prompted Emperor Guangxu to issue an edict in 1897. The edict stated, "The majority of manufacturing bureaus and factories were established in the coastal areas in the past. Because the lack of warships for coastal defense has made the coastal areas vulnerable to foreign military attack, however, we must prepare for what may be coming by establishing and relocating manufacturing bureaus and factories in the interior provinces." The edict also sanctioned Rong Lu's suggestion to relocate Jiangnan Arsenal to Hunan province and ordered the provincial governor-generals and governors to "make conscientious effort to implement" the edict.[17] The new imperial policy appears to have contributed to the establishment of ten new arsenals between 1895 and 1900, as all the new arsenals were located in the interior.[18]

Ordnance officials also developed a new strategic plan in an attempt to implement the new imperial policy. Soon after Emperor Guangxu issued his edict, Liu Kunyi, then southern commissioner and governor-general of Jiangsu, Jiangxi, and Anhui provinces, reported that since Jiangnan Arsenal had been established many years earlier and had been expanding for more than a decade, it would be very difficult to relocate it to Hunan province. Furthermore, the cost for reconstruction would be very high, and most buildings would be useless once the arsenal relocated. Six months later, Liu submitted a memorial to Emperor Guangxu, further defending his decision to keep Jiangnan Arsenal where it was.[19] The matter was effectively dropped for the time being.

It was not until 1903 that Zhang Zhidong, in his capacity as acting governor-general of Jiangsu, Jiangxi, and Anhui provinces, renewed the effort to relocate Jiangnan Arsenal to China's interior. Admitting the problems and costs associated with relocation, Zhang proposed the establishment of a new branch factory instead of the wholesale relocation of Jiangnan Arsenal. He also outlined a plan for establishing the branch factory in Anhui province. According to Zhang, Jiangnan Arsenal should be reorganized as a "private enterprise" once the new factory became operational.[20] Emperor Guangxu referred the matter to the Bureau of Government Affairs (zhengwuchu) for deliberation.[21] The bureau completed deliberations three months later and submitted a written opinion in favor of Zhang's proposal to Emperor Guangxu. The emperor gave his approval a few days later.[22]

The story did not end there. Early in 1904, Zhang Zhidong decided to establish the new factory in Hunan province instead of Anhui province. In another memorial submitted in June, Zhang discussed issues such as fund raising, selecting a new site, purchasing machinery, appointing personnel, selecting weapons for manufacturing, sending talented people for training abroad, and consolidating Jiangnan Arsenal.[23] Now it was up to the newly created Bureau of Military Reorganization *(lianbingchu)* to deliberate on the memorial.[24] According to the bureau's report, "Jiangnan Arsenal has been in existence for a number of years, and occasionally there have been problems with management. It has often been pointed out that the arms and ammunition it produced are of poor quality and yet they cost huge amount of money to manufacture. Given the instability in the coastal frontier and the destruction of Fuzhou arsenal and the attack on Lushun shipyard, we believe Jiangnan Arsenal should relocate to the interior."

On the other hand, the Bureau of Military Reorganization had serious doubts about funding, the location of the new factory, and the purchase of new machinery. Consequently, it recommended the appointment of a special commissioner to investigate proposed sites before reaching definitive conclusions.[25] One month later, Emperor Guangxu sent Tie Liang, vice-president of the board of war, to Jiangnan Arsenal, and the two proposed sites for the new factory. In a report dated February 1905, Tie severely criticized management problems and abuses in Jiangnan Arsenal and endorsed wholeheartedly earlier proposals for relocation. In Tie's view, "one or two arsenals are simply inadequate" in meeting the needs for arms and ammunition for "all of China." He then proceeded to prescribe what he called a "comprehensive solution" for Chinese ordnance industry: the establishment of a southern factory in Hunan province as Zhang Zhidong had proposed earlier; the creation of a northern factory at a location to be chosen in Zhili and Henan provinces; and the continued operation of Hanyang Arsenal in Hubei province between the southern and northern factories.[26] Emperor Guangxu again referred the matter to the Bureau of Military Reorganization for deliberation. About three months later, the bureau completed its deliberation and recommended approval of Tie Liang's "comprehensive solution." Emperor Guangxu approved the recommendation.[27] In short, a new strategic plan for the ordnance industry had finally emerged one decade after China's disastrous defeat in the first Sino-Japanese War. Unfortunately, the imperial government, lacking financial resources, did not implement this well-conceived plan.[28]

Even before the new strategic plan emerged in 1905, the imperial government had begun centralizing its military organizations, including the ordnance industry. The first major move in this direction was the creation in 1903 of the Bureau of Military Reorganization, an important deliberation and decision-making agency in charge of military reform. Before its creation, provincial authorities controlled various ordnance bureaus and factories, with governor-generals exercising supervision over their operation. Afterward, the imperial government placed these provincial arsenals under the jurisdiction of the Bureau of Military Reorganization.[29] In other words, the modern provincial arsenals established before 1903 were now subject to the control of a central government agency. In 1906 the Board of War *(bingbu)* and the Bureau of Military Reorganization merged to form the Ministry of War *(lujunbu)*.[30] According to its organizational regulations, the Ministry of War consisted of ten departments *(si)*, one of which was the Department of Military Supply *(junshisi)*. It was charged with manufacturing, inspecting, storing, and distributing arms and ammunition produced in government arsenals.[31] Two years later, the Ministry of War expanded to twelve departments,[32] but when the ministry drafted new organizational regulations in early 1911, it reduced the number of departments to six. It also renamed the Department of Military Supply as the Department of Military Establishment and Manufacturing *(junzhisi)*.[33] The Qing dynasty had now created a new institutional framework for centralizing military organizations before it collapsed in 1911.

After 1911, postrevolutionary governments continued earlier efforts to centralize military organizations. According to the *Revised Official System of the Ministry of War* promulgated in 1914, the head of the Ministry of War was to assume the "responsibility of supervising and directing provincial governors and highest administrative officials in various regions in executing tasks that fall within the purview of the Ministry of War." The Department of Military Weaponry *(junxiesi)* was among the eight departments that came under the control of the Ministry of War.[34] In the following year, the Department of Military Weaponry made plans to take over five major ordnance factories in Shanghai and in the provinces of Hubei, Sichuan, Guangdong, and Henan, and to gradually relocate coastal factories in Shanghai and Guangdong province to the interior.[35] Later the Ministry of War presented another plan for consolidating ordnance factories. Among other things, the plan explained the rationale for further centralization of ordnance production:

Although our country's ordnance factories are under the jurisdiction of the Ministry of War, they are all located in the provinces, and the authority of factory directors is limited. In fact these factories have to rely on military commanders for operation. Furthermore, the factories were financially dependent on the provinces as the latter served as the source of manufacturing expenditures for these factories, a fact that resulted in repeated interference and all kinds of abuses. Therefore we now request that all ordnance factories be placed under the direct control of the Ministry of War; that responsibilities and authorities be clearly defined, and that sources of manufacturing expenditures be unequivocally stipulated, so as to prevent interference by military commanders and departments of finance in the provinces.[36]

Despite the best of intentions, the effort to centralize the ordnance industry did not succeed because China soon disintegrated into a loose federation of competing warlords. Instead, conditions in the ordnance industry continued to deteriorate, a development that manifested itself most clearly in the persistent lack of funding for ordnance factories. In January 1919, a Ministry of War report complained that manufacturing expenditures for ordnance factories were cut repeatedly after 1913. In addition, until 1917 the Ministry of Finance allocated a mere Ch$190,000 monthly for all three ordnance factories in Shanghai, Hubei and Henan provinces, which caused a sharp decrease in production and made it difficult to maintain existing operations.[37] According to another report written five months later, the Ch$190,000 figure was so inadequate that the three factories could not even produce enough cartridges for one year's target practice by the regular army. As for rifles, the entire annual output could replenish the weaponry of only one army division.[38] By the early 1920s, the situation had become desperate. A 1921 internal report of the Ministry of War stated that the Ministry of Finance had delayed payment of over Ch$5,000,000 for four major ordnance factories for two years.[39] Because no funding was forthcoming, production in many ordnance factories had stopped,[40] even employees of an entire factory had to be dismissed.[41]

The Consolidation of the Ordnance Industry

Such was the condition of the ordnance industry when the Nationalist Party came to power in 1928. Shortly afterward the Nationalist government created the Ministry of Military Administration *(junzhengbu)*. It controlled five bureaus: the army, navy, air force, military supplies, and ordnance.[42] According to its organizational regulations, the Bureau of Ordnance was "in charge of administering national ordnance affairs and all matters concerning ordnance reconstruction." Within the Bureau of Ordnance were four sections *(ke)* and two commissions *(weiyuanhui):* the sections were general affairs, planning, inspection, and supervision, and the commissions were those of ordnance research and purchase of ordnance material.[43] Within three years, increased needs led the Bureau of Ordnance to reorganize itself by creating three new departments *(si):* resources, administration, and technology. In July 1934 the department of military weaponry, formerly under the jurisdiction of the Bureau of Army, was incorporated into the Bureau of Ordnance.[44] By 1935 the organizational structure of the Bureau of Ordnance had finally taken shape: it now consisted of departments of manufacturing, technology, and military weaponry.[45]

The directorship of the Bureau of Ordnance also changed hands several times after the Nationalists came to power. When the Nationalist government created the Bureau of Ordnance in November 1928, it appointed Zhang Qun its first director.[46] Zhang Qun served only five months when Chen Yi replaced him.[47] Three years later, in 1931, Hong Zhong moved into the position when Chen Yi left the Bureau of Ordnance, but Hong left after only nine months. Finally, the Nationalist government appointed Yu Dawei the bureau's new director on January 26, 1933. Yu remained in that position until the abolition of the Ministry of Military Administration in May 1946.

Yu Dawei (1897–1993) was born in 1897 in Shaoxing, Zhejiang province. After graduating from St. John's University in Shanghai, he studied in the United States at Harvard University for three years, earning a Ph.D. in philosophy. Immediately afterward, in 1921, he went to Germany to continue study at Berlin University. There he took up German philosophy and mathematics, and even published an article on mathematical logic in 1925 in *Mathematische Annalen,* edited by Albert Einstein and David Hilbert. After four years of study he earned another Ph.D. in mathematics. However, he did not want to spend the rest of his life teaching; he had bigger ambitions.

It so happened that in early 1928 Chiang Kaishek (Jiang Jieshi) sent a team headed by Chen Yi to Germany to invite retired German military officers to serve as advisers in China and to "recruit talent" among Chinese students studying in Germany. Although Chen Yi failed in the first part of his mission, he did discover some talents, including the then thirty-one-year-old Yu Dawei. With Chen Yi's strong recommendation, the Nationalist government appointed Yu director of the Department of Commercial Affairs stationed in Germany, whose primary responsibility was the purchase of armaments. Yu worked in this capacity until early 1930 when, at the suggestion of German military adviser Max Bauer, he returned to Germany again as a student. He did not study philosophy or mathematics at any university, however. Instead, he engaged retired German military officers to teach him in the Chinese legation in Berlin. The subject was the knowledge and technology of arms and munitions manufacturing and training of staff officers. Yu returned to China in June 1932 upon completing his studies. In January of the following year, he was appointed director of the Bureau of Ordnance when Hong Zhong left that position. For the next thirteen years, Yu's name was associated with all the major changes that took place in the Chinese ordnance industry. Theodore H. White, a prominent American journalist stationed in wartime Chongqing, praised him as one of only three men in the Nationalist government with "glowing integrity and ability."[48]

When Yu Dawei became director of the Bureau of Ordnance in January 1933, the Nationalist effort to consolidate the ordnance industry was already under way. As early as 1928, Chen Yi had drafted a plan for developing the ordnance industry.[49] The major stimulus for development, however, was the Japanese invasion of Manchuria in 1931 and the subsequent attack on Shanghai in January 1932. In response to Japan's increasing threats to China's national security, the Bureau of Ordnance drafted a plan for establishing new ordnance factories in July 1932. The record of the planning meeting indicates that the new ordnance factories were "designed to achieve autarky and self-sufficiency in ordnance and materials." Specifically, these factories, along with the existing ones, were to produce "new armaments for the replenishment of the needs for five army divisions annually." Zhuzhou in Hunan province was chosen as the site for constructing new ordnance factories, with the total cost estimated at US$16 million.[50]

The Bureau of Ordnance submitted the draft plan to Chiang Kaishek, who responded by making several suggestions for revision. Chiang pointed out that US$16 million was roughly the equivalent of Ch$80 million, and it was impossible for the government to appropriate such a huge amount within two years. Chiang suggested that the plan's implementation could perhaps be carried out within a period of five years with an estimated

funding of Ch$20 million each year, in addition to regular annual manu-
facturing expenditure of Ch$30 million. Chiang also stated bluntly that with
limited revenues the proposed plan to purchase new weaponry for five
divisions annually was simply out of the question, although it was possible
to purchase enough weapons for one division annually. Chiang expressed
the hope that the new weaponry purchased abroad and produced by newly
established ordnance factories would adequately equip ten army divisions
within five years.[51]

Following Chiang's instructions, the Bureau of Ordnance submitted a
five-year budget beginning with the 1932 fiscal year, requesting government appropriation in the amount of Ch$374,723,634. The Bureau of
Ordnance planned to allocate annual appropriations to ordnance manufacturing of existing factories, construction of new factories, and ordnance
manufacturing of newly constructed factories.[52] At the same time, the Bu-

Figure 1. Yu Dawei (1946), director of the Bureau of Ordnance, 1932–1945.
Courtesy Taiwan Daily News.

reau of Ordnance submitted a plan for constructing new ordnance factories to the General Staff of the Military Affairs Commission. Among other things, the plan proposed relocating several ordnance factories, including Jinan and Jinling arsenals, to interior provinces.[53]

Within a month, the General Staff drafted a comprehensive new plan for consolidating ordnance factories. The plan explained the guiding principles and key elements of consolidation and contained information on output after consolidation. In order to "meet the need for national defense," the Bureau of Ordnance was to consolidate and expand existing ordnance factories with "minimum financial resources and the least amount of disruption" while taking into consideration the "international situation as well as the reality of domestic political economy." Once the consolidation was complete, the ordnance factories should develop a capacity for manufacturing enough weapons and ammunition to supply five army divisions annually and special forces, as well as forces engaged in "domestic pacification campaigns."[54]

The plan also revealed key components of ordnance consolidation. It provided for the "immediate and complete relocation" of Shanghai Arsenal, for the Japanese attack on Shanghai early in the year had exposed its vulnerability. In contrast to the relocation of Jinan and Jinling arsenals as proposed in the earlier draft submitted by the Bureau of Ordnance, the new plan recommended against relocating the two arsenals for the time being for fear of "reducing the supply of ammunition for pacification campaigns." In addition, the plan explained ways to consolidate and expand existing arsenals, and it proposed the establishment of several new ordnance factories in Zhuzhou in Hunan province for manufacturing heavy artilleries, artillery shells, smokeless powder, and explosives. Finally, the plan provided detailed estimates of output after the consolidation of existing ordnance factories and the establishment of new ones.[55]

Precise figures on how much funding the Bureau of Ordnance received annually from the state treasury are not available, but archival sources indicate that funds for consolidating the ordnance industry were substantial during the early 1930s. For the 1934 fiscal year, the state budget allocated Ch$14 million for national defense reconstruction and Ch$12 million for purchasing foreign armaments.[56] For the same fiscal year, the operating expenditure of the five centrally controlled arsenals—Hanyang Arsenal, Jinling Arsenal, Hanyang Powder Plant, Gongxian Arsenal, and Jinan Arsenal—was roughly Ch$12.16 million, a figure that reflected the same level of state support for ordnance manufacturing.[57] For the 1935 fiscal year, the Bureau of Ordnance expected to receive an appropriation of Ch$33 million for weapon purchase and ordnance manufacturing.[58]

The steady flow of state funds permitted the Bureau of Ordnance to begin working toward establishing new ordnance factories. In April 1932, the Bureau of Ordnance sent Wu Qinlie, a prominent chemical engineer with a B. S. from the Massachusetts Institute of Technology and a M. S. from the University of Chicago to the United States to purchase machinery and equipment and to recruit technical personnel for a planned chemical plant. While in the United States, Wu signed contracts with Monsanto Chemical Works, Westvaco Chlorine Products Incorporation, and the Lake Erie Chemical Company. He also engaged six American experts to help establish the new plant in Gongxian, Henan province.[59] Construction began in the summer of 1933. The factory was first named Gongxian Chemical Arsenal and then Shihe Branch Arsenal. An April 1934 report indicates that the construction of seven factory buildings, along with a hospital and an employees' dormitory, was almost complete.[60] In May 1934, Shihe Branch Arsenal was renamed Gongxian Branch Arsenal. By the beginning of 1936, the arsenal had become operational.[61] Thus China's first chemical arsenal came into existence in less than three years.

At about the same time, the Bureau of Ordnance attempted to consolidate existing ordnance factories. After the bureau's establishment in November 1928, the Nationalist government immediately placed Shanghai, Hanyang, Jinan, and Gongxian arsenals under its jurisdiction.[62] All other arsenals remained under the control of provincial authorities. Data compiled by the Bureau of Ordnance reveal the existence of thirteen arsenals in 1931 in Jinling, Shanghai, Jinan, Hanyang, Gongxian, Huayin, Liaoning, Taiyuan, Guangdong, Chengdu, Kaifeng, Yunnan, and Hengyang.[63] Even as late as 1931, however, the Bureau of Ordnance had direct jurisdiction over only six of the thirteen arsenals.[64] Naturally the Nationalist government attempted to bring more ordnance factories under its control. On September 22, 1932, in a telegram to He Yingqin and Chen Yi, minister and deputy minister of the Ministry of Military Administration, respectively, Chiang Kaishek stated that "the central government should take over Taiyuan Arsenal for the purpose of national defense." Chiang also asked them to make representation to Yan Xishan of Jiangxi province.[65] Four years later, the Bureau of Ordnance sent Yang Jizeng, head of the bureau's manufacturing department, to negotiate with Yan Xishan but without success.[66]

At the same time that the Nationalist government tried to centralize control of ordnance factories, it sought to consolidate existing ones that were already under the direct control of the Bureau of Ordnance. Shortly after the conclusion of the Sino-Japanese military conflict in Shanghai early in 1932, military authorities decided to dismantle Shanghai Arsenal and allocate its equipment and personnel elsewhere. On June 24, 1932, Chen Yi sent a telegram to Chiang Kaishek suggesting that Shanghai Arsenal relocate to Hangzhou. Chiang did not object but stated emphatically, "The restoration of the old Shanghai Arsenal can never be allowed to happen."[67] Two months later, the relocation of Shanghai Arsenal became part of the comprehensive plan drafted by the General Staff of the Military Affairs Commission. Eventually, Shanghai Arsenal's equipment was divided among three arsenals: the equipment for making artillery went to Hanyang Arsenal; the equipment for making artillery shell went to Gongxian Arsenal; and the equipment for making rifles and machine guns went to Jinling Arsenal. Only the steel-making plant, later renamed the Third Arsenal, remained in Shanghai. By October 1932 the Bureau of Ordnance had completely dismantled and relocated Shanghai Arsenal,[68] a move reformers had been demanding for almost four decades!

The effort to modernize China's ordnance industry had produced marked changes by the early 1930s. A little more than a decade earlier, government arsenals could produce only enough cartridges for one year's target practice and the weaponry for only one army division. By the early 1930s, however, a number of positive changes had occurred. As early as 1932, the ordnance factories under the direct jurisdiction of the Bureau of Ordnance had already developed the capacity to produce weaponry for replenishing more than five army divisions.[69] As a result of the substantially increased capacity, during the 1934 fiscal year the bureau's four ordnance factories produced 58,800 rifles, 576 heavy machine guns, 87,532,200 cartridges, 160 mortars, 134,400 mortar shells, 61,144 mountain artillery shells, and 1,077,000 hand grenades. From June 1933 to June 1935 they also made over 54,100 bombs of different types and sizes for bombers. At the same time, the bureau began introducing cost accounting in ordnance factories. As a result, the four ordnance factories saved over Ch$4 million out of their regular funding, which was then used in building infrastructure, purchasing new machinery, and undertaking technical innovation.[70]

Despite the Bureau of Ordnance's persistent effort and the positive changes it brought about, not every plan was carried out in a timely fashion. In 1932, the Bureau of Ordnance made plans to establish new ordnance factories in Zhuzhou in Hunan province, including the establishment of an artillery factory.[71] This planned artillery factory was also the only one listed in the military program of implementation drafted by the Military Affairs Commission for the 1933 fiscal year.[72] There is no evidence to indicate that the Bureau of Ordnance took any concrete step to implement the plan before 1935, however, owing partly to funding constraints and partly to the bureau's focus on the consolidation of existing factories. As late as 1935 the bureau was still trying to upgrade the artillery plant of Hanyang Arsenal. According to its own estimate, improvement of existing facilities in the artillery plant would "cost three times less the money and two times less the time than the establishment of a brand-new plant."[73]

By the mid-1930s, the increasingly dangerous international situation prompted the Nationalist elite to further revise their existing mental model and use the newly formed shared mental model to guide their efforts to build a strong national defense industry. This revision of the mental model manifested itself in a joint proposal that four members of the Central Political Commission of the Nationalist Party submitted to the commission's Secretariat on June 17, 1935: "Since the Japanese invasion of Manchuria in 1931, the survival of the state and the life of the nation have sunk into a most dangerous and miserable condition . . . The reasons for such a condition are many, including the lack of effective weapons for modern wars, the absence of a solid foundation for heavy industry, and the underdevelopment of light industry . . . It is our belief that we will not succeed in saving China from the danger of being extinguished unless we immediately formulate a national policy and make a determined and concentrated effort by undertaking fundamental reconstruction of national defense heavy industry." Specifically, the proposal suggested drafting a five-year plan for developing national defense industries, selecting an industrial region for national defense in locations such as Hengyang and Zhuzhou in Hunan province, and raising revenues to implement national defense plans.[74]

In response, the General Staff of the Central Military Commission, the National Resources Commission, the Ministry of Industries, and the Ministry of Financial Administration all submitted reports describing their efforts in developing national defense industries.[75] Then, in February 1936, representatives of these four organizations and the Bureau of Ordnance met twice to discuss issues concerning national defense industries. Eventually, these acts of communication—reports, discussions, and deliberations—created a shared mental model among leaders of the Nationalist government. This model explained the increasingly dangerous international situation and prescribed the development of national defense industries as the top priority on the Nationalist agenda. Specifically, at the February meetings representatives of the General Staff, the National Resources Commission, the Bureau of Ordnance, the Ministry of Industries, and the Ministry of Financial Administration reached a consensus on creating an industrial region for national defense, on developing national defense industries, and on handling ordnance factories and general heavy industries. They agreed that they would choose appropriate areas in Sichuan, Hunan, and Jiangxi provinces to create "an industrial region for national defense" (guofang gongye quyu), and that the Bureau of Ordnance and the National Resources Commission would draft plans for developing national defense industries. They also agreed that they would differentiate between ordnance factories and general heavy industries: the plan drafted by the National Resources Commission would guide general heavy industrial reconstruction, whereas the five-year plan proposed by the Ministry of Military Administration would direct the effort to expand ordnance factories.[76]

In a formal letter to the Central Political Commission of the Nationalist Party on March 5, 1936, Chiang Kaishek summarized the decisions of the meetings. He stated that the representatives decided "for the sake of safety, to choose appropriate areas in Hunan, Jiangxi and Sichuan provinces" [note the order of the three provinces] in order to create "an industrial region for national defense." Chiang also reiterated the need to differentiate between ordnance factories and general heavy industries. He pointed out that the plan drafted by the National Resources Commission would guide general heavy industrial reconstruction, whereas the five-year plan proposed by the Ministry of Military Administration would direct the effort to expand ordnance factories. In submitting the draft three-year plan to the Central Political Commission for approval, Chiang emphasized that "ordnance materials, air materials, instruments of transportation and communications, and fuels are most urgently needed in heavy industries for national defense," that most planned factories would be located in "safe zones," and that all the factory plans were "based on thorough investigation and research conducted by the National Resources Commission."[77]

With regard to the cost of the five-year plan for the ordnance industry, the total expenditure was estimated at Ch$360 million. Although establishing new ordnance factories was part of the plan, the projected cost was only Ch\$60.8 million for a three-year period. The purpose of establishing new factories was to supply weapons and ammunition for thirty army divisions and twenty-two artillery regiments for a period of ten months in battle.[78] One month later, a Special Commission of National Defense reviewed the plan and made important changes. It revised the schedule for constructing new ordnance factories from three to two years and reduced estimated expenditure for new factory construction from Ch\$60.8 million to Ch\$57.2 million. It also concluded that once the plan was carried out, the weapons and ammunition produced would be able to supply only one-fifth of the battlefield need of thirty army divisions and twenty-two artillery regiments.[79]

Even before the Central Political Commission of the Nationalist Party adopted the plan, the Bureau of Ordnance had appointed Zhuang Quan director of the newly created Research Division of Artillery Technology in preparation for building the planned artillery factory.[80] Between March and June of 1936, the Research Division of Artillery Technology purchased land in Zhuzhou in Hunan province and proceeded to purchase machinery from Germany and other countries.[81] On June 15, 1936, its organizational establishment received the approval of the Bureau of Ordnance, which consisted of sections of general affairs, civil engineering, work affairs, planning, accounting, and purchase. Under the section of work affairs were an artillery plant, an artillery shell plant, a cartridge plant, a machine plant, and a power plant. In November the Research Division of Artillery Technology took over the artillery plant of the Hanyang Arsenal. It was meant to be the largest modern ordnance factory in China. Construction of the new factory was well under way when the Sino-Japanese War broke out the following year.[82]

Overall, the effort to build a modern ordnance industry had produced remarkable results by 1936. Statistics compiled by the Bureau of Ordnance show that between 1932 and 1936, the ordnance factories under its jurisdiction produced 325,942 rifles, 3,497 machine guns, 976 82mm mortars, 402,267,200 cartridges, 335,162 75mm mountain artillery shells, 773,582 82mm mortar shells, 5,451,533 hand grenades, 105,480 fighter bombs, 332,055 signal flares, and 57,034 gas masks. The same statistics also reveal a steady increase in output between 1932 and 1933, a slight decline between 1934 and 1935 in certain areas, and then a major upsurge in 1936, more than doubling the output for 1932 in most areas.[83] Still, the Bureau of Ordnance did not rely exclusively on domestic weapons and ammunition. For the 1934 fiscal year, the bureau purchased from abroad 2,000 Browning light machine guns, 5,000 light machine guns made in Czechoslovakia, 20 mountain artillery pieces, 5,000 Mauser pistols, and 10,000 Mauser 1935 model rifles.[84] These purchases made up to some extent for the deficiencies of domestic ordnance manufacturing.

To summarize, the Nationalist government began to modernize the ordnance industry as soon as the Nationalist Party came to power. Fundamentally, however, the Nationalists were motivated by Japan's invasion of Manchuria and attack on Shanghai during 1931 and 1932, together with the continued Japanese encroachment on Chinese sovereignty after 1935. Japanese aggression led the Bureau of Ordnance to plan for the establishment of new ordnance factories, the consolidation of existing ones, and the immediate relocation of the Shanghai Arsenal. The Japanese threat compelled the Nationalists to revise their existing mental model and form a new one that would guide their renewed effort in building a modern ordnance industry. Unfortunately, the modernization process was interrupted by the all-out Japanese invasion of China in 1937. That invasion triggered a sustained systemic crisis and forced a massive relocation of ordnance factories into China's interior and their expansion and centralization.

Relocation and Expansion of the Ordnance Industry

Li Hongzhang was the first official in the history of Chinese ordnance industry to raise the question of relocating ordnance factories to the interior. After the first Sino-Japanese War, general consensus was reached to relocate ordnance factories, especially the Jiangnan Arsenal (later renamed the Shanghai Arsenal), and so relocation became imperial policy. Still, it took a direct Sino-Japanese military confrontation in Shanghai in 1932 for the Nationalist government to finally relocate Shanghai Arsenal. Many important ordnance factories, such as Jinling Arsenal and Guangdong Arsenal, remained in coastal areas.

On July 7, 1937, Japan launched an all-out invasion of China proper. The invasion forced the majority of China's ordnance factories, over twenty in all, to relocate to five interior provinces: Sichuan, Yunnan, Guizhou, Hunan, and Guangxi. Sichuan province was the destination for fifteen factories: the First, Second, Tenth, Twentieth, Twenty-first, Twenty-third, Twenty-fourth, Twenty-fifth, Twenty-sixth, Twenty-seventh, Twenty-eighth, Twenty-ninth, Thirtieth, Fortieth, and Fiftieth Arsenals. Six ordnance factories relocated to Yunnan and Guizhou provinces; these factories were the Twenty-second, Forty-second, Forty-fourth, Fifty-first, Fifty-second, and Fifty-third Arsenals. The remaining three ordnance factories, the Eleventh, Forty-first, and Forty-third Arsenals, moved to Hunan and Guangxi provinces.

This massive relocation occurred in three distinct phases. The first began in September 1937 with the relocation of the Shanghai Steel Plant. It had been part of Shanghai Arsenal, but in 1929 the Ministry of Military Administration had separated the Steel Plant from the Shanghai Arsenal and placed it under the direct control of the Bureau of Ordnance.[85] After the Japanese troops launched the attack on Shanghai in early August 1937, the Bureau of Ordnance twice ordered the Shanghai Steel Plant to "transport important materials and machinery to Wuhan."[86] Between September and December, the bureau issued relocation orders to seven other ordnance factories and units: Jinan Arsenal, Gongxian Arsenal, Jinling Arsenal, Gongxian Branch Arsenal, Central Weapon Repair Shop, Division of Military Optical Instrument, and Guangdong First Arsenal.[87] During the first phase, then, relocation was apparently confined to factories and units that were exposed to the immediate threat of the Japanese forces in Shanghai, Nanjing, and north China. Their destination indicates that less than one year after the outbreak of the Sino-Japanese War, the center of Chinese ordnance industry had begun to move away from coastal areas to central and interior provinces. Such a move was consistent with the Nationalist plan of developing an industrial region for national defense in Hunan, Jiangxi, and Sichuan provinces.

The rapid advance of Japanese troops and the subsequent Japanese attack on Wuhan in the summer of 1938 shattered this Nationalist dream and forced the ordnance factories in central China to relocate more deeply into the interior.[88] During this second phase, which lasted from April to November of 1938, nine ordnance factories and units moved from provinces such as Guangdong, Hunan, and Hubei to new destinations in the interior provinces. They included the Guangdong Second Arsenal, Jinan Arsenal, Guangdong Mask Plant, Hanyang Powder Plant, Hanyang Arsenal, Research Division of Artillery Technology, Shanghai Steel Plant, Central Weapon Repair Shop, and Guangxi First Arsenal.[89] Except for the few ordnance factories and units that had relocated to the southwest in 1937, the majority of them were involved in the second phase of relocation. Some factories and units had to relocate twice as a result of changes in the military situation. The Shanghai Steel Plant, Jinan Arsenal, and Central Weapon Repair Shop are cases in point. Six out of the nine factories and units relocated to Chongqing, making Chongqing the undisputed center of Chinese ordnance industry.

The last relocation phase began with the dismantlement of Gongxian Arsenal in Changsha in Hunan province. The Japanese attack on Changsha in the fall of 1939 exposed its vulnerability and forced its relocation in December.[90] Four ordnance factories—Gongxian Arsenal, Guangdong First Arsenal, Hanyang Arsenal, and Hanyang Powder Plant—were involved in this final phase, and three of the four factories relocated to Chongqing between December 1939 and October 1940.[91] Because many ordnance factories and units had moved from their original locations and their names did not correspond to those of their destinations, in the interest of convenience and safety in February 1938 the Bureau of Ordnance decided to use numbers to designate them.[92] Because some factories and units relocated again, however, their locations changed after their redesignation. Appendix Table 1.1 shows the name, location, relocation process, and the original name of sixteen ordnance factories and units as of April 1941.

On the whole, the data reveal three very significant facts. First, the massive relocation of the ordnance factories and units fundamentally altered the spatial structure of China's ordnance industry. Coastal areas and central China had been centers of the ordnance industry. Despite numerous debates on the matter over a period of several decades, the basic geographical configuration remained unchanged before the outbreak of the second Sino-Japanese War. The all-out Japanese invasion of China forced the relocation of ordnance factories and units to three interior provinces in the southwest. As Appendix Table 1.1 shows, twelve of the sixteen factories and units were concentrated in the wartime capital Chongqing. The center of gravity for China's ordnance industry shifted to the southwest by the early 1940s. Second, Nationalist preparation and mobilization for war also led to an unprecedented centralization of the ordnance industry. As late as 1935, the Bureau of Ordnance had only seven factories under its direct control.[93] Within five years, however, the bureau had under its jurisdiction sixteen factories and units, having taken over province-run factories and establishing new ones. Third, the successful relocation of so many ordnance factories and units made possible the preservation of the productive capacity of an industry that proved vital for China's war of resistance against Japanese aggression.

How did factory officials and workers accomplish the daunting task of removing and relocating an entire ordnance industry from coastal and central China to southwestern China? The examples of the Twenty-first and Fiftieth Arsenals highlight the industry's dramatic spatial movement during the Sino-Japanese War.

The Twenty-first Arsenal had its origins in the Jinling Manufacturing Bureau that Li Hongzhang had established in 1865. After that, the bureau went through a period of expansion. By the time the first Sino-Japanese War broke out in 1894, the bureau had over 1,200 employees and nearly thirty different types of ordnance products. After the 1911 Revolution, the provisional government took over the bureau, which had suffered serious decline with only about 500 employees by this time. In March 1928, the newly established Nationalist government changed the bureau's name to the Jinling Branch Plant of Shanghai Arsenal. However, the difficulty of managing it from Shanghai led the government to rename it Jinling Arsenal in June 1929. By this time its workforce had increased to over 1,000.[94] According to a 1931 survey by the Bureau of Ordnance, Jinling Arsenal consisted of a weapons plant, a cartridge plant, and a powder plant, and employed 1,100 workers, with a monthly output of thirty-five Maxim machine guns, 2,700,000 cartridges, and 700 fighter bombs.[95]

In July 1931, the Bureau of Ordnance appointed Li Chenggan director of Jinling Arsenal. For the next five years Li implemented a series of reforms, notably the introduction of cost accounting, technical innovation, purchase of new machinery, and improvement of employee welfare. By 1936, these reforms had given a new life to this seventy-year old arsenal.[96] For the decade between 1927 and 1937, Jinling Arsenal manufactured a total of 3,904 Maxim heavy machine guns, 1,100 82mm mortars, 616,080 82mm mortar shells, and 203,580,000 7.9mm rifle cartridge clips.[97]

In August 1937, Japanese forces launched an attack on Shanghai. Although Chinese forces offered heroic resistance, Shanghai fell in November.[98] The fall of Shanghai immediately exposed Nanjing as a potential target and forced the Bureau of Ordnance to order Jinling Arsenal to relocate on November 16. Under Li's effective leadership, it took only sixteen days for the employees to dismantle over 4,000 tons of machinery, equipment, materials and semifinished products and load them on cargo trains, trucks, and steamships. Through their extraordinary effort, the entire arsenal was relocated in only three and a half months. The arsenal resumed operations in Bojishi of Chongqing on March 1, 1938, making it the first ordnance factory to do so after relocation.[99]

On April 14, 1938, the Jinling Arsenal formally changed its name to the Twenty-first Arsenal.[100] Under the director were one office and three divisions (chu)—the general office and the divisions of work affairs, accounting, and employee welfare.[101] Over the next few years the arsenal greatly expanded its size and capacity by annexing whole plants and equipment. It took over the rifle plant of Hanyang Arsenal in July 1938; the light machine gun plant of the Twentieth Arsenal in January 1939; and German-made equipment for manufacturing artillery shells in March 1939, which led to the establishment of a branch arsenal in Anning of Yunnan province in 1940.[102] At the same time, the number of employees increased dramatically—from 2,539 in 1937 to 5,039 in 1940. By the time the Sino-Japanese War concluded in 1945, the Twenty-first Arsenal employed a total of 8,769 employees, making it China's largest ordnance factory.[103]

This expansion led to a sharp increase in production during the war. Between 1938 and 1945, the Twenty-first Arsenal manufactured a total of 18,068 heavy machine guns, 9,833 light machine guns, 7,011 82mm mortars, 3,212,252 82mm mortar shells, 293,364 rifles, and 311,500 hand grenades.[104] A comparison of the total output of selected products before and during the war is even more revealing. As Appendix Table 1.2 demonstrates, the Twenty-first Arsenal produced no light machine guns, hand grenades, or rifles before the war. But during the war, it manufactured 9,833 light machine guns, 311,500 hand grenades, and 293,364 rifles. Although the arsenal began producing heavy machine guns, 82mm mortars, and 82mm mortar shells before the war, during the war their output was dramatic, with an increase of output of 363 percent, 537 percent, and 421 percent for respective categories. It is estimated that the output of the Twenty-first Arsenal constituted roughly half of the total output of the entire ordnance industry.[105]

The Fiftieth Arsenal, as noted earlier, was also important in the spatial movement of the ordnance industry. In contrast to the Twenty-first Arsenal, whose date of establishment can be traced to 1865, the Fiftieth Arsenal came into existence only in the 1930s. After the Nationalist Party came to power in 1928, factional tensions within the party intensified and by 1931, had caused a split in the Nationalist Party, with Chen Jitang and Li Zongren establishing a de facto separatist regime in Guangdong and Guangxi provinces, respectively. In order to expand their military capabilities, in 1933 their representatives signed a contract with a representative of Hapro, a German company, for the construction of four ordnance factories that would manufacture artillery, artillery shell, poisonous gas, and gas masks.[106] Pajiangkou of Qingyuan County, which was about thirty miles north of Guangzhou, was selected as the site for the planned arsenal.[107] Construction for the artillery plant and artillery shell plant was complete within two years. In December 1935, the two plants merged to form what became known as Pajiangkou Arsenal with about 340 new machines and equipment imported from Germany. The arsenal designed an organizational structure that included an office and three divisions under the director—the general office and divisions of work affairs, accounting, and employee welfare.[108] At this time, the arsenal employed over twenty German engineers and foremen, as many Chinese technicians, and roughly 300 Chinese workers. According to the arsenal's first director, the major drawback was its lack of steel and powder plants, which meant that the arsenal had to rely on Germany for raw materials for manufacturing artillery and artillery shells.[109]

Unfortunately for Chen Jitang and Li Zongren, their alliance against Chiang Kaishek failed. Chen Jitang fled to Hong Kong in July 1936. Four months later, the Bureau of Ordnance took over Pajiangkou Arsenal and renamed it Guangdong Second Arsenal in June 1937. At the same time, the bureau appointed Jiang Biao, then the bureau's head of the technology department, as its director.[110] Partly as a result of these changes, the arsenal was not fully operational when the Sino-Japanese War broke out in July. Within a month the arsenal began to suffer losses in infrastructure because of repeated Japanese bombing. The arsenal's workers began dismantling machinery and equipment in the winter of 1937.[111]

It took much longer to relocate the Guangdong Second Arsenal than the Jinling Arsenal, owing at least in part to the difficulty of finding an acceptable site. The Bureau of Ordnance first ordered it to relocate in late 1937. The arsenal sent personnel to explore potential sites for relocation in Hunan, Guizhou, and Yunnan provinces. In March 1938, the arsenal received another, more specific order to relocate to Chongqing. Shortly afterward, Jiang Biao selected Guojiatuo in Jiangbei County as the relocation site. This site had the advantage of being both close to Chongqing proper—a distance of about ten miles—and within easy access of mountains, where expensive machinery and equipment could be installed in man-made caves.[112]

Adding to the difficulty of finding an acceptable site was the challenge of transporting heavy machinery and equipment from the coastal city of

Guangzhou to the inland city of Chongqing. First, workers had to transport machinery and equipment to the train station in Guangzhou, where they loaded them onto cargo compartments of railroad cars. Once the equipment arrived in Zhuzhou in Hunan province, it was loaded on steamboat-pulled barges on the Yangzi River, to be shipped to the port city of Yichang. Upon unloading there, it was loaded on Minsheng Corporation's steamboats, to be shipped to their final destination, Chongqing. Between March and the end of 1938, the arsenal shipped 3,000 tons of machinery and equipment.[113] The arsenal was renamed the Fiftieth Arsenal during its relocation to Chongqing.

After the factory officials and workers arrived in their new location, they were immediately confronted with the new challenges of constructing factory buildings and shelters for employees, resuming production within the shortest possible time, and avoiding Japanese bombing. Between 1938 and 1941, the arsenal constructed forty-three regular factory buildings for installing ordinary machinery and equipment, twenty man-made caves for installing expensive machinery and equipment and storing weapons and ammunition, and 115 employee apartments and dormitories.[114]

Unlike the Twenty-first Arsenal, the Fiftieth Arsenal had established division-level units before the Sino-Japanese War, with a general office and the three divisions of work affairs, accounting, and employee welfare.[115] Still, the Fiftieth Arsenal expanded considerably during the war. The number of its employees increased dramatically during its first five years in Chongqing, from 1,323 in 1939 to 3,822 in 1943.[116] At the same time, the Fiftieth Arsenal did its best to maximize its artillery and artillery shell manufacturing capacity despite the lack of artillery materials. Between 1939 and 1941 the arsenal focused on the production of artillery shells. Beginning in 1942 it started manufacturing anti-tank artillery, which contributed to the Allies' operations in the Burma theater. As military operations shifted to mountainous terrains, the arsenal concentrated on the manufacturing of 60mm mortars. Despite its limited capacity and output, the Fiftieth Arsenal served as the Nationalist government's main artillery and artillery-shell factory.

The massive relocation, reconstruction, and expansion of ordnance factories such as the Twenty-first and Fiftieth arsenals required consistent state support. Although materials for the wartime period are scanty, archival sources indicate that the Chinese state devoted considerable resources to developing the ordnance industry. According to its 1939 budget estimate, the Bureau of Ordnance was to receive Ch$51,078,864 to cover regular manufacturing expenses, Ch$56,500,000 to defray the cost for constructing new ordnance factories and reconstructing relocated factories, and Ch$129,318,600 to pay for the manufacturing of additional weapons and ammunition.[117] In other words, the bureau requested a total of Ch$236,897,464 for its 1939 fiscal year (Ch$78,965,821 in 1936 constant price),[118] a figure that represented 52.85 percent of the total budget for national defense and 13.89 percent of the total national budget, which were Ch$448,204,144 and Ch$1,705,512,879, respectively, for the same fiscal year.[119]

The 1942 budget estimate of the Bureau of Ordnance reveals equally significant state support for the ordnance industry. According to a budget report prepared by the Ministry of Military Administration and marked "extremely secret," state appropriations earmarked for the ordnance industry was Ch$1,765,000,000 (Ch$27,578,125 in 1936 constant price) out of a Ch$3,302,980,582 total budget for national defense for the 1942 fiscal year.[120] This figure represented 53.44 percent of the total budget for national defense and made up 10.2 percent of the total national budget, which was Ch$17,310,618,343 for the same fiscal year.[121] If these 1939 and 1942 figures of state appropriation accurately reflected state investment in the ordnance industry, one can infer that the Chinese state allocated 10 percent or more of its annual expenditure to the development of the ordnance industry during the Sino-Japanese War.

As a result of the considerable state support and the tremendous efforts made by officials, managers, and employees, the wartime period saw a significant increase in the total output of ordnance factories. Appendix Table 1.4 documents the output increase of the ordnance industry during the war. Between 1940 and 1945, the number of rifles increased by 2.4 times, machine guns by 4.7 times, 82mm mortars by 2.7 times, 7.9mm cartridges by 2.2 times, 75mm artillery shells by 2.3 times, 82mm mortar shells by 2 times, and hand grenades by 1.3 times. If we compare the output in 1945 and that of 1936, the result is even more striking. Appendix Table 1.5 provides the output figures for both 1936 and 1945 and the proportion of increase in output. It shows that during the ten-year period, the output of rifles increased 1.3 times, machine guns 20.3 times, 82mm mortars 4.3 times, 7.9mm cartridges 2 times, 75mm artillery shells 1.6 times, 82mm mortar shells 5.3 times, and hand grenades 2.4 times.

The output of the ordnance industry met the needs of the Nationalist forces for weapons and ammunition in a number of important categories. Appendix Table 1.6 documents the monthly average of the number of weapons and ammunition lost or damaged, produced, and replaced, and the percentage of the number of weapons and ammunition produced vis-à-vis the number lost or damaged. It demonstrates that the weapons and ammunition produced not only met between 63 and 99 percent of the needs for cartridge, rifles, light machine guns, and mortar shells, but also completely replaced the losses of heavy machine guns, mortars, grenade launchers, and grenades. Although the Nationalist government had to import some ordnance, it was primarily these China-made weapons and ammunition that sustained Chinese resistance against the much better equipped Japanese forces during the Sino-Japanese War.

To a large extent, crisis shaped the development of China's ordnance industry. Domestic and foreign crises led to the establishment of the modern ordnance industry in the 1860s. The Sino-French War and the first Sino-Japanese War exposed the vulnerability of coastal arsenals, forced imperial officials to respond by revising their existing mental model to one that emphasized the interior as the ideal location for government arsenals, which in turn guided the imperial government to formulate a policy in favor of establishing and relocating arsenals in interior provinces. Because of the local nature of these crises, however, the imperial government did little to implement its policy.

As a modernizing elite, the Nationalists began modernizing the ordnance industry as soon as they came to power. The major stimuli for modernization, however, came from the Japanese invasion of Manchuria, their attacks on Shanghai in 1931 and 1932, and the state of impending crisis after 1935. These escalating crises compelled the Nationalists to form a new mental model that explained the increasingly dangerous international situation and also prescribed the development of national defense industries as the Nationalists' top priority. Still, it was the sustained systemic crisis provoked by the second Sino-Japanese War that forced the massive relocation of ordnance factories into China's interior and their development and centralization.[122]

CHAPTER 2

Expansion of
Heavy Industries

Crisis not only led to the development of the state-owned ordnance industry during the Sino-Japanese War, it also motivated the expansion of state-owned heavy industries. In this chapter I contend that the sustained systemic crisis led to the creation, expansion, and centralization of resources in major state-owned heavy industries. The Japanese invasion of Manchuria gave rise to the National Defense Planning Commission and to resource investigation. The deepening of the national crisis brought about both the reorganization and reorientation of the National Defense Planning Commission. Ultimately the war-triggered sustained systemic crisis compelled the Nationalist elite to develop a new mental model, which in turn led them to undertake large-scale heavy industrial reconstruction. As was the case with the ordnance industry, the changes that occurred in heavy industries were path dependent as crisis strengthened the existing model of state ownership and management.

The National Resources Commission

Sun Yatsen (Sun Zhongshan), leader of the Nationalist Party, did not live to see the completion of China's unification and the establishment of the Nationalist regime, but his idea of economic planning left a lasting legacy for the Nationalists.[1] After achieving national unification in 1927, the newly established Nationalist regime created various government organizations to foster planned economic development. In addition to relevant ministries in the central bureaucracy, the government created a National Reconstruction Commission in 1929 and a National Economic Commission in 1931.[2] Between 1928 and 1931, the government drew up at least four major economic plans. In 1928, in his capacity as head of the Railroad Ministry, Sun

Ke (Sun Fo), Sun Yatsen's son, attempted to set a time limit and estimate a budget for his father's elaborate plan for China's economic development. According to Sun Ke, it would take fifty years with a minimum budget of Ch$25 billion to complete his father's scheme. Subsequently Sun Ke drafted a *Ten-Year Plan* as the first step toward its implementation.[3]

In March 1929, the Nationalist Party held its third national congress. With regard to economic reconstruction, the congress adopted a resolution on political affairs, which stated that "economic reconstruction is the material foundation of the Three Doctrines of the People. Without a solid material foundation, it will be impossible for China to secure its national independence, to actually develop people's democracy, or to truly resolve the problem of people's livelihood."[4] Following Sun Yatsen's plan for industrial development, the congress made "communications and water conservancy the first priority of economic reconstruction."[5]

Such a policy found confirmation in the *Outline Program for Implementing Economic Reconstruction during the Period of Political Tutelage* which the Central Executive Committee of the Nationalist Party adopted in April 1929. According to this program, "the criteria for determining the procedure of implementing material reconstruction should be based on the principles and policies formulated in the plan for industrial reconstruction by Sun Yatsen in his *International Development of China*, with the development of communications being the most important."[6] Two years later, the third Nationalist Party congress adopted a *Six-Year Plan*, which again emphasized that "the plan for industrial reconstruction by Sun Yatsen in his *International Development of China* shall be recognized as the highest principles for the material reconstruction of Republican China, and the whole plan shall be carefully carried out by the national government stage by stage."[7]

These early plans share two characteristics in common. Although they emphasized the role of the state and the development of basic industries, they aimed at long-term domestic economic development and nation-building. National defense was not a primary consideration. In addition, the majority of these plans were drafted on the basis of Sun Yatsen's *International Development of China* by bureaucrats working within regular government ministries without conducting thorough research and investigation.

By the early 1930s, leading scholars such as Weng Wenhao had pointed out those weaknesses. Weng Wenhao (1889–1971) was born in Qin County of Zhejiang province. In 1903, at the age of fourteen, he passed the traditional civil service examination at the prefectural level and became a "received talent" *(xiucai)*. In 1909 he went to Belgium to study physics and geology at Louvain University, where he received a doctorate in 1913. Upon returning to China in the same year, he became one of the foremost pioneers in Chinese geological research. He joined the China Geological Research Institute and served as its acting director from 1921 until 1926, when he became director. At the same time, he taught at the Geology Department at Qinghua University and served as the university's acting president in 1931. In November 1932, he was appointed secretary-general of the newly created National Defense Planning Commission and continued to serve in that position until 1935. After the National Defense Planning Commission was renamed the National Resources Commission in the same year, he served as its director until 1946. After the outbreak of the Sino-Japanese War in 1937 and the reorganization of the central government, he was appointed minister of the Ministry of Economic Affairs. He served in that position until 1946. After the war concluded, he served as president of the Executive Yuan for a brief period in 1948. He joined the Communist government in 1951.[8]

Writing in early 1932, Weng Wenhao pointed out that "The necessity of planning has been widely accepted in China today, thus we hear about plans almost daily, although we have not made much progress in reconstruction in the last few years. On the other hand, the contents of these plans are often far from based on facts, consequently we end up in failure once these plans are carried out . . . [Therefore] Reconstruction had to be preceded by plan, and plan in turn had to be based on hard facts." As a remedy for the situation, Weng suggested that since planning required special technical expertise, relevant data had to be gathered and actual conditions investigated before one could make plans. In his view, a viable plan could "never be made by a regular administrative agency that has no data or reference materials."[9]

Nevertheless, major changes were under way by the time Weng's essay appeared in June 1932. The Japanese invasion of Manchuria in 1931 and their attack on Shanghai in 1932 shocked the nation. Japanese aggression aroused strong Chinese nationalism and forced the Nationalist government to take a firm stand against Japan. In a speech delivered in October 1932, Chiang Kaishek stated that "the Chinese nation has reached a critical moment and the fate of the nation is about to be decided"; his only purpose was to "revive the nation and save China." He proposed economic reconstruction and education as two means of saving China.[10] What Chiang failed to mention in his public speech, however, was the fact that he was about to create a secret national defense planning commission as a first step toward resistance against Japan.

The decision to create such an agency had been made almost a year earlier, as a result of a suggestion made by Qian Changzhao. Qian Changzhao (1899–1988) was born in Changshu, Jiangsu province. Having graduated from high school, he went to England to study political economy at the University of London, graduating with a M. A. degree. Between 1922 and 1924 he continued to study economics at Cambridge University. Among the subjects he studied was Fabianism, which advocates the gradual socialization of land and industrial capital through state power. Fabianism soon exerted a profound influence on his thought. Upon returning to China in the mid-1920s, he visited several prominent warlords in an attempt to find the political backing to implement Fabian socialism in China. He entered the Nationalist government in early 1928 to serve as secretary in the

Figure 2. Weng Wenhao (1943), secretary-general of the National Defense Planning Commission, 1932–1935; director of the National Resources Commission, 1935–1945; minister of the Ministry of Economic Affairs, 1938–1946. Courtesy Weng Xinjun and Weng Xinhe.

Ministry of Foreign Affairs as well as in the Bureau of Civil Service. Three years later he was appointed deputy minister of the Ministry of Education. In 1932, he was appointed deputy secretary of the National Defense Planning Commission, and when it was renamed the National Resources Commission in 1935 he was made deputy director. In 1938, the Nationalist government placed the National Resources Commission under the Ministry of Economic Affairs, but he continued to serve as its deputy director. He served in that position until 1946 when he became its director. He joined the Communist government in 1949.[11]

Beginning in June 1931, Qian served as deputy minister of the Ministry of Education, which allowed him easy access to Chiang Kaishek because

Figure 3. Qian Changzhao (1943), deputy secretary of the National Defense Planning Commission, 1932–1935; deputy director of the National Resources Commission, 1935–1945. Courtesy Chongqing Municipal Archives.

Chiang was then both president of the Nationalist government and minister of the Ministry of Education. Qian developed a close personal relationship with Chiang. Qian recalled that he would "work in the Ministry of Education in the morning, and meet with guests with Chiang at Chiang's residence in the afternoon."[12]

During the evening of a cold winter day in late 1931, Qian suggested to Chiang that a national defense planning agency be created. He pointed out that "national defense planning should be defined broadly to include military affairs, international relations, education and culture, finance and economy, raw materials and manufacturing, transportation and communication, land and food supply, and survey of population with professional expertise." Chiang accepted the suggestion and asked Qian to draw up a list of would-be members of the proposed agency. Two weeks later, Qian presented the list to Chiang, who accepted it without making major changes. They decided that Qian would contact those on the list and make arrangements for some members to meet Chiang.[13]

During the spring, summer, and autumn of 1932, Qian arranged for more than twenty scholars and experts to meet with Chiang in Nanjing, Lushan, and Wuhan. Among those who met with Chiang or lectured for him was Weng Wenhao. When Weng met with Chiang in Lushan in the summer of 1932, he tried to convince Chiang that "the government has an intrinsic obligation in protecting China's territorial integrity" in the face of increasing Japanese aggression: "Japan has not only occupied the Northeast but invaded North China. It is only logical that it will continue to move south into the area along the Yangzi River. Now people are even more frightened, because they fear that the government would only seek temporary peace in the unoccupied territory and would not take upon itself the responsibility for the entire country. Clearly this is critical for the survival of the government. If the government could take its responsibility, it will certainly have the support of the whole nation and be able to gain new strength. Furthermore, once the government assumes its responsibility, definite goals can also be set for economic reconstruction."[14]

Chiang then expressed a willingness to strengthen national defense and told Weng that he intended to create a national defense planning commission to devise plans to save China outside the purview of military affairs. Chiang volunteered to serve as president for the new agency but asked Weng to serve as secretary-general. Weng first declined the offer but eventually accepted it.[15]

The National Defense Planning Commission was formally established on November 1, 1932. According to its organizational regulations, the commission was designed to make specific plans for national defense, to plan reconstruction projects with a focus on national defense, and to prepare and plan measures for national defense.[16] The agency was placed under the General Staff of the Military Affairs Commission, but it reported directly to Chiang Kaishek, who served as president of both commissions. Weng Wenhao was appointed secretary-general, and Qian Changzhao deputy secretary-general. At the time the National Defense Planning Commission was established, it had thirty-nine members, most of them members of the educated elite.[17]

Compared with earlier planning agencies, the National Defense Planning Commission took on a number of new characteristics. Its primary purpose was to devise plans for national defense against Japan. According to the commission's work program, "there is no longer a need to create a hypothetical enemy at the present time . . . the enemy country of China today is of course Japan."[18] Following this assumption, the commission would "devise comprehensive plans for national defense according to the needs of modern national defense and domestic materials and situation."[19]

The National Defense Planning Commission conducted a series of investigations in preparation for defense planning. Until 1934 the commission consisted of a secretariat and seven sections: military affairs, international affairs, economics and finance, raw materials and manufacturing, transportation and communications, land-population-foodstuff, and cultural affairs.[20] The commission conducted investigations and gathered statistics in areas of raw materials and manufacturing, transportation and communications, and economics and finance. According to the commission's 1934 work report, "statistics have been sorely lacking in the past. Even when we find them occasionally in government agencies . . . they are not very useful for our purpose. Consequently, all the preliminary work of the commission has aimed to gather factual information."[21]

Finally, technocrats of various professions staffed the National Defense Planning Commission. In 1934, the commission recruited many new members, raising the original thirty-nine to well over one hundred.[22] Among the commission members were humanists and social scientists Hu Shi, Fu Sinian, and Jiang Tingba; geologists Ding Wenjiang and Weng Wenhao; economists Liu Dajun and Sun Cheng; industrial and financial leaders Wu Dingchang, Zhang Jiaao, and Xu Xinliu; mining experts Sun Yueqi and Jin

Kaiying; electrical engineers Yun Zhen and Wang Congzhi; chemical experts Wu Chengluo and Fan Xudong; weaponry experts Hong Zhong and Yang Jizeng; and central government officials Chen Lifu and Huang Fu. Most already held government or nongovernment positions at the time of their appointment. Still, the National Defense Planning Commission was anything but a regular administrative bureaucracy. It was a genuine technocracy owing to the technical expertise of most of its members.[23]

In April 1935, the National Defense Planning Commission was renamed the National Resources Commission and placed under the jurisdiction of the Military Affairs Commission. Although Chiang Kaishek continued to serve as president, and Weng Wenhao and Qian Changzhao remained secretary-general, and deputy secretary-general, respectively, changes were clearly discernible in the commission's organizational structure and definition of functions. In addition to the original investigation and statistics divisions, the National Resources Commission created three new offices and two divisions: the offices of electrical engineering, metallurgy, mining, a secretariat, and a planning division. At the same time, the commission's mission was redefined as investigation, statistical survey, and study of human and material resources; planning and reconstruction of resources; and planning of resource mobilization.[24]

What occurred in April 1935 was more than a name change. It marked an important change in purpose and direction. The original three departments in military affairs, international affairs, and education and culture ceased to exist. During the next three years, the National Resources Commission changed its orientation from resource investigation and planning to heavy industrial reconstruction. In effect, the organization was transformed from Chiang Kaishek's brain trust to an organization in charge of industrial development.[25] The development of a *Three-Year Plan for Heavy Industrial Reconstruction* in 1936 best embodies these changes.[26]

The making of the *Three-Year Plan for Heavy Industrial Reconstruction* had begun under the National Defense Planning Commission, although it was not completed until early 1936.[27] Compared with earlier government plans, it had several distinct characteristics: It was based on a large amount of data experts had gathered through systematic investigation. Heavy industry would receive the lion's share of investment capital. Geographically, most planned factories were to be built in interior provinces such as Hunan and Jiangxi for fear of further Japanese aggression. Finally, unlike previous plans, most projects "went according to the plan."[28] Among some thirty planned factories and collieries, twenty-one had begun construction by the time the Sino-Japanese War broke out in July 1937.[29]

The outbreak of war and the relocation of the Nationalist government to Chongqing led to further changes in the organization and activities of the National Resources Commission. In March 1938 the Nationalist government placed the commission under the jurisdiction of the newly created Ministry of Economic Affairs. Although Weng Wenhao and Qian Changzhao continued to lead the organization, their official titles were changed from secretary-general and deputy secretary-general to director and deputy director, respectively. More importantly, the function of the National Resources Commission was redefined to include the creation and management of basic industries, the development of mining resources and management of important collieries, and the creation and management of power plants.[30]

The change of function gave rise to corresponding changes in the commission's organizational structure. Under the director and deputy director were four new divisions, four sections, and one committee: the secretariat, divisions of industry, mining, electric power, sections of technology, economic research, accounting, material purchase, and a committee of finance.[31] Four years later, the commission further modified its organizational structure to reflect its expansion of activities. By now it had seven divisions and two sections under its jurisdiction: the secretariat, the divisions of industry, mining, electric power, material purchase, finance, accounting, and the sections of technology and economic research.[32] By 1938, the National Resources Commission had become a bona fide technocracy in charge of directing heavy industrial development as well as managing enterprises under its jurisdiction. But exactly how did it plan and direct heavy industrial development during the war? To answer this question, I will examine the process of planning and financing heavy industrial development.

Planning and Financing Heavy Industrial Development

Although the development of China's state-owned heavy industries began with the *Three-Year Plan for Heavy Industrial Reconstruction* in 1936, planning for the development of national defense industries began soon after the creation of the National Defense Planning Commission. By early 1933, the commission had drafted plans for the development of heavy industries and the ordnance industry. The plans called for creation of "industrial regions for national defense" within the provinces of Hunan, Hubei, and Sichuan. It was estimated that the plan for general heavy industries would cost Ch$101 million, and the plan for the ordnance industry would cost Ch$57 million.[33] By July 1935 the National Resources Commission had drafted separate proposals based on reliable data. It had also begun integrating these proposals to make a comprehensive plan for developing national defense industries.[34]

By all indications, the commission had completed a draft of the comprehensive plan by early February 1936. Subsequently representatives of the General Staff, the National Resources Commission, the Bureau of Ordnance, the Ministry of Industries, and the Ministry of Financial Administration met twice and reached a consensus on the creation of industrial regions for national defense, the procedures for developing national defense industries, and the treatment of ordnance factories and general heavy industries.

After some modification, the preliminary three-year plan became final in June 1936. The revised *Three-Year Plan for Heavy Industrial Reconstruction* provided that the Nationalist government would spend Ch$101 million for the establishment of factories and collieries in metallurgical, fuel, chemical, electric, machine, and hydroelectric-generating industries.[35] In reality, the Nationalist government appropriated Ch$10 million for the National Resources Commission to begin implementing the *Three-Year Plan for Heavy Industrial Reconstruction,* presumably in addition to the commission's regular budget of Ch$5.49 million for the 1936 fiscal year.[36] Although the sum total of the two figures combined was less than half the projected expense for the first year in the three-year plan, the commission now had enough funding to begin implementation. As indicated earlier, twenty-one out of the thirty planned factories and collieries had begun construction by the time the Sino-Japanese War erupted.

The war caused serious disruptions in implementing the three-year reconstruction plan and forced some of the half-finished factories to relocate to the interior. Despite the disruptions and forced relocation, the National Resources Commission continued to rely on the mechanism of planning for heavy industrial reconstruction. If anything, wartime military and economic mobilization added a greater sense of urgency for planned and coordinated development. Thus, after relocating and constructing factories in the interior between late 1938 and early 1939, the commission started developing a new *Three-Year Plan for Heavy Industrial Reconstruction.* According to this plan, between 1939 and 1941 the commission would establish new factories or expand existing ones in the metallurgical, chemical, liquid fuel, and machine industries, transportation and communication equipment, and the leather and rubber industries. The total cost of these projects was estimated at Ch$57.98 million and US$38.22 million.[37] Although precise figures on total government spending are unavailable, existing documents indicate that the government appropriated Ch$329.97 million (Ch$28.21 million in 1936 constant price) for heavy industrial reconstruction during the three-year period.[38]

In early 1941, the National Resources Commission drafted another comprehensive economic plan, the *Outline of Three-Year Plan for National Defense Industries*. The Eighth Plenary Session of the Fifth Central Executive Committee of the Nationalist Party adopted it in April 1941. According to this plan, between 1942 and 1944 the National Resources Commission would establish new factories or expand existing ones in the metallurgical, machine, electric, chemical, food, and energy industries.[39] The total initial capital needed was estimated at Ch$735.32 million and US$18.34 million, in addition to Ch$361.74 million in liquid assets.[40] Three months later, the commission revised the early plan. The total initial capital needed was now estimated at Ch$816.69 million and US$25.56 million, in addition to Ch$259.74 million in liquid assets.[41]

Where did the National Resources Commission receive the investment capital? How did it finance heavy industrial projects? Did it receive all the investment capital it requested? Archival documents indicate that the commission received investment capital from three sources: annual budget appropriation from the state treasury; short-term loans and investment from state-run banks; and profits from export of mineral resources. Annual budget appropriations from the state treasury constituted the major source of investment capital. Appendix Table 2.1 documents the annual appropriations for the National Resources Commission between 1938 and 1940 and the distribution of appropriations among various industries. It shows that the commission received Ch$42 million from the state treasury through annual appropriations (Ch$ 12.91 million in 1936 constant price) during the three-year period. The two industries that benefited most were the energy and the iron and steel industries. The energy industry received Ch$11.32 million, whereas the iron and steel industry received Ch$11.24 million. The share of the two industries combined accounted for over half (53.71 percent) of the commission's total appropriations.

The National Resources Commission also received capital in the form of short-term loans and investment from state-run banks. There were four major state-run banks before the outbreak of the Sino-Japanese War: the Central Bank of China, the Bank of China, the Bank of Communications, and the Farmers' Bank.[42] Soon after the war broke out, the Nationalist government established a Joint Administrative Agency of the Four Banks (*silian zongchu*). During the first two years of the war, the Joint Administrative Agency of the Four Banks functioned primarily to coordinate the operations of its affiliates. In September 1939, the Nationalist government reorganized the Joint Administrative Agency of the Four Banks and gave it broad powers to make national financial and economic policies.[43] According to the *Measures to Strengthen Wartime Central Financial Institutions*, the Joint Administrative Agency of the Four Banks would establish a board of directors with a chairman appointed by the Nationalist government.[44] As it turned out, the board of directors consisted mostly of heads of central ministries. The government "appointed" none other than Chiang Kaishek to serve as chairman.[45]

In March 1940, Chiang Kaishek ordered the Joint Administrative Agency of the Four Banks to draft a three-year national economic and financial plan. In a handwritten instruction to the agency, he emphasized that "the success of the war of resistance against Japan depends entirely on the achievement of the economy and finance. Thus the Four Banks' responsibility will no longer be confined to financial matters, it will extend to [the making of] economic policies and plans. The Four Banks will also serve as the sole economic foundation [for implementing these economic policies and plans]."[46]

Subsequently, the Joint Administrative Agency of the Four Banks drafted two separate national plans: a three-year economic plan and a three-year financial plan. With regard to the *Three-Year Economic Plan*, after "making industry and mining the top priority," the board of directors decided to invest Ch$166.54 million in state-owned industries through appropriations from the state treasury and loans and investment from the Joint Administrative Agency of the Four Banks.[47] Furthermore, although 68.55 percent of the planned investment capital came from budget appropriations, almost one-third of the total capital came in the form of loans and investment from the Joint Administrative Agency of the Four Banks.[48] Whereas bank investments aimed at making a profit, bank loans were designed to provide circulating capital for existing state-owned enterprises. From the perspective of the National Resources Commission, it only "borrowed piecemeal" from state-run banks before 1943.[49] As inflation became serious after 1942, it resorted more and more to bank loans to keep its enterprises operational. In 1943, the commission received Ch$680 million bank loans from the Joint Administrative Agency of the Four Banks.[50] In 1944 and 1945, the amount of bank loans it received increased to 13.2 billion and 20 billion, respectively.[51] In terms of 1936 constant price, however, the amount it actually received decreased from Ch$2.73 million for 1943 to Ch$1.8 million and Ch$845,666 for 1944 and 1945, respectively.

In addition to state appropriations and loans and investment from the Joint Administrative Agency of the Four Banks, the National Resources Commission used profits it obtained from selling ores such as tungsten and antimony as investment capital. Government regulations provided that the commission could keep 20 percent of the profit from tungsten and antimony trade as "operating expenses."[52] In 1939, the Ministry of Economic Affairs established a Supervisory Committee for the Special Fund of Tungsten and Antimony to keep track of the revenue and expenditure in marketing these ores.[53] The committee's records show that between 1939 and 1943 the National Resources Commission gained Ch$45.69 million (Ch$4.02 million in 1936 constant price) from tungsten and antimony trade, and that most profits were reinvested in industrial and mining enterprises.[54] From 1936 to 1943 the commission reinvested Ch$66.13 million (Ch$6.42 million in 1936 constant price) in various enterprises out of the profits from tungsten and antimony trade,[55] although inflation pressure led to a rapid decline of the value of the amount reinvested after 1939.

Despite the increasing needs for bank loans and the use of profits from the sale of tungsten and antimony, the National Resources Commission relied primarily on appropriations from the state treasury for heavy industrial reconstruction. Appendix Table 1.3 shows the absolute figures of annual state appropriations between 1936 and 1945 as well as the amount of annual state appropriations in terms of 1936 constant price. The table reveals that after experiencing a steady rise from 1936 to 1941, the value of annual state appropriations suffered a steep decline from 1942 to 1945. The share of the National Resources Commission in the state budget indicates a similar trend: after reaching a high of 2.8 percent in 1940, it declined rapidly.

Still, state appropriations for heavy industrial reconstruction constituted the major source of investment for the National Resources Commission. To better understand the role of state appropriations for heavy industrial reconstruction, we need to determine the percentage of the special fund allocated to the National Resources Commission out of the total amount of the Special Fund for Reconstruction Projects (*jianshe shiye zhuankuan jijin*) the Nationalist government created in 1937. As a new category in the national budget, the Special Fund for Reconstruction Projects was intended to provide investment capital for all reconstruction projects in national defense, heavy industries, transportation and communications, water conservancy, and education and culture.[56] As Appendix Table 2.2 shows, the Special Fund for Reconstruction Projects made up anywhere from 20 to 50 percent of the total national budget between 1937 and 1943. Although the fund earmarked for heavy industrial reconstruction was low at times, the special fund allocated to the National Resources Commission averaged 8.8 percent of the Special Fund for Reconstruction Projects between 1941 and 1942, when the Special Fund's percentage in the national budget was reduced to an average of 20.49 percent. In other words, on average, the special fund allocated to the National Resources Commission accounted for 42.95 percent of the total Special Fund for Reconstruction Projects for 1941 and 1942.

Once the appropriations from national budget were made available, the National Resources Commission distributed them among heavy industries such as the energy, coal, petroleum, metal, iron and steel, machine, electric, and chemical industries. The commission's own statistics reveal that between 1936 and 1945 it received Ch$119.21 billion investment capital, which amounted to Ch$71.78 million in 1936 constant price. Among the nine industries, the energy industry received Ch$50.73 billion, which counted for 42.6 percent of the commission's investment capital. The industry that received the second largest share was petroleum (15.8 percent) with a total of Ch$18.87 billion.[57]

A closer examination reveals an unprecedented increase in the energy industry's share of investment capital in 1945, which constituted 91 percent of all the investment capital it received during the ten-year period. Thus, if we only consider the nine-year period between 1936 and 1944, a different picture emerges. As Appendix Table 2.3 demonstrates, the National Resources Commission received Ch$ 26.70 billion for investment between 1936 and 1944. Among the nine industries, the petroleum industry, instead of the energy industry, received Ch$ 10.90 billion, counting for 40.8 percent of the investment capital the commission received. The industry that received the second largest share was the energy industry (16.3 percent) with Ch$4.34 million.

In terms of importance, then, the energy and petroleum industries experienced a complete reversal of order. Appendix Table 2.3 reflects the National Resources Commission's investment priority. In descending order, they are the petroleum industry (40.8 percent), energy industry (16.3 percent), iron and steel industry (12.5 percent), electric industry (8.3 percent), coal industry (7.1 percent), machine industry (4.9 percent), metal industry (4.7 percent), chemical industry (3.3 percent), other industries (1.8 percent), and the cement industry (0.2 percent).

The Process of Heavy Industrial Expansion

After making plans and obtaining investment capital, the National Resources Commission began heavy industrial reconstruction in 1936. Between 1936 and July 1945, the commission established or took over 130 enterprises and organizations in heavy industries: nine in metallurgy, seven in machine, five in electric equipment, thirty-seven in chemicals, thirty-eight in mining, twenty-seven in energy, and seven service organizations. Among them, the commission wholly owned and managed seventy-five enterprises and organizations, partially owned and managed thirty-seven, and invested in eighteen. In addition, the majority were established between 1938 and 1942. Among those enterprises and organizations whose dates of establishment are available, four were established in 1936, three in 1937, eleven in 1938, nineteen in 1939, fifteen in 1940, twenty-four in 1941, sixteen in 1942, nine in 1943, ten in 1944, and one in early 1945.[58] The process of heavy industrial expansion can be highlighted through case studies of a number of key enterprises.

Energy The National Resources Commission established its first power plant in July 1937. By August 1945, the commission had twenty-five power plants under its control. Over half (fourteen) were established during the first five years of the war (1937–1941). Most were located in interior provinces.[59] The commission's own report stated that the war saw the "establishment of a foundation of energy enterprises in all political and economic centers with the exception of those locations where small-scale power plants had already existed."[60]

Several factors explain the establishment of power plants in the interior provinces. First, as Japanese troops occupied more and more territory in China, the Nationalist government retreated deeper and deeper into the interior, making the interior provinces China's political and economic centers and "base areas" *(genjudi)* for resistance. Hundreds of factories relocated to the interior in order to avoid being destroyed or confiscated by the Japanese. Most factories resumed production once they completed relocation. Moreover, new factories sprang up like mushrooms during the first few years of the war. All these abrupt changes created a tremendous need for electricity in a region where little previously had been available.

For instance, the National Resources Commission's budget plan for 1940 revealed the commission's rationale for its decision to fund ten power plants, including the Guiyang plant: "Since the eruption of the war Guiyang became the hub of overland transportation and communications, and the original direct current generator of 150 kilowatts was no longer adequate to meet the increasing needs. After the provincial government of Guizhou requested assistance, the National Resources Commission set up another power plant with the capacity of generating 320 kilowatts, which began providing electricity on March 20, 1939. Since then, the city of Guiyang has seen rapid municipal development, and the industrial need for electricity has also been increasing. Consequently the newly completed power plant has already become inadequate, and so a decision has been made to establish a new power plant in 1940 with the capacity of generating 1,000 kilowatts of electricity."[61]

A similar situation existed in Kunming. There had been a power plant in Kunming since 1904, but it was mainly designed to provide electricity for urban residents. After the war began, numerous factories relocated to Kunming, including the Central Machine Works, the Central Electric Works, and the Central Airplane Manufacturing Works. Their relocation created a tremendous need for electric power. To meet this need, the National Resources Commission in June 1939 set up a new power plant, the Kunhu Power Plant, on the outskirts of Kunming. It had 4,000 kilowatts of electricity-generating capacity.[62] On average, the plant barely generated more than 50,000 kilowatt-hours (*du*) of electricity a month during the latter part of 1939. Beginning in January 1940, however, the number of kilowatt-hours generated increased dramatically, from 50,000 to 500,000 by December 1940.[63] Given the dramatic increase in demand, the National Resources Commission allocated Ch$1.5 million to expand the power-generating capacity of the existing plant. Even in places such as Lanzhou, where few industries had existed but which were strategically important, the commission established and later expanded a power plant for the purpose of "laying a solid foundation for industrial reconstruction in the Northwest."[64]

In Sichuan, which had the greatest concentration of industrial enterprises, the National Resources Commission established nine power plants to meet wartime needs for electricity. In late 1937, the commission launched a joint venture with the provincial government of Sichuan to expand an existing power-generating facility in Wanxian. By June 1939, the power-generating capacity of the plant had increased from the original 180 kilowatts to 320 kilowatts.[65] Despite the increase, the need for electricity continued to grow. In 1941, the commission installed new equipment with the capacity to generate an additional 340 kilowatts of electricity. The commission's plan for the 1943 fiscal year called for the "completion of a power network within Sichuan province to meet industrial needs."[66] By 1945, the total power-generating capacity of the commission's power plants had reached 26,975 kilowatts, out of which 24,000 kilowatts resulted directly from the establishment and expansion of new plants.[67] As a result, the amount of electricity increased from 1,533 thousand kilowatt-hours in 1937 to 70,136 thousand kilowatt-hours in 1945.[68]

The bulk of electric energy that these power plants produced went to factories in heavy industries and the ordnance industry. In 1944, heavy industries (the chemical, electric, iron and steel, machine, and coal mining industries combined) consumed 43.9 percent of the total electric energy produced, whereas the ordnance industry consumed 19.6 percent.[69] In other words, heavy industries and the ordnance industry consumed close to two-thirds (63.5 percent) of electricity produced. It is little wonder that the National Resources Commission spent 16.73 percent of its investment capital on the energy industry between 1937 and 1944.

Petroleum As Appendix Table 2.3 shows, the National Resources Commission invested Ch$10.90 billion in the petroleum industry, almost half of its total investment capital for the period from 1937 to 1944. Unlike the story of the energy industry, which involves some twenty-five plants, the story of the petroleum industry is essentially that of one oil field in China's northwest.

The story began to unfold in late 1937. After returning from a visit to Moscow and London, Weng Wenhao made an important suggestion to Chiang Kaishek. Weng said that "since we have already given up the littoral and coastal areas and devoted our attention to reconstruction in the interior provinces, we could only rely on trucks for transporting materials, machinery, and personnel from the coastal areas to the interior. However, since trucks must use gas and the coastal areas have all been blocked and import of gas from foreign countries has become impossible, the problem of the shortage of liquid fuel has become extremely serious. There are only two solutions to this problem: establishing alcohol factories mainly in Sichuan province . . . and opening oil fields in Gansu province. Gansu province has a rich source of oil. Although we do not have complete confidence in the exploitation of oil fields, we must take the risk in order to solve the problem of shortage of liquid fuel." Chiang agreed.[70]

On June 12, 1938, Weng Wenhao presided over the ceremony for creating the Gansu Oil Field Preparatory Division in Hankou, which marked the beginning of exploiting the Gansu oil field.[71] To cover operating expenses, the National Resources Commission allocated Ch$200,000 from the Special Fund for Heavy Industrial Reconstruction for the 1938 fiscal period. For the 1939 fiscal year, the commission set aside Ch$2.3 million from profits made in tungsten and antimony trade.[72] Still, the Gansu Oil Field Preparatory Division faced a major obstacle—the lack of drilling rigs for oil exploration. At the time of the division's creation, the National Resources Commission already had two divisions: the Sichuan Division of Oil Exploration and the Shanbei Division of Oil Exploration. The Sichuan Division had rotary rigs purchased from Germany, but they were being used in Sichuan. The only other drilling rigs available were those left in Yanchang by the Shanbei Division of Oil Exploration when the Communists took over Shanbei in 1935. Consequently, Weng Wenhao met with Zhou Enlai, then Communist representative in Hankou, to explain the importance of oil exploration for resistance against Japan, hoping that Zhou would agree to the removal of the two drilling rigs and other equipment from Yanchang. Zhou not only agreed but promised full support for the equipment's removal and transportation.[73] Weng's recollection written in 1949 confirmed the "Communists' active assistance" in the process.[74] Because of the lack of transportation facilities, however, it took five months to ship the equipment to Yumen oil field in northwestern Gansu. On May 6, 1939, workers at the Yumen oil field began using the drilling rigs to drill wells, and by August 11 they had discovered an oil layer between 100 and 300 meters below the surface.[75] Between July and November the Gansu Oil Field Preparatory Division drilled five oil wells and established a simple oil refinery. By the end of 1939 it had produced 428 tons of crude oil and 71 tons of refined oil. In the following year the amount of crude and refined oil increased to 1,346 and 1,505 tons, respectively.[76]

The discovery of China's first major oil reservoir prompted the National

Resources Commission to allocate Ch$1.5 million for the Yumen oil field in its budget plan for the 1940 fiscal year. Nevertheless, the Gansu Oil Field Preparatory Division actually received Ch$10.34 million that year, which was almost 4.5 times its funding for 1939.[77] Later in 1940 the National Resources Commission won approval of additional US$5 million government appropriations and used them to order twelve rotary rigs and other heavy equipment from the United States. Unfortunately, after the Pacific War broke out, the Japanese destroyed or confiscated most of the equipment while it was still in transit.[78]

In March 1941, the National Resources Commission reorganized the Gansu Oil Field Preparatory Division as the Gansu Petroleum Administration and appointed Sun Yueqi, mining expert and member of the National Resources Commission, as general manager. Because the Japanese invasion of Vietnam and Burma effectively blocked the transportation of much needed equipment, the Gansu Petroleum Administration had to rely on domestic technologies to make equipment such as furnaces for oil refining. Still, it succeeded in developing the Yumen oil field. From 1939 to 1945, the oil field produced 78,667,120 gallons of crude oil, 13,033,549 gallons of gas, 5,116,273 gallons of kerosene, and 717,277 gallons of diesel oil.[79] With the exception of kerosene, the distribution of gas and diesel oil was placed under the control of the Commission for the Management of Liquid Fuel. The commission used information on the amount of gas and diesel oil available as a basis to distribute coupons to organizations in the military and government and to reconstruction enterprises in the northwest.[80] A 1942 report by the National Resources Commission reveals that out of the monthly total of 35,500 gallons of gas allocated to these organizations between April 1940 and March 1942, the military received 13,500 gallons (38 percent) and government organizations 1,450 gallons (4.1 percent), whereas reconstruction enterprises received 20,550 gallons (57.9 percent).[81] These petroleum products made a significant contribution to the resistance against Japan and economic reconstruction in the Northwest.[82]

Iron and steel   The National Resources Commission began building iron and steel enterprises in 1936 under the *Three-Year Plan for Heavy Industrial Reconstruction*. It chose Xiashesi in Hunan province as the site for a central iron and steel works. Unfortunately, Japan's military advances forced the commission to stop construction in July 1938, although "all the preliminary work had been completed."[83] Between 1938 and the war's end, the commission established eight iron and steel factories, mostly in Sichuan and

Yunnan provinces: one in 1938, one in 1939, three in 1941, one in 1943, and two in 1944.[84]

The National Resources Commission and the Bureau of Ordnance established the largest of their enterprises, the Relocation and Reconstruction Committee of Iron and Steel Works, in Hankou in March 1938. As the name of the organization suggests, it was designed to dismantle and relocate the equipment of existing iron and steel works, including Hanyang Iron and Steel Works, Daye Iron Works, Liuhegou Iron Works, and Shanghai Steel Works.[85] Between June 1938 and December 1939, the Relocation and Reconstruction Committee of Iron and Steel Works shipped 56,800 tons of materials and equipment to Chongqing.[86] Once the resources were there, the construction of a new iron and steel works began at Dadukou along the bank of the Yangzi River. Between 1939 and 1940, the Relocation and Reconstruction Committee of Iron and Steel Works received Ch$19.33 million from the government for reconstruction in its new Dadukou location.[87] After that, the Relocation and Reconstruction Committee of Iron and Steel Works became popularly known as the Dadukou Iron and Steel Works (DISW).[88]

By March 1943, the DISW had emerged as the largest state-owned enterprise in the Nationalist-controlled areas, with 21,691 employees, including 6,994 at its Chongqing headquarters. The DISW consisted of seven manufacturing plants. The first plant had two power generators that generated and supplied power to the entire factory. The second had two iron-smelting furnaces that produced pig iron. The third had two open-hearth furnaces, two electric furnaces, one Bessemer furnace, and five iron-smelting furnaces, all used to make steel and cast iron. The fourth was in charge of steel rolling, making steel plates and other steel products. The fifth was a coal washery. It had a coal cleaning machine that made coal fit for iron smelting. The sixth made refractory materials such as refractory bricks. The seventh made and repaired machine tools. The DISW also had a large transportation unit responsible for shipping raw materials and equipment.[89]

For the purpose of supplying raw materials for making iron and steel, the DISW established its own iron mine and coal mine. Both were located in Sichuan province in areas less than 100 miles from Chongqing. The DISW embarked on explorations at the two sites in early 1938. By the end of 1940, the two mines had begun to provide a regular supply of iron ore and coal to the Chongqing manufacturing plants.[90] In fact, the DISW achieved an effective vertical integration of the various stages of production because it had "achieved complete self-sufficiency in its supply of raw materials."[91]

Between 1940, when the DISW became operational, and 1945, the DISW produced 34,021 tons of pig iron, 18,159 tons of steel ingots, 6,660 tons of steel products, and 332 tons of cast steel.[92] In comparison, the other seven iron and steel factories under the National Resources Commission produced 76,331 tons of pig iron and 24,077 tons of steel ingots during the same period. In other words, as Appendix Table 2.4 shows, the DISW output of pig iron was almost half (44.6 percent) of the total output of all other enterprises of the National Resources Commission in pig iron. Moreover, the DISW output in steel ingot and other steel products consistently outnumbered that of all other enterprises of the National Resources Commission in steel ingot and other steel products.

Machinery   During the Sino-Japanese War, the National Resources Commission established five machine works: one in Yunnan province, one in Sichuan province, one in Gansu province, and two in Jiangxi province.[93] Among them the largest and most important was the Central Machine Works, located in the outskirts of Kunming in Yunnan province.

The Central Machine Works was conceived as part of the *Three-Year Plan for Heavy Industrial Reconstruction* of 1936 and was designed to manufacture airplane engines, power machines, and tool-making machines. In November 1936, the National Resources Commission established a Preparatory Committee for the purpose of coordinating activities in founding the machine works. Subsequently the committee chose Xiashesi of Xiangtan in Hunan province as the site for the new factory. Construction began in earnest in January 1937. One year later, work on the engine, power, and machine tools plants was well under way, when Japanese advances forced the factory to relocate to Yunnan province.[94] By May 1938, over 5,000 tons of machinery and equipment and more than 200 technical personnel and workers had arrived at Ciba, the new location in the outskirts of Kunming. One year later, the construction of the new factory buildings was complete, and on September 9, 1939, the factory was named the Central Machine Works.[95]

At the time of its establishment in 1939, the Central Machine Works consisted of five plants: a steam turbine plant, steam boiler plant, gas engine and gas furnace plant, power generator and motor generator plant, and automobile plant.[96] The vital importance of the Central Machine Works led the National Resources Commission to allocate more than Ch$6.37 million to it between 1936 and 1939.[97] During the next two years the commission continued to invest heavily in the Central Machine Works, with Ch\$4 million in 1940 and Ch\$4.53 million in 1941.[98] These investments led to the establishment of two new manufacturing plants in 1942—one for spinning and weaving machines and one for tool-making machinery. At the same time, the steam turbine plant was designated as an iron and steel plant because the projected manufacturing of airplane engines in the original plan was canceled on orders from the government.[99]

The National Resources Commission's sustained investment made the Central Machine Works one of the largest state-owned enterprises in Yunnan province. In 1939 the Central Machine Works had Ch\$7.41 million in assets and 727 employees.[100] Two years later, its total assets increased from Ch\$7.41 million to Ch\$12.64 million. The number of permanent employees also increased from 727 to 1,415.[101] By September 1943, the Central Machine Works had a total of Ch\$35.32 million in assets and 1,648 permanent employees, which more than doubled the number of employees for 1939.[102]

Figure 4. Panoramic view of the Dadukou Iron and Steel Works in Chongqing during the Sino-Japanese War. Courtesy Chongqing Municipal Archives.

The expansion of the Central Machine Works brought about a substantial increase of its productive capacity.[103] Between 1939 and 1945, the Central Machine Works manufactured fifty different power machines of different capacities (such as diesel engines, water tube boilers, and power generators), 250 tool-making machines, 18,590 precision instruments, sixty-five spinning machines, 4,517 units of transportation equipment, 1,403,980 units of special equipment, and 249,650 miscellaneous products.[104] These products were widely distributed among different sectors of the economy. Between July 1944 and June 1945, for example, 37.7 percent of its products

Figure 5. Hundred-ton blast furnace of the Dadukou Iron and Steel Works in Chongqing during the Sino-Japanese War. Courtesy the Second Historical Archives of China.

went to military, transportation, and educational organizations, 23.2 percent to enterprises of the National Resources Commission, 7.2 percent to province-run enterprises in Yunnan, 24.4 percent to private enterprises, and 7.5 percent to branch factories of the Central Machine Works.[105]

Alcohol   As was the case with the machine industry, the National Resources Commission began making plans to develop an alcohol industry in 1936. According to its *Program for Self Sufficiency in Liquid Fuel*, the com-

Figure 6. Cowper stoves for the 100-ton blast furnace of the Dadukou Iron and Steel Works in Chongqing during the Sino-Japanese War. Camouflage netting is visible on top of the stoves. Courtesy the Second Historical Archives of China.

mission planned to invest Ch$4 million to establish alcohol factories with a projected output of 4 million gallons of alcohol.[106] This plan was never implemented because war broke out the following year. Nonetheless, leaders of the National Resources Commission understood the critical importance of liquid fuel to the Chinese war effort and were determined to solve the problem of fuel shortages by establishing alcohol factories and oil fields in the interior provinces. Because the Yumen oil field was so far away from the political and economic centers and did not begin producing in large quantities until 1942, establishing alcohol factories became a top priority on the commission's agenda.

Shortly after the war began, the National Resources Commission sent personnel to Sichuan to investigate whether it was feasible to establish an alcohol factory. Soon the commission established such a factory in Neijiang in cooperation with the Department of Reconstruction of Sichuan province, with an initial capital of Ch$140,000. It was named the Sichuan Alcohol Factory. By September 1938, the alcohol factory had begun producing alcohol and gas substitutes. Almost all the products went to

Figure 7. Panoramic view of the Central Machine Works on the outskirts of Kunming during the Sino-Japanese War. Courtesy Jiaoda Kunji High-Tech Company Limited.

military, transportation, and other government organizations.[107] After this initial effort, the National Resources Commission established eight other alcohol factories in Sichuan, Yunnan, Guizhou, Gansu, and Shanxi provinces.[108] Between 1938 and 1944, these factories produced 10,407,105 gallons of alcohol. Because wartime demand for alcohol often exceeded supply, the provincial government strictly controlled the distribution and price of alcohol.[109]

Electric products   During the Sino-Japanese War, the National Resources Commission established five factories to manufacture electric products. Two were located in Yunnan province, one in Sichuan province, one in Gansu province, and one in Jiangxi province.[110] Among them, the largest and most important was the Central Electric Works located in Kunming in Yunnan province.

The Central Electric Works was conceived as part of the *Three-Year Plan for Heavy Industrial Reconstruction* of 1936. According to the plan, the Central Electric Works was to develop the capability of manufacturing electric products such as electric wires, electron tubes and bulbs, telephones, and power

Figure 8. A machine operator of the Central Machine Works during the Sino-Japanese War. Courtesy Yunnan Provincial Archives.

generators. It was designed to "meet the needs of the military and the national economy and gradually achieve self-sufficiency in electric products for both military and civilian use." The plan called for the creation of three factories in three years with an initial capital of Ch$14.5 million. In July 1936, the National Resources Commission created a Preparatory Committee and entrusted it with the responsibility of planning and coordinating factory construction in Xiashesi of Xiangtan in Hunan province. Construction began in March 1937. By December 1937, the construction was partially complete, and a fourth factory was built in March 1938. Because of increasing Japanese military threats, however, the Preparatory Committee began relocating its factories in early 1938.[111]

Eventually, the first factory, which made electrical wires, relocated to Kunming in Yunnan province. The second factory, which produced electron tubes, electric bulbs, radio transmitters, and receivers, relocated to Guilin in Guangxi province. The third factory, which focused on the manufacturing of telephones and switchboards, also relocated to Kunming. The fourth enterprise was divided into four branch factories, with locations in Kunming, Guilin, Chongqing, and Lanzhou. The Kunming branch made transformers, switch equipment, electric meters, and electric motors above 50 horsepower; the Guilin branch produced power generators, electric mo-

Figure 9. "Resource" model trucks made by the Central Machine Works during the Sino-Japanese War. Courtesy the Second Historical Archives of China.

tors below 50 horsepower, dry cells, and batteries; the Chongqing branch manufactured dry cells and batteries; and the Lanzhou branch specialized in the manufacturing of dry cells.[112]

On July 1, 1939, the National Resources Commission abolished the Preparatory Committee and formally established the Central Electric Works.[113] Because of its important position in heavy industrial reconstruction, the National Resources Commission allocated more than Ch$6.34 million to the Central Electric Works between 1936 and 1938.[114] For the 1939 fiscal year, the commission invested Ch$2 million in it, followed in 1940 by the investment of another Ch$4.98 million.[115] The continued allocation of resources not only contributed to the enterprise's dramatic expansion but made it the largest enterprise in the electric industry. The number of its employees increased from a mere 535 in 1939 to 4,066 in 1943.[116] The Central Electric Works' predominant position also manifested itself in the output of electric products. With the exception of its output of power generators, its output of other products accounted for 82 to 97 percent of the total output of all five factories in the electric industry.[117] Factory records reveal that its products enjoyed a large share of market throughout China's southwest, with the bulk going to government organizations (44.9 percent) and enterprises of the National Resources Commission (23.2 percent) for fiscal 1942.[118] During the following year, 40 percent of its products went to military organizations, 10 percent to government and transportation organizations, and 22 percent to state-owned enterprises. In terms of regional distribution, the statistics for 1943 show that 47 percent went to Chongqing region, 34 percent to Kunming region, 13 percent to Guilin region, 2 percent to Guiyang region, and 4 percent to Lanzhou region. The Central Electric Works also provided its products to American troops stationed in China.[119]

In short, the war-triggered crisis led to major expansion of the state-owned heavy industries. But how significant was the state sector in China's overall heavy industrial development? To address this question let us turn to a comparison between public and private enterprise in heavy industry.[120] I will first discuss the structure of Chinese industry and the position of heavy industry within that structure before the Sino-Japanese War. I will then compare public enterprise with private enterprise in heavy industry during the war.

Public and Private Enterprise in Heavy Industry

In the spring of 1933, the National Defense Planning Commission launched a survey of Chinese industry as part of its mission of resource investigation. Between April 1933 and October 1934, a group of researchers from the China Economic Statistics Institute inspected firms in fourteen provinces and more than 120 municipalities and counties. The statistics they gathered were then compiled and published by the National Resources Commission in early 1937 as the *Report on Conditions of Chinese Industry*. The report did not cover Gansu, Xinjiang, Yunnan, Guizhou, Ningxia, and Qinghai provinces; nor did it include Manchuria, which was now under Japanese occupation. Moreover, the report excluded government arsenals and firms that did not use mechanized power and employed fewer than thirty workers.[121] Still, the *Report on Conditions of Chinese Industry* was the most comprehensive industrial census for prewar China.

The census takers found that China had 2,435 factories under Chinese ownership, which had a capital of Ch$406,872,634 and employed 435,257 workers.[122] At the time of the census, the Chinese economy was "predominantly private, and the role of the state sector, though increasing over time, remained small."[123] Within what was essentially a market-oriented private economy, light industry dominated. Food–beverage–tobacco and textile products made up more than 70 percent of the total output of China's manufacturing industry in 1933, whereas basic metals (iron and steel) and other metal products such as machinery counted for less than 9 percent.[124]

Contemporary statistics from the Ministry of Industries also show the dominant position light industry occupied in the overall structure of Chinese industry. Appendix Table 2.5 reveals that, between 1932 and 1937, the number of registered factories reached 3,885, had a capital of Ch$377,848,000, and employed 457,143 workers. As far as the proportion between heavy and light industry is concerned, light industry (such as the food processing, textile, and chemical industries) accounted for 3,305 factories or 85.1 percent of the total, Ch$308,643,000 in capital or 81.68 percent, and 432,049 workers or 94.5 percent. In sharp contrast, heavy industry (such as the hydroelectric-generating, metallurgical, machine, electric, and the ordnance industries) accounted for only 580 factories or 14.8 percent of the total, Ch$69,205,000 in capital or 18.3 percent, and 25,094 workers or 5.5 percent.

Within the light-industry dominated industrial structure, the proportion of public enterprise was even smaller than private enterprise. The *Report on Conditions of Chinese Industry* notes that, out of the 2,435 factories surveyed, only sixty-six were public enterprises, and most of them were in the hands of provincial authorities.[125] Data compiled in 1935 by the Ministry of Industries reveals an even clearer picture of the share of public enterprise. The data show a total of seventy-two public enterprises in China, with Ch$30,297,726 in capital, 40,669 workers, 38,779 horsepower, and Ch$74,828,733 in value of output.[126] Among them, fifty-one were in either heavy industry or the transportation industry. As Appendix Table 2.6 shows, they had Ch$18,075,979 in capital, 26,966 workers, 33,169 horsepower, and Ch$61,870,831 in value of output. What is more, of all the public enterprises, only seventeen were in heavy industry proper (metallurgical, metal, machine, and energy industries), with Ch$12,320,992 in capital, 8,258 workers, 23,376 horsepower, and Ch$53,365,723 in value of output. Appendix Table 2.7 summarizes the comparison between public and private enterprise in heavy industry in the mid-1930s. The table reveals that public enterprises made up only 2.9 percent of all the factories, 17.8 percent of all the capital, and 32.9 percent of all the workers.

The decade between 1935 and 1945 witnessed a fundamental change in the existing position of public and private enterprise. According to a statistical survey conducted by the Bureau of Statistics of the Ministry of Economic Affairs, the relative position of public and private enterprise had changed radically by 1942. Appendix Table 2.8 illustrates the different positions public and private enterprise occupied as of 1942 in terms of number of factories, amount of capital, number of workers, and power equipment. The result is more revealing when we compare the average capital, number of workers, and power equipment in public and private enterprise in heavy industry. By 1942, public enterprise had overtaken private enterprise in the amount of capital, number of workers, and power equipment. As Appendix Table 2.9 shows, on average the amount of capital of a public enterprise was 18 times that of a private enterprise, the number of workers 3.7 times that of a private enterprise, and the power equipment 2.2 times that of a private enterprise.[127]

Statistics on the increase in output of major products in heavy industry provide further evidence of the dominant position public enterprise achieved during the Sino-Japanese War. Appendix Tables 2.10a and 2.10b show an increase in output of major products in heavy industry and the share of public enterprise in the increase. The output of public enterprise in some industries was very small one year after the war began; yet by the time the war ended, their share of the total output had increased dramatically. For instance, in 1938 the share of output of state-owned iron and steel industries was only 5.8 percent and 20 percent, respectively. By the end of 1945, these figures had increased to 64.8 percent and 96.4 percent. Moreover, the manufacturing of a number of heavy industrial products was from the very beginning a monopoly of state-owned industries. Finally, the average figures of the share of product of public enterprise show a steady increase during the eight-year period: 55.6 percent in 1938, 61.9 in 1939, 62.7 in 1940, 65.5 in 1941, 70.5 in 1942, 75.5 in 1943, 77.9 in 1944, and 79.9 in 1945.

To summarize, all the evidence points to a significant expansion of state-owned heavy industry during the war. One could even argue that the share of public enterprise products in heavy industry as well as light industry expanded significantly during the war. After analyzing the output statistics of seventeen major products of heavy and light industries, Xu Dixin and Wu Chengming concluded that the share of public enterprise products was 21.2 percent in 1938. By 1944, however, the share of public enterprise products had reached 53.7 percent.[128] In other words, public enterprise had achieved a dominant position by the end of the Sino-Japanese War.

A sustained systemic crisis developed in China after Japan invaded Manchuria. This crisis led to the creation and reorganization of a central planning bureaucracy and the tremendous expansion of heavy industry, a process that ultimately led to the dominance of state-owned heavy industry in twentieth-century China.

CHAPTER 3

Enterprise Governance Structure

Path dependence also characterizes the evolution of the enterprise governance structure. Although crisis caused resource creation, expansion, and centralization in the ordnance and general heavy industries, it strengthened both the existing model of state ownership and management and the existing model of bureaucratic organization of enterprises within these industries due to the nature of China's institutional endowments.

An essential component of China's institutional endowments is the organizational model of state administrative bureaucracy. Within the Chinese historical and institutional context and as an ideal type, a government bureaucracy is an administrative structure characterized by a hierarchy of positions filled with appointed officials, with graded ranks and corresponding emoluments, whose lines of authority and responsibility are defined by administrative codes or written rules. A pervasive institutional endowment, the organizational model of formal administrative bureaucracy served as the only institutional resource when China began establishing ordnance factories in the 1860s. As a result, most ordnance factories established between the 1860s and 1890s bore the name of "manufacturing bureaus," and traditional bureaucrats ran them as they would any other government bureaus. Even the establishment of the Chinese republic in 1912 did not alter the fundamentally bureaucratic nature of the state machinery and the governance structure of state-owned enterprises. Although Nationalist leaders explored different organizational forms of economic reconstruction, the war-triggered sustained systemic crisis of the 1930s and 1940s strengthened the organizational model of formal administrative bureaucracy as state-owned enterprises developed and expanded a bureaucratic governance structure similar to that of the formal administrative bureaucracy.

By 1945 a large state-owned enterprise had developed a governance structure characterized by administrative units made up of divisions *(chu)* and departments *(ke)*, ranked according to their size and importance within the administrative hierarchy. All division and departmental heads had official ranks, as well as classes within ranks with corresponding privileges. Nevertheless, as a result of the introduction of a modern educational system early in the twentieth century, the increasing availability of educational opportunities abroad, and the requirement for technical expertise essential for developing national defense industries, a new class of technocrats replaced the traditional bureaucrats in state-owned enterprises in the ordnance and heavy industries.

The Enterprise Governance Structure in the Ordnance Industry

Between 1860 and 1894 China established at least twenty-two ordnance bureaus and factories and after 1894, another fourteen ordnance bureaus and factories came into existence. More importantly, all of these enterprises were owned and operated by the imperial government or provincial governments. As a result of state ownership and management, the forms these enterprises took represented an extension of the organizational model of the formal administrative bureaucracy.

The bureaucratic nature of enterprise organization found expression in the name of ordnance factories. Li Hongzhang established the Jiangnan Arsenal in 1865 and named the new arsenal the Jiangnan General Manufacturing Bureau.[1] The majority of ordnance factories established during this period carried the term *bureau* in their titles, indicating the bureaucratic nature of their establishments.[2]

The bureaucratic aspect of ordnance factories is also reflected in their organizational structure and the ability of their officials and functionaries to move to comparable positions in the state bureaucracy. For instance, the Jiangnan Manufacturing Bureau's director and associate director, as well as its administrative and management staff, had not only official titles but also ranks. As of 1910, almost all the officials worked on a short-term basis, preparing to take a permanent position at a moment's notice.[3] Such a practice found confirmation in the recommendations for consolidating the Sichuan ordnance factory made by Zhu Enba, a high-ranking official in charge of ordnance affairs. According to Zhu, "There are frequent transfers among expectant appointees serving in the provinces. However, deputies in the business of manufacturing ordnance cannot be treated as regular deputies of temporary assignment. Especially because of the need to deal with all kinds of matters, they must work in the factory for an extended period of time before they could function effectively. Frequent transfer makes it difficult for new deputies to understand how the factory operates."[4] Still, the practice of assigning expectant officials temporary duties existed in numerous ordnance bureaus and factories, such as the Jilin Machine Manufacturing Bureau,[5] the Jinling Manufacturing Bureau,[6] and the Sichuan New Machine Factory.[7] In a way, these expectant officials were deemed "interchangeable parts" in the bureaucratic machinery because they could be, and in fact were, assigned to any official positions commensurate with their rank.

The bureaucratic structure of state-owned enterprises gave rise to a number of problems that were unique to a government bureaucracy. First, factory officials tended to "administer the arsenals as they would any other bureau of the traditional government" without regard to cost-effective management, which resulted in overstaffing, misuse of personnel, and malfeasance in the handling of funds.[8] An 1895 investigation of the Jiangnan Manufacturing Bureau revealed that with each change of directors it was customary for the new director to bring in thirty to forty of his personal friends as officials and staff. By the end of 1895, the arsenal had employed as many as 200 officials and staff.[9]

Bureaucrats who were in charge of managing ordnance factories generally received training grounded in the Confucian and Neo-Confucian classics. As a result, they had neither the educational background nor the experience necessary to run manufacturing bureaus as modern business enterprises. A 1909 report by Zhu Enba noted that the Sichuan Machine Bureau had eighteen deputies, but "none of them know anything about manufacturing."[10] Zhu's remarks on the Jiangnan Manufacturing Bureau were equally unflattering. In his view, the bureau "uses too many incompetent personnel. Moreover, the officials neither understand the method of manufacturing nor have any idea about management, although they see their positions as excellent assignments."[11] In November 1910, having inspected two ordnance factories in Hubei province, Zhu again wrote: "There are no clearly defined responsibilities for the administrative and management staff in the factories. Moreover, no one really understands the method of manufacturing. Consequently the administrative and management staff has to rely on foremen and artisans to make decisions. Because the foremen and artisans neither confer with one another nor conduct research for improvement, however, they simply try to shift responsibility onto others when problems arise."[12]

After the 1911 Revolution, ordnance officials and managers made renewed efforts to improve factory management. For example, the Shanghai Manufacturing Bureau, the successor to the Jiangnan Manufacturing Bureau, abolished twelve units in December 1912. These units included divisions of reimbursement, statistics, general inspection, price control, civil engineering, general affairs, assignment, reception, library, academy of translation, academy of learning, and academy of training.[13] By the following summer, the Ministry of War regarded the situation at the Shanghai Manufacturing Bureau as hopeless because it dismissed all the deputies, administrative and management staff, and artisans. In issuing its order the Ministry of War stated that "the administrative and management staff and artisans have been working in the Bureau for a number of years, and they believe they have seniority status. Although they may have once been hard working, at present many of them simply draw their salary without actually doing anything. It has also been said that they recommend and appoint only their relatives and friends in order to consolidate their positions. As a result, the administrative and management staff dare not impose discipline on the artisans, and the director cannot make the administrative and management staff carry out his orders and instructions."[14]

Still, the organization of ordnance enterprises remained bureaucratic as a result of the re-creation of the formal administrative bureaucracy and its application in state-owned enterprise. As early as May 1912 the government adopted a system of ranks by classifying civil service into selected appointment (jianren), recommended appointment (jianren), and delegated appointment (weiren).[15] Then, in January 1913, the government enacted a *Draft Administrative Law Governing Civil Service Appointments*, which provided for classifiying the civil service into four ranks of special appointment (teren), selected appointment, recommended appointment, and delegated appointment.[16] This ranking system applied to various branches of the civil service, including ordnance factories under the Ministry of War.[17]

When the Nationalist Party took power in 1927, "it invented neither personnel classifications nor the basic structure of its civil service system from thin air; it drew heavily from the immediately preceding Beiyang and Yuan Shikai governments."[18] In 1933, the Nationalist government promulgated a slightly modified version of the ranking system which the Yuan Shikai government had used. Three years later, the Nationalist government issued a revised version, which continued to classify civil service into four ranks: special appointment, selected appointment, recommended appointment, and delegated appointment. In addition, as Appendix Table 3.1 shows, all officials with a first rank had the same grade. There were different grades, however, for officials with the other three ranks: eight grades for the second rank, twelve grades for the third rank, and sixteen grades for the fourth rank, for a total of thirty-six grades.

Gradually this system of ranks extended to all branches of government administration, including the Ministry of Military Administration. In 1928 five bureaus were established under the Ministry of Military Administration: army, navy, air force, military supplies, and ordnance. There were no indications of the use of a ranking system at this time.[19] Among them, the Bureau of Ordnance was in charge of administering national ordnance affairs and all matters concerning ordnance reconstruction. Four departments and two commissions were established within the Bureau of Ordnance: the departments of general affairs, planning, inspection, and supervision, and commissions of ordnance research and purchase of ordnance materials.[20] Increasing needs soon led to reorganization and expansion. In December 1931, the Bureau of Ordnance created three new departments: the departments of resources, administration, and technology.[21] In June 1934, the Ministry of Military Administration decided to place the department of military weaponry, formerly a department in the Bureau of Army, under the jurisdiction of the Bureau of Ordnance. By 1935, the organizational structure of the Bureau of Ordnance had finally taken shape. It consisted of departments of manufacturing, technology, and military weaponry.[22]

A 1935 draft of the organizational law of the Ministry of Military Administration indicates that the ministry applied the ranking system to positions in its subordinate organizations, including the Bureau of Ordnance, within two years of the organizational law's promulgation. The document stipulated that the head of the Ministry of Military Administration would be an appointment at the first rank (special appointment); officials such as bureau chief, and department and division heads appointments at the second rank (selected appointment); officials such as lieutenant colonel and major at the third rank (recommended appointment); and officials such as captain and first and second lieutenants at the fourth rank (delegated appointment).[23] In January 1938, the Bureau of Ordnance adopted the provisional regulations which the Nationalist government had promulgated in July 1937, regulations that established appropriate ranks for civilian officials and technical personnel employed by the military, including those employed by the Bureau of Ordnance.[24]

A similar bureaucratic governance structure obtained within ordnance factories. According to the organizational law for ordnance factories promulgated by the Executive Yuan in 1929, there were three divisions and one department under the director and associate director of an ordnance factory: divisions of general affairs, work affairs, and inspection, and a department of auditing. The division of general affairs oversaw departments of correspondence, accounting, general affairs, purchasing, medicine, in addition to an ordnance warehouse and a security guard unit. Under the division of work affairs were the cartographic office, various manufacturing plants, and a power plant. Finally, the division of inspection supervised a material warehouse and a laboratory. According to the same organizational law, the director and associate director were appointments at the second rank (selected appointment), a division head at the second or third rank (selected or recommended appointment), a department head at the third rank (recommended appointment), and administrative and management staff at the third or fourth rank (recommended or delegated appointment).[25] A revised organizational law of ordnance factory promulgated about two years later confirmed the bureaucratic governance structure in the ordnance industry.[26]

This bureaucratic governance structure expanded during the 1930s and 1940s. As provided in the regulations for ordnance factories, until 1935 Jinling Arsenal had a governance structure that included three divisions of general affairs, work affairs, and inspection, and a department of auditing under its director. By 1936, however, Jinling Arsenal had established, on a trial basis, a new organizational structure that included not only the three existing divisions but a full-fledged division of accounting under its director.[27]

By the early 1940s, a major expansion of bureaucratic organization had taken place in the ordnance industry and is documented in Appendix Table 3.2. The table shows that by early 1943, a typical ordnance factory had, under the director and chief secretary, divisions of work affairs, technology, accounting, and welfare, as well as a general office. In addition, both the divisions and the general office had several subordinate departments or units under their jurisdiction. In reality, the form of factory organization varied from factory to factory. Appendix Table 3.3 reproduces the organizational structure of the Twenty-first Arsenal. It shows that the arsenal had no division of technology, but there were more units under the general affairs office and the divisions of work affairs and welfare.

The Enterprise Governance Structure in Heavy Industry

The enterprise governance structure in heavy industry followed a similar pattern. Whereas the ordnance industry originated in the 1860s, state-owned heavy industry only began to develop on a large scale in the late 1930s. Moreover, whereas the bureaucratic governance structure in ordnance factories evolved gradually, state-owned enterprises established a similar bureaucratic structure within a short period of time. Since the National Resources Commission was the government agency charged with establishing and managing state-owned heavy industry, it was also responsible for determining the organizational form of state-owned enterprises.

The immediate predecessor of the National Resources Commission was the National Defense Planning Commission, established in 1932. After the reorganization of 1935, the National Resources Commission created three new offices and two divisions: offices of electrical engineering, metallurgy, mining, and a secretariat and planning division, in addition to the existing divisions of investigation and statistics.[28] Shortly after the Sino-Japanese War erupted, the National Resources Commission made important changes to its organizational structure. Now under the director and deputy director were four divisions, four sections, and one committee: the secretariat, divisions of industry, mining, and energy industry, sections of technology, economic research, accounting, and material purchase, and a committee of finance.[29] In 1942 the commission further modified its organizational structure to reflect the expansion of its activities. By then it had under its jurisdiction seven divisions and two sections: the secretariat, divisions of industry, mining, energy, material purchase, finance, and accounting, and sections of technology and economic research.[30]

The National Resources Commission acquired its bureaucratic character in part because it had the status of a central ministry within the administrative hierarchy of the Nationalist government.[31] In February 1938 the Nationalist government promulgated the organizational law of the National Resources Commission, which stipulated that the director, deputy director, chief secretary, and division heads would be appointments at the second rank (selected appointment). The same ranking system applied to the appointment of officials in charge of technical matters such as chief engineer, associate engineer, and assistant engineer.[32]

The National Resources Commission issued its own statutes during the Sino-Japanese War, which were published in 1947 as the *Statutes of the National Resources Commission*. The statutes reveal that the commission made appointments "according to existing stipulations of official ranks and emoluments for the Five Yuan (branches of government) and various ministries and commissions."[33] Appendix Table 3.4 documents the implementation of the ranking system in the National Resources Commission and shows that the ranking system the commission used was a carbon copy of that of the central administrative bureaucracy.[34] In addition, the National Resources Commission established a corresponding system of ranks for commissioners and researchers recruited outside its formal establishment.[35]

More importantly, the National Resources Commission extended the organizational model of the administrative bureaucracy to state-owned enterprises under its jurisdiction. As early as 1938, the National Resources Commission promulgated provisional regulations for factory organization, which stated that the commission would designate subordinate organizations as "division, bureau, factory, plant, or company in accordance with their nature and character." The regulations provided general formats consisting of divisions and departments for organizing industrial, mining, and energy enterprises.[36] Three years later, the National Resources Commission revised its provisional regulations, but the basic provisions for enterprise organization remained unchanged.[37]

In practice the organizational structure varied from enterprise to enterprise, but most enterprises followed the general guidelines in establishing their governance structure. The evolution of the organizational structure of the DISW is a good case in point. At the time of its establishment in 1938, the DISW's organizational structure was simple. It had two offices—accounting and technology—and eight sections: waterways, transportation, construction, power, steel rolling, steel furnaces, iron furnaces, and general affairs.[38] During the next four years, the need for increased wartime production led to an expansion of the DISW and its central administration. In late 1939, the DISW began to reorganize sections into divisions. According to a December 1939 draft, the DISW would have a general office, an accounting division, and a welfare division.[39] By March 1940, the DISW had developed a more elaborate governance structure, with five division-level units: a general office, a work affairs division, an accounting division, a welfare division, and a material-purchasing committee. Each division-level unit contained three to six departments. All seven manufacturing plants were placed under the work affairs division.[40]

In December 1941, in an attempt to rationalize its governance structure, the DISW decided to change the name of all division-level units to divisions, effective in January 1942, and to create two new division-level units. As a result, the DISW now consisted of two division-level units—an office of chief engineer and a secretariat—and five divisions: a work affairs division, an accounting division, a construction engineering division, a purchasing division, and a welfare division (see Appendix Table 3.5). Moreover, the seven manufacturing plants were removed from the work affairs division and placed directly under the jurisdiction of the DISW. Finally, the DISW created four affiliated units in material production and transportation.[41] Although further adjustments were made at the department level in March 1943, no major changes took place in organizational structure before the Sino-Japanese War concluded.[42]

The Gansu Petroleum Administration offers another example of the expansion of bureaucratic organization in heavy industry. The National Resources Commission created the Gansu Oil Field Preparatory Bureau in Hankou in June 1938. Only three years later, the Gansu Oil Field Preparatory Bureau had evolved into a large bureaucratic organization known as the Gansu Petroleum Administration. As Appendix Table 3.6 shows, by late 1941 the Gansu Petroleum Administration had established two offices, secretariat and accounting, and divisions of work affairs, transportation, construction engineering, electric machinery, general affairs, and finance.

The rapid expansion of the administrative bureaucracy led to the creation of an entire category of factory personnel called *zhiyuan*. As a generic term, the *zhiyuan* included division and department heads, those who occupied various administrative and management positions, and technical personnel such as engineers. Typically, the *zhiyuan* of state-owned enterprises were regarded as "officials." As late as October 1944 the DISW director declared, "There is nothing inappropriate about promoting workers to positions of *zhiyuan* . . . although conferring official titles is not necessarily the best means of rewarding workers."[43] In an essay written after the war, Qi Zhilu, former secretary of the Ministry of Economic Affairs, explained, "State-owned enterprises . . . treated *zhiyuan* as officials. In addition, they paid little attention to issues of efficiency,"[44] although identification of management personnel as officials was not unique to China's state-owned enterprises.[45]

Given the rapid expansion of the administrative bureaucracy in state-owned enterprises, the ratio of *zhiyuan* to workers was high. For example, the Central Machine Works had 1,415 permanent employees, which in September 1941 included 335 *zhiyuan*, 640 skilled workers, and 440 unskilled workers. In other words, the ratio of *zhiyuan* to workers was 1 to 4.2. By September 1943, the number of permanent employees at the Central Machine Works had increased to 1,648, with 456 *zhiyuan*, 853 skilled workers, and 339 unskilled workers.[46] As a result, the ratio of *zhiyuan* to workers increased from 1 to 4.2 to 1 to 3.6.

A similar ratio of *zhiyuan* to workers obtained at the DISW: roughly 1 to 3 during 1943 and 1 to 3.5 during 1944.[47] Such a ratio is confirmed by an investigative report written by American engineer Max Kanner, who served as an engineer for the Fifty-first Arsenal from 1939 to 1942. He moved to the DISW during the following year.[48] In 1943 Weng Wenhao, head of the Ministry of Economic Affairs and concurrently director of the National Resources Commission, asked Kanner to write a report on the existing problems of state-owned enterprise. Subsequently Kanner's report was translated into Chinese and published in *Crashing Waves (taosheng)*, the official journal of the DISW.

Kanner began his report with a caveat: "I believe that criticism is inappropriate unless one could also show how improvement can be made. The problems that I shall discuss below are in most cases the ones known to management; the fact that they are tolerated is merely because circumstances make changes impossible at the present time." He then outlined five major problems that confronted China's state-owned enterprises. They included the lack of machinery and equipment; the insufficient supply of power; a plethora of *zhiyuan*; a high labor turnover; and an attempt to achieve economic self-sufficiency. With regard to the number of *zhiyuan* in state-owned enterprises, Kanner was "almost certain that the ratio of *zhiyuan* to workers is 1 to 4 or 1 to 5, which is clearly not very economical."[49] Contemporary sources suggest that the high ratio of *zhiyuan* to workers was common knowledge among officials and managers of state-owned enterprises. For example, a National Resources Commission report stated that "as a rule, state-owned enterprise employs more people than does private enterprise." As far as the ratio of *zhiyuan* to workers was concerned, the report revealed that "in private enterprise the ratio is as low as 1 to 10, whereas in state-owned enterprise the ratio is as high as 1 to 3.3, with 1 to 5 being the average."[50]

In addition, many *zhiyuan* in state-owned enterprise had official ranks and gradations in salary. As Appendix Table 3.7 shows, the DISW had a total of 521 *zhiyuan* at the end of 1940. Among them 9 had the status of second rank (selected appointment), 47 the status of third rank (recommended appointment), and 329 the status of fourth rank (delegated appointment). They represented, respectively, 1.7 percent, 9 percent, and 63.2 percent of the total number of *zhiyuan*. Also listed are 136 *zhiyuan* with no formal ranks, which represented a substantial 26.1 percent of *zhiyuan*.

And just who was appointed at what rank? Within the structure of official rank, class, and salary, the DISW *zhiyuan* were divided into six grades.[51] In nine cases *zhiyuan* with a second rank (selected appointment) were appointed as division heads, chief secretaries, and chief engineers. In 47 cases *zhiyuan* with a third rank (recommended appointment) were appointed as plant directors, department heads, administrative commissioners, department secretaries, engineers, and associate engineers. And in 329 cases *zhiyuan* with a fourth rank (delegated appointment) were appointed as officials ranging from department heads, section chiefs, assistant engineers, staff, office personnel, and technicians to staff assistants, librarians, school teachers, nurses, office clerks, and junior clerks.[52]

The pervasive bureaucratization of state-owned enterprise finds further confirmation in contemporary sources. In a 1943 essay exploring the management of state-owned enterprise, Yun Zhen, general manager of the Central Electric Works, pointed out that a major problem that confronted state-owned enterprise was that "the government treats state-owned enterprise the same way it treats the regular administrative bureaucracy." For example, "existing regulations treat *zhiyuan* of state-owned enterprise as regular [government] officials and applied the same classification of selected, recommended, and delegated appointments to *zhiyuan* for the purpose of determining their ranks and compensation."[53] As late as 1945 a government report stated, "our state enterprise system has yet to separate itself from the regular administrative system. In fact, every law code and regulation governing the regular administrative system is applicable to state-owned enterprise, which hinders its development."[54]

Organizational Change in State-Owned Enterprises

The bureaucratization of enterprise governance was a phenomenon that transcended national boundaries as modern business enterprises increasingly took on a bureaucratic character. For instance, the acquisition of such a character had already taken place in American business enterprises by the 1920s.[55] Despite the seeming similarity between China's state-owned enterprise and the modern private enterprise as a "bureaucratic institution,"[56] they were fundamentally different economic entities. In contrast to the emergence of modern business enterprise in the United States as an "organizational response to fundamental changes in processes of production and distribution," hence "little affected by public policy, capital markets, or entrepreneurial talents,"[57] the rise of the state-owned enterprise in China was an organizational response to the fundamental challenge to the survival of the Chinese nation-state, and hence had everything to do with public policy and initiative. In contrast to the fundamental profit motive of modern business enterprise, the state-owned enterprise in China was motivated primarily by the urgent need to "establish a foundation for national defense."[58] In contrast to the modern business enterprise's substitution of the "visible hand" of management for the "invisible hand" of the market in coordinating production and distribution in the United States, the "visible hand" of management in China's state-owned enterprise extended the state's economic function into the organization of productive activities. In contrast to the gradual acquisition of the bureaucratic character by the private business enterprise in the United States as a result of the "managerial revolution," the state-owned enterprise in China was a bureaucratic institution at the very time of its creation owing to the application and extension of the organizational model of the formal administrative bureaucracy. In contrast to the role of managers in the modern business enterprise in the United States as representatives of the interest of the investors and stockholders, officials and managers in state-owned enterprises in China served as the agents of the exclusive stakeholder—the Chinese nation-state.

China's state-owned enterprises acquired a bureaucratic character because the nation's institutional resources were limited. As far as political tradition is concerned, Chinese civilization developed several distinct features, including a centralized bureaucratic system of government. A pervasive institutional endowment, the organizational model of formal administrative bureaucracy served as the only institutional resource when China began establishing ordnance factories in the 1860s. Consequently, most ordnance factories established between the 1860s and 1890s bore the name of "manufacturing bureaus," and traditional bureaucrats ran them as they would any other government bureau.

During the last decades of the Qing dynasty, reform-oriented bureaucrats began to search for new organizational forms in pursuit of economic development, restoration of economic sovereignty, and regulation of economic changes. The results were mixed. In 1903, the Qing government established the Ministry of Commerce with four departments *(si):* trade, agriculture and forestry, industry, and auditing. Although the establishment of the Ministry of Commerce "represented the state's acknowledgement that commerce and industry had a proper place in Chinese society," the organizational form of the new ministry represented an extension of the organizational model of the traditional Six Boards.[59] In the following year, the Qing government enacted the Company Law, which provided for four types of companies: partnership, limited partnership, joint-stock company, and limited shareholding company. In reality, however, "the formal, corporate form remained rare even during Chinese capitalism's 'golden age.'"[60]

Despite the 1911 Revolution and alterations in terminology, the fundamentally bureaucratic nature of China's state machinery remained unchanged. In fact, shortly after the establishment of the Chinese Republic, the new government enacted the *Draft Administrative Law Governing Civil Service Appointments,* which provided for the classification of the civil service into the four ranks of special appointment, selected appointment, recommended appointment, and delegated appointment. After the Nationalist Party came to power in 1927, the new regime made important innovations in state structure by establishing a Five Yuan (that is, five branches) system of government. It also created a number of commissions outside the regular structure of central ministries, especially in the administration of national economic affairs. For example, the Nationalist government created a National Reconstruction Commission in 1928, which was delegated the responsibility of planning national economic reconstruction and managing "model enterprises."[61] In 1931 the Nationalist government established a National Economic Commission for the purpose of "promoting economic reconstruction, improving people's livelihood, and coordinating national finance." When the government revised its organizational law in

September 1933, it entrusted the National Economic Commission with the duty of planning, directing, and supervising national economic reconstruction.[62]

Still, there were substantial institutional continuities between the Nationalist government and the previous governments as the Nationalist government adopted and adapted the organizational model of its predecessors. The Nationalist government promulgated only a slightly modified version of the ranking system that the Yuan Shikai government had used, and continued to classify the civil service into four ranks (special appointment, selected appointment, recommended appointment, and delegated appointment). For example, the newly created Ministry of Industries (1930) managed eight departments (si) and one bureau (shu): departments of general affairs, agriculture, industry, commerce, fishery and animal husbandry, mining, labor, and cooperative, and a bureau of reclamation and forestry. Each department's function and responsibility were listed in detail, with stipulations of the prescribed number of officials and zhiyuan as well as their titles and ranks.[63] The National Reconstruction Commission and the National Economic Commission established similar provisions concerning the number of officials and zhiyuan and their titles and ranks.[64]

In 1932 the Nationalist government, spurred to action by the Japanese invasion of Manchuria, began making preparations for developing national defense industries. However, leaders of the Nationalist government and prominent intellectuals had serious doubts as to whether regular government bureaucrats were capable of carrying out such a mission and whether such a bureaucratic system of administration should be used for the purpose of undertaking economic reconstruction. In a 1933 speech, Chiang Kaishek expressed deep suspicion of the capabilities of the regular administrative bureaucracy when he stated that "whenever a new organization is created, it always degenerates into a huge government bureaucracy. Within the bureaucracy many people are assigned positions, a substantial amount of money is spent, and yet these people only engage in empty talk or idle theorizing. Nothing is really accomplished . . . Because of the environment in which they find themselves, both their minds and practices have ossified. . . . Consequently, it is extremely difficult to bring about changes in the regular administrative organization."[65]

Far more important in this context is an essay published in *Independent Review* in November 1932. The author, writing under the pseudonym "Da," focused on the question of whether the regular administrative bureaucracy should manage important economic enterprises. Reviewing China's administrative system from the late Qing period, he wrote:

> Since the Republican revolution of 1911, there have been many reforms and experiments in China's political system such as presidential system, cabinet system, and commission system. However, there have seldom been any changes in government administration, especially in the various ministries of the Executive Yuan. Government administration in China has always been quite general. It was only under the pressure of foreign intrusion during the last decades of the Qing dynasty that the imperial government realized the inadequacy of the traditional six boards in carrying out complex administrative functions needed in modern times. As a result, the imperial government gradually created nondescript organizations, such as the Office for the Management of Foreign Affairs and the Bureau of Railway and Mining. . . . After several rounds of observation and investigation abroad, the imperial government finally established a new-style Ministry of Education, Ministry of Posts and Communications, and Ministry of Agriculture, Industry and Commerce. Despite these changes, however, their internal system remained as before; their organizations and fundamental principles remained unchanged. They were nothing more than additions to the existing administrative bureaucracy.
>
> During the first few years of the Chinese Republic, the central government changed the names of some organizations; it even adopted certain names from the Japanese. Still, no fundamental changes were made in these organizations. After the Northern Expedition succeeded, the Nationalist forces chose Nanjing as the site for the new central government, bringing with them the traditional government organizations to Nanjing. Because these administrative organizations consistently followed the traditional organizational forms, they could not function without the help of a few "old hands." In fact, during the first few years of the Chinese Republic the various ministries of the Beijing government had to seek advice from former Qing bureaucrats, who had been formerly responsible for drafting memorials or court documents. The same was true with the Nationalist government in Nanjing. At the time of its establishment the government had to select a few old secretaries and old department heads from the former Beijing government.[66]

Following this review of China's administrative system, "Da" addressed four major problems of model bureaucratic organizations in the central administration: the absence of differentiation between political affairs *(zhengwu)* and administrative affairs *(shiwu);* the lack of practical and sensible distribution of responsibility in managing administrative affairs within the central government ministries; the lack of specific budgets within the overall government budget; and the preoccupation with written documents in managing administrative affairs and the corresponding lack of any real effort to implement policies. This last problem, "Da" stated, was the "most common shortcoming of bureaucratic organizations."[67]

Having set up the parameter and context for the reader, "Da" introduced the central issue of his essay. He pointed out that, in the recent past, the government's main function had been to provide direction and supervision of the enterprises owned by the people. Many world governments had now begun to manage their own enterprises, however. It was certainly the case with the Soviet Union, where the government had abolished private property and placed all enterprises under state ownership. According to "Da," these changes meant that government organizations had assumed direct enterprise management as their primary responsibility, while radically reducing or eliminating their former responsibility of directing and supervising private enterprise.[68]

"Da" noted that China was not yet a Communist state, but he believed that "state socialism seems to be central to the Three Doctrines of the People." In addition, "as people all over the country recognize the extreme backwardness of Chinese industry, everywhere one hears the call for rapid economic reconstruction." As a result, "everybody takes state-owned and province-run enterprises for granted, without detecting any contradictions between state-owned and private enterprise. Until now, however, no one knows for sure as to the kind of administrative agency or organization that we should use for managing these public enterprises."[69]

In reality, however, as "Da" pointed out, the government had already assumed "two types of responsibilities: the assistance and supervision of private enterprise and the establishment and management of state-owned and province-run enterprise." This gave rise to two sets of problems: "whether the imposition of these responsibilities on one administrative agency would result in due consideration to each and appropriate coordination between the two, and whether regular administrative organizations (such as ministries and departments) and their conventional way of handling affairs were competent or adequate for managing enterprises." "On the surface," according to "Da," "it appears the Nationalist government does intend to separate administrative organizations from reconstruction organizations. Consequently the government established the National Reconstruction Commission in the capital and departments of reconstruction in the provinces." Regardless of the effect of this separation, for "Da" the fundamental question remained: "for the purpose of managing major reconstruction enterprises, should we continue to use the hierarchical administrative system consisting of bureau chiefs and department heads or should we create a sounder and more effective organization?"[70]

It turned out that "Da" was none other than Weng Wenhao, the newly appointed secretary-general of the National Defense Planning Commission.[71] He continued to serve as director when the National Defense Planning Commission became the National Resources Commission in 1935. By the time this essay appeared in the *Independent Review* on November 6, 1932, Weng had met with Chiang Kaishek at least three times. He also had agreed to serve as secretary-general of the proposed National Defense Planning Commission, which was formally established on November 1, 1932.[72] In other words, what Weng attempted to accomplish in this essay was the establishment of a theoretical foundation for developing more effective administrative organizations for economic reconstruction.

It seems that the kind of organization Weng had in mind would embody various forms of commissions, such as the National Defense Planning Commission. Others also saw the commission form of organization as a viable alternative to the regular administrative bureaucracy. For example, in an essay published in *Independent Review* in September 1933, another prominent scholar wrote, "it appears that the solution to the question Weng Wenhao raised lies in the creation of more effective organizations. Hence the creation of the National Economic Commission."[73] In any case, Weng and other leaders did try to make the National Resources Commission an effective organization and to avoid the pitfalls of the regular administrative bureaucracy. The National Resources Commission was indeed one of the most effective organizations during the war. Still, the evidence shows that the commission was unable to prevent either its own bureaucratization or that of its enterprises.

The Rise of Technocrats in the Enterprise Governance Structure

Despite the bureaucratic character of state-owned enterprises, significant changes had taken place within the enterprise governance structure by the early 1940s, notably the rise of technical and professional experts. If Confucian scholar-officials had dominated state-owned enterprises until the collapse of the Qing dynasty, then technocrats rose to positions of power in state-owned enterprises during the 1930s and 1940s.[74]

During the late nineteenth century, many officials and managers of ordnance factories were recruited from those who had succeeded in passing the traditional civil service examinations. Because of their training in Confucian and Neo-Confucian classics, they had neither the educational background nor the experience necessary to run the manufacturing bureaus as modern business enterprises. As Zhu Enba, a high-ranking official in charge of ordnance affairs, noted in 1910, few officials and managers understood the method of manufacturing. Consequently, they had to rely on foremen and artisans to make decisions.[75] Unfortunately the majority of foremen and artisans possessed no more knowledge of ordnance manufacturing then did their superiors. According to an investigative report cited by a 1911 memorial by the Ministry of War, among the 1,100 artisans who took an examination during the previous year, fewer than thirty showed a "real grasp" of the subject matter of ordnance manufacturing.[76]

During the next two decades, successive governments attempted to recruit and train technical personnel to fill positions in the ordnance factory. In June 1914, the Ministry of War of the Beiyang government sent twenty-eight recent graduates from the Shanghai Ordnance School to work in five major ordnance factories under its jurisdiction.[77] Seven months later the Ministry of War sent an official letter to various provinces and ordnance factories requesting them to provide information on "people with specialized knowledge" who had studied either abroad or in China.[78] In order to train specialized technical personnel for ordnance manufacturing, the Ministry of War of the Beiyang government approved the creation of the Hanyang Special School of Ordnance Manufacturing in January 1917. Of the one hundred students admitted, however, only eighteen students had graduated by 1921.[79] At the same time the Ministry of War made an effort to recruit students who had studied abroad.[80]

It was only after the Nationalist regime had been established in 1927 that government agencies began to recruit people with specialized knowledge in ordnance production and appoint them to management positions on a large scale.[81] As a modernizing elite, the Nationalists were keenly aware of the urgent need to acquire technical personnel through training in special schools of ordnance manufacturing. In 1926 the Nationalist forces took over the Hanyang Special School of Ordnance Manufacturing from the Beiyang government and placed it directly under the Nationalist government.[82] In May 1929 the government formally renamed it the Hanyang Special School of Ordnance Manufacturing of the Ministry of Military Administration, its objective being the "training of specialized professional personnel in ordnance manufacturing."[83] According to statistics compiled by the Bureau of Ordnance, 128 students graduated from this school between 1925 and 1935. During the following decade, another 151 students graduated with a bachelor's degree, in addition to 136 graduates with an associate degree between 1934 and 1941.[84]

At the same time, the Nationalist government made a major effort to recruit talent from students who had studied abroad. In early 1928 Chiang Kaishek sent Chen Yi to Germany for the purpose of engaging retired Germany military officers and recruiting talent among Chinese students studying there. It was during this trip that Chen discovered Yu Dawei, who later served as director of the Bureau of Ordnance. But Yu was only one among many who entered the ordnance industry upon completing their studies abroad. Shortly after the establishment of the Nationalist government in 1928, Chiang Kaishek appointed Zhang Qun to serve as the first director of the Bureau of Ordnance. Zhang also served concurrently as director of the Shanghai Arsenal.[85] During his tenure as director of the Shanghai Arsenal, Zhang broke with the convention of promoting only administrative personnel to managers by appointing a number of technical personnel to management positions, many of them having studied in Germany and Japan or having graduated from Chinese universities.[86] As a result of this precedent-setting practice, most ordnance factories soon filled management positions with technical personnel who had received advanced training in colleges and universities.

Although systematic data on ordnance factories are unavailable for the period before the Sino-Japanese War, the personnel composition of the Bureau of Ordnance in early 1929 serves as a good indication of the direction of future development. Among the sixty-two *zhiyuan* whose biographical information was given, roughly thirty-one had a bachelor's degree, nineteen had an associate degree, and twelve had a high school diploma, representing, respectively, 50 percent, 30 percent, and 20 percent of the total number of *zhiyuan*.[87] Moreover, twenty of the thirty-one *zhiyuan* with a bachelor's degree—a high 65 percent—received their education in universities in Germany, Japan, United States, and France. Finally, the record indicates that fourteen of these twenty *zhiyuan* earned degrees in fields such as metallurgy, engineering, and ordnance manufacturing.[88]

The major change, however, took place during the Sino-Japanese War, when many technical personnel joined ordnance factories to serve in management positions. A 1944 roster of directors of all subordinate organizations of the Bureau of Ordnance shows that out of sixty-six directors whose biographical information was given, forty-six had a bachelor's degree and twenty had an associate degree or a degree from a military academy, representing, respectively 70 percent and 30 percent of the total number of directors. Moreover, among the directors who had a bachelor's degree, thirty-nine received their education in universities in Germany, Japan, United States, and France. More importantly, among the thirty-four directors of organizations of ordnance manufacturing and research, twenty-nine—a high 85 percent—earned degrees in fields such as metallurgy, engineering, and ordnance manufacturing in universities in Germany, Japan, United States, and France.[89] Their leadership position in the overwhelming majority of ordnance factories and research units and their advanced technical education demonstrate that technocrats had established a dominant position in ordnance factories by the early 1940s.

A similar development took place in state-owned enterprises in heavy industry. From the very beginning, the National Defense Planning Commission was composed primarily of technocrats. It had thirty-nine members at the time of its establishment in 1932, but in two years the number reached well over 100. The majority of commissioners had received training in universities either in China or abroad, and most had occupied important positions in government or nongovernment organizations at the time of their appointment.

In 1935 the newly renamed National Resources Commission drafted the *Three-Year Plan for Heavy Industrial Reconstruction*. In order to implement this plan, the commission recruited a number of technocrats from the National Reconstruction Commission; from technical personnel who had studied in Germany; and from Weng Wenhao's former colleagues in the Geological Institute.[90] It soon became painfully clear to leaders of the National Resources Commission that it "did not have enough human talent for allocation" among heavy industrial enterprises. Moreover, its lack of human talent was "not limited to technical personnel; there was also an insufficient supply of human talent in enterprise management."[91] In order to meet the urgent need for human resources, in 1936 the National Resources Commission adopted several policies, which Qian Changzhao, deputy director of the commission, summarized in a 1939 essay on the lessons learned in heavy industrial reconstruction:

First of all, we would help create leadership talent. Whoever had a solid foundation in learning and experience and could make a real contribution to heavy industrial development in the future, we would provide funding to make it possible for them to conduct research and investigation either in China or abroad, so that they could develop a good understanding of actual situations. We would invite them to join our work when opportunity presents itself. We had about twenty such personnel in 1936. Second, we would train people to become cadres. We would invite talented graduates from colleges and universities to seek employment in our factories or collieries, or in the National Resources Commission. After an extended time period we would promote those who have an outstanding service record or send them abroad for further studies. We had anywhere from eighty to ninety such people in 1936. Finally, we would establish cooperative agreements with various colleges and universities, whereby we would provide additional funding to them so that these schools could purchase new facilities and hire more teachers. The agreement would also provide for internship in our factories or collieries for students in their junior and senior years. In 1936 we entered into such a cooperative agreement with twelve colleges and universities.[92]

After the Sino-Japanese War began, the National Resources Commission continued to underscore the importance of cultivating talent. An instruction the commission issued in 1938 made it clear that "talent is vitally important for enterprise management . . . Consequently every constituent part should engage individuals with the most professional expertise, and every professional expert should have under his leadership a number of promising youth so that the expert could give full play to his professional knowledge." Unfortunately, the emphasis on professional expertise also gave rise to management problems: "many directors of our enterprises are technical experts, a fact that may have contributed to their lack of attention devoted to business operation."[93]

Although the National Resources Commission acknowledged the existence of problems resulting from its reliance on professional experts, it had yet to fully recognize the importance of management in the late 1930s. The expansion of heavy industrial enterprises exposed the need for managerial talent as well as professional experts and forced industrial leaders to revise their existing mental model to one with dual emphasis on technical knowledge and management. Contemporary sources reveal the rationale behind this revised mental model. In a speech delivered in 1942, Qian Changzhao pointed out the need to cultivate different types of talent, including "management and technical talent."[94] In an important petition submitted to Chiang Kaishek one year later, Qian explained the need to prepare for postwar reconstruction of heavy industry, including the need for "simultaneous cultivation of technical and managerial talent." In Qian's view, "during the early phase of reconstruction we placed much emphasis on technology but ignored management. Actually, we must give equal weight to management and technology."[95] Qian continued to stress the importance of management during the immediate postwar period. In responding to a reporter's question about potential management difficulties in developing large-scale industries, he asserted that "if China's industrial reconstruction were to fail, the failure will not result from technical incompetence but from managerial incompetence. Management is more difficult [to learn] than technology. The object of management is people whereas that of technology is things. Consequently we must place a great deal of emphasis on management if we were to become an industrialized nation."[96]

This revised mental model—the dual emphasis on technology and management—led the National Resources Commission to implement policies of recruiting college and university graduates to state-owned enterprises as well as sending technical and management personnel to receive advanced training in the United States. In June 1941, the National Resources Commission drafted provisional regulations on assisting educational and research institutions in the area of industrial and mining technology. According to the regulations, the National Resources Commission would provide funding to these institutions for conducting experiments in industrial and mining technology, establishing lecture series, and providing financial assistance to students in fields related to industrial reconstruction.[97]

In July 1942, in order to "encourage the cultivation of talent in technology and management in heavy industrial reconstruction," the National Resources Commission drew up provisional regulations for providing financial assistance (Ch$800) to outstanding undergraduate students in engineering departments as well as departments of economics, accounting, and business management. The regulations stipulated that students who received financial assistance were required to first consider job offers by the National Resources Commission upon graduation, in addition to receiving practical training in the commission's subordinate enterprises before graduation.[98] Two months later, the commission issued another set of provisional regulations on assisting educational institutions, which would provide funding to these institutions for conducting experiments in industrial and mining technology, establishing lecture series, and providing financial assistance to students in related fields.[99] As a result of implementing these and other programs, the National Resources Commission and its subordinate enterprises recruited 780 college graduates between 1944 and 1946, with 81 for 1944, 308 for 1945, and 391 for 1946.[100]

In addition to recruiting talented college graduates, the National Resources Commission sent technical and management personnel to the United States for observation and practical training. The commission's first group to the United States, sent in 1942, consisted of thirty-one men drawn from the commission itself and its subordinate enterprises, such as the Central Machine Works, the Central Electric Works, and the Gansu Petroleum Administration.[101] Group members received several internships over a two-year period in organizations such as Westinghouse, RCA, DuPont, Monsanto, the Tennessee Valley Authority, the U.S. Bureau of Reclamation, and U.S. Steel.[102] Most returned to China upon completing their training and served in technical and managerial positions. In 1945, the Ministry of Economic Affairs sent another group of 143 persons to the United States, among them ninety-nine from the National Resources Commission.[103] A senior *zhiyuan* of the National Resources Commission recalled that the majority of those from the commission were either directors or managers of its heavy industrial enterprises.[104] Between 1942 and 1947, the commission sent a total of 450 men to study or receive training abroad, with the overwhelming majority in the United States.[105]

The policy of recruiting college graduates and training technical and management personnel contributed to the rise of technocrats to leadership positions in heavy industrial enterprises by the early 1940s. Available evidence indicates that the National Resources Commission and its subordinate enterprises had 7,550 *zhiyuan* in August 1941, 11,055 in August 1942, 13,290 in August 1943, and 11,408 in August 1944.[106] Despite the decrease in 1944, by mid-1946 the number of *zhiyuan* had increased to 18,000, with 58 percent possessing a college degree.[107]

Statistics from large state-owned enterprises such as the DISW demonstrate even more clearly the dominant position of the technocrats. As Appendix Table 3.8 shows, in 1943 the percentage of DISW *zhiyuan* with a college (both four-year and two-year colleges) degree accounted for 27.3 percent of the total number of *zhiyuan*, those with a high school diploma

33.8 percent, and those with a junior-high school diploma 38.9 percent. One year later, the percentage increased to 31.7 percent, 26.2 percent, and 42.1 percent, respectively. Moreover, by 1945 the DISW *zhiyuan* with advanced technical education occupied leadership positions. Appendix Table 3.9 documents the name, official title, and educational background of the top cadres of the DISW as of September 1945. It shows that seven of the fifteen officials graduated from universities in Germany, Japan, France, and Scotland, whereas eight graduated from major Chinese universities. More importantly, the table reveals that all fifteen officials earned their degrees in engineering, mining, metallurgy, or accounting.

The evolution of the enterprise governance structure was path-dependent because China's existing institutional resources confined and limited the enterprise governance structure to the organizational model of the formal administrative bureaucracy. The crisis of the 1930s and 1940s

Figure 10. Convention dinner of Chinese engineers of the National Resources Commission in Knoxville, Tennessee, July 12–15, 1943. Courtesy the Second Historical Archives of China.

brought about the expansion of the bureaucratic enterprise governance structure in state-owned national defense industries. At the same time, as a result of the introduction of a modern educational system early in the twentieth century, the increasing availability of educational opportunities abroad, and the requirement for technical expertise essential for the development of national defense industries, a new class of technocrats replaced traditional bureaucrats in state-owned enterprises in the ordnance industry as well as heavy industries.[108] The rise of technocrats contributed to the introduction of new management mechanisms, a topic to which I shall turn in the following chapter.

CHAPTER 4

Enterprise Management and Incentive Mechanisms

In response to the crisis surrounding the Sino-Japanese War, officials and managers of state-owned enterprises introduced new management and incentive mechanisms, including a new accounting system, a work emulation campaign, and a system of delegating responsibility according to administrative levels. If the evolution and expansion of the bureaucratic governance structure of state-owned enterprises were largely path-dependent because of the constraints of limited institutional endowments, the creation of enterprise management and incentive mechanisms was primarily path-independent because of these mechanisms' foreign origins and their ability to overcome the limits of existing institutional endowments. Using the case study of the DISW, the largest state-owned enterprise in Nationalist-controlled area, this chapter examines how officials and managers introduced and implemented the new accounting system and the work emulation campaign. The system of delegating responsibility according to administrative levels will be discussed in a later chapter.

A New Accounting System in the Ordnance Industry

During the Sino-Japanese War, state-owned enterprises in the ordnance industry adopted a new accounting system. Although factory officials and managers had introduced new accounting practices before the war, it was during the war that they replaced the old system of government accounting (*guanting kuaiji*) with a new one characterized by cost calculation.[1]

The earliest available document concerning changes in ordnance accounting during the Nationalist era was the *Draft Trial Regulations on Ordnance Accounting* drawn up by the Bureau of Ordnance in September 1933. It was revised twice, first in November 1933 and again in May 1934. The

101

earliest document consisted of three sections: budget, annual statistics and cost calculation, and profits and losses. The revisions contained two new sections on reimbursement of product expense and verification of expenditure and materials. All of the documents had similar provisions in the first three sections. Budget regulations stipulated that early in a given fiscal year, the Bureau of Ordnance would draft a budget for constant expenses for the following fiscal year. They differentiated between the budget for manufacturing weaponry and the budget for manufacturing raw materials. The expenditures for manufacturing weaponry would come from the state treasury, but ordnance factories responsible for manufacturing raw materials would not receive expenditures from the state treasury. As a rule, the Bureau of Ordnance would determine the unit cost for manufacturing weaponry on the basis of past cost calculations or newly derived estimates. As for statistics and cost calculation, the regulations provided that, at the end of each fiscal year, each ordnance factory would submit to the Bureau of Ordnance statistics on assets and liabilities, profits and losses, price changes for by-products, depreciation and repair charges, annual reports of revenue and expenditure, annual reports on products, and cost calculations based on the cost of direct wages and direct materials. Finally, at the end of a fiscal year the Bureau of Ordnance would determine what to do if the ordnance factories made a profit or incurred a loss.[2] Provisions on reimbursement of product expense in the revised trial regulations provided that each ordnance factory should submit monthly expense accounts to the Bureau of Ordnance for transmission and eventual reimbursement. At the same time, each ordnance factory should compile monthly or quarterly reports on expenditure and materials for verification by the Bureau of Ordnance. Furthermore, personnel from the Ministry of Military Administration and the Ministry of Auditing would audit the account of each ordnance factory every three months.[3]

The adoption of the *Draft Trial Regulations on Ordnance Accounting* did not lead to immediate implementation. According to an April 1934 report, "After the adoption of the *Draft Trial Regulations on Ordnance Accounting* in 1933, only Jinling Arsenal had tried to implement them. Consequently the Bureau of Ordnance convened an accounting conference on January 10, 1934. It was hoped that ordnance factories would all adopt a system of auditing so as to comply with the trial regulations. The goal was to develop cost accounting through cost calculation." The conference representatives agreed that Hanyang Arsenal would take the lead in establishing the new accounting system. Despite the joint effort by officials of the Bureau of Ordnance and Hanyang Arsenal, the experiment in cost accounting at Hanyang Arsenal failed. A Bureau of Ordnance official attributed this failure to the arsenal's "lack of personnel to guide implementation and functionaries to conduct calculation."[4]

In July 1934 the Bureau of Ordnance issued another report, which stated that the *Trial Regulations on Ordnance Accounting* was "designed to establish a system of auditing and gradually unify accounting regulations. It was also intended to create cost accounting for the purpose of precise calculation and scientific management." The report noted that the system of auditing was being carried out among ordnance factories, whereas cost accounting would be implemented in the latter part of 1934. The report also pointed out the absence of any provision on equipment depreciation in existing accounting regulations and suggested two methods of depreciation for old and new equipment.[5]

All the same, a 1935 report by the Bureau of Ordnance indicates that the bureau did not follow its schedule in implementing the trial regulations. On the one hand, the report stated that several ordnance factories had satisfactorily implemented the trial regulations. On the other hand, the report indicated that cost accounting had not been implemented as planned earlier. Although the report regarded cost accounting as the "guiding principle for scientific industrial management," the authors determined that it was difficult to apply cost accounting to an ordinary factory. It would take an extended period of time for an ordnance factory with complicated production process to adopt cost accounting. Consequently, the ordnance factories were still making preparations for the transition from the old accounting practice to cost accounting. On July 1, 1935, the Bureau of Ordnance established a Committee of Unified Ordnance Accounting to study the integration of general accounting and cost accounting and draft regulations for ordnance accounting and auditing.[6]

Archival sources seem to support the report's conclusion. According to a March 1935 report by the Shanghai Steel Plant, "As far as the accounting system is concerned, our plant had always used the method of calculation for reimbursement. During the last fiscal year, we planned to implement cost accounting on a trial basis for the purpose of arriving at precise calculation of product value and profits and losses. For example, wage records, the amount of raw materials, the productivity of steel smelting, and the capacity of the lathe, all of them are essential for cost calculation. Due to limits of the authorized size for our plant, however, we simply did not have enough personnel for allocation. Consequently, we have not been able to sort everything out and calculate cost in a systematic manner, although we are moving forward in the right direction."[7]

The mid-1930s witnessed a similar transition from old accounting practices to new ones in other ordnance factories. Jinan Arsenal, the predecessor of the Thirtieth Arsenal, came under the control of the Bureau of Ordnance in May 1929. Between 1929 and June 1935, the traditional government accounting served as the basis of Jinan Arsenal's entire accounting system. Following the unified accounting system of the central government, the arsenal worked out monthly budgets and submitted them along with receipts to the Bureau of Ordnance, which in turn transmitted them to the Ministry of Auditing for removal from the account after verification. In July 1935, Jinan Arsenal began introducing new accounting methods for calculating profits and losses, although it continued to use the old system of government accounting in other areas.[8]

Despite the introduction of new accounting practices before the Sino-Japanese War, it was during the war that ordnance factories finally replaced the old system of government accounting with a new system characterized by cost calculation. The exigencies of war put state-owned enterprises to the ultimate test of efficiency. In large state-owned enterprises such as the DISW, factory officials and managers recognized a lack of efficiency, revised their existing mental model, and introduced cost calculation through the systematic use of vouchers. In the following section, I shall focus on the DISW's implementation of cost accounting during the Sino-Japanese War.

The war delayed the implementation of cost calculation, however, for the leaders of the DISW were preoccupied with factory relocation in 1938. In October they decided "not to apply cost accounting before the DISW became operational."[9] It was not until the end of 1939 that the DISW completed the transportation of materials and equipment to its Chongqing location, and it did not begin the work of reconstruction until the beginning of 1940.[10]

Gradually the DISW created an institutional framework for the adoption of new accounting methods. It reorganized its accounting office into an accounting division in March 1940 and separated the division into departments of auditing, compensation calculation (payroll by 1942), cost calculation, and bookkeeping. The responsibilities of the department of cost calculation included estimating and calculating product cost, verifying and calculating the cost of direct materials consumed, analyzing and apportioning manufacturing and other expenses, and studying and comparing product costs.[11] Less than two months later, the accounting division provided detailed regulations on the procedure for conducting accounting business.[12]

The creation of the department of cost calculation was only the first step toward implementating cost calculation. In December 1940, the DISW held its first cost accounting meeting. Among the issues addressed by the director were procedures for purchasing, checking, transporting, storing, and distributing raw materials for use in the production process, and for recording raw materials in a ledger. With regard to cost calculation, the director stated that, ideally, the accounting division would carefully record and precisely calculate the cost for direct and indirect labor and materials. Under the extraordinary wartime circumstances, however, this was not easy to accomplish. Short of that, according to the director, the accounting division should assign an account to each manufacturing unit and enter all labor and material costs associated with a given manufacturing unit on its account. Then, at the end of each month, the accounting division could calculate the unit cost of various products by dividing total labor and material cost by the number of products.[13]

By 1942, the DISW apparently was conducting systematic cost calculation in line with current accounting standards. In today's managerial accounting, manufacturing cost is made up of direct materials, direct labor, and manufacturing overhead. A DISW accounting division report for the 1942 fiscal year used the same categories. The cost for direct materials *(cailiaofei)* was Ch$35,510,000; the cost for direct labor *(gongfei)* was Ch$2,940,000; and the cost for manufacturing overhead *(tanfei)* was Ch$63,970,000.[14] In other words, the total manufacturing cost *(zhizaofei)* for the 1942 fiscal year was Ch$102,420,000, with 35 percent for direct materials, 2 percent for direct labor, and 63 percent for manufacturing overhead. According to the same report, the manufacturing overhead included indirect salary, wages, and bonuses, indirect materials, repairs and maintenance, depreciation on facilities, and administrative expenses, which is how manufacturing overhead is currently defined.[15]

An integral part of cost calculation was the systematic use of vouchers *(chuanpiao)* to record transactions. Of course, the use of vouchers was nothing new in modern industrial development. In the United States, Carnegie Steel and several other manufacturing enterprises had introduced the voucher system of accounting as early as the 1880s. At Carnegie Steel, for instance, each department listed the amount and cost of materials and labor used on each order as it passed through the subunit. The information obtained became Carnegie's primary instrument of cost control.[16]

There is no evidence to suggest that the voucher system was introduced in China's state-owned enterprises before the Sino-Japanese War, however. Instead, it developed during the war as factory officials and managers recognized the lack of efficiency, revised their existing mental model, and implemented the voucher system. In the case of the DISW, officials and managers did so as a mechanism of calculating profits and losses in response to the perceived need to maintain economic viability, to deliver to higher authorities the number of finished products requested in a timely manner, and to improve the efficiency of the DISW as a business enterprise. Several archival sources lend support to this argument, but the strongest evidence comes from an essay written in September 1944 by Yang Junya, head of the accounting division. According to Yang, at the time the DISW was promoting the implementation of "the voucher system for calculating profits and losses," which was designed to "achieve a balance between revenue and expenditure among the constituent parts in production and service and to consolidate the DISW's economic foundation."[17]

Yang then proceeded to elaborate on the purpose of calculating profits and losses by using vouchers to record transactions. His logic was that an economic enterprise should sustain itself and that a balance between revenue and expenditure was a minimum requirement regardless of the nature of the enterprise.[18] Calculating profits and losses would also "transform production into planned activities." For various reasons, the DISW was unable to rigorously execute manufacturing orders from higher authorities. This led to delays in delivering finished products or an inability to produce the number of finished products requested. These problems, combined with a drastic inflation in the price of raw materials and labor, caused the DISW to sustain heavy financial losses. Yang expressed the hope that production would be conducted according to plan once the DISW implemented the calculation of profits and losses, because each constituent part would have to make up for its own losses in the case of delays in delivering its finished products.[19]

Finally the calculation of profits and losses was meant to "promote commercialization in the management of state-owned enterprise." "In principle," Yang stated, "a state-owned factory is an economic organization. We accept manufacturing expenditure from higher authorities. In return we deliver finished products to higher authorities. There is no difference between a state-owned factory and a privately-owned factory in terms of the nature of business enterprise." In Yang's view, "every business organization seeks maximum returns with a minimum cost. At the same time, the success or failure of every business organization is determined by its cost. Consequently we should adopt a commercial spirit in business management— seeking product improvement and stressing work efficiency." Yang expressed the hope that cost calculation would lead to the establishment of a reasonable unit price for every product and the supply of necessary statistics for making management decisions.[20]

Although systematic implementation of the voucher system began three months before Yang published his essay, the DISW had experimented with the use of vouchers two years earlier. The DISW used 11,031 vouchers during the 1942 fiscal year, roughly 920 vouchers per month or thirty per day.[21] The accounting division must have had some mixed feelings about the voucher system because in March 1943 it decided "in principle not to use vouchers anymore unless it is essential" for accounting purposes.[22]

It appears that certain negative consequences of this decision convinced the leadership of the indispensability of vouchers for cost calculation, because they reversed the earlier decision and reintroduced vouchers shortly afterward. In July 1943, Yang Jizeng, director of the DISW, told factory officials and managers, "The DISW and its affiliated organizations must make an effort to improve work efficiency and increase production. From now on, every business transaction must be recorded with a voucher from the beginning to the end."[23] Between May and September 1943, the DISW issued 12,136 vouchers, more than the number used for the entire 1942 fiscal year.[24]

By the end of 1943 Yang Jizeng had decided to expand the use of vouchers for calculating profits and losses throughout production and service units. In a decree *(yu)* issued in December 1943, Yang gave the following instructions:

Beginning next year, the constituent parts in production and service must adopt the voucher system in order to calculate profits and losses. The clinics and hospital, the school for employees' children, the farm and other welfare parts, should especially be among the first constituent parts to adopt it. The principles for adopting the voucher system are as follows: (1)

There has to be a balance between revenue and expenditure in the constituent parts in production and service. (2) The product and labor of the constituent parts in production and service ought to have a unit price. (3) The constituent parts should make the initial determination on various unit prices and then submit them to the office of the director for final determination and approval . . . (4) The constituent parts should prepare income statements in three carbon copies for the earnings from their product and labor. (5) The DISW will establish a committee for cost control, which will determine the form for income statements and the method for calculating profits and losses. (6) The constituent parts should settle their account of profits and losses on a monthly basis and submit their reports to the office of the director for examination.[25]

A few days later, the DISW took steps to carry out the director's instructions.[26] After several months' preparation and personnel training, the DISW was ready in May 1944 to implement the voucher system in production and service units. On May 14, the head of the accounting division gave a lecture at the DISW's second management forum on "the voucher system as an instrument in ascertaining profits and losses in factory management."[27] By the end of May, the accounting division made available various voucher forms needed for recording transactions. It also published the unit price of a variety of raw materials as a reference for the manufacturing units in determining their new unit prices.[28] Yang Jizeng ordered the implementation of the voucher system as of June 1, 1944.[29]

By the end of July, the DISW had calculated profits and losses through the voucher system for two months. By then, according to another accounting division report, the calculation of profits and losses was "roughly in shape," and the trial implementation "proved that the method of calculation was feasible." The same report noted that the calculation of profits and losses had a positive impact on the investigation of market prices of finished products and on cost comparison for unit prices, on the examination and understanding of the nature of profits and losses, and on the smooth drafting of the operating budget.[30] When the DISW calculated the profits and losses of thirteen units for the period June and September 1944, nine units had made a profit while four units had operated at a loss. The same report offered high unit price as an explanation for profits and cited low unit price as the cause of losses.[31]

By the end of October 1944, Yang Jizeng had become convinced of the feasibility of making the voucher system a permanent feature of the DISW's accounting system. At a meeting of factory officials and managers, Yang declared, "The system of calculating profits and losses should become a standard procedure by the year's end at the latest. . . . Beginning next year, the profits and losses of the various constituent parts will serve as a basis for reward and punishment. Therefore, every constituent part in production should pay attention to this principle."[32]

According to the bulletin issued by the secretariat, the DISW implemented systematic calculation of profits and losses throughout the 1945 fiscal year. It did so first by dividing revenues and expenditures into categories of production, service, and management. The DISW then calculated the profits and losses of the production and service units based on the expenditure and revenue received. There were roughly twenty production units, eight service units, and ten management units. Whereas production and service units had profits and losses to calculate, management units incurred only losses (see Appendix Table 4.1).

The DISW conducted calculation of profits and losses consistently during the 1945 fiscal year. The production units generated monthly earnings during only four months out of the twelve-month period. In comparison, the service units generated monthly earnings during six months of the same time period. Still, by the end of 1945, the DISW had generated cumulative earnings of $83,725,019 in the production units while incurring a cumulative deficit of $14,433,952 in the service units. Figures from income statements show that the DISW incurred losses during nine months of the twelve-month period (see Appendix Table 4.1).

Despite its lack of solid performance, the DISW still made effective use of calculating profits and losses in factory management. In January 1945 the accounting division reported that after the DISW began calculating profits and losses in June 1944, there had been a number of cumulative losses. Delays in checking and delivery procedures for finished or repaired products, an overstock of raw materials for a given month, and a low unit price for finished products were believed to be the reasons for these losses. Consequently the DISW issued supplemental provisions to remedy the situation.[33]

A few months later, Yang Jizeng responded to the huge deficit incurred during the month of June by ordering each unit to uncover the causes. He wrote in a memo to unit leaders, "If the unit price is the cause for the deficit, we should make adjustments so that we can set a reasonable unit price. If the lack of human effort is responsible, we should establish a standard to which we can all make an effort to conform."[34] Shortly after that, the unit leaders held a meeting and adopted a resolution to make necessary changes.[35] It appeared that the various units overreacted to the situation and made overly drastic adjustments. As Appendix Table 4.1 shows, the monthly earnings of production units jumped from a negative $183,382,006 in the month of June to a positive $438,245,603 in the month of July. The earnings for the month of July were so large that despite a monthly deficit for August, October, November, and December, the production units still maintained cumulative earnings of $83,725,019 at the end of 1945.

Significant differences exist between the ways the DISW operated and assigned cost and those of a private enterprise. At best, the DISW operated in an incomplete, if not closed, market. An "organization designed to manufacture ordnance materials," the DISW accepted manufacturing expenditures from the Bureau of Ordnance and delivered finished products to it for use by other ordnance factories.[36] As a result, and in sharp contrast to privately owned industrial organizations in China and the United States, the DISW did not have a marketing division, as both its funding and market were guaranteed.[37] In addition, the mechanism of purchasing raw materials affected how the DISW assigned product cost. Although the DISW had a purchasing division, the Bureau of Ordnance also purchased raw materials through its purchasing commission and assigned product cost before it delivered them to the DISW. The Bureau of Ordnance "allocated manufacturing expenditure to the DISW on the basis of predetermined product quantity and unit cost of raw materials."[38] As a result, the DISW assigned cost for raw materials either by using the unit cost provided by the Bureau of Ordnance or by using their market prices.[39] Given the rising inflation during the early 1940s, the DISW published the unit cost of a wide variety of raw materials in its *Bulletin of Secretariat* periodically once it began implementing the voucher system.

Despite these differences, the evidence shows that the DISW calculated profits and losses during the early 1940s. As Yang Junya explained in September 1944, "normal cost calculation often loses its effectiveness due to the drastic price fluctuation of raw materials during this extraordinary time . . . but that does not mean that we need to change the method of calculating cost." Yang pointed out that product cost "included direct materials, direct labor, and manufacturing overhead. The various constituent parts regularly record the quantity of materials and labor needed for various products. What they do not know is the unit price of raw materials." As a remedy, Yang suggested that the DISW would publish the unit price of raw materials "every three months" and that the various constituent parts should "assign cost for raw materials by using the unit cost provided by the Bureau of Ordnance as well as that obtained from purchase in the market." Yang concluded that the various constituent parts would be able to determine a product's "unit cost" once they had calculated the cost of direct material, direct labor, and manufacturing overhead.[40]

In summary, traditional government accounting prevailed in ordnance factories until the late 1920s. By the early 1930s, the Bureau of Ordnance had begun introducing new accounting methods, including the method of cost accounting. Nonetheless, it was only during the Sino-Japanese War that the new accounting system replaced traditional government accounting. The case of the DISW demonstrates that ordnance factories implemented a new system of cost accounting and used vouchers for cost calculation. By mid-1945 the voucher system had not only become a standard procedure in cost calculation but a major instrument in making management decisions.[41]

A New Accounting System in Heavy Industry

In contrast to the early introduction of the new accounting system in the ordnance industry, the National Resources Commission did not begin drafting accounting regulations until 1936. Although archival materials are far less systematic for heavy industry, available evidence indicates that during the Sino-Japanese War, leaders of the National Resources Commission revised their existing mental model of institutional requirements for heavy industrial reconstruction, which in turn led them to develop and implement a comprehensive accounting system in heavy industrial enterprises.

The adoption of the *Three-Year Plan for Heavy Industrial Reconstruction* in June 1936 made it necessary to establish an accounting system. Consequently, the National Resources Commission drafted its first accounting regulations in November of the same year. The regulations consisted of nine sections: general regulations, accounts receivable and accounts payable, categories of accounts and journals, receipts, bookkeeping procedures, auditing, budget estimates and accounting reporting, documents transfer, and supplementary regulations. The regulations stipulated that the National Resources Commission would appoint accounting personnel to its subordinate organizations and that the provisions of the accounting regulations were applicable to these organizations.[42]

After the Sino-Japanese War began, the Nationalist government placed the National Resources Commission under the jurisdiction of the Ministry of Economic Affairs and redefined its function to include the creation and management of basic industries, the development of mining resources and management of important collieries, and the creation and management of power plants. As the number of enterprises in the southwestern and northwestern provinces multiplied, leaders of the National Resources Commission came to recognize "the importance of accounting administration."[43] Hence they revised their existing mental model of institutional requirements for heavy industrial reconstruction. For example, in instructions to its subordinate organizations dated December 1938, the National Resources Commission criticized its officials for the "lack of attention devoted to business operations." In order to remedy the situation, the commission ordered the officials to draft operational plans and submit them for evaluation and approval before establishing enterprises, to submit budget estimates at the beginning of a fiscal year, to submit monthly reports of business operations, and to submit annual reports containing statements of profits and losses in order to "improve efficiency and reduce cost."[44]

The same problem apparently prompted Qian Zuling, full-time commissioner of the National Resources Commission, to write an essay on the "urgent necessity" to develop an accounting system for the commission's subordinate enterprises. According to Qian, an accounting system was essential for the operation of a business enterprise because its accounting record not only reflected changes of the enterprise's financial conditions but indirectly served as a means of assessing its performance. Although heavy industrial enterprises needed to establish such a system, "they must pay special attention to cost analysis" in order to reduce product cost. Unfortunately, although the railroad and energy administrations made considerable progress in developing an accounting system, "such a system has yet to be established in heavy industries."[45]

This revision of the mental model—the recognition of the necessity of an accounting system—led the accounting section of the National Resources Commission to draw up a draft version of the *Accounting System for Subordinate Organizations of the National Resources Commission* in June 1939, with sections on general explanations, organizational system of bookkeeping, accounting reporting, categories of accounts and journals, accounting bookkeeping, accounting receipts, and accounting procedures. Upon completing the draft version, the accounting section submitted it to Qian Zuling for examination. He endorsed it in December of the same year.[46]

In August 1939, the National Resources Commission distributed a revised draft version to its subordinate organizations for discussion and feedback. At the same time, Zhang Jun, then head of the accounting section of the National Resources Commission, embarked on an inspection tour of the commission's subordinate organizations.[47] Zhang's telegrams revealed that implementation of the new accounting system was uneven. He pointed out that although the Central Machine Works in Kunming had already "established a foundation for cost accounting," three other enterprises in the same metropolitan area "lack vigor in their management of raw materials, have not established any link between the management of raw materials and accounting sections, and have not developed any effective mechanisms for internal checks. These conditions not only make it difficult to precisely calculate cost; they will adversely affect these enterprises' operations."[48]

By August 1940 the National Resources Commission had completed the revision of the draft version of *Accounting System for Subordinate Organizations of the National Resources Commission* based on the lessons learned and materials Zhang Jun had acquired during the inspections. In January 1941, the Chief Accounting Office of the Nationalist government approved its implementation on a trial basis. Six months later, the National Resources Commission ordered its formal implementation in its enterprises.[49]

The *Accounting System for Subordinate Organizations of the National Resources Commission* was a lengthy document of 429 pages. It consisted of sections on general explanations, an organizational system of bookkeeping, accounting reporting, categories of accounts and journals, accounting bookkeeping, accounting receipts, accounting procedures, and supplemental articles. With regard to cost accounting, the document defined production cost as "all expenses incurred in the manufacturing of a product," including direct materials, direct labor, and direct and indirect expenses. Moreover, the document stipulated that the various organizations should record production cost in a subsidiary cost ledger.[50] In 1943 the National Resources Commission revised the document, but the basic provisions remained unchanged.[51]

Although the *Accounting System for Subordinate Organizations of the National*

Resources Commission was designed for use in heavy industrial enterprises, it was not radically different from the accounting system prevailing in the ordnance industry. For instance, the *Accounting System of the DISW* included sections similar to those of the *Accounting System for Subordinate Organizations of the National Resources Commission,* such as an organizational system of bookkeeping, categories of accounts and journals, and accounting procedures. In fact, the *Accounting System of the DISW* stated that "there is no significant difference" between the DISW accounting system and that of the National Resources Commission.[52]

Reports of the National Resources Commission suggest that the commission largely succeeded in its effort to implement its accounting system. A work plan of the commission stated that "80 percent of the commission's enterprises had implemented the accounting system by early 1943." The same plan also placed "the establishment of a system of cost accounting" as the commission's number-one priority for the 1943 fiscal year.[53] By the beginning of 1944, the commission had focused its attention on "establishing the system of cost accounting in various industrial enterprises." According to Zhang Jun, now head of the accounting division, the National Resources Commission had established the system of cost accounting in the alcohol, electric, and mining industries by September 1944, with the purpose of "making accounting a truly effective instrument of management."[54]

Available evidence seems to confirm the commission's assessment. In explaining the plan and objectives of the Central Electric Works for the 1943 fiscal year, Yun Zhen called for "speedy implementation of cost accounting."[55] By the end of 1943, the individual plants of the Central Electric Works had indeed implemented cost accounting as evidenced by statistics compiled by the second plant, which show the unit cost of forty different products for the 1943 fiscal year.[56] By the end of 1944, at least two dozen subordinate enterprises of the National Resources Commission had implemented cost accounting as evidenced by the commission's statistics, which show the estimated unit cost of 130 different products made by twenty-five of its subordinate enterprises for January 1945.[57]

The Work Emulation Campaign

Despite the adoption of an accounting system characterized by cost calculation, state-owned enterprises lacked the fundamental profit motive of the modern capitalist enterprise. As the war dragged on and as a combination of a shortage of workers and rising inflation led to serious disruption of production, leaders of the Nationalist government searched for ways to increase productivity. One result of this search was the Work Emulation Campaign.

The Nationalist government developed the campaign mechanism with its New Life and National Economic Reconstruction Campaigns during the early 1930s.[58] To date, the National Economic Reconstruction Campaign has not received any scholarly attention, but several studies of the Nationalist period do offer insights into the New Life Campaign.[59] Lloyd E. Eastman argues that the New Life Campaign was designed to implant a "fascist spirit" among the Chinese people, but he also sees it as "the classical example of the Guomindang's administrative incompetence."[60] In contrast to Eastman's argument, Arif Dirlik regards the New Life Campaign as the "Guomindang version of a 'cultural revolution' for China," and as such it "represented the Guomindang effort to overcome public alienation from the government, to mobilize the public not only to support the state but also to help in its reform. Its basic intention was to substitute 'political mobilization' for social mobilization, thus replacing revolutionary change from the bottom with closely supervised change orchestrated from the top."[61] Finally, William C. Kirby suggests that the New Life Campaign was designed to "instill in the Chinese people a new social and political consciousness through a merger of Confucian moral virtues and the modern military ethic."[62]

These works, however, do not fully address the questions of the New Life Campaign's historical context, cause, and method. I submit that both endeavors took place in the context of a national crisis in social and economic life, both resorted to the campaign method to achieve their respective objectives, both utilized bureaucratic mobilization to implement their programs, and both were launched by Chiang Kaishek. During the Sino-Japanese War, a similar endeavor launched by Chiang occurred in a similar context and used the same method and the same bureaucratic mobilization: the Work Emulation Campaign.

The New Life Campaign began in the midst of a national crisis. Between 1931 and 1933, the Nationalist government launched four "extermination campaigns" against the Communist forces. None succeeded. Shortly after launching a fifth campaign in October 1933, Chiang Kaishek stated that "the success of the extermination campaign does not depend on the military; rather it depends on party work and political strength." He believed that "political reform is the only solution for saving the nation from doom and for ensuring its survival." In other words, the Nationalist Party must "completely transform the old society unsuited for survival into a new society."[63]

Less than four months later, Chiang seemed to have found an appropriate instrument for effecting the fundamental transformation of Chinese society. In two speeches delivered in Nanchang, Jiangxi province on February 17 and 19, 1934, Chiang launched the New Life Campaign. The logic for the campaign was revealed by Deng Wenyi, a leader of the New Life Campaign, in a speech delivered later in the month. Deng stated that the Nationalists were confident in their ability "to exterminate the red bandits. Exterminating the red bandits would not lead to the resolution of many problems in China, however. We must have morality, order, discipline, and cleanliness before fundamental improvement can be made."[64] In the words of Arif Dirlik, the "immediate aim" of the New Life Campaign "was the rehabilitation of Jiangxi province, ravaged by years of warfare and now on the verge of recapture by the government."[65]

More broadly, the New Life Campaign aimed to transform Chinese society and rejuvenate the Chinese nation at a time of national crisis by utilizing two existing ideological resources: Confucian moral and ethical values, and the so-called national spirit, which was seemingly best embodied by the German military. The New Life Campaign attempted to inculcate the masses with a basic set of Confucian values—propriety, righteousness, integrity, and consciousness (li, yi, lian, chi)—and a sense of discipline and devotion to the needs of the nation through militarization of national life. According to Chiang Kaishek, the "New Life Campaign which is in accordance with propriety, righteousness, integrity, and consciousness and modern survival is at present the most basic and most effective revolutionary campaign for saving and building our nation and for national regeneration."[66] In other words, the New Life Campaign was concerned with "saving the nation and the people with a campaign to revolutionize social custom and habit."[67] One year later, Chiang further characterized the New Life Campaign as a "reconstruction campaign for spiritual defense of the Chinese nation."[68]

From the very beginning, the Nationalist government relied on bureaucratic mobilization as the chief instrument to promote the campaign and carry out its objectives. Shortly after Chiang launched the campaign, the Nationalist government established the Nanchang New Life Campaign Promotional Association. On July 1, 1934, the association was reorganized as the Central New Life Promotional Association for the purpose of coordinating activities in various provinces and municipalities. By the first anniversary in February 1935, fifteen provinces, three municipalities, and 1,132 counties had established organizations designed to promote the New Life Campaign.[69] By 1936, twenty provinces had established the New Life Promotional Association, and the number of counties with branch organizations had increased to 1,355.[70] More importantly, at each level of the Nationalist government the New Life Promotional Association was placed under the leadership of chief civil and military officials. Chiang himself served as president of the Central New Life Promotional Association. At the provincial level, the provincial governors served as presidents of the New Life Promotional Association of their provinces. Similarly, county magistrates served as presidents of the New Life Promotional Association of their counties.[71]

Ultimately the crisis of national life shaped the dynamics of the New Life Campaign. In a speech delivered on the second anniversary of the New Life Campaign, Chiang stated that "the national spirit, morality, and mental attitude are unsuited for modern life. What is more, because of the grave crisis we are confronted with, the survival of our entire nation is at stake. That is why I wanted to transform national life and seek national regeneration." For Chiang, "the New Life Campaign is not simply a regular campaign for social reform; i t is a crucial campaign designed to save the nation from doom and ensure its survival."[72] As the *Program for the New Life Campaign* put it, "at this critical moment of national survival, if we do no want to fold our hands and await destruction, we should not simply wait for the natural evolution of society; on the contrary, we must use extraordinary means in order to rejuvenate society. . . . Only the New Life Campaign is capable of accomplishing such a great mission."[73]

The very same logic applied to the National Economic Reconstruction Campaign. In launching the campaign in April 1935, Chiang stated that "in order to meet the challenge of our national crisis and relieve the suffering of the masses of people, we must launch a campaign in the wake of the New Life Campaign, namely the National Economic Reconstruction Campaign."[74] About four months later, Chiang elaborated on the theme of crisis and the need for a National Economic Reconstruction Campaign: "The fundamental crisis China faces today lies in the bankruptcy of the economy. As a result, the material life of the people is getting worse, and the fate of the nation is consequently in imminent danger. . . . Therefore the most urgent task is to prevent the national economy from collapse and to substantially improve people's lives. . . . In order to complete such a task I believe that we must launch a campaign in the wake of the New Life Campaign, namely the National Economic Reconstruction Campaign." Chiang then proceeded to explain the relationship between the New Life Campaign and the National Economic Reconstruction Campaign. For Chiang, the two campaigns were truly complementary to each other: "Whereas the New Life Campaign aims at the nation and individual cultivation with an emphasis on morality and spirit, and consequently serving as the essential principle of the National Economic Reconstruction Campaign, the National Economic Reconstruction Campaign is directed toward the people's livelihood and production with an emphasis on action and the material aspect, and consequently serving as the practical application of the New Life Campaign. In other words, while the New Life Campaign is designed to lay the spiritual foundation of the Chinese nation, the National Economic Reconstruction Campaign is intended to establish the material foundation of the Chinese nation. Both campaigns are indispensable."[75]

Concern for China's national security appears to have been an important factor in Chiang Kaishek's decision to launch the National Economic Reconstruction Campaign. More than two years earlier, Chiang had created a National Defense Planning Commission to investigate national resources and to draft plans for national defense against Japan. During the same month (April 1935) Chiang launched the National Economic Reconstruction Campaign, he also reorganized the National Defense Planning Commission as the National Resources Commission and redefined its responsibility from resource investigation and planning to reconstruction of the national defense industry. Although Chiang did not explicitly refer to the need to strengthen national defense in his public speech made in April 1935, one would be naïve to assume the absence of a connection between the National Economic Reconstruction Campaign and national defense.[76]

Five months after his April 1935 speech, Chiang made explicit the link between the New Life Campaign, the National Economic Reconstruction Campaign, and China's national defense in a speech delivered at the Officer Training Corps. The speech focused on what Chiang called the "vitality of a modern state," which he believed consisted of education, economy, and military force. In order to strengthen the vitality of the modern state and build a new nation, China needed to undertake the New Life Campaign in education, the National Economic Reconstruction Campaign in the economy, and the expansion of a labor conscription system in the armed forces. For Chiang, "a nation can expect to maintain its independence in the modern world only if it possesses the qualities of the modern state."[77] According to a prominent scholar of the Nationalist economic policy, the National Economic Reconstruction Campaign was "designed not only to promote national economic development during peace time but to prepare for economic mobilization at a time of war." Given the grave reality of international relations in 1935, China "could not afford to raise openly the banner of establishing a quasi-wartime economic system; it had to use the National Economic Reconstruction Campaign as a disguise in order to make preparations for general national economic mobilization during the wartime period."[78]

As in the case of the New Life Campaign, the Nationalist government relied on bureaucratic mobilization to achieve its goal of national economic reconstruction. In December 1935, the Fifth Nationalist Party Congress passed a resolution that called for implementation of the *Outline Program for National Economic Reconstruction*. The resolution stated that the outline program was designed not only to "promote national economic development during peace time but to prepare for economic mobilization at a time of war and to lay a foundation for long-term resistance."[79] Six months later, having been appointed president of the Executive Yuan, Chiang Kaishek created the Central Commission for the National Economic Reconstruction Campaign. According to its regulations, the commission aimed to "help promote planning for economic reconstruction of both the central and local governments, advocate the development of various economic enterprises, and recruit and train specialized personnel for economic reconstruction." In addition, the Nationalist government would establish a Commission for the National Economic Reconstruction Campaign at the provincial, municipal, and county levels. Finally, the chief executive leader of the central government would serve as commission chairman at the national level, whereas the chief executive leaders of the provincial governments would be named the commission chairmen at the provincial level. As it turned out, the chairman of the Central Commission for the National Economic Reconstruction Campaign was none other than Chiang Kaishek himself, and, not surprisingly, leaders of the National Resources Commission such as Weng Wenhao and Wu Dingchang were among the leading figures of the central commission.[80]

Although the National Economic Reconstruction Campaign was more successful than the New Life Campaign, the two campaigns shared similar characteristics in their crisis context, in their use of campaign method, in their utilization of bureaucratic mobilization, and in their source of leadership.[81] These same characteristics found expression in another campaign that the Nationalist government undertook during the Sino-Japanese War: the Work Emulation Campaign.[82]

During the early phase of the war, the Nationalist government led the military resistance against Japan and developed the heavy and defense industries. As the war continued, it became apparent that a quick military victory was not possible. Consequently the Nationalist government focused more and more on the economic front in order to prepare for long-term resistance. As early as 1939, Chiang called on the economic bureaucracy to "increase material production" so as to implement "economic plans of national defense."[83] By early 1940 Chiang had placed the overwhelming emphasis on the economic front because the "most effective weapon for the war of resistance is [a strong] economy." Consequently, China must fight the war with "30 percent military power and 70 percent economic power."[84]

The emphasis on the economy did not immediately lead to an increase in productivity. On the contrary, the combination of a shortage of workers and rising inflation caused "serious disruption of production activities" during the first two years of the war. In order to "strengthen China's ability for a prolonged war of resistance against Japan," Chiang was determined to find a "method to provide workers with effective management and training, raise their living standard, improve work efficiency, and increase production."[85]

It did not take Chiang long to find such a method—"work emulation." As early as January 1939 Chiang submitted a *Program for the Work Emulation System* to the fifth plenary session of the Fifth Nationalist Party Congress for deliberation and implementation.[86] The program was designed to "apply and extend the method of campaign and emulation to agriculture, industry and all other trades and professions in order to increase production and improve work efficiency." It listed different methods for work emulation such as that between different teams of workers within a factory for achieving production increase or cost reduction, or that between different factories for fulfilling assigned tasks more quickly. It also stipulated the honors and material awards winners of work emulation would receive for their achievements.[87]

Not long after January 1939 when Chiang submitted the *Program for the Work Emulation System*, Gan Naiguang, then deputy-secretary of the Nationalist Central Party Headquarters, attempted to explain the rationale for the work emulation system because of his belief in the system's "profound implications." According to Gan, "the free competition of capitalism" had led to "blind and irrational production," which explains the emergence of a socialist theory and a controlled economy. However, "both socialism and controlled economy have now come under criticism by scholars who believe the abolition of production based on laissez fair and free competition is tantamount to the abolition of incentives for industrial progress. I have to say that such criticism is quite to the point. In fact, during the early stages of the Soviet state-owned farm, the farmers did not have much incentive to increase production; similarly the Soviet industry also suffered. If incentives were lost, that would certainly be a fatal blow to industrial development. In China the National Economic Reconstruction Campaign suffered from a similar problem. The Soviet Union began promoting the Stakhanovite Campaign after a coal miner named Stakhanov produced more coal than other workers during the same work hours. This campaign is essentially an industrial emulation campaign. It substitutes psychological incentive for the loss of profit incentive under free competition. It is not an exaggeration to say that the Work Emulation Campaign is designed to remedy the defect of the socialist system of production. In other words, in developing state-owned enterprises in China, the work emulation system is a very important theoretical and institutional supplement. If we could implement the work emulation system then state-owned enterprise will not degenerate or become corrupt because of the loss of capitalist-style free competition."[88]

In order to promote work emulation, the Nationalist Central Training Commission in late 1939 drafted a *Preliminary Proposal for Work Emulation*, which included topics such as typology, procedure, and organization of work emulation, emulation and reward and punishment, and work emulation within factories. As its preface indicates, the proposal "drew its inspiration from the socialist emulation principles of the Soviet Union."[89]

By early 1940 Chiang Kaishek had made up his mind about the need to utilize work emulation for improving productivity. In a radio address delivered on March 12, 1940, he stated that the Nationalist government "should advocate work emulation as a way to increase production and bring to fruition the task of reconstruction, [because] having fought the war of resistance for more than two years, the war is no longer a question of a purely military operation. Consequently we must, from now on, begin the work of nation building in earnest. We must encourage our fellow countrymen to look forward, to raise their level of energy to the maximum so that we could improve our work efficiency." To realize the goal of increasing productivity, Chiang called for "a rigorous implementation of work emulation" in all government organizations, schools, factories, and farms.[90]

Within a week of Chiang's radio address, Gan Naiguang published an essay in the Nationalist *Central Daily News*. In addition to repeating much of his earlier arguments, Gan underscored the need to "establish the work emulation system in all organizations and enterprises. Although China has yet to establish a planned economic system, we must get ready for its eventual establishment, which means that all these organizations and enterprises ought to work out detailed methods of emulation."[91]

For the next three years, the government took steps to discuss, consider, and implement the Work Emulation Campaign. In the process, the Nationalist elite not only developed a shared mental model on the rationale, methods, and objectives of the Work Emulation Campaign; they also began to reorder the reality of political and economic life according to that model. During the summer of 1940, Chiang Kaishek ordered Zhang Qun and Gu Zhenggang, secretary-general of the Supreme National Defense Commission and head of the Ministry of Social Affairs, respectively, and several others to study how to implement work emulation. Out of their study was drafted a *Program for Implementing Work Emulation*.[92] Subsequently, Chiang approved the program. In September 1941, he ordered the creation of a Commission for Promoting Work Emulation. It was formally established in January 1942 with Gu Zhenggang serving as director. At the time of its creation it belonged to the Commission for National Spiritual Mobilization, but in May 1943 it came under the control of the Party and Government Work Evaluation Commission.[93]

The process of forming a shared mental model continued in March 1942 when the newly established Commission for Promoting Work Emulation organized seven panels to discuss issues involved in work emulation, including panels on national spiritual general mobilization and work emulation, on work emulation and the demonstration effect of party members, on work emulation in industrial and mining enterprises, and on work emulation in agricultural reconstruction. According to Gu Zhenggang, the objective of work emulation was to change people's attitudes toward work and to improve work efficiency. For Gu, "in order to succeed in the great enterprise of the war of resistance against Japan and nation building, China must mobilize all of its human and material resources. Among the many mobilization methods spiritual mobilization is the most important, and work emulation clearly belongs to this kind of spiritual mobilization."[94] As Gu saw it, "the Work Emulation Campaign is a campaign that Chairman Chiang designed to meet the needs of the war of resistance against Japan and nation building."[95]

Beginning in 1942, the Commission for Promoting Work Emulation undertook numerous work emulation campaigns in the areas of production, transportation, and government administration. In a speech delivered at the first awards ceremony for national work emulation held in the summer of 1943, Gu Zhenggang listed the campaigns conducted in agriculture, industry, mining, transportation and communications, government administration, and cultural institutions. He pointed out that organizations and enterprises in transportation and communications "have frequently adopted the method of emulation. What is more, work emulation has almost become institutionalized in post and telecommunications organizations."[96] A total of five hundred individuals and two hundred organizations received awards for their achievements at the awards ceremony.[97]

According to a comprehensive survey conducted by the national Commission for Promoting Work Emulation, the Work Emulation Campaign extended to almost all major areas of social, economic, and political activity between 1940 and 1945. In agriculture, there were emulation campaigns in grain production, cultivation of plants and cotton, and irrigation networks. In the industrial sector, the textile, machine manufacturing, flour making, and coal mining industries had undertaken work emulation. In transportation and communication, work emulation took place at all levels of railroad and highway administration, telecommunications, and the postal service. Finally, work emulation was organized in cooperative and welfare enterprises, cadre training, trade unions, chambers of commerce, and in the area of national education and school administration.[98]

It was in the context of the national Work Emulation Campaign that the DISW initiated its own campaign to increase productivity. In March 1942, the DISW received a copy of the Nationalist Central Training Commission's booklet *A Preliminary Proposal for Work Emulation* from the Bureau of Ordnance. The DISW printed one thousand copies of it and distributed them among *zhiyuan*. The leaders decided to get the campaign started by publicly soliciting essays with the topic, "how should the DISW put work emulation into practice?"[99] Apparently no one responded to the call for almost two years.[100]

Finally, in March 1944, Xiong Shiping, a midlevel *zhiyuan*, wrote an essay on how to implement work emulation in response to a request for essays from *Crashing Waves*, the official journal of the DISW. In this essay he first pointed out existing problems, such as the lack of training, a high labor turnover, and poor living conditions. He proposed work emulation as a way to solve these problems. According to Xiong, the DISW should set up a committee, establish a propaganda team within each "large unit" *(da danwei)*, and then promote work emulation. Xiong suggested that work emulation could make consumption of raw material and utilization of waste material more efficient and could reduce the amount of time spent completing certain tasks.[101] On April 8, 1944, the DISW announced the methods to be used in the Work Emulation Campaign.[102]

Five months later, the DISW designated Xiong as chair of the newly established Committee for Promoting Work Emulation. At the committee's first meeting in September, Xiong stated: "Work emulation is designed to increase production and improve product quality. It is equivalent to America's scientific management campaign, continental Europe's rationalization campaign, England's efficiency campaign, and the Soviet Union's Stakhanovite campaign." Xiong also explained that the director "felt deeply the urgency of ordnance production, but due to production inefficiency, the wartime need for ordnance is not being met. Thus the director was determined to launch the Work Emulation Campaign to boost morale and increase production."[103] What Xiong failed to point out was the equally important factor of wartime inflation. Under the pressure of rising inflation, the DISW provided workers with a variety of nonwage benefits and welfare so that "wages constituted only a small percentage of workers' income." As a result, material incentives such as money awards and bonuses were "no longer sufficient to motivate workers to make strenuous effort at work."[104]

According to the preliminary plan drafted in September 1944, the Work Emulation Campaign sought to "improve work efficiency and raise the level of technical proficiency." To accomplish these objectives, the DISW would conduct or coordinate a propaganda campaign to increase awareness among *zhiyuan* and workers, a campaign for self-examination of shortcomings by various "work units" *(gongzuo danwei)*, an investigation of the technical expertise of skilled workers, an investigation of production efficiency, and a campaign to select model workers.[105]

Less than a month later, the DISW held its first panel discussion on the Work Emulation Campaign. At the beginning of the discussion, Yang Jizeng underscored the importance of adopting a practical approach: "work efficiency is of vital important to a factory. Work efficiency is derived from people's interest in work, and we can enhance people's interest in work with work emulation. However, we should not simply shout slogans; we should approach work emulation in a practical manner." After the director spoke, a number of plant directors and division heads made suggestions on how to conduct work emulation. In the end, the panel made a number of decisions on issues related to work emulation.[106]

After the first three months, the Committee for Promoting Work Emulation declared the Work Emulation Campaign to be a success. For example, the output of sterilized jars in the department of refractory brick increased 131 percent over a three-month period. At the same time, the monthly output of steel strips in the fourth manufacturing plant increased to 288,677 tons in October, breaking the previous record of 280,044 tons. Having listed these and several other achievements, Xiong Shiping concluded, "The Work Emulation Campaign has indeed led to improved efficiency and increased production."[107]

Gradually the Work Emulation Campaign extended to activities not directly related to production. These activities included business and personnel management, document drafting, copying, proofreading, and processing, archival management, property management, environmental hygiene, and academic research.[108] For example, at the end of 1944 the Committee for Promoting Work Emulation inspected work emulation in the maintenance of factory buildings and machinery, storage of raw materials in warehouses, office hygiene in various "units" (danwei), hygiene in residential housing and dormitories, and environmental hygiene such as the conditions of roads and lavatories. The Committee for Promoting Work Emulation then published a detailed report during February and March of 1945.[109]

By March 1945, the DISW had conducted the Work Emulation Campaign for more than five months, and the time had come for the Committee for Promoting Work Emulation to summarize its lessons and achievements. In a report published in Crashing Waves in June 1945, the commission found that the method of selecting model workers did not work well, in part because it subjected them to "jealousy and ridicule" by fellow workers and contributed to work slowdowns and an unwillingness to assume responsibility. Consequently the various departments had chosen the "method of team emulation" because it "not only encouraged worker sympathy and mutual assistance among one another but served to strengthen ties and cooperation in the workplace."

The same report also offered statistics on the achievements of the Work Emulation Campaign. The use of coal, it showed, decreased from 2.56 kilograms to 2.18 kilograms between July 1944 and February 1945, a savings of 13 percent over a seven-month period. Worker productivity in the iron-smelting plant also improved during the same period. The statistics show that a particular product required the labor of 34.4 workers in June 1944, but only 20.2 workers by February 1945. Because of the improvement in productivity, a major boost in production took place: the product index allegedly increased 347 percent between June 1944 and February 1945.[110]

Both the new accounting system and the Work Emulation Campaign were rooted in changes the Nationalist government initiated during the 1930s: the Bureau of Ordnance began introducing cost accounting in ordnance factories, whereas the Nationalist government conducted the New Life Campaign and the National Economic Reconstruction Campaign. Fundamentally and despite their different origins, it was the sustained systemic crisis of the 1930s and 1940s that shaped the creation of management and incentive mechanisms in state-owned enterprises such as the DISW. In response to the wartime need for efficiency and increased production, the DISW implemented the new system of cost accounting which had its origins in the "managerial revolution" in the United States. The same national crisis also called for the adoption of nonconventional means to increase productivity. As in the case of early campaigns, the Work Emulation Campaign was an emergency response to a crisis. It was also an incentive mechanism modeled on the Stakhanovite Campaign in the Soviet Union. In comparative terms, whereas the sustained systemic crisis strengthened the existing organizational model of the formal administrative bureaucracy and led officials and managers to expand the bureaucratic enterprise governance structure, the same crisis forced officials and managers to expand existing institutional resources as well as to appropriate institutional resources abroad in developing enterprise management and incentive mechanisms.

CHAPTER 5

Enterprise Provision of
Social Services
and Welfare

The provision of social services and welfare was a final defining characteristic which state-owned enterprises acquired during the Sino-Japanese War. Although social service and welfare institutions first emerged during the 1920s, the wartime crisis in social and economic life led directly to their development and expansion. As was the case with the creation of enterprise management and incentive mechanisms, path independence also characterizes the evolution of enterprise provision of social services and welfare.

Prewar Evolution of Institutions of Social Services and Welfare

Some private firms had already adopted social service and welfare measures during the 1920s. By 1928, at least twenty-five private firms in industry and mining offered some kind of service and welfare facilities, with apartments and dormitories at twenty-one firms, dining halls at ten firms, clinics or hospitals at twenty-one, recreational or sports facilities at eight, and primary schools at seven.[1] Five years later, the number of firms providing service and welfare facilities had more than doubled. According to incomplete information gathered by the Factory Inspection Division of the Ministry of Industries, within the manufacturing industry forty-six firms had apartments and dormitories, twenty-eight had dining halls, thirty-three had bathhouses, fifty had medical treatment facilities including clinics and hospitals, and three had child-care centers. In the mining industry, seventeen collieries had apartments and dormitories, and twelve had clinics or hospitals.[2]

The national government also played a role in promoting workers' welfare. As early as 1920, the Ministry of Communications promulgated an

Outline for Educating Railroad Workers,[3] and subsequently established twelve schools along four major railroad lines. The schools supplied students with textbooks and charged no tuition and fees. For the purpose of educating the children of railroad employees, the Ministry of Communications established its first primary school in 1918. By 1925 the number had increased to thirty-four. An internal investigation during the same year reveals that these schools had 7,103 students, with 6,207 being children of railroad employees.[4]

The best statistics on enterprise provision of social services and welfare comes from a 1936 survey of five railroads and forty-four industrial and mining enterprises. Of these forty-nine enterprises, ten were state-owned, eight were province-run, and thirty-one belonged to private enterpreneurs. The survey took place between March and June of 1936 and was "limited to large-scale enterprises with a long history and the best record of achievement in the provision of social services and welfare."[5] Four years later the findings were published in the form of a book entitled *A Survey of Social Services and Welfare in China.*

The author of this report, Wu Zhixin, found "substantial improvement" in the provision of social services and welfare in these enterprises. Social service and welfare facilities already encompassed many aspects of workers' lives, such as room and board, sanitation, education, and recreation. Of the forty-nine enterprises, thirty-eight provided medical facilities, and thirty-eight offered apartments and dormitories. Other services and welfare facilities included sports facilities, savings plans, schools for employees' children, recreational facilities, consumer organizations, and public dining halls. Wu found that the availability or lack of goods and materials where factories were located was the "most important factor in determining the priority when establishing service and welfare facilities." Most enterprises and collieries located in rural areas had relatively well-equipped hospitals and schools for employees' children, which was not the case with enterprises and collieries located in urban areas.[6]

This comprehensive survey also confirms the existence of a variety of service and welfare facilities in some medium to large private enterprises. Dasheng No. 1 Cotton Mill in Nantong had provided company housing for its employees at least by 1920.[7] During the early 1930s, the family enterprise founded by the Rong Brothers in Shanghai created a "workers' self-governing community" that included a primary school, dormitories, a dining hall, a bathhouse, a theater, a consumer cooperative, and a rabbit farm.[8] The Jiuda Salt Refinery at Tanggu provided comprehensive service and welfare facilities such as dormitories, a dining hall, a hospital, a workers' school, a primary school for employees' children, a consumers' cooperative store, and recreational facilities.[9] An investigation by the Department of Reconstruction of Shandong province in 1936 reveals that the two cotton mills in Jinan provided employeees with apartments and dormitories, dining halls, hospitals, bathhouses, reading rooms, recreation facilities, and consumer cooperatives.[10]

Yet another example of company welfarism was the Commercial Press in Shanghai, China's largest modern printing enterprise. In 1931 it had about 4,500 employees in its Shanghai headquarters alone. The company did not provide housing for its employees, but it offered a wide range of other service and welfare facilities: a school for employees, a primary school for employees' children, a child-care center, a kindergarten, a library, a clubhouse, an annual bonus, pensions for retirement, employees' savings plan, free medical treatment at a designated hospital, and paid maternity leave for female employees.[11] Gail Hershatter finds that the cotton mills in Tianjin were also "planned communities complete with a full range of welfare services." Government and academic surveys lauded one of the cotton mills for its dormitories, dining hall, clinic, schools for employees and their children, consumer cooperative, bathhouse, athletic field, and martial arts society, as well as its paid maternity leave, disability benefits, funeral subsidy, and the bonus paid to workers so they could purchase melons in the summer.[12]

Among the state-owned enterprises included in the *Survey of Social Services and Welfare in China*, roughly half were enterprises in the ordnance industry. Available archival materials confirm that some ordnance factories did provide social services and welfare for their employees. The Shanghai Steel Plant already had a primary school for employees' children in early 1936.[13] Jinling Arsenal in Nanjing had a school for employees' children as well as a department of medical care.[14] In January 1937 the Ministry of Military Affairs promulgated *Provisional Regulations on the Treatment of Workers in Ordnance Factories*. Among other things, the regulations stipulated that ordnance factories should establish schools for employees' children, promote workers' legitimate recreation, and provide pensions for retirement and for the injured.[15] On May 31, the Ministry issued *Regulations on Schools for Employees' Children in Ordnance Factories*. The regulations provided that each ordnance factory should establish a primary school, which should admit children of workers free of tuition and other miscellaneous charges. The cost of running schools would come from the budget for manufacturing expenses.[16]

The Second Arsenal of Guangdong province offers an example of well-developed institutions of social services and welfare existing in ordnance factories before 1937. Following the German model of organizing ordnance factories, the Pajiangkou Arsenal—the immediate predecessor of the Second Arsenal of Guangdong province—created a welfare division at the time of its establishment in 1935. When the Bureau of Ordnance took it over and renamed it the Second Arsenal of Guangdong province in June 1937, it retained the welfare division and under it created a training department, a service department, and a hospital.[17] According to the organizational regulations of the welfare division, the training department was responsible for providing workers' education and training, planning for the creation of schools for apprentices and employees' children, promoting the New Life Campaign, and organizing sports activities. The service department was in charge of setting up a consumer cooperative, a library, a reading room, and a photo lab. The hospital was to take epidemic prevention measures, spread hygienic knowledge, in addition to providing physical examinations, diagnoses, and treatment for employees.[18]

The service and welfare facilities in the Second Arsenal of Guangdong province were an exception rather than the rule, however. By its own admission, "only the Second Arsenal has a welfare division among all ordnance factories."[19] That may have had to do with the early adoption of the German organizational model and the unhealthy geographical environment in which the arsenal found itself. The arsenal was located in Pajiangkou and was surrounded by "undulating hills and mountains" during its formative period.[20] According to a report submitted to the Bureau of Ordnance, over one thousand workers died due to subtropical diseases such as pernicious malaria and insect stings. At the time the arsenal drafted the report in the summer of 1937, several dozen people still became sick daily. Such a "peculiar," inhospitable environment required extensive service and welfare facilities. The arsenal drafted the report to defend its organizational structure in the spirit of "seeking truth from fact."[21]

Expansion of Social Service and Welfare Institutions in the Ordnance Industry

Despite these developments, "only a minority of factories and collieries undertook social service and welfare enterprise" by the eve of the Sino-

Japanese War.[22] In addition, among the state-owned enterprises included in this survey, none manufactured basic products such as those of iron and steel, a fact that reflected the lack of state-owned heavy industries during the early 1930s. What led to the rapid expansion of social service and welfare institutions was the sustained systematic crisis triggered by the war.

After the war began, more than twenty ordnance factories relocated to Sichuan, Yunnan, Guizhou, Hunan, and Guangxi provinces. Of the fifteen factories relocated to Sichuan province, the overwhelming majority concentrated in Chongqing.[23] Once relocation was complete, factories began building apartments and dormitories for their employees. The DISW began housing construction shortly after its relocation to Chongqing. By November 1941, it had constructed 189 units of apartments, dormitories, and temporary shelters.[24] Two years later, the DISW had enough apartments and dormitories to accommodate about three thousand people, roughly half of the DISW employees at its Chongqing headquarters.[25] The Twentieth Arsenal provided apartments for married employees and dormitories for single ones.[26] The Twenty-first Arsenal solved housing problems over a period of several years. It constructed some apartments and dormitories but obtained others through purchase from private owners.[27] Its Kunming branch had a total of seventeen dormitory units.[28] From 1938 to 1945, the Twenty-fifth Arsenal built thirty apartments and seventy dormitory units.[29] Four other arsenals that relocated to Kunming (the Twenty-second Arsenal, Fifty-first Arsenal) and Guizhou province (the Forty-first Arsenal, Forty-second Arsenal) also provided housing as well as dining halls for their employees.[30] Because "every factory provides apartments, dormitories, dining halls, and bathhouses," many chose not to include them in their description of welfare facilities.[31] That was the case with the Twenty-first Arsenal, even though it was among the first ordnance factories to provide apartments, dormitories, and dining halls.[32]

Many ordnance factories also established schools for employees' children. The DISW established a primary school in August 1939 with 275 students and twelve teachers. Two years later the number of students increased to 541 and that of teachers to twenty-five.[33] In order to prevent the interruption of education for primary school graduates, the DISW established a middle school in June 1943.[34] The DISW experience was typical of ordnance factories during this period. For example, a list of school names reveals that fourteen ordnance factories had established schools for employees' children by July 1940.[35] In July 1942 the Bureau of Ordnance changed the name of "school for employees' children" to "primary school for employees' children," apparently in anticipation of the establishment of middle schools in the near future. In order to prevent possible mistakes in identifying schools of different factories, the Bureau of Ordnance published a list of primary schools for employees' children in November 1942, which included a total of thirty such schools at the time.[36] In January 1944 the Bureau of Ordnance promulgated *Regulations Concerning the Establishment of Employee Children's Middle Schools in Ordnance Factories,* which stated that the purpose of establishing middle schools was to "prevent children from being deprived of further education and to reduce the burden of employees so that they can keep their minds on work." As in earlier provisions for primary schools, the regulations provided that the middle school children of employees would not need to pay tuition and miscellaneous charges and that the cost of running schools would come from the budget for manufacturing expenses.[37] The regulations were but a belated recognition of a number of middle schools that had come into existence earlier. For instance, the Twenty-first Arsenal established Ninghe Middle School in September 1943. It not only admitted employees' children free of charge but also offered room and board to students.[38] The Fiftieth Arsenal established a middle school for employees' children during the same year.[39]

Along with housing and schools for employees' children, medical services also expanded during the Sino-Japanese War. The DISW established a medical office during the summer of 1939. By April 1941, the DISW operated two outpatient clinics that together treated about four hundred patients daily.[40] Wartime living and working conditions were such that 15 to 30 percent of all employees visited the clinics at least once between May and September of 1943.[41] Among those treated at the clinics, most were infected with malaria. The second most frequent ailment was the common cold, with enteritis, gastritis, and tuberculosis farther down the list.[42] The Tenth Arsenal did not have a hospital when it relocated to Chongqing in August 1938, but established one in the summer of 1941.[43] The Twentieth Arsenal also established a hospital, which included departments such as internal medicine, surgery, gynecology and obstetrics, and dentistry.[44] The Twenty-first Arsenal, the largest ordnance factory during the war, had a department of medical care when it relocated to Chongqing in 1938. Two years later the factory established a hospital, and the department of medical care ceased to exist. By 1948, the hospital had departments of internal medicine, surgery, and gynecology and obstetrics, with 120 beds and a medical team of more than eighty personnel. The hospital also engaged two doctors of traditional Chinese medicine for those who preferred Chinese medicine to Western medicine.[45]

The Twenty-fifth Arsenal established a hospital in 1939, and its authorized size continued to expand over the next few years.[46] The Thirtieth Arsenal established a hospital in September 1940. It had three outpatient clinics because the factory was scattered in three different locations.[47] The Fiftieth Arsenal established a hospital in early 1939, less than one year after it relocated to Chongqing. At the time of its establishment, the hospital had one small building, and the facilities were "extremely simple and crude."[48] Over the next nine years, the hospital evolved into a sizable institution, with departments of internal medicine, surgery, gynecology and obstetrics, and dentistry. It also had an X-ray room, laboratory, operating room, and forty beds.[49] The Forty-first Arsenal relocated to Tongzi in Guizhou province in 1938. During the war it also established a hospital with an inpatient department, two outpatient clinics, and one mobile medical team.[50]

Another welfare institution that flourished during the war was the consumer cooperative. In April 1939 the DISW founded a consumer cooperative designed to make it possible for members to "purchase low-priced daily necessities."[51] Because of the increasing volume of transactions, two branch cooperatives came into existence by June 1942.[52] The Twentieth Arsenal also established a consumer cooperative in order to "reduce the burden of living" for employees. It provided daily necessities such as edible oil, salt, and general merchandise as well as services for laundry, hair-cutting, tailoring, and picture-taking.[53] Another ordnance factory that established a consumer cooperative was the Twenty-first Arsenal. The cooperative also provided cheap goods to its members, but because its supply of daily necessities and sundry articles was limited, members could purchase them only with coupons. Affiliated with the cooperative were service facilities run by contractors, such as a dining hall, a pastry room, a tailor's room, a shoemaker's room, a photo-lab, a barber's room, and a meat and vegetable market.[54] The Fiftieth Arsenal had a consumer cooperative before the war. The arsenal not only resumed operation after it relocated to Chongqing in 1938, but it established a branch store in a newly constructed residential area. Subsequently the cooperative's business continued to expand. By early 1948 the cooperative had developed a retail department, a shoe department, a tailor's room, and a laundry room.[55] The Forty-first Arsenal, the Twenty-second Arsenal, and the Fifty-first Arsenal each established a consumer cooperative during the war.[56]

Many ordnance factories developed farms in order to assure adequate supply of daily necessities such as meat and vegetables. The DISW developed its factory farm in December 1939. Between April and August of 1943, the farm produced a monthly average of 27,568 pounds of vegetables. Farm workers also raised hogs and sheep, and produced bean curd, soybean milk, and bean sprouts.[57] The Tenth Arsenal, Twentieth Arsenal, Twenty-first Arsenal, Twenty-second Arsenal, Forty-first Arsenal, Fiftieth Arsenal, and Fifty-first Arsenal all set up farms in close proximity to the factories. The farm of the Twentieth Arsenal, for example, grew crops and vegetables, cultivated flowers and plants, made soybean oil and pickled vegetables, and raised hogs and dairy cows. It sold produce to employees at reasonable prices.[58] The farm of the Fiftieth Arsenal produced soybean milk, soybean curd, fermented soybeans, soy sauce, pickled vegetables, and sweet sauce in addition to growing vegetables.[59] The farm of the Twenty-first Arsenal provided similar produce and farm products.[60] In his memoir Li Chenggan, director of the Twenty-first Arsenal, summarized the situation in these words: "The drastic price fluctuation during the war caused a great deal of privation and hardship in the lives of *zhiyuan* and workers. As a result we had to find some kind of remedy to the situation. What we did was to grow vegetables and raise hogs in order to meet the needs of *zhiyuan*, workers, and their families of over ten thousand people. In addition to growing vegetables and raising hogs, we made soybean curd, soy sauce, and solid food. The objective was not to eat delicious food, but rather to simply allay hunger and acquire minimum nutrition . . . Eventually we were so successful in raising large numbers of hogs that we had meat to eat every week. At the same time our farm grew all kinds of vegetables, even vegetable roots were quite tasty. All these led to a substantial increase of productivity."[61]

Finally, at least two ordnance factories established a cemetery and a crematorium during the war. After its relocation from Nanjing to Chongqing in 1938, many employees in the Twenty-first Arsenal died. For several years the arsenal buried the dead in the wilderness. The burial site took up a large tract of land, and in addition the graves became unrecognizable within a few years. Consequently the arsenal established a cemetery to which many coffins were moved for reburial. The arsenal also set up a crematorium so that family members or relatives of the dead could take the ashes back to their hometowns in other provinces. In addition, the crematorium served as a public mourning hall when a member of a family died.[62] The DISW also established a cemetery in order for the deceased to have a permanent resting place.[63] The establishment of the cemetery by these two enterprises is all the more remarkable, as only five public cemeteries were reportedly established in Chongqing during the war.[64]

Out of the formation of these institutions of social services and welfare emerged a number of self-contained, factory-run communities. Employees lived in factory apartments and dormitories, bought their daily necessities at factory cooperatives, purchased vegetables grown at factory farms, and went to factory clinics and hospitals for medical treatment. Employees' children received their education in factory schools. When employees died, they sometimes were buried in factory cemeteries.[65]

The rapid development of these institutions necessitated the establishment and expansion of welfare administration in ordnance factories. The Tenth Arsenal is a good case in point. When the arsenal relocated to Chongqing in 1938, it had a section of general affairs but no specific department in charge of welfare. Two years later the arsenal created a welfare section in its administrative structure. After its reorganization in July 1941, the welfare section expanded into a welfare division, under which were created a service department, a training department, a hospital, a farm, and a school for employees' children.[66] A similar arrangement developed in the Twentieth Arsenal, where a training department, supply department, hospital, school for employees's children, farm, and consumer cooperative came under the jurisdiction of the welfare division.[67]

The record of the Twenty-first Arsenal tells a similar story. During its days as Jinling Arsenal before 1937, it had a department of medical care and a school for employees' children under the general affairs division.[68] It created a welfare department between 1937 and 1939.[69] Soon afterward, the department of welfare expanded into a welfare division, which oversaw a training department, supply department, hospital, farm, grain shop, consumer cooperative, and accounting office.[70] The DISW had only a medicine room and a library room under the general affairs section in 1938.[71] It created a welfare division in January 1940, under which were established a hygiene department, training department, supply department, hospital, school for employees' children, consumer cooperative, library, and farm.[72] In 1942 the DISW's welfare division added a real estate department responsible for housing allocation, repair, and maintenance.[73]

The experience of the Thirtieth Arsenal offers another example of organizational growth. The Thirtieth Arsenal, formerly the Jinan Arsenal, did not have a welfare department until it relocated to Chongqing in 1938. In

February 1939 it enlarged its welfare department to include sections for supply and training. Three years later the welfare department expanded to become a welfare division, which included a supply department, training department, hygiene department, farm, hospital, and school for employees' children.[74] Although detailed information for the Forty-first and Fifty-first arsenals is scarce, available evidence indicates that both established similar structures of welfare administration.[75] A history of the Fiftieth Arsenal stated that after it relocated to Chongqing in 1938, "the business of the welfare division continued to expand with a corresponding development of welfare oganizations." By 1948 the Fiftieth Arsenal had a total of eight "units" *(danwei)* under its welfare division: a business department, training department, farm and forestry center, hospital, consumer cooperative, joint administration of primary and middle schools, an accounting section, and an office of traditional Chinese medicine.[76] Overall, the evidence indicates that the majority of large ordnance factories had established a welfare department by August 1939,[77] only to expand to a full-fledged welfare division between 1940 and 1942 to meet rapidly increasing needs.[78]

Causes for the Expansion of Social Service and Welfare Institutions

The factory-run communities in the ordnance industry were a product of the war-triggered crisis. The crisis exposed the inadequacy of existing social service and welfare insitutions, and forced factory officials and managers to change their mental model of socioeconomic reality. This in turn led them to reorder that reality by developing and expanding social service and welfare institutions.

Many ordnance factories relocated to the interior after the war broke out, but they were not at liberty to choose whichever sites they desired. They had to take into consideration factors such as safety, availability of raw materials, and transportation. As a result, almost all the ordnance factories in Chongqing were located in the outskirts, far from the city proper. The Fiftieth Arsenal chose a site in a mountainous area eleven miles east of Chongqing.[79] The Twenty-third Arsenal was located in Luxian, where it had all its important workshops built in man-made mountain caves.[80] The Twenty-fifth Arsenal also chose a site in a mountainous area to the west of Chongqing where the factory had as many as 40 workshops in man-made caves.[81] The Kunming branch of the Twenty-first Arsenal was located at the foot of a mountain valley thirteen miles away from Kunming, and all the important manufacturing work was done in two man-made caves.[82] As an iron and steel works, the DISW had to have access to a deepwater wharf to unload heavy machinery and equipment and to obtain good water transportation for coke and ore. The DISW therefore chose Dadukou along the Yangzi River at the time of its relocation. Still, it was a long way to the city proper during the 1940s. Because of the abrupt relocation to areas where either few social services were available or those provided by urban centers were inaccessible due to long distance, or because of their relatively large organizational scale, officials and managers of ordnance factories recognized that they had to establish institutions of social services and welfare.

A high labor turnover resulting from a shortage of skilled labor also contributed to the development of social service and welfare institutions. Before the war, China's southwest was predominantly an agricultural region with little industry. Although Chongqing, one of the largest urban centers in the region, had forty-one industrial enterprises with eight thousand workers during the mid-1930s, it was primarily a regional center for commerce and finance.[83] What made Chongqing an industrial center was the

Figure 11. Panoramic view of a branch factory of the Central Electric Works in a mountainous area during the Sino-Japanese War. Courtesy the Second Historical Archives of China.

relocation necessitated by the Sino-Japanese War. Statistics compiled by the Division of Industry and Mining Regulations *(gongkuang tiaozhengchu)* reveal that by the end of 1940, a total of 448 enterprises had relocated to interior provinces such as Sichuan, Hunan, and Guangxi.[84] Of those 448 enterprises 254 relocated to Sichuan province, which accounted for 57 percent of all relocated enterprises. Furthermore, the majority of those enterprises that relocated to Sichuan province were concentrated in Chongqing. Statistics published in June 1940 reveal that of the 247 relocated enterprises, over 90 percent were located in Chongqing and its vicinities, not to mention the fact that a substantial majority of ordnance factories were also located in Chongqing.[85] As a result, Chongqing suddenly emerged as the single most important industrial center in China's interior.

The rapid concentration of hundreds of factories in a predominantly agricultural region created a severe shortage of skilled labor. Chongqing was in no position to provide an adequate supply of skilled labor, and not all skilled laborers in the coastal provinces chose to migrate. A 1938 report by

Figure 12. Residential area of a branch factory of the Central Electric Works during the Sino-Japanese War. Courtesy the Second Historical Archives of China.

the Division of Industry and Mining Regulations indicates that only about 2,300 skilled laborers from metropolitian areas such as Shanghai and Beijing chose to relocate with their firms.[86] Having recognized that the shortage of skilled labor was the "main labor problem in the southwest," the Division of Industry and Mining Regulations encouraged enterprises to establish schools to provide training to apprentices. In addition, the division set out in 1938 to help relocated factories recruit skilled workers.[87] The targets for recruitment included turners, fitters, forgers, carpenters, casters, and other categories of skilled laborers. The division would loan Ch$30 to Ch$80 to prospective skilled laborers for them to travel to the interior.[88] Gradually this program paid off: 1,793 skilled laborers reported to the division by the end of 1938. Over the course of the next couple of years that figure increased dramatically: 10,912 by the end of 1939 and 12,664 by the end of 1940.[89]

In the meantime, the severe shortage of skilled laborers, competition for skilled laborers among public and private enterprises, and the consequent labor turnover caused serious disruptions of wartime production in government arsenals, which led officials and managers to recognize the urgent

Figure 13. Group photo of apprentices who received training at the Central Machine Works during the Sino-Japanese War. Courtesy Yunnan Provincial Archives.

need for change. As early as July 1938 an order by the Bureau of Ordnance stated: "Because of the shortage of technical personnel and skilled laborers and the difficulty of recruitment, sometimes organizations would offer very high salaries and wages to recruit technical personnel and skilled laborers, which led other employees to become discontented and desirous of job changes. The smart ones would find excuses to ask for leave from which they would never return; the less smart ones would deliberately slow down in order to leave their present jobs. There are even those who would arrogantly threaten to leave if their demands for high salaries and wages are not met. Obviously this kind of practice cannot be encouraged and something must be done about it."[90]

As another order by the Bureau of Ordnance revealed nine months later, that "something" was to make the workers subject to military law. Yu Dawei, the bureau chief, stated in his order that "the majority of factory workers understand their responsibility and work hard. Still, due to material inducement from the outside many have left their factories or have chosen not to observe factory discipline in the hope of being dismissed. In the factories located in Chongqing these workers far outnumbered those in factories located elsewhere." Having petitioned the Ministry of Military Administration twice and received the permission to proceed, Yu issued notices to the effect that workers could be subject to military law at the discretion of the factory; and if workers "absconded" from the factory they would be arrested as army deserters and punished accordingly.[91] In October 1939 the Bureau of Ordnance issued another order, which instructed ordnance factories not to simply dismiss workers who broke factory regulations at a time when skilled labor was in short supply. Instead, those who violated the regulations would be punished according to military law.[92]

The arrest and punishment of disobedient workers constituted only part of the answer of the ordnance factories to the problem of high labor turnover. In June 1939, in a major effort to prevent workers from leaving ordnance factories, the Bureau of Ordnance proposed a comprehensive program that included measures for management and control of workers and the establishment of social service and welfare institutions. In the following month, the Bureau of Ordnance sent the program to all ordnance factories for implementation.[93] After that, officials and managers of ordnance factories consistently associated problems of labor turnover with the need to improve social services and welfare. These officials and managers assumed a causal relationship between the lack of social services and welfare and job-hopping *(tiaochang)*. In September 1939, the Bureau of Ordnance again called for expansion of social services and welfare in order to prevent workers from being influenced by "outside inducement."[94]

Wartime inflation, not labor turnover, proved to be the most important factor in the development of social service and welfare institutions. As Appendix Table 5.1 shows, there was a moderate increase in retail price and cost of living between 1937 and 1939. Moreover, during 1938 the real wages for industrial workers rose more rapidly than the cost of living, which may have resulted from labor shortages and competition for skilled laborers among enterprises.[95] By 1939, both retail prices and the cost of living increased more rapidly, and workers' real wages had fallen behind the cost of living by a large margin. All the figures indicate that the year 1939 was a critical turning point in wartime inflation.

Growing inflation caused great pain and suffering for the general population and led directly to the development of more social service and welfare institutions.[96] Archival materials show the conceptual connection between inflation, the revision of the existing mental model, and the establishment of these institutions in ordnance factories. A survey of the Twentieth Arsenal pointed out that "the cost of living kept rising. . . . It was very difficult for workers to make a living despite wage adjustments." "In order to increase production and to keep workers content, [the arsenal] created a welfare division to run housing, meal service, education, and sanitation for employees and their families."[97] A survey of the Thirtieth Arsenal indicated that "in 1939 commodity prices skyrocketed, and we felt an urgent need to establish service and welfare facilities for employees and their families."[98]

The strongest evidence of the causal relationship between rising inflation, mental model revision, and the establishment of social service and welfare institutions comes from the comprehensive program the Bureau of Ordnance adopted in June 1939. Entitled *Program for Stabilizing Workers' Lives and Schedule for Implementation*, it meant to "stabilize workers' lives, prevent workers from being influenced by outside inducement, and put an end to workers' restlessness and flight with practical methods, minimum cost, and within a short period of time." In other words, the program aimed to "combat the symptoms and attack the root causes" of these problems.[99]

This program had three components. The first part dealt with the management of workers and was subdivided into three sections. Section one called for workers' organization and training to strengthen both their physical power and willpower because those who lacked will tended to be vulnerable to outside inducement. Section two called for strict regimentation of workers' lives by introducing military organization and training for single employees. For employees with families, the program called for the creation of "mutual security" *(baojia)* organizations in the residential districts so that people could "watch over each other's private lives, making it impossible for outside inducement to penetrate." Section three repeated an earlier order by the Bureau of Ordnance, which stated that workers could be subject to military law at the discretion of the factory; and if workers absconded from a factory, they would be arrested as army deserters and punished accordingly.

The second part of the program addressed the need for social service and welfare facilities and was subdivided into five sections. Section one addressed the spiritual well being of workers. With regard to workers' moral education *(deyu)*, the program called on factories to instruct workers to devote their energy to their work and skill development and to avoid involvement in political activities. For workers' intellectual development *(zhiyu)*, the program required factories to set up libraries and recreation facilities so that workers could undertake independent studies or recreational activities. As for workers' physical training *(tiyu)*, the program directed factories to purchase sports equipment and to promote sports activities so as to build up workers' physical strength.

Section two listed several material benefits factories should offer to workers. Ordnance factories should establish an "employees' welfare society" because existing consumer cooperatives were small in scale and unable to meet workers' needs. Under the supervision of the welfare department in each factory, the employees' welfare society would be in charge of constructing apartments and dormitories, running public dining halls for single employees, purchasing and distributing daily necessities, and managing public bathhouses, barber's rooms, and laundry rooms. The program also called for the adjustment of workers' wages and the establishment of workers' savings plans.

Section three explained concrete measures needed for promoting employee health. Section four emphasized the necessity to strengthen the education of employees' children. It called for the expansion of schools for employees' children to accommodate more students who were unable to attend school due to limited school facilities. It also required ordnance factories to give graduates of schools for employees' children priority when hiring apprentices. Section five pointed out the desirability to recruit workers' spouses so as to lighten workers' burden.

The third part of the program set a schedule for implementation. The schedules were different for different components of the program, but over-all the ordnance factories "must complete the program's implementation within a period of one year."[100]

On June 7, 1939, the Bureau of Ordnance convened a meeting of officials of various ordnance factories to consider the *Program for Stabilizing Workers' Lives and Schedule for Implementation*. After careful deliberations, the Bureau of Ordnance adopted it and urged the ordnance factories to "implement the program as soon as possible."[101] The implementation order issued to all ordnance factories one month later further establishes the causal relation-ship between the wartime crisis, mental model revision, and development of social service and welfare institutions: "Since the outbreak of war and military mobilization, workers in various ordnance factories have relocated to the interior provinces. Due to the rapid increase of the cost of living, most workers find it hard to maintain a decent standard of living. It is even more so for workers with families. Because of this and the change of social environment and outside inducement, workers have become restless, which in turn has led to numerous incidents of flight and job-hopping among the workers. If we allow this to continue it will definitely have an adverse effect on our work. Consequently this bureau drafted a program for stabilizing workers' lives for the purpose of both management of workers and provision of workers' welfare."[102] In September the Bureau of Ordnance again called for the expansion of service and welfare facilities in order to prevent workers from being influenced by "outside induce-ment."[103]

These efforts did not stop workers from leaving ordnance factories and finding employment elsewhere. Incidents of flight and job-hopping con-tinued despite the establishment of social service and welfare institutions. In December 1939, the Thirtieth Arsenal reported that eighteen workers had absconded, and all but two were skilled workers.[104] In June 1942, an-other forty-one workers reportedly absconded from ordnance factories, thirty of whom were skilled workers.[105] Two months later, another seventy-six workers escaped. Again most of them were skilled workers.[106] According to a 1942 program to improve welfare drafted by the Fiftieth Arsenal, the job-hoppers not only left ordnance factories for employment in private en-terprises; they also changed jobs within the ordnance industry: "At the present time there is neither permanent funding nor a unified plan or co-ordination in the provision of services and welfare in the ordnance factories. As a result, there are sometimes huge gaps between two ordnance factories in the provision of services and welfare even though the two factories are located in the same area. Consequently when the technical personnel and skilled workers leave an ordnance factory, they not only hope to leave the ordnance industry altogether and join private enterprises; even within the ordnance industry they often leave one ordnance factory to join an-other."[107]

The most revealing evidence linking the problem of labor turnover, rising inflation, alteration of the mental model, and establishment of social service and welfare institutions comes from the DISW. The DISW recognized labor turnover and rising inflation as major obstacles for factory construction. For example, the DISW pointed out the "difficulty of recruiting experienced skilled workers" as a main reason for failing to implement its 1939 plan.[108] Worse still, many of these skilled workers left the DISW "under the impact of skyrocketing inflation and the offer of higher wages by other enterprises (especially private enterprises)," which contributed to the lack of progress in factory construction for 1940.[109] A DISW document shows that, between December 1940 and October 1941, a total of 144 single workers left the DISW but still owed money to the dining halls.[110] The DISW archives also contain orders by the Bureau of Ordnance to arrest 348 workers who ab-sconded between December 1940 and late 1941. The description of their positions reveals that the overwhelming majority were skilled workers.[111]

These documents indicate but the tip of the iceberg of a constant labor turnover that forced officials and managers to revise their mental model and devise solutions by expanding institutions of social services and welfare. In a meeting held in October 1942, for example, the DISW director asked, "why are there so many incidents of worker flight recently? What is the situation with outside inducement? . . . The welfare division must make every effort to improve workers' welfare in housing, meal service, health, and recreation, so as to make workers content with their conditions and reduce the incidence of abnormal moves."[112]

Following the director's instruction and inquiry, Tong Shude, head of the work affairs division, investigated how the skilled workers were treated in six enterprises in the vicinity of Chongqing and submitted a report on Oc-tober 29, 1942. The report reveals that "the skilled workers in private en-terprises all receive higher wages than their counterparts in ordnance factories. On average the skilled workers in the private enterprises actually received Ch$1,500 per month," whereas those in the Twentieth Arsenal received only Ch$650 to 850 per month. In a separate report submitted the following day, Tong Shude summarized the causes for worker escape and offered prescriptions to address the problem. The report stated that the rising cost of living, the lack of differential treatment of skilled and unskilled workers, and the inadequate service and welfare facilities were to blame for the high labor turnover at the DISW. As a remedy, the report recommended raising the wages of outstanding skilled workers, offering differential treatment of skilled workers, and expanding service and welfare facilities such as provision for housing, supply of daily necessities, and improvement of medical care. The report also suggested establishing a production bonus to reward efforts to improve work efficiency.[113]

At the same time, the welfare division offered solutions to deal with inflationary pressure and labor turnover. The welfare division report reveals that each person needed Ch$320 per month to maintain a minimum standard of living, but on average a *zhiyuan* received only Ch$140 per month, a skilled worker Ch$300, and an unskilled worker Ch$150. In other words, even the skilled workers' earnings only barely met the minimum living standard, while the *zhiyuan* and unskilled workers could not even support themselves, much less their family members. The report stated what must have been obvious when it attributed "the lack of enthusiasm for work" and "the desire to change jobs" to "increasing economic pressure and the difficulty of eking out a living."[114]

After describing the harsh reality of daily life, the welfare division presented two plans "designed to improve work efficiency, stabilize employee life, and avoid worker flight and frequent turnover." Under Plan A, employees with families would receive low-priced daily necessities, whereas single employees would receive cash subsidies for board expenses. In Plan B, all employees would receive minimum cash subsidies in accordance with price fluctuations.[115] Despite the lack of archival materials concerning the fate of these recommendations and plans, available evidence suggests that the DISW adopted many elements of these reports. For example, the DISW continued to expand institutions of social services and welfare during the early 1940s. It raised the wages of foremen and skilled workers in November 1942.[116] Four months later, the DISW developed a system of bonuses to reward workers for production increases and implemented it on a monthly basis for the next three years.[117]

Despite these efforts, the DISW continued to suffer from serious labor turnover. Its own statistics show that a total of 2,571 workers left the DISW in 1943, which constituted 44.6 percent of all DISW workers. In the following year, the number of workers who left the DISW increased to 2,710, which accounted for 53.5 percent of all DISW workers. In other words, the number of workers leaving increased in both absolute and relative terms. The same source also reveals a significant difference between skilled and unskilled workers. On average 690 skilled workers left the DISW during 1943 and 1944, which meant a turnover ratio of 31.7 percent. In contrast, on average 2,316 unskilled workers left the DISW, a turnover ratio of 71.8 percent.[118]

In short, the rising cost of living and the high labor turnover served as a constant source of "inspiration" for expanding social service and welfare institutions. Factory officials and managers revised their mental model by linking outside inducement to worker flight and job-hopping. In addition, they often sought remedies in the improvement of social services and welfare. In early 1940 Yu Dawei asserted in a hand-written memorandum that "we must study the issue of employee welfare carefully as it is of vital importance to the Bureau of Ordnance."[119] It turns out that they not only studied employee welfare, but they put it into practice. In a period of eight years, the institutions of social services and welfare expanded so greatly in the ordnance industry that even Yu was immensely impressed during his inspection of the DISW shortly before the Japanese surrender in 1945. With a smile, he told the head of the welfare division, "a factory should put welfare first, production second."[120]

Development of Social Services and Welfare Institutions and Policies in Heavy Industries

The dynamics that shaped the expansion of social service and welfare institutions in the ordnance industry also gave rise to the development of similar institutions in heavy industries. The Central Electric Works, for example, established a medical office in Xiashesi in Hunan province four months after construction began in March 1937.[121] After it relocated to Kunming and Guilin in 1938, all its branch factories constructed apartments and dormitories for their employees and established medical offices, consumer cooperatives, and schools for employees and employees' children.[122] A 1940 investigation confirms that the Kunming branch factory had two mess halls, three dormitories, a dispensary, and some recreational facilities.[123] These service and welfare facilities expanded, and new ones came into existence during the next few years. Both the Kunming and Guilin factories established child-care centers in 1942.[124] The Guilin factory even developed a farm that supplied vegetables for employees.[125] The Central Electric Works set up similar service and welfare facilities after it established branch factories in Chongqing and Lanzhou.[126]

The Yunnan Iron and Steel Works was another heavy industrial enterprise that developed comprehensive social service and welfare institutions during the Sino-Japanese War. Formally established in August 1941, the Yunnan Iron and Steel Works was a "joint venture" of sorts by the National Resources Commission, the Bureau of Ordnance, and Yunnan provincial government.[127] It was located in a rural setting, about eighteen miles west of Kunming.[128] The Yunnan Iron and Steel Works was also small in comparison to many of the National Resources Commission's enterprises: it had a total of 516 employees as of October 1943.[129] Still, the enterprise established a number of social service and welfare facilities, including apartments and dormitories, six dining halls, a medical office, a school for employees' children, library, consumer cooperative, producers' cooperative, and farm.[130]

Another compelling case of a factory-run welfare community was the Gansu Petroleum Administration located in Yumen in Gansu province. At the time of its establishment in March 1941, the Gansu Petroleum Administration had 1,972 employees. As petroleum production expanded, the number of employees increased to 4,168 by December 1941, 5,864 by October 1943, and 7,467 by October 1944.[131] Eventually the combination of this dramatic expansion, rising inflation, and the remote location of the Gansu Petroleum Administration—the closest city was Jiuquan about sixty miles to the east—led to the establishment of numerous social service and welfare facilities, which included apartments and dormitories, dining halls, a hospital, a school for employees' children, a consumer cooperative, a farm, a granary, a flour mill, a bakery, facilities for making tofu, soysauce, soybean oil, barber's and tailor's shops, and a bathhouse. The social service and welfare facilities were so comprehensive that General Manager Sun Yueqi described the Gansu Petroleum Administration as "a self-contained society."[132]

The same dynamics that were at work at the enterprise level also led the National Resources Commission to formulate a set of unified welfare policy in response to the sustained systemic crisis. The commission became aware of the need for a welfare policy as it began implementing its *Three-Year Plan for Heavy Industrial Reconstruction* drafted in 1936.[133] In order to formulate a policy of employee welfare, the commission sent Wu Zhixin, one of its full-time commissioners, to investigate social service and welfare facilities in leading industrial, mining, military, and railroad enterprises. Wu completed his investigation in June 1937 and published his findings three years later.[134]

Despite the prewar effort by the National Resources Commission to gather materials on labor welfare, it was the war-triggered crisis of social and economic life that led the commission to formulate a systemic welfare policy. As early as 1938, the commission directed its subordinate enterprises to provide information on employee recruitment, hours of work, calculation of wages, and employee welfare.[135] As inflation pressure increased in 1939, the commission drafted an *Outline of Employee Spiritual Guidance and Welfare Work* and promulgated it in February 1940. The document stated that subordinate enterprises should "provide spiritual guidance to their employees and promote employee welfare." On one hand, enterprises should strengthen employee belief in the Three Doctrines of the People in the cause of resistance war against Japan, in the value of service, and in the spirit of mutual help by delivering speeches, by providing books and journals, and by promoting healthy recreational activities. On the other hand, the enterprises should promote employee welfare by providing a safe and sanitary workplace, the convenience of room and board, the purchase of daily necessities, medical treatment, and the education of employees and their children.[136]

Toward the end of 1940, the National Resources Commission ordered its subordinate enterprises to report on "their welfare facilities and current welfare regulations."[137] About three months later, the commission issued *Measures for Managing Funds of Employee Welfare Enterprises,* which stipulated, among other things, that the commission and its subordinate enterprises might use funds of employee welfare enterprises to establish schools for employees and their children, libraries, hospitals, clinics, child-care centers, cooperatives, and employee insurance.[138] As inflation continued to rise, the commission expanded the scope of welfare undertakings and made some service and welfare facilities mandatory. In order to help employees "keep their minds on work," in February 1942 the commission promulgated a *Standard for Implementing Welfare Work,* which distinguished between welfare enterprises that its subordinate organizations "must undertake" from those that the subordinate organizations could "undertake at their discretion." The mandatory welfare enterprises included public dining halls, apartments and dormitories, consumer cooperatives, and hospitals, whereas the discretionary welfare enterprises included life insurance, savings plans, loans, farms, and the education of employees and their children. The document stipulated that the various organizations should furnish these service and welfare facilities to employees either free of charge or at minimum cost.[139]

That rising inflation pressure served as a fundamental motive force for formulating a comprehensive welfare policy also found expression in another directive the National Resources Commission issued in April 1942: "Recently commodity prices have skyrocketed, a change that has placed an increasingly heavy burden on employees' lives. The National Resources Commission has paid a great deal of attention to employees' lives and actively promoted all forms of welfare enterprise. The commission already issued the *Standard for Implementing Welfare Work*. At present the top priority is to establish consumer cooperatives so that enterprises can lighten the burden on employees by supplying them with daily necessities. The *Standard for Implementing Welfare Work* already listed consumer cooperatives in the category of welfare enterprise that subordinate organizations must undertake. Attached please find a copy of instructions on how to establish a consumer cooperative. It is hoped that subordinate organizations will follow these instructions and establish consumer cooperatives as soon as possible."[140]

Archival sources suggest that these subordinate organizations complied with these directives and effectively transformed themselves into welfare communities. At the end of 1942, the National Resources Commission had ninety-two enterprises under its jurisdiction. The overwhelming majority developed social service and welfare institutions similar to those of the Central Electric Works and the Yunnan Iron and Steel Works.[141] The social service and welfare institutions expanded so much that in April 1943 the commission warned that "the objective of welfare enterprise is to lighten employees' burden, not to increase their income. Consequently, welfare enterprises should be limited to those related to basic necessities of employees' lives."[142]

Apparently the subordinate organizations ignored the warning and continued to expand social service and welfare institutions. Given "the increasing expansion of service and welfare facilities," the National Resources

Commission found its existing form of welfare survey inadequate, which in January 1944 led the commission to devise a more inclusive form with a total of fourteen categories. Included in these categories were welfare organizations, public dining halls, apartments and dormitories, consumer cooperatives, producer cooperatives, farms, life insurance, savings plans, medical facilities, employee education, education of employees' children, and recreation.[143] Eventually the commission felt it necessary to draft a comprehensive report to explain the objectives and principles of welfare enterprise, the categories of employee welfare, and the management of welfare administration.[144]

Beyond National Defense Industries

The institutional and organizational response to the crisis of social and economic life was not limited to state-owned ordnance and heavy industries. In late 1944 the Ministry of Social Affairs received reports on the number of social service and welfare institutions from 558 industrial and mining enterprises. The reports indicate that there were 2,813 such institutions in thirteen provinces and in the Nationalist capital of Chongqing. Among these institutions were 433 dining halls, 431 dormitories, 189 apartments, 56 hospitals, 286 clinics, 112 schools and classes for workers, 94 schools for employees' children, 190 bathhouses, 138 barber's rooms, 12 child-care centers, 2 employment agencies, 81 laundry rooms, 194 libraries, 198 recreational clubs, 148 athletic fields, 36 information centers, 137 consumer cooperatives, 49 life insurance plans, and 27 "others."[145]

By the end of 1945, the number of social service and welfare institutions had increased to 5,561 in 973 enterprises across seventeen provinces and in Chongqing. Among those institutions were 856 dining halls, 850 dormitories, 424 apartments, 527 clinics, 285 sports grounds, 252 schools for workers, 194 schools for employees' children, 350 bathhouses, 169 laundry rooms, 273 barber's rooms, 48 child-care centers, 203 consumer cooperatives, 381 libraries, 65 life insurance plans, 30 savings plans, 32 farms, 342 recreational clubs, 19 tea rooms, 213 information centers, 5 postal agencies, 6 social activity rooms, 22 subsidy programs for weddings and funerals, and 21 employment agencies.[146] The number of social service and welfare institutions continued to rise during the next year and a half, with 7,598 in 1,085 enterprises at the end of 1946 and 10,890 in 1,354 enterprises in June 1947.[147]

The development and expansion of social service and welfare institutions in public and private enterprises seem to have helped the formation of a new mental model that placed the responsibility of providing social welfare, of which the welfare of labor was a central component, on the Chinese state. As early as January 1941, Gu Zhenggang, head of the newly created Ministry of Social Affairs, pointed out that, "China's social enterprise lags far behind others. Part of what we have achieved results from the efforts by the Christian community. As to China's own social enterprise, we have many relief institutions to take care of the old and the young. What has motivated these institutions, judging from what they have done in various localities, however, is the notion of charity, not responsibility; more of a passive nature, not of a positive nature. As far as social welfare or social service is concerned, their achievements are few and far between. Now that the Ministry of Social Affairs is in charge of social administration, we shall provide guidance to programs of social relief in various parts of the country, but we shall place the emphasis on advocating and promoting programs of social welfare and service. Our main objective is to promote social welfare by transforming social enterprise from one motivated by the notion of charity to one guided by that of responsibility, and by replacing the passive method with a positive one."[148]

Three years later, Xie Zhenglu, head of the Department of Social Welfare within the Ministry of Social Affairs, further elaborated on the theme of state responsibility for social welfare.[149] In Xie's view, "Social welfare enterprise is designed to promote public well being, stabilize social order, safe guard social interest, so that the state will bring its social policy to fruition. All the advanced countries in Europe and North America regard social welfare enterprise as an important responsibility of government administration, and so does our country. . . . In the past, however, people tended to subscribe to the notion of charity. Now with political progress, the constitutions of various countries have typically defined social welfare as the responsibility of the state toward its people. Article thirty-four, forty-one, and forty-two of our country's constitution during the tutelage period clearly stipulated that the state should actively promote the establishment of welfare facilities for peasants and workers, protect women and children, and to provide relief to the old, weak, and disabled. Therefore, we must develop a correct new notion of social welfare enterprise by replacing the [old] notion of charity with the [new] notion of absolute [state] responsibility." According to Xie, it was the very concept of "absolute responsibility" that had guided the promotion of social welfare after the creation of the Ministry of Social Affairs.[150]

Although social service and welfare institutions emerged during the 1920s and 1930s, it was the sustained systemic crisis engendered by the Sino-Japanese War that shaped the development and expansion of these institutions. Changes in the conditions of social environment, high labor turnover, and rising inflation led directly to the revision of the mental model of factory officials and managers and indirectly to the development of social service and welfare institutions in state-owned enterprises. The evidence demonstrates that enterprise officials and managers in the ordnance and heavy industries shared similar mental models as they created, developed, and expanded institutions of social services and welfare. By the end of 1945, these institutions had become a defining characteristic of state-owned enterprises.

CHAPTER 6

Danwei Designation of State-Owned Enterprises

At the same time that state-owned enterprises established the bureaucratic governance structure, created distinctive management and incentive mechanisms, and provided social services and welfare to their employees, they were also designated as *danwei* (units). In other words, not only did the defining characteristics of the post–1949 state-owned enterprises take shape before the Communists took over China; the post–1949 *danwei* identity of state-owned enterprises also originated in the Nationalist era.

This chapter presents the argument that the Sino-Japanese War witnessed the most intensive Nationalist effort at state-building characterized by the rationalization of state institutions, an endeavor that ultimately led to the *danwei* designation of state-owned enterprises.[1] The chapter begins by tracing the intellectual origins of key elements of Nationalist rationalization of state institutions to theories of public administration in the United States.[2] It then describes how the Nationalists pushed for institutional rationalization by creating a Central Planning Board *(zhongyang shejiju)* and a Party and Government Work Evaluation Commission *(dangzheng gongzuo kaohe weiyuanhui)*.[3] In order to rationalize the Nationalist administrative bureaucracy, Chiang Kaishek introduced a three-in-one administrative system *(xingzheng sanlianzhi)* and entrusted the Central Planning Board the Party and Government Work Evaluation Commission with the responsibility for establishing the new system. The chapter then analyzes the Nationalist efforts to establish and implement the three-in-one administrative system, especially the effort to establish a system of delegating responsibility according to administrative levels *(fenceng fuze zhidu)*. Despite its mixed record, the Nationalist struggle to rationalize the state bureaucracy began the process of designating political, economic, and administrative organizations as *danwei*. As was the case with the creation of enterprise management and incentive mechanisms and the evolution of enterprise provision of social services and welfare, path independence characterizes wartime Nationalist institutional rationalization because of its intellectual roots in American theories of public administration as well as its ability to overcome the limits of existing institutional endowments.

Origins of the Nationalist Institutional Rationalization

Of all the characteristics that define the twentieth-century, the dramatically increased availability of intellectual and ideological resources across national boundaries is one of the most important. Such availability is crucial for developments within national boundaries, as individuals and groups often used the resources developed in other national contexts to promote their own causes. That was the case for China during the 1930s and 1940s, when the Nationalist elite attempted to reform China's administrative bureaucracy by adopting and adapting American theories of public administration.

The central figure responsible for transmitting these theories of public administration was Gan Naiguang, one of the principal architects of China's administrative reform during the 1930s and of institutional rationalization during the 1940s. Born in 1897 in Guangxi province, Gan graduated from Lingnan University of Southern China in 1922 with a degree in economics. Two years later he began serving as English secretary and political instructor in Chiang Kaishek's Huangpu Military Academy. In 1926 he was elected to the Nationalist Central Executive Committee and the Standing Committee of the Central Executive Committee.[4] He held several important positions in 1927 and was again elected to the Nationalist Central Executive Committee in 1928 before leaving China for the United States.[5] Gan recalls being "confused and depressed" after the 1927 split between the Nationalists and the Communists. This confusion and depression made him aware of the inadequacy of his learning and prompted him to escape China's political reality by going to the United States to pursue further studies. Once there, he "began to pay attention to issues of reforming China's administrative system" while studying public administration at the University of Chicago.[6]

The 1920s and 1930s were a time of transformation for the public administration field in the United States. During those decades political scientists developed new theories of public administration that, among other things, included an emphasis on administrative efficiency, a desire for a system of delegating responsibility, and a focus on the work unit as a mechanism to improve management. These elements served as essential intellectual resources for the Nationalist rationalization of China's administrative bureaucracy.

The field of public administration in the United States began with the publication in 1886 of Woodrow Wilson's essay "The Study of Administration." But the "first full-fledged textbook" did not appear until 1926, when the Macmillan Company published the *Introduction to the Study of Public Administration* by Leonard D. White, a professor of political science at the University of Chicago.[7] A decade later White elaborated its themes in a revised edition.

Certain aspects of White's *Introduction* contributed directly to Nationalist reform of the administrative bureaucracy during the early 1930s. In writing this book, White was concerned primarily with methods of improving administrative efficiency. The objective of public administration, White stated, was the most efficient utilization of the resources at the disposal of officials and employees. In every direction, good management sought to eliminate waste, to conserve and effectively use materials and energy, and to protect employee welfare.[8] As one reviewer put it, "Professor White's study of his subject is dominated by the idea of efficiency."[9]

White also emphasized that appropriately locating and delegating authority and responsibility was essential for a smoothly working organization, insisting that authority must be commensurate with responsibility. White coined the term *system of responsibility*, which he defined as "the sum total of the constitutional, statutory, administrative and juridical rules and precedents and the established practices by means of which public officials may be held accountable for their official actions."[10]

Finally, the scope of the term *unit*, used to refer only to administrative organizations in the first edition of White's book, was expanded in the second edition to the discussion of "the formation of administrative units," "the types of management units," and the types of "government units" as well.[11] White even used such phrases as *work unit*, as in his description of the lines of authority and responsibility of the administrative organization: "[T]he whole organization is bound together as a work unit by the power of command, expressed in regulations, minutes, circulars, individual orders, and precedents."[12]

White's use of the term *unit*, and, more particularly, *work unit*, reflects not just a fashion in the choice of vocabulary but a new focus in the study of public administration in the United States. In *American City Government* published in 1925, William Anderson noted that "at various times in history . . . the city or city-state has been the chief if not the only political unit known to man."[13] About a decade later, in the booklet *The Units of Government in the United States*, Anderson addressed such questions as "the total number of units," the definition of "a unit of government," "layers or levels in the system of government units," "central and local units of government," and "classes of local units;"[14] reprinted or revised editions subsequently appeared in 1936, 1942, 1945, and 1949.

The concept of *work unit* also came into widespread use during the 1930s as a result of the movement to improve business management and public administration, although it carried several different connotations. In 1936 the *Society for the Advancement of Management Journal* published an essay that called for "the establishment of units, methods and means of measurement of industrial, economic phenomena."[15] By the end of the year, "a number of federal agencies had worked out advanced systems of administrative control through work units and unit-cost accounting." Reflecting this new emphasis, the February 1937 meeting of the Washington Chapter of the Society for the Advancement of Management focused exclusively on the work unit in federal administration. A careful reading of the ten papers presented reveals that contemporaries typically conceived of *work unit* as a standard or criterion of measuring work performance. For example, in describing "the development of work units in public administration," William E. Mosher of Syracuse University suggested that "if budget bureaus and budget officers were accustomed to think in terms of units of work and performance . . . the determination of the new budget could be handled on a much more realistic basis and with closer reference to known facts and reliable predictions." Similarly, Oliver Short of the Census Bureau explained that the bureau "finds it necessary to define work units and to compute unit costs," though at different phases of census taking *work unit* meant variously the individual schedule, the individual card, or the man-hour. Short believed that "analysis of the job in terms of work units serves as a basis of administrative control" in the Census Bureau.[16]

In other cases, the phrase was used to designate administrative organizations, as White had done. Thus, after pointing out that the Farm Credit Administration was "more or less in the first stages of developing standards and measurements of work performance," R. W. Rigsby, the agency's acting executive officer, stated that "the work of this unit (the General Service Section of the Division of Finance and Research) falls into three broad types of functions: coding and filing; punching and verifying; sorting and tabulating." He later referred to the section's "photographic unit" and its "graphic unit."[17] In another publication of the same year, Luther Gulick, director of the Institute of Public Administration at Columbia University, also noted that "the theory of organization . . . has to do with the structure of co-ordination imposed upon the work-division units of an enterprise." In fact, Gulick's work included an analysis of "aggregating the work units."[18]

The terms, ideas, and concepts addressed in the two editions of White's *Introduction to the Study of Public Administration,* Anderson's study of government units, and other scholarly studies of work units in federal administration served as the intellectual resources for Nationalist rationalization of China's administrative bureaucracy. Gan Naiguang became thoroughly familiar with White's works during his stay in Chicago during the late 1920s. According to Gan, he not only "met" White but "translated White's *Introduction to the Study of Public Administration* into Chinese and submitted his manuscript to the Commercial Press for publication" after he returned to China.[19] Unfortunately, during the war between Japan and China in 1932, Japan bombed the city of Shanghai and destroyed the Commercial Press, including Gan's manuscript.[20] Nevertheless, in translating White's *Introduction* Gan undoubtedly gained a thorough understanding of the ideas and concepts summarized above.[21] Gan went beyond acknowledging that "the orthodox theory of administrative efficiency is derived from the study of public administration," as he explicitly recognized the "important contributions" of White and William F. Willoughby, another leading scholar, whose *Principles of Public Administration* appeared in 1927.[22]

Gan intended to apply American theories of public administration to the reform of China's administrative system. In 1933, he formally proposed the creation of a society to study administrative problems.[23] His proposal found support among advocates of administrative rationalization and led to the establishment of the Society for Studying Administrative Efficiency *(xingzheng xiaolü yanjiuhui)* in 1934. Shortly afterward the organization was renamed the Commission for Studying Administrative Efficiency *(xingzheng xiaolü yanjiu weiyuanhui).*[24] In explaining the subject of administrative study in July 1934, Gan pointed out that although both White and Willoughby analyzed "problems of organization and personnel," Willonghby also examined issues of "finance and material." Gan then listed problems of organization, personnel, finance, and material as the first four subjects of administrative study.[25]

As he drew on American theories of public administration, Gan made it clear in early 1935 that the Commission for Studying Administrative Efficiency was not established for "purely theoretical research." On the contrary, the commission "must create its own theory based on China's administrative reality."[26] Toward that end, between 1934 and 1936 the commission published periodicals containing articles on administrative efficiency and reform, hosted conferences, and drew up a multitude of plans for reforming the central archives, the provincial governments, and local tax administration, as well as for the integration of "bandit suppression areas."[27]

In adapting American theories to Chinese administrative reality, Gan developed ideas and concepts during the early 1930s that became central to the later creation of the three-in-one administrative system during the Sino-Japanese War, a system that was characterized by the integration of planning, execution, and assessment. For example, in a 1934 essay Gan outlined four phases in administrative procedures: the drafting of plans, the execution of administrative orders, the direction and supervision of that execution, and the assessment of its outcome. He also described the lack of a clear definition of authority and responsibility in central ministries. He pointed out that "within a given ministry the authority and responsibility all concentrate in the head of the ministry, with no clear definition of the authority and responsibility of the deputy-minister in charge of policies *(zhengwu cizhang)* and the standing deputy-minister in charge of administration *(changwu cizhang)*, not to mention the fact that public servants from the department head *(sizhang)* down have no authority but all the responsibility." In order to remedy the situation, the Commission for Studying Administrative Efficiency drew up a *General Regulations for Conducting Business* for the ministries, commissions, and divisions of the Executive Yuan.[28]

By early 1937 Gan had already developed the concept of "delegating responsibility according to organizational levels" *(fenji fuze)*, an idea consistent with White's emphasis on allocating authority and responsibility within the administrative bureaucracy. At the same time, Gan began using the term *danwei* to refer to administrative organizations. For example, in discussing provincial administration in 1937, he pointed out that "the various provinces differ not only in wealth and size; the number of administrative *danwei* at the lowest level, namely counties and municipalities, also varies considerably." Thus provinces such as Anhui and Jiangsu had roughly sixty or seventy counties, whereas "the province of Sichuan had more than 150 *danwei*."[29]

The ideas and concepts developed by Gan and his Commission for Studying Administrative Efficiency may have contributed to the creation of a secret Party-Government-Military Investigating and Planning Commission *(dangzhengjun diaocha sheji weiyuanhui)* in Chiang Kaishek's Nanchang military headquarters in November 1933. Chiang saw this new organization as his "brain trust" *(guwentuan)* responsible for investigating conditions and planning reconstruction in "bandit suppression areas."[30] Although Gan served as deputy-minister in charge of policies in the Ministry of Interior Administration from May 1932 to February 1935, he joined Chiang's military headquarters in Wuhan as soon as he left the Interior Ministry.[31] In any event, Gan attributed administrative reforms in the "bandit-suppression areas" to the attention Chiang devoted to "administrative research and experiments." In a 1942 essay Gan traced the origins of wartime "administrative innovations" to the Nationalist practices in the "bandit suppression zones" during the early 1930s.[32]

The Three-in-One Administrative System

Although American theories of public administration and prewar reform of the Nationalist administrative bureaucracy contributed to wartime institutional rationalization, it was the sustained systemic crisis triggered by the Sino-Japanese War that shaped Nationalist institutional rationalization characterized by the creation of new state institutions and the implementation of the three-in-one administrative system.

As early as 1938, the Nationalists had recognized the inadequacy of the administrative bureaucracy for effectively responding to the national crisis. Resolutions introduced to the provisional party congress pointed to numerous problems in administrative organizations at various levels.[33] Even more serious problems existed in the Nationalist Party. "Our party," Chiang Kaishek declared at the opening session of the provisional party congress, "has become virtually an empty shell, without any real substance; the form of the party persists, but the spirit of the party has almost completely died out." For Chiang, "the most obvious defects of our party are that organization is so lax and discipline so loose that the spirit of the party is feeble and dissipated, and the foundation of the party is wholly lacking in substance."[34]

The recognition of these problems prompted Nationalist leaders, in its *Program for the War of Resistance and Nation Building* promulgated in July 1938, to call upon party and government organizations to improve administrative efficiency in order to "meet wartime needs."[35] Still, the problems that Chiang described remained. Two years later, in response to the lack of effort to implement party and government policies, Chiang lashed out at what he called "bureaucratic malpractice," which he defined as "shifting responsibilities onto others when problems arise and an unwillingness to assume responsibility." For Chiang, "the problems with party and government officials are that they have become bureaucrats and have consequently lost their revolutionary spirit."[36]

In addition to the perceived failure of party and government officials to assume responsibility, which spurred the attempt to establish a system that would systematically delegate responsibility within the administrative bureaucracy, Chiang blamed the lack of overall planning and systematic assessment for administrative inefficiency. In a speech delivered in February 1941, he explained how the lack of planning and assessment contributed to inertia and even to the corruption of party work and politics.[37] In order to solve these problems, in July 1940 Chiang recommended the creation of a Central Planning Board and a Party and Government Work Evaluation Commission under the Supreme National Defense Council *(guofang zuigao weiyuanhui)*, the top party-government coordinating body that had been established in January 1939. In submitting his recommendation to Nationalist Central Executive Committee, Chiang summarized the lessons learned from China's reconstruction and revealed the rationale for creating these institutions:

In recent years, China's reconstruction enterprises have daily increased, and our central party and government organizations have established corresponding agencies and recruited needed planning personnel. However, in the absence of an overall system it becomes difficult to undertake comprehensive planning and to demonstrate the efficacy of collaborative effort. With regard to work assessment, other than the superior organ of an agency, no other organization exists to provide overall assessment of discrete organizations, a fact that contributes to organizational inertia and inefficiency. In order to remedy these deficiencies, it is recommended that a Central Planning Board be created under the Supreme National Defense Council with the responsibility of formulating and deliberating plans for national political and economic reconstruction. . . . In addition, it is recommended that a Party and Government Work Evaluation Commission be created to take charge of the assessment of the work, economy, and personnel of party and government organizations. The Party and Government Work Evaluation Commission should work closely with the Central Planning Board in order to avoid the drawback of separation between planning, execution, and assessment, to establish a foundation for a three-in-one administrative system, and to initiate planned modern political and economic development.[38]

Following Chiang's recommendation, the Nationalist Party created the Central Planning Board and the Party and Government Work Evaluation Commission in October and December 1940, respectively.[39]

Central to the work of both organizations was instituting the three-in-one administrative system. Shortly after the establishment of the Central Planning Board, Chiang Kaishek elaborated on the system's meaning and importance. In his view, the three-in-one administrative system consisted of three basic interrelated elements—planning, execution, and assessment. Administrative planning was crucial for the successful execution of plans, and the outcome of their execution had to be assessed or evaluated to enable new plans to be made on a solid basis. According to Chiang, "the three-in-one administrative system serves as a basis for implementing a planned political and economic [system]."[40]

As the institutional embodiment of the first element of the three-in-one administrative system, the Central Planning Board conducted considerable planning during the war. In accordance with the decision of the eighth plenary session of the fifth Nationalist Party congress, the Central Planning Board began drafting a three-year reconstruction plan in June 1941.[41] Between 1942 and 1945, the Central Planning Board examined the annual plans and budget estimates of 146 central-level *danwei* and eighty-six provincial and municipal *danwei*. At Chiang Kaishek's request, the Central Planning Board deliberated or drafted 162 plans, programs, and policy recommendations, with twenty-four dealing with military affairs, thirty political affairs, sixty-three economic affairs, and forty-five other matters. Prominent on the agenda of the Central Planning Board were issues of administrative reorganization and consolidation, scientific management of the administrative bureaucracy, improvement of the planning and assessment system, economic reconstruction, and the development of national defense industries.[42]

One of the most important planning activities undertaken by the Central Planning Board was the drafting of a plan for postwar economic reconstruction. As early as late 1941, Chiang ordered the Central Planning Board to draw up such a plan,[43] and by June 1942, he had approved the procedure for drafting what was being called the Postwar Five-Year Plan for National Defense and Economic Reconstruction.[44] Subsequently the ministries and commissions of the Executive Yuan and the Central Military Commission submitted their respective draft plans to the Central Planning Board at its request.[45] According to a Central Planning Board document marked "extremely secret," the main points of the Postwar Five-Year Plan included the possible designation of Xian as China's postwar capital, the formation of primary and secondary centers of national defense industries, and the development of a self-sufficient economy.[46] Throughout 1943 and 1944, the Central Planning Board deliberated on the nature and scope of the proposed Postwar Five-Year Plan. In the end, the Central Planning Board decided to draft separate plans for political, economic, and military reconstruction.[47] With regard to economic reconstruction, in December 1944 the Supreme National Defense Council approved the *Principles of Economic Reconstruction for Phase One*, which the Central Planning Board had drafted.[48] Eventually the Central Planning Board formulated a Five-Year Draft Plan for Material Reconstruction. After Chiang approved it, the Central Planning Board sent the plan to the Supreme Economic Commission for implementation in 1945.[49]

In addition to being responsible for planning for wartime and postwar reconstruction, the Central Planning Board was entrusted with the task of facilitating execution, the second element of the three-in-one administrative system, by designing administrative regulations. Of all the regulations intended to aid policy implementation, the *Principles and Methods for Drafting Regulations for Conducting Business by Delegating Responsibility according to Administrative Levels* (hereafter referred to as *Principles and Methods*) was the most important.

The idea of drafting regulations for conducting business came from earlier reform of the Nationalist administrative bureaucracy, but it was Chiang who issued the order to draft them. In a speech delivered at a meeting of the Executive Yuan in 1939, he declared that since heads of ministries could not personally assess the work of department heads or members of a department, they must ensure that officials such as division and department heads "assume responsibility according to their administrative levels."[50] One year later, in introducing the three-in-one administrative system, Chiang pointed out that in order to successfully execute administrative plans, party and government organizations must implement a system of delegating responsibility according to administrative levels. He described what such a system would entail: "Regardless of their size, government organizations at all levels must stipulate detailed regulations for conducting business. In addition, these regulations should include a section with detailed provisions on the responsibility of officials and functionaries at various administrative levels. . . . Once such a system is established, all decisions do not have to be made by a leading official alone; instead, decisions on certain matters should be made by officials at lower administrative levels. Because the authority and responsibility of officials are thus clearly defined in legal terms, we will not only be able to avoid the malpractice of shifting responsibilities onto others or unwillingness to assume responsibility when problems arise, we will be able to deal with administrative matters much more efficiently and effectively, because we will no longer need to write overlapping instructions on official documents at every administrative level."[51]

The Supreme National Defense Council apparently responded to Chiang's directive by ordering the Central Planning Board to formulate "principles and methods" to guide party and government organizations in establishing a system of delegating responsibility according to administrative levels.[52] Once the Central Planning Board drew up the *Principles and Methods*, the Supreme National Defense Council promulgated it in February 1941.[53]

The *Principles and Methods* explained which party and government organizations needed to draft detailed regulations and which needed to draft general regulations. The document also defined the responsibility of party and government officials at various levels, ranging from high-ranking officials in central party and government organizations to division and department heads in provincial and county governments.[54] In the view of Gan Naiguang, the Central Planning Board's deputy-secretary, "the system of delegating responsibility according to administrative levels constitutes an extremely important reform in the Chinese system of personnel administration." Gan expressed the hope that various party and government organizations would be imaginative enough in drafting their regulations for conducting business so as to "bring to fruition the new administrative system within a short period of time."[55]

In accordance with the provisions of the *Principles and Methods*, various party and government organizations began drafting regulations for conducting business. The Judicial Yuan drafted its general regulations in March 1941, followed by the Central Executive Committee in April 1941.[56] The Party and Government Work Evaluation Commission drafted its detailed regulations in August 1941,[57] the Organizational Department of the Central Executive Committee in May 1942,[58] the Ministry of Military Administration in March 1943,[59] the Ministry of Financial Administration in April 1943,[60] and the Planning and Assessment Committee of the Secretariat of the Central Executive Committee in August 1943.[61] By May 1943 seventeen provinces had also drafted detailed regulations for conducting business.[62]

Equally critical for effective policy execution was the need to establish a system of unified personnel management because the Nationalists recognized that "administrative efficiency cannot be improved without strengthening the existing system of personnel management."[63] In order to establish such a system, in December 1941 the Supreme National Defense Council approved the *Outline of Unified Management for Personnel Organs of Party, Government, and Military Organizations*, which identified organizations and mechanisms for managing both these organs and the personnel within them. The outline provided that the Secretariat of the Central Party Headquarters was responsible for managing these personnel matters within the party, whereas the Ministry of Personnel of the Examination Yuan was in charge of managing government personnel matters. These two organizations were also delegated the authority to assess, appoint, and dismiss those working in party and government personnel organs. In addition, the outline stated that party, government, and military organizations "should establish personnel organs as soon as possible, if none existed. Moreover, they should determine the size of these *danwei* according to the volume of their business, the size of their establishment, and the number of their affiliated organizations."[64]

This *Outline of Unified Management for Personnel Organs of Party, Government, and Military Organizations* served as the basis for drafting *Measures for Implementing Unified Management among Personnel Organs of Central Party Organizations*, which the Committee of Central Party Affairs approved in March 1942. Article Two of the document provided that personnel organs of the central ministries, commissions, divisions, and bureaus be placed "directly under the jurisdiction of the head of these organizations and are subject to the unified management of the central secretariat."[65]

Following the approval of the *Measures for Implementing Unified Management among Personnel Organs of Central Party Organizations*, the Nationalist government issued additional regulations on personnel management in September 1942.[66] By June 1943 most central party, government, and military organizations had established personnel organs within their organizations. Provincial party and government organizations followed suit after July 1943. By May 1945, a total of 2,310 personnel organs had come into existence nationwide.[67]

The last major component of the three-in-one administrative system was assessment. On July 4, 1941, the Supreme National Defense Council promulgated the *Methods for Assessing Party and Government Work*, which was designed to "improve their efficiency." These methods were divided into political assessment *(zhengwu kaohe)*, or the examination of an enterprise's overall success or failure, and administrative assessment *(shiwu kaohe)*, or the examination of work, expenditure, and personnel within an organization. The same document also provided that party and government organizations should assess their work according to organizational levels *(fenji kaohe)*, and that those at various levels should submit annual self-assessments of their achievements.[68] In a speech delivered in January 1942, Chiang Kaishek placed heavy emphasis on implementing the three-in-one administrative system and strengthening the assessment of party and government work, declaring these among "the most important tasks for 1942."[69]

At the urging of Chiang Kaishek and other Nationalist leaders, a number of central party and government organizations drafted regulations for assessing their work and achievement. The Ministry of Interior Administration promulgated regulations for implementing measures to assess party and government work in November 1941.[70] Six months later, the Ministry of Auditing issued regulations for implementing measures of work assessment.[71] A Supreme National Defense Council report indicates that by October 1942 eleven central party organizations and nineteen government organizations had drafted such regulations. The same number of government organizations had also created organs for work assessment.[72]

In order to institutionalize this process, in February 1943 Chiang Kaishek ordered that planning and assessment commissions be established at all levels of central, provincial, municipal, and county party and government organizations. According to the *General Regulations for Party and Government Planning and Assessment Commissions*, these commissions were entrusted with the promotion of the three-in-one administrative system, the drafting or deliberation of their administrative programs and annual plans, the deliberation of plans drafted by their subordinate organizations, the integration of plans with budget estimates, the assessment of the work and performance of their own organizations, and the assessment of the work and performance of their subordinate organizations.[73] Following Chiang's order, various party and government organizations soon established planning and assessment commissions.

According to a comprehensive report by the Party and Government Work Evaluation Commission, between 1941 and 1945 the commission examined and assessed the work and achievement of 160 central and provincial party organizations, 2,495 plans and reports of central party organizations, and 1,787 plans, reports, and meeting records of provincial and municipal party organizations. During the same period, the commission examined and assessed the work and achievement of 1,427 central, provincial, and municipal government organizations and financial and economic reconstruction enterprises, as well as 4,853 reports and records of central, provincial, and municipal government organizations.[74]

Chiang Kaishek was the driving force in the Nationalist institutional rationalization. It was he who introduced the three-in-one administrative system; it was he who recommended the creation of the Central Planning Board and the Party and Government Work Evaluation Commission; and it was he who served as the director-general of the Central Planning Board as well as the chairman of the Party and Government Work Evaluation Commission. Nevertheless, he could not have succeeded in this effort without the contribution of trusted lieutenants such as Gan Naiguang, one of the principal architects of the three-in-one administrative system.

Perhaps in recognition of Gan's contribution to administrative reforms before the Sino-Japanese War, Chiang appointed him deputy-secretary of the Nationalist Central Party Headquarters in 1938.[75] In October 1940 Chiang appointed him the first deputy-secretary of the Central Planning Board at the time of its establishment.[76] Gan's own writings suggest that Gan played a crucial role in creating the new system. For example, in an essay written after the sixth plenary session of the Central Executive Committee in November 1939, Gan made a rare revelation about his thought process: "in recent months the director-general instructed us to study personnel issues in order to get to the source of administrative problems. Consequently I have devoted a considerable amount of time to thinking about it . . . Exactly where do we begin to address personnel problems?"

Among the solutions he came up with were an examination system, a system of delegating responsibility according to administrative levels, and legislation guaranteeing the livelihood of public servants.[77] A few months later, Chiang introduced the three-in-one administrative system, which greatly emphasized the delegation of responsibility according to administrative levels.[78]

Six months after Chiang introduced the new system, Gan summarized the three methods of delegating responsibility: "delegating responsibility according to the type of business *(fenshi fuze)*, delegating responsibility according to organizational levels, and delegating responsibility according to administrative levels." Although for obvious reasons Gan credited Chiang with creating "the system of delegating responsibility according to administrative levels," he emphatically pointed out that "this system marks the beginning of implementing the politics of responsibility."[79] Gan's writings followed the pattern of a Chinese institutional innovator: he would help design a new system, elements of a new system, or a set of new regulations; then, after Chiang and the Nationalist Party had adopted them, he would attempt to promote their implementation by explaining them in writing.[80]

The *Danwei* Designation

Nationalist rationalization of state institutions produced an unintended consequence for the formation of China's *danwei* system.[81] To understand how and why the Nationalist institutional rationalization contributed to the *danwei* system's formation, it is necessary to understand the dual meaning of the *danwei* system.

The existing literature typically defines the *danwei* system as "a hierarchy of state-owned workplace units" that provides employees "a variety of perquisites denied to peasants in the countryside: secure jobs, affordable housing, inexpensive medical care, [and] a range of subsidies."[82] Most scholars seem to subscribe to this definition. Wen-hsin Yeh, for example, believes that "the distinguishing feature of a *danwei* was a lifetime social welfare system virtually from cradle to grave, and a network of relationships encompassing work, home, neighborhood, social existence, and political membership."[83] Following such a definition, many scholars trace the origins of the *danwei* to the Communist free supply system, to the heritage of labor protest, to the management practice of a major bank, and to the evolution of labor management institutions.[84]

The *danwei* system can also be defined more broadly as the prevailing administrative system encompassing virtually all government, business, and educational institutions in urban China after 1949. Such a definition emphasizes that these institutional entities were integral parts of the overall state administrative structure, a character that cannot be explained by any of the specific traditions or institutions scholars have heretofore examined. The existing literature also fails to offer any insight into the historical usage of the term *danwei*, although such an insight is indispensable for understanding the *danwei* system. What the evidence strongly suggests is that the origins of the *danwei* system in the sense of the prevailing administrative system can be traced to the Nationalist struggle to rationalize the administrative bureaucracy during the Sino-Japanese War, when the Nationalists used the term *danwei* to designate political, economic, and administrative organizations.

The definition offered by the authoritative dictionary of Chinese language published by the Commercial Press in 1937 limits the term's meaning to "unit as a standard of measurement."[85] As a result of the Nationalists' use of *danwei* to designate political, economic, and administrative organizations undergoing rationalization, the term acquired a meaning it had not possessed before the Sino-Japanese War. With a dramatic suddenness, the term, in its new sense, began appearing in a variety of contexts, beginning with its use in the *Principles and Methods*, which the Supreme National Defense Council promulgated in February 1941. The document used the phrase "organizations as *danwei*" in identifying the leading official as the highest-ranking official of a particular organization. It also defined the responsibility of such a leading official as "supervising, directing, and assessing the work of various *danwei*." The document made it clear that the term *danwei* referred to these organizations as well as to constituent parts within them.[86]

The term seems to have had a strong connection to the objective of Nationalist institutional rationalization—to improve the efficiency and effectiveness of the state bureaucracy. Less than two weeks after the Supreme National Defense Council promulgated the *Principles and Methods*, Gan Naiguang wrote an essay on planned political development in which he argued that "one cannot effectively administer a country and make it a fighting *danwei* unless one develops a comprehensive plan. In modern terms, the various branches of government ought to establish mobilization organizations and draft detailed plans, and only when they accomplish these tasks could one expect to mobilize these branches to meet the need of war."

Fortunately for Gan, "the entire country has become an effective fighting *danwei*" within four years of the outbreak of the Sino-Japanese War.[87]

Following the provisions of the *Principles and Methods,* many party and government organizations drafted regulations in which the term *danwei* is frequently used. The regulations issued by the Organizational Department of the Central Executive Committee referred to the divisions, offices, and committees of the organizational department as *danwei.* The document actually used the word thirty-two times.[88] Similarly, in the regulations issued by the Planning and Assessment Committee of the Secretariat of the Central Executive Committee, it appeared twenty-four times.[89]

In March 1942, the Committee of Central Party Affairs approved the *Measures for Implementing Unified Management among Personnel Organs of Central Party Organizations,* which again referred to the central ministries, commissions, divisions, and bureaus as *danwei.* Article Three stipulated that "personnel administrators of the various *danwei* should be placed under the direction and supervision of the central secretariat." Article Five provided that "the various *danwei* should establish personnel management organs or appoint personnel administrators or strengthen their existing personnel management organs or increase the number of their personnel administrators depending on the volume of their business." In fact, seven out of the ten articles in the original document begin with the phrase "various *danwei.*"[90]

Other contemporary writings also labeled political, economic, and administrative organizations as *danwei.* In a speech delivered in November 1942, Chiang Kaishek expressed concern over the expansion of administrative organization at the county level. According to Chiang, even though the New County System *(xin xianzhi)* was being implemented, there were still too many *danwei* in some county governments. After noting that some had as many as eight departments and seven offices, he asserted that "for a competent authority at the grass-roots level, five is the most reasonable number of *danwei;* at most the number of *danwei* cannot exceed six."[91]

By the early 1940s economic organizations such as state-owned enterprises had also been identified as *danwei.* Speaking in January 1942, Qian Changzhao, deputy-director of the National Resources Commission, declared: "The existing reconstruction enterprises of the National Resources Commission can be divided into categories of industry, mining, and electric products. We have forty-one *danwei* in industry, . . . forty-three *danwei* in mining, . . . [and] twenty-four *danwei* in electric products. All in all, we have a total of 108 *danwei*. Although the staff of the various *danwei* work hard, there is still room for improvement in our work."[92]

As a result of the designation of such organizations as *danwei*, by the early 1940s the word had acquired the same status as *jiguan*, a well-established term in the lexicon of government administration meaning "organizations." Government agencies routinely used the phrase "various *jiguan* and *danwei*" in their reports.[93] An editorial of the Nationalist *Central Daily News* spoke of the need for "self-assessment by various *jiguan* and *danwei*." The same editorial also pointed out that assessment by the central government "cannot replace the self-assessment of various *danwei* and *jiguan*."[94] That the term *danwei* had gained the status of superstar in the administrative lexicon was confirmed in the same paper a few days later. In discussing how administrative organizations really work, another editorial asked rhetorically, "How many functionaries can execute their tasks efficiently? Within the department, which is the basic *danwei* of an administrative organization, how many are actually familiar with their cases, conscientiously handling documents or fulfilling their duties?"[95] And the word appeared at least thirteen times in different contexts in an article on the Nationalist personnel system published in the *Central Daily News* in April 1943.[96]

In addition, the phrase *work unit (gongzuo danwei)* was already being used to mean "workplace" as early as 1940.[97] Enterprise officials and managers, like American scholars of public administration, also employed it in the sense of a standard or criterion for measuring performance, as they explored how to "improve efficiency of a particular work unit." They believed that "the size of work unit" was "an urgent topic for study" because "it was essential for the improvement of work efficiency."[98]

By late 1945, use of the term *danwei* had become so widespread that the Ministry of Social Affairs felt obligated to define its categories in the *General Knowledge of Statistics* published in late 1945: "The use of the term *danwei* is quite extensive, such as the *danwei* of the United Nations, the various *danwei* of China's administrative districts, the various *danwei* under the Executive Yuan, the various *danwei* of the Ministry of Social Affairs, the various *danwei* under investigation, the *danwei* of the cooperative, the institutional *danwei* of social service, social relief and social welfare, the material *danwei* of rationing for distribution. . . . From the perspective of statistics, all of these *danwei* are considered statistical *danwei*."[99]

Danwei at the Dadukou Iron and Steel Works

While the Nationalists were in the process of rationalizing state institutions at the central level, officials and managers in state-owned enterprises also attempted to rationalize management administration in part by implementing the system of delegating responsibility according to administrative levels. Within the DISW such an endeavor gave rise to the *danwei* designation of administrative organizations.

Since state-owned enterprises followed the organizational model of the administrative bureaucracy, officials and managers wrestled with similar problems in factory administration and management. In response to calls by Nationalist leaders to improve administrative efficiency and to solve existing problems within its factories, the DISW leaders undertook a major reform in management administration during the early 1940s.

As early as February 1940, Yang Jizeng, the DISW director, stated at a meeting of top administrators, plant directors, divisional heads, and technical engineers, "Since the establishment of our organization in early 1938, we have encountered many difficulties. Because of the large number of people we have hired and the large sum of money we have spent, we have been subject to frequent censure from the outside. We should feel ashamed of ourselves when we compare the effect of our work with the amount of money we spent."[100] In written instructions to the DISW employees one year later, Yang confirmed the existence of the very bureaucratic malpractice Chiang Kaishek described when Yang stated that there were "quite a few irresponsible people, who either shift responsibility onto others or procrastinate and keep putting things off."[101]

Yang apparently attributed the inefficiency and other problems to the lack of cooperation and bureaucratic red tape. At the eighty-seventh meeting of the DISW in March 1941, Yang stated, "most of our construction projects have not been completed as planned. We need to examine the reasons for such delays." According to him, "the various divisions should consult with one another whenever necessary so that we can reduce the necessity of sending official documents back and forth. From now on, once an important document has been approved, it should be returned to the division from which it originated and other relevant divisions within one working day."[102]

By the summer of 1942, the DISW leadership understood the need for reform in management administration. According to its report prepared for government inspectors, the DISW "had now entered a period of consolidation," and it would undertake necessary reform in "management administration" at the headquarters and its affiliated organizations, including "reorganization of personnel, supply of material, allocation of manufacturing work, implementation of cost accounting, emulation [campaign] for increased production, and the promotion of employees' welfare enterprise . . . so as to bring to fruition scientific management."[103]

A central and consistent theme in reforming management administration was how to reduce overload in decision making at the top by improving the handling of official documents and delegating responsibility to officials at various administrative levels. The terms used to designate these administrative levels were the same as those used by Leonard White and other American scholars of public administration. For instance, in November 1942, the DISW promulgated regulations concerning the handling of official documents and the delegation of responsibilities to officials at various administrative levels. The regulations used the term *management unit (guanli danwei)* to designate the seven large *danwei*, namely, secretariat, accounting division, welfare division, purchasing division, business division under the chief engineer, work affairs division, and division of construction engineering, and stipulated that documents sponsored by these seven large *danwei* had to be drafted within the units themselves. The same regulations also provided that in dealing with incidents within the DISW, "a system of delegating responsibility according to administrative levels must be rigorously implemented." The head of these *danwei* no longer needed to submit petitions for instructions in cases when incidents were solvable, when these incidents fell within the purview of their authority, and when they could solve them according to existing regulations or by invoking precedents.[104]

These regulations were frequently ignored in practice. As a result, Yang Jizeng gave the following instructions to the head of various units on May 10, 1943: "First, you should make more use of telephone in conducting official business. . . . Second, with regard to work-related matters, the various plants should avoid submitting petitions for instruction. Instead, you should consult the division of work affairs as the occasion demands. If the latter views the matter problematic, the various plants may then petition the associate director for instructions, or report directly to me during our weekly meetings for solutions. Third, the head of the various administrative divisions should convene a daily meeting and distribute the official documents received by the department of correspondence for processing. . . . And finally, there are too many report forms with regard to personnel matters and that an effort should be made to reduce the number of these forms."[105]

In an attempt to reduce decision-making overload and improve administrative efficiency, the DISW adopted a new and standardized procedure for all internal communications in June 1943. The official instructions provided that all petitions to the director and associate director were to use the new and standardized form. In addition, these petitions were to use a prescribed procedure. If a *zhiyuan* needed to submit a petition or report, he or she must submit it to his or her direct superior. If a large *danwei* needed written forms to conduct business, the said *danwei* was to submit its documents directly to the management units in charge. If incidents or routine matters fell within the purview of their authority, the officials in charge at a given administrative level were to make decisions at their discretion, without having to submit petitions to the office of the director. Finally, it was the responsibility of the head of a large *danwei* to submit petitions to the office of the director if the need arose. To underscore the need for officials at various administrative levels to take their responsibility seriously, brief instructions and "subtle" reminders were printed on the margins of the new form for internal communication, with the font for the character *fuze* (assume responsibility) at least one size bigger than that for other characters in the same sentence.[106]

About a week later, *Crashing Waves* published an essay written by the chief secretary. He discussed the ways officials and administrators could improve their administrative efficiency. These included goal setting, understanding the nature and limits of one's responsibility, prioritizing work in terms of importance and urgency, determining sequence and procedure, allocating responsibility according to administrative levels, and being direct in conducting business.

More importantly, the essay summarized two indirect ways of conducting business within the DISW—"climbing the ladder" *(pa tizi)* and "beating around the bush" *(dou quanzi),* which the chief secretary considered "the root cause of all evils." According to the chief secretary, "climbing the ladder" meant that officials and managers pushed a given matter upward within the administrative hierarchy from the lower level to the intermediate level, and then pushed from the intermediate level to the upper level, and even all the way to the highest level. Sometimes, however, high-level officials did not understand what was going on. Consequently, they pushed the matter all the way back to the lowest level within the administrative hierarchy. In contrast to the vertical movement of a given matter described in ladder climbing, "beating around the bush" depicted the horizontal movement of a given matter in a circlelike fashion, so that it often wound up in a totally unrelated administrative unit. Eventually the unit pushed the matter all the way back to where it began without ever making a decision or getting a problem solved.[107]

The pervasive bureaucratic malpractice that the chief secretary described likely prompted the director to order the use of vouchers to record transactions in factory administration and management. In addition, the director appointed the chief secretary to draft detailed measures for implementing the system of delegating responsibility according to administrative levels.[108] Then within one month of the appointment, in an attempt to define precisely the "authority and responsibility of the large *danwei* and small *danwei*," Yang Jizeng issued the following instruction in August 1943: "First of all, a division *(chu)* or its equivalent is a management unit. On all matters concerning hiring and dismissal of personnel, assessment of employees' work, and the allocation of bonuses among various departments or their equivalents, the department head shall make a recommendation to the division head; the division head in turn, shall submit a report to the office of the director based on overall coordination and assessment. Second, a department *(ke)* is a work unit *(gongzuo danwei)*.[109] On all matters that fall within the purview of a given department, the department head shall, on his accord, take on the responsibility in their planning, preparation, allocation, execution, supervision, and assessment with the head of the large *danwei* providing guidance, supervision, and solution to difficult problems."[110]

This instruction marked a serious step in defining the authority and responsibility of the administrative units within the DISW. And, too, for the first time it defined the term *work unit* in regard to China's state-owned enterprises. Moreover, that the concepts of management unit and work unit were used here just as they had been by Leonard White and other leading scholars suggests their possible American origins.

At the same time, the chief secretary began drafting the document on implementing the system of delegating responsibility according to administrative levels. By early February 1944 he had produced a draft ready for the director and the associate director to consider. Once the chief secretary incorporated their suggestions, the document was made official and promulgated on March 21, 1944.[111]

This document, known as *Measures for Implementing the System of Delegating Responsibility according to Administrative Levels*, divided the responsibility of DISW officials, managers, and other *zhiyuan* into three administrative levels: management unit, work unit, and operating personnel. Thus, "The first administrative level is the management unit, which refers to the division head and plant director. It is also called large *danwei*. The second administrative level is the work unit, which refers to the department head and technical personnel of various constituent parts with the rank of a department head. It is also called small *danwei*. The third administrative level is the operating personnel, which refers to all officials and functionaries who perform routine tasks, excluding the division and department heads mentioned above."

The document went on to carefully define the authority and responsibility of the three administrative levels. The management unit had the authority and responsibility to establish criteria for its entire business operation, to draft plans and programs for implementation, to determine its budget and draft regulations concerning business or manufacturing procedures, to make decisions on petitions submitted by the work unit, and to supervise and direct its work. For its part, the work unit had the authority and responsibility to carry out all the tasks assigned in accordance with the principle and plan provided by the head of the large *danwei*, to handle routine matters that fell within its purview as defined by laws, regulations, and precedents, to supervise and accelerate the completion of tasks assigned to the operating personnel, and to thoroughly understand the operating personnel. With regard to the operating personnel, they had the authority and responsibility to handle matters or cases according to the instructions of the division and department heads, to handle routine matters in a timely manner and on their own accord, to request instructions from the work unit if they did not understand the laws, regulations, and precedents that applied to the cases at hand, and to fulfill assigned tasks on time.[112]

The *Measures for Implementing the System of Delegating Responsibility according to Administrative Levels* was an ambitious attempt by the DISW leaders to bring about bureaucratic rationalization of management administration. By elaborately defining the authority and responsibility of officials, managers, and other *zhiyuan*, the DISW leadership hoped to establish accountability and ultimately to improve administrative efficiency.[113] The DISW leadership consistently pushed to implement the *Measures for Implementing the System of Delegating Responsibility according to Administrative Levels* after its promulgation. For example, during the first informal discussion on management among the officials and managers of various management units and work units, the director urged department heads to carefully coordinate and allocate work, rigorously train and supervise personnel in their departments, and do their best to guarantee the efficient fulfillment of the assigned tasks by operating personnel—all "according to the spirit of the system of delegating responsibility according to administrative levels."[114]

Beginning in July 1944, the DISW conducted an intensive propaganda campaign through its daily *Bulletin of the Secretariat* in an attempt to publicize among *zhiyuan* key concepts and procedures outlined in the *Measures for Implementing the System of Delegating Responsibility according to Administrative Levels*. On the nature of official communication, the bulletin explained, "there are three different types of internal communication at the DISW. The informal note is one type and is used for making requests or arrangements. Consequently, it should not be sent to the department of correspondence, but should go directly to the administrative unit in charge." The second type of internal communication, the petition, "is used when it becomes difficult to make a decision about a given case, or when a given level of administration does not have the necessary authority to make a decision. In cases such as these, the petition form of communication is used, and the petition shall be sent to the department of correspondence for distribution." The third type of internal communication, the report, "is used when there is a need to describe and explain how a given case is handled, or when the head of a large unit must submit something in writing about an important case to the office of the director for examination and approval. The report shall also go to the department of correspondence for distribution."[115]

The end of July 1944 marked the one-year anniversary of the DISW director's order to the chief secretary to draft the *Measures for Implementing the System of Delegating Responsibility according to Administrative Levels*. More than four months had passed since its promulgation. Between the end of July 1944 and the conclusion of the Sino-Japanese War in August 1945, the DISW leadership continued to push for its implementation in an effort to reduce decision-making overload, establish accountability, and improve administrative efficiency.

Although the attempt to implement the system of delegating responsibility according to administrative levels may have contributed to the utilization of the DISW's productive capacity, the DISW leadership was disappointed in the pace of the system's implementation. They openly admitted that they had failed to realize their goal almost one year after they introduced the system. In December 1944, the director pointed out that "our staff and workers still lack a spirit of cooperation. They act in a perfunctory manner and pass the buck when problems arise. They even engage in mutual attack and slander, which clearly has a negative effect on our work."[116]

In the month that followed, the director delivered a more revealing indictment of the pervasive bureaucratic inertia: "Our system of delegating responsibility according to administrative levels is a very good system, but its implementation is not good. Probably most people have not acted in accordance with the system; perhaps some have never understood what it means. More recently I have also discovered an attitude of conjecture and doubt, which is clearly a malady resulting from the system. One manifestation of this malady is that when people compose petitions, they like to begin with the phrase 'in accordance with the oral decree *(mianyu)* of the director.' Once such a phrase is inserted in the text, it seems that everyone, from the composer of the report to the head of his administrative unit, is no longer accountable. And once the head of a given administrative level affixes his seal to the report and passes it on to his superior, it seems he does not have anything to do with the case anymore. . . . Consequently, one individual is forced to make all the decisions on all matters, however trivial they might be. This is diametrically opposed to the spirit of the system of delegating responsibility according to administrative levels."[117]

Although the director was deeply frustrated, he did not give up hope for change. He continued to remind officials and managers of their responsibilities, urging them to "get rid of the outmoded bureaucratic malpractice and improve work efficiency."[118] To his credit, there is evidence to suggest that the system of delegating responsibility according to administrative levels did work in certain cases. An April 1945 editorial of the *Crashing Waves* pointed out that one of the DISW's affiliated *danwei*—the Management Division of Jijiang Waterways—had greatly improved its administrative efficiency after implementing the system of delegating responsibility according to administrative levels. However, the editorial echoed the director's earlier indictment of the system's implementation: " 'The system of delegating responsibility' is not a new term anymore; the key is how to take one's responsibility seriously. . . . Despite the easily recognized demarcation line between different administrative levels, however, a serious commitment to responsibility has not clearly manifested itself. For one thing, this has something to do with the lack of a clear definition of authority and responsibility. Consequently, too much work is placed on the shoulders of the operating personnel below the level of the work unit. However, because the pressure on the operating personnel is sometimes overwhelming, the operating personnel tend to avoid responsibility altogether. . . . Even the heads of some large *danwei* downplay their responsibility so that they might avoid trouble whenever possible, seeking not to perform meritorious service but instead merely to avoid blame, seeking not to outshine others but instead merely to acquire their own peace of mind."[119]

Despite the failure to implement the system of delegating responsibility according to administrative levels, the DISW campaign to bring about bureaucratic rationalization of management administration led to the definition of administrative organizations as management units as well as work units. Officials and managers began using the term *work unit* after the director defined it in 1942. Although they often used the term when referring to a workplace,[120] they also used it to mean a standard or criterion. In June 1944, for example, the DISW's transportation team decided to "use small teams and groups as work unit in implementing a [work] emulation system."[121] Specifically, the managers of this transportation team identified a crane and three workers as one "work unit" in one area of work and a locomotive and three workers as one "work unit" in another.[122]

DISW's internal documents conveyed a sense that employees identified various organizations within the DISW as *danwei*. According to an April 1945 editorial of the *Crashing Waves,* "now various organizations all have establishments and prescribed structures, with the department being a mid-level organization or work unit, with those above the level of the department being a *danwei*-in-charge or management unit, and with those below the level of the department being the operating personnel."[123] As the daily *Bulletin of the Secretariat* reveals, the DISW used the term *danwei* hundreds, if not thousands, of times between October 1942 and November 1949 when the bulletin was published. In other words, by the time the Chinese Communists took over the DISW and other state-owned enterprises, the *danwei* designation of these enterprises had been firmly established in countless official documents and routinely used by officials and managers.

In response to the crisis brought on by the Sino-Japanese War, the Nationalists engaged in an extraordinary struggle to rationalize state institutions.

In order to rationalize the state bureaucracy, the Nationalists consistently pushed for implementation of the three-in-one administrative system, especially the system of delegating responsibility according to administrative levels, in the central administrative bureaucracy as well as in state-owned enterprises. Wartime Nationalist institutional rationalization resulted in the *danwei* designation of political, economic, and administrative organizations, including state-owned enterprises.

CHAPTER 7

Nationalist Ideology of
the Developmental State

The crisis that shaped the making of the state enterprise system also gave rise to an ideology of the developmental state, emphasizing state-owned enterprise, heavy industry, national defense, and the creation of a planned socialist economic system.[1] As a radically altered mental model, this ideology provided an interpretation of China's institutional environment as well as a prescription of how to reorder that environment.[2] Ultimately this new mental model formed the ideological underpinnings of the state enterprise system and led directly to its formation. However, unlike the cases with the creation of enterprise management and incentive mechanisms, with the evolution of the enterprise provision of social services and welfare, and with wartime Nationalist institutional rationalization, the formation of the Nationalist ideology of the developmental state was both path-dependent and path-independent. It was path-dependent because the Nationalist ideology of the developmental state represented an extension of Sun Yatsen's Three Doctrines of the People.[3] It was path-independent in part because this ideology transcended the Three Doctrines of the People with the ideology's focus on national defense as a critical new element.

State-Owned Enterprise versus Private Enterprise

A key component in the Nationalist ideology of the developmental state is the emphasis on state-owned enterprise vis-à-vis private enterprise. This emphasis found expression in *Jianguo Fanglüe*, written by Sun Yatsen in 1918. The second part of it was later translated into English and published in 1922 as *International Development of China*.[4] In this "general plan for reconstructing a New China," Sun offered the classic statement on the scope and function of state-owned and private enterprise: "The industrial development of China should be carried out along two lines: (1) by private enterprise and (2) by national undertaking. All matters that can be and are better carried out by private enterprise should be left to private hands, which should be encouraged and fully protected by liberal laws . . . All matters that cannot be taken up by private concerns and those that possess monopolistic character should be taken up as national undertakings . . . In this national undertaking, foreign capital has to be invited, foreign experts and organizers have to be enlisted, and gigantic methods have to be adopted. The property thus created will be state owned and will be managed for the benefit of the whole nation."[5]

If this declaration of principles suggests an equal emphasis on state-owned and private enterprise, Sun's other statements indicate a clear preference for state-owned enterprise. As early as 1912, he stated that "all major industries in our country, such as railroads, electricity, waterways, ought be owned by the state, so that no private individuals will be able to reap all the profits [from these undertakings]."[6] Later that year, Sun further stated that "the railroad, streetcar, electric light, gas, running water, canal and forest industries should all be owned by the state."[7] His other articles and speeches contain similar arguments for the necessity of establishing state-owned enterprise.[8] In short, less than one year after the 1911 Revolution, Sun had already developed one of the central concepts in the Nationalist ideology of the developmental state.

If Sun Yatsen recognized the necessity of state-owned enterprise by 1912, the issue of private ownership largely eluded his attention, owing perhaps to his concern about the abuses of "capitalist monopoly" and to the lack of a clearly defined boundary between state and private ownership in his mind. For him, "public ownership means state ownership. Furthermore, since the state belongs to the people, what is the difference between state ownership and private ownership!"[9] Whatever the case may be, by the time Sun completed his *Jianguo Fanglüe* in 1918, private enterprise certainly had a place in his plan. On the surface at least, both state and private enterprise had a role to play in China's economic development.

After its reorganization in 1923, the Nationalist Party incorporated many of Sun's views into its platform, including those on the scope and function of state-owned and private enterprise. Thus, the 1924 *Manifesto of the First Nationalist Party Congress* provided that "enterprises which are monopolistic in nature and the development of which lies beyond private means, such as railroad and navigation, ought to be undertaken and managed by the state."[10] Later, in a series of lectures on his Three Doctrines of the People, Sun again called for the "development of state-owned industries." That is to say, "the state should lead in business enterprises and set up all kinds of productive machinery which will be the property of the state."[11]

Sun Yatsen did not live long enough to witness the success of the Nationalist Revolution. Nonetheless, the party's leadership accepted his vision of economic development and made it part of the dominant ideology of the Chinese state after 1928.[12] A 1929 resolution of the Third Nationalist Party Congress stated that "the criteria for determining the procedure of implementing material reconstruction should be based on the principles and policies Sun Yatsen formulated in his plan for industrial reconstruction . . . with the development of communication being the most important."[13] Two years later, the Nationalist Central Executive Committee again declared that "Sun Yatsen's plan for industrial reconstruction . . . is the highest principle for material reconstruction for Republican China."[14]

Sun Yatsen's emphasis on state-owned enterprise also found expression in Nationalist statements. A 1930 resolution of the Nationalist Central Executive Committee stated that "the state should undertake reconstruction projects such as railroad construction, water conservation projects, shipbuilding, and iron and steel making in accordance with Sun Yatsen's doctrine of regulating capital."[15] Although the government established state-owned enterprises during the 1930s, they were admittedly limited in number. What led to the expansion of state-owned enterprises were the crisis triggered by the Sino-Japanese War and the corresponding changes in the Nationalist elite's mental model.

During the late 1930s and 1940s, and in response to the escalating crisis, leading figures of the Nationalist government such as Weng Wenhao developed and elaborated on Sun Yatsen's views. On one hand, Weng "found in Sun's writings the theoretical underpinnings of his own work. Like Sun, he noted that in theory government should manage only those enterprises essential to the national well-being and which government could best run." On the other hand, Weng's statements suggest that the type of enterprises government could undertake was "vague" and "potentially very large."[16] In a 1938 report, Weng divided state-owned enterprises into four broad categories: enterprises necessary for supplying basic materials for national defense; enterprises necessary for the creation of basic manufacturing industries; enterprises that sought to improve and develop important mineral products; and enterprises supplying power for civilian and industrial use. Weng declared emphatically that these enterprises "aim to increase the productive capacity of the nation; they are not designed to compete for profit with the people."[17]

A few months later, Qian Changzhao summarized the experience and lessons of heavy industrial reconstruction in an important essay that revealed Nationalist preoccupation with state-owned enterprises. In Qian's view, the state should manage enterprises in the following categories: enterprises needed for national defense; enterprises necessary for unified overall planning; enterprises whose specialized products enjoyed a virtual international monopoly; enterprises beyond the means of private entrepreneurs; enterprises whose precision products were essential for achieving self-sufficiency; and enterprises whose products were inadequate in quality or quantity. Qian warned that "we should not repeat the mistake of capitalist countries in offering unlimited encouragement to private enterprise. There are not very many big capitalists in China today and consequently we may not have an urgent need to regulate capital. When the time for regulating capital finally arrives, however, we cannot afford to be excessively liberal about it."[18]

In an official announcement on New Year's Day 1939, Weng Wenhao attempted to further define the scope of state-owned enterprises. He stated that while government organizations assumed the management of some enterprises, they "aim to increase the productive capacity of the nation; they are not designed to compete for profit with the people." For Weng, this meant that the state should limit its activity to the following types of enterprise: those urgently needed for national defense; those requiring central planning or control; those requiring extraordinary financial resources; those urgently needed for national defense and the people's livelihood but offering no guarantee of returns to investment; and those supplying energy to private industry.

Weng cautioned that "all government enterprises must meet these criteria. Moreover, these government enterprises will not be monopolistic in nature. If private investors wish to invest their money in government enterprises, they could reach an agreement with government enterprises for joint operation. The government will allow private entrepreneurs complete freedom to engage in fields of enterprise in which it also is engaged, except in cases where restrictive action is justifiable for special reasons . . . Our most urgent need at present is to increase production enormously in order to meet the demands of the front and the rear. If we define government enterprise too broadly now, and if the government is financially incapable of developing to the fullest extent the enterprises within the prescribed area of government economic activities, there is a danger that the country's productive power will be needlessly curtailed. Thus, while we try our best to establish government enterprises . . . we also consider private enterprises essential to the national economy. Consequently we must make an earnest effort to promote the development of private enterprise."[19]

These 1939 announcements revealed the Nationalist government's determination to develop heavy industrial enterprise in response to the war-triggered crisis. To dispel the perception that state-owned enterprise competed with the people for profit, Weng defended government action by stating the government's intention to limit the activities of state-owned enterprise to those directly related to national defense. Over time, the activities of state-owned enterprises would become more and more inclusive as government officials defined and redefined their scope in response to the deepening national crisis.

In addition, Weng's explanation for his relatively narrow definition of the scope of state-owned enterprise suggests that he preferred state-owned to private enterprise. That he did not define the scope of state-owned enterprise "too broadly" appears to have resulted from his fear that China's productive power might be reduced, for the government might be unable to fully develop state-owned enterprise. That seems to explain why the government "consider(s) private enterprises essential to the national economy." To put it differently, in contrast to Weng's primary goal of developing state-owned enterprise, encouraging private enterprise was secondary on his agenda.

By 1942, Weng's position had shifted to one that overwhelmingly emphasized state-owned enterprise, as evidenced by his speech delivered at the Central Training Corps. Weng summarized his arguments by saying that, "First, China must industrialize. Second, in order to bring industrialization to fruition, we must proceed according to plan and focus on heavy industry. Finally, instead of counting entirely on private enterprise, the government must rely on state-owned enterprise to lay the foundation for China's heavy industrial development."[20] Less than a year later, Weng offered a more concrete definition of the scope of state-owned and private enterprise. "In principle," he wrote, "basic industries such as those of iron and steel, petroleum, large machinery, electric products, and chemistry and energy, as well as basic transportation and communications industries . . . should be owned and managed by the state." In contrast to the large scope of state-owned enterprise in these industries, "light industries such as those of textile, food-processing, flour-making . . . should in principle be owned and managed by private enterprise."[21] The scope of state-owned enterprise expanded at the expense of that of private enterprise as a result of re-drawing the conceptual boundary between the two.

In a 1943 speech, Weng recognized that the scope of state-owned enterprise was broad. He described three different types of economic systems: the democratic system represented by England and the United States, the Communist economic system embodied by the Soviet Union, and the controlled economic system practiced by Nazi Germany. Weng saw these economic systems as "entirely different from that of China." Nevertheless, he acknowledged that under China's existing economic system, "the scope of state-owned enterprise is very broad." For Weng, "promoting the development of state-owned enterprise constitutes an important agenda in nation building."[22]

Other leaders of the Nationalist government shared Weng Wenhao's view on the primary importance of state-owned enterprise. Sun Ke, son of Sun Yatsen and a leading figure of the Nationalist government, did not just agree with Weng; he went farther than Weng in placing a heavy emphasis on state-owned enterprises.

Sun Ke expressed his views on state-owned enterprise in a series of lectures he delivered between 1940 and 1942. Some of these lectures were translated into English and published in 1944 in the United States as *China Looks Forward*. In these lectures he elaborated on the implications of his father's Three Doctrines of the People for the Chinese economy. For example, in a lecture delivered in November 1940, he stated: "The Doctrine of People's Livelihood proposes . . . to institute a planned economy. All large-scale enterprises are to be operated and managed by the state for supplying the needs of the whole nation, so that even if there is loss, no factories would be shut down, provided there is demand for their products . . . In the second place, the means of production in capitalist countries are private property, whereas in the economy of People's Livelihood, these would ultimately belong to the whole nation. Through the control of capital during the period of the rapid expansion of our economy and its transition from agriculture to industry, we shall prevent the growth of large privately owned corporations and companies of a monopolistic nature. Medium-sized capitalist enterprises will be tolerated, but the decisive role must be played by state-owned enterprise." Even more suggestive of the future direction of the Chinese economy was Sun Ke's prediction that "gradually the private entrepreneur will find that he cannot compete with large state-owned enterprises, and he will disappear and be absorbed by the national section of industry."[23]

In another speech delivered in the following month, Sun Ke continued to underscore the critical importance of state-owned enterprise. He believed that the "rise and fall of the modern state are contingent to a large extent on the conditions of state-owned enterprise. If state-owned enterprise is developed, the state will be rich and strong; if state-owned enterprise is not developed, the state will be poor and weak." Consequently not only must the state rely on state-owned enterprise to develop heavy industry, but it must own and manage domestic as well as foreign trade.[24]

All the same, it would be a mistake to conclude that Sun Ke left no room for private enterprise. In another lecture delivered in September 1942, he affirmed that "with the exception of communications and large-scale enterprises connected with national defense, which will be managed by the state, the people are welcome to invest in all other industries."[25] Sun Ke distinguished heavy industry from light industry and argued that whereas heavy industry should be owned and managed by the state, light industry should be left to private enterprise. In his words, "All basic industries and national defense industries with a monopolistic character must be owned and managed by the state, whereas light industries and consumer-goods industries shall be left in the hands of the private concerns. The production of unnecessary luxuries and consumer-goods must be restricted, and whatever capital left will be invested in urgently needed projects of national reconstruction. This will lead not only to the creation of a planned economy in the postwar period but to the realization of the Doctrine of People's Livelihood."[26]

Although the Nationalist leaders placed a premium on state-owned enterprise and sought to foster its development by expanding the scope of state-owned enterprise and by redefining the boundary between state-owned and private enterprise, the issue of state ownership also received serious attention within the scholarly community. As early as 1934, for example, a leading scholar called on the Nationalist government to "make active development of state-owned enterprise the central task while promoting the development of private enterprise."[27]

After the Sino-Japanese War began, scholars continued to discuss the scope and function of state-owned enterprise. In August 1938, Wu Ban-nong, a prominent economist, wrote: "we believe that in principle the state should own and manage business enterprises in heavy industry, energy industry, and basic chemical industry . . . while allowing private ownership in light industry by encouraging investment by overseas Chinese and Chinese entrepreneurs within China."[28]

By early 1941, Wu had developed his ideas into an elaborate argument. In his view: "Economic reconstruction in China should not follow the path of private capitalism under a laissez faire economy; rather it should choose the path of state capitalism based on the Doctrine of People's Livelihood. Such a system of state capitalism is characterized most importantly by the rapid development of our national economy on the basis of China's existing private economy, and by using the means of 'managing and developing state capital.' In other words, state-owned enterprise will occupy an extremely important position in China's reconstruction, but private enterprise will also achieve substantial development under state control."

Still, Wu had little doubt about the state's vital role in Chinese industrialization: "In order to lay a sound foundation for China's industrialization, we must make and implement economic plans on a large scale and gradually make the transition from economic planning to a planned economic system. However, if we intend to implement economic plans on a large scale, we will need to exercise control over private economic activities to ensure their compliance with state policies, but above all, we will need government participation in the work of reconstruction on a large scale, making government the principal actor in economic reconstruction."[29]

In an attempt to define the scope of state-owned enterprise, Wu set forth "ten principles of state ownership" in a 1942 booklet. He argued that enterprises in the following categories should be owned by the state: key industries such as mining, metallurgical, machine, basic chemical, energy, and transportation and communications industries; military industries directly needed for national defense; manufacturing industries needed to provide supplies for government organizations and state-owned enterprises; important industries that must be placed under unified planning and government control; public utilities that were natural monopolies; enterprises not conducive to generating returns but important for the national economy and the people's livelihood; enterprises urgently needed but too large in scale; enterprises that enjoyed political and cultural importance;

monopolistic industries such as poisonous products and lacquer; and monopolistic industries important for generating state revenue. For Wu, "these ten principles define the criteria of China's state-owned enterprise. Any enterprise that is not covered by these principles should be managed by private enterprise."[30]

Toward the end of the Sino-Japanese War, some scholars went even further than what amounted to Wu's program of industrial nationalization. In August 1943, Chen Bozhuang, another prominent economist and part-time commissioner of the Central Planning Board,[31] wrote that the state should control heavy industry as well as "light industrial enterprises that are of critical importance and national in scope." Moreover, he maintained that private enterprises in light industry should be nationalized through purchase when necessary. For example, he considered textile production a centralized, critical, and large-scale industry. Consequently textile industry should be owned and managed by the state. According to Chen, state-owned enterprise should occupy such a dominant position in China's overall economy that private entrepreneurs would be reduced to the following types: peasant farmers; small entrepreneurs; transport merchants; wholesale merchants; and retail merchants.[32]

To summarize, although Sun Yatsen and the Nationalists emphasized the importance of state-owned enterprises during the 1920s and early 1930s, it was the crisis unleashed by the Sino-Japanese War that led the Nationalists to expand the scope of state-owned enterprise through definition and redefinition. Through extensive communications, Nationalist leaders and members of the intellectual community developed during the war a shared mental model on the scope and function of state-owned enterprise. This model points to state ownership as a fundamental principle of the Nationalist ideology of the developmental state.

Heavy Industry versus Light Industry

Within the Nationalist ideology of the developmental state, the relationship between heavy and light industry corresponds roughly to the relationship between state-owned and private enterprise. According to this ideology, heavy industry must be owned and managed by the state, whereas light industry can be left to private ownership.

Again, it was Sun Yatsen's *International Development of China* that laid the foundation for the Nationalist conception of heavy industry. Sun devoted major portions of the book to a discussion of "key and basic industries."[33] Later on, in his 1924 lectures on the Three Doctrines of the People, Sun continued to emplasize "state-owned industries."[34] Fundamentally, however, it was the increasing Japanese threat to China's national security after the mid-1930s and the war-triggered crisis that caused the Nationalists to underline the importance of heavy industry. The recognition of the vital importance of heavy industry—hence the revised mental model—led first to the drafting of the 1936 *Three-Year Plan for Heavy Industrial Reconstruction.* As the National Resources Commission expanded heavy industrial enterprises following the outbreak of war, Nationalist leaders began to define and elaborate on the meaning of state-owned heavy industry. In a speech delivered in late 1939, for example, Weng Wenhao identified heavy industry as the government's first priority in economic reconstruction.[35]

In an essay published in 1940, Weng attempted to explain why the Nationalist government gave top priority to heavy industry. In his view, "heavy industries constitute the main pillar of national defense. The strength and weakness of a country may often be gauged by the increase or decrease of its productive capacity. This explains why progressive nations the world over have spared neither time nor efforts in expanding and developing heavy industries." According to Weng, these heavy industries included the following in order of importance: metallurgical industries; energy industry; machine industry; electric products; and chemical industry.[36] In another speech delivered in 1941, Weng admitted that the Nationalist government "attaches great importance to heavy industry."[37]

By 1942 heavy industry had become a core component in the Nationalist ideology of the developmental state. As Qian Changzhao stated, China "must make industrialization the central task of its economic reconstruction, must make heavy industrial reconstruction the central task of industrialization, and must make the development of the state-owned enterprise the central task of heavy industrial reconstruction."[38] Weng Wenhao made a similar statement a few months later. He declared, "First, China must industrialize. Second, in order to bring industrialization to fruition, we must proceed according to plan and focus on heavy industry. Finally, instead of counting entirely on private enterprise, the government must rely on state-owned enterprise to lay the foundation for China's heavy industrial development."[39]

The same view of heavy industry also found expression in Sun Ke's speeches and writings. In a lecture delivered in 1942, he commented on the opposing argument regarding the priority of industrial development: "There are people who think light industry is easier to start with, while heavy industry requires too much capital and technically trained specialists. At the same time, it is argued that it is easier to make money in light industry, while it is difficult to make money in heavy industry, and consequently, people are unwilling to invest in heavy industry. These people use the example of advanced industrial nations to make their point. . . . They point out that both England and the United States and even Japan began with light industry. These countries built heavy industry only when they had laid a foundation for light industry and when they had accumulated enough wealth to invest in heavy industry . . . Consequently, they believe that China should follow the footsteps of these advanced industrial nations."

Sun pointed out that the same logic did not apply to China. For him, the big mistake in this line of reasoning was that "it overlooks the elements of timing and opportunity. It is well known that English industry has a history of a century and three-quarters. American industry has a history of a century. Japanese industry has a history of at least sixty years. If we also had such a long period of time to develop industry without being invaded by foreign enemies and without having to fight a war of resistance, then there would be nothing terribly wrong with such an approach. If we have only five to ten years' respite, however, it would be dead wrong to follow the example of advanced industrial nations by developing light industry first."

Thus, Sun Ke concluded, "we must assume that we have only a limited time period in which to build our industry. Consequently we ought to concentrate our energy in undertaking heavy industrial reconstruction. Once we establish a foundation for heavy industrial reconstruction, we would then be in a strong position to develop light industry, as the machine used in light industry is produced by heavy industry. In other words, economic reconstruction is but an illusion without the foundation of heavy industry."[40]

Sun Ke's argument is quoted in full because it represented the major argument on both sides of the issue, because it would later resonate among Communist planners during the 1950s, and because it echoed strongly among the intellectual elite during the 1930s and 1940s. Luo Dunwei, a well-known economist, wrote a book on the controlled economic system *(tongzhi jingji)* in the early 1930s, in which he argued against developing light industry first.[41] While admitting the importance of light industry, he contended that "without the development of basic industry, light industry will always be without foundation and will of necessity be dependent on external force," namely, heavy industrial products from foreign countries.[42]

After the outbreak of war, a large number of scholars placed top priority on heavy industrial development. In a 1940 article, Wu Bannong argued that China must develop heavy industry first. In his view, "not only was the first five-year plan of the Soviet Union entirely a plan for heavy industrial development, its second and third five-year plans also stressed the development of heavy industry." Moreover, Nazi Germany's "two four-year plans also underscored heavy industrial development as its first priority." Wu conceded that in the early stages of heavy industrial development the state could not expect returns from its investment. In addition, the Chinese people had to be prepared to make sacrifices. The lack of financial returns and the need for sacrifice, however, did not change Wu's belief in the primary importance of heavy industry. Wu approvingly quoted Lenin as saying that "we cannot expect to establish any industry without rescuing and restoring heavy industry, and without industry we can never hope to achieve independence and will be doomed to destruction."[43]

This emphasis on heavy industry also struck a responsive chord in the writings of Fang Xianting (H. D. Fong), one of the most prominent scholars during the 1930s and 1940s. As early as 1936, Fang had expressed his dissatisfaction with the conditions of Chinese industry: "The modern industries that have grown up to some extent in China are mainly of the light type, neither heavy nor basic. The main branches are cotton spinning and weaving, silk reeling, woolen spinning and weaving, hosiery knitting, flour milling, oil pressing, match making, printing, cigarette making, etc. Heavy or basic industries such as iron and steel, machine making, shipbuilding, electric power generation, making of acids, etc. have failed either to grow or to succeed in the Chinese environment."[44]

Writing after the outbreak of the Sino-Japanese War, Fang maintained that "in the transition from an agricultural nation to an industrial nation, the process of industrial reconstruction is unavoidable. Even in such a predominantly agricultural nation as ours, industrial reconstruction is of vital importance for the integrity and independence of the national economy. . . . Since heavy industry or basic industry is the mother of all other industries, the development of heavy industry is all the more urgent."[45] Furthermore, "heavy industries, which China must establish in order to satisfy her minimum defense needs as a modern nation, must be owned and operated by the state. . . . These industries require a large capital outlay which private enterprise, still in its infancy in China, is not in a position to furnish. They are usually risky and not profitable; they are too vital to the needs for national defense to be left to develop in an uncontrolled manner by private enterprise and free competition. In heavy industries, as well as in large-scale public works and public utilities, state ownership and operation seem to offer the best solution."[46]

Jian Guansan, a scholar and one-time legislator in the Nationalist government, was equally vocal in insisting on heavy industrial development. Writing in 1945, he approvingly quoted one scholar as saying that "national defense cannot be established without heavy industry, and a new nation cannot be created without national defense. This fact is crystal clear and we do not need to repeatedly demonstrate that. Although the methods of 'commercial wars' of the modern nations are subtle and fierce beyond description, ultimately these nations will have to rely on their national defense created by industry to back them up. Otherwise, their fate will not be much different from that of the Jewish people: even though they are the most successful businessmen, they nevertheless have not been able to create their own nation."[47]

During this period scholars did not all speak with one voice regarding the proper relationship between heavy industry and light industry. Liu Dajun, a well-known scholar at the Institute of National Economy, recognized the potential conflict between heavy industry and light industry and linked that conflict to the relationship between national defense and people's livelihood: "if we lay stress on national defense, then in industry we should pay close attention to heavy industrial reconstruction; if we emphasize the importance of people's livelihood, then we should actively promote light industry." In Liu's view, "since China has no intention of waging wars of aggression against other nations, the importance of national defense is a function of the international environment." If all nations wanted peace and reduced armaments after World War II, then there would be no need to actively promote national defense industry, that is, heavy industry. For Liu, "the improvement of people's livelihood should be given first priority."[48] Even though Liu and a few other scholars challenged the perception of heavy industry and light industry as a zero-sum relationship,[49] Chen Zhenhan expressed the predominant view when he stated in 1943 that "our fundamental national policy in the postwar period is economic reconstruction, particularly heavy industrial reconstruction."[50]

In short, despite Sun Yatsen's emphasis on heavy industry, it was the war-triggered sustained systemic crisis set off by the war that caused leading figures of the Nationalist government and the intellectual community to recognize heavy industry as vital for national defense and nation-building. By the time the Sino-Japanese War concluded, the Nationalist elite had little doubt as to what the preference should be between heavy industry and light industry in China's postwar reconstruction.

National Defense versus People's Livelihood

As was the case with the emphasis on state-owned enterprise and the stress on heavy industry, the focus on national defense was also the product of several decades. Unlike the emphasis on state-owned enterprise and the stress on heavy industry, however, the focus on national defense did not find explicit expression in Sun Yatsen's Three Doctrines of the People. The lack of focus on national defense can be explained in part by the absence of either a unified national government or an imminent external threat to China during the 1920s.

Even during its first three years in power (1927–1930), the Nationalist Party was concerned primarily with China's long-term economic development. None of the party's major policy statements and resolutions touched on the issue of national defense. For example, a resolution of the third Nationalist Party congress adopted in March 1929 stated that "economic reconstruction is the material foundation of the Three Doctrines of the People. Without a solid material foundation, it will be impossible for China to secure its national independence, to actually develop people's democracy, or to truly solve the problem of people's livelihood." Following Sun Yatsen's plan for industrial development, the party congress made "communications and water conservancy the first priority of economic reconstruction."[51]

This orientation toward long-term economic development found confirmation in the *Outline Program for Implementing Economic Reconstruction during the Period of Political Tutelage*. According to this program, which the Nationalist Central Executive Committee adopted in April 1929, "the criteria for determining the procedure of implementing material reconstruction should be based on the principles and policies Sun Yatsen formulated in his plan for industrial reconstruction . . . with the development of communication being the most important." Important reconstruction projects, listed according to priority, included "railroads, national highways, other communications industries, coal-mining and iron-making industries, other basic industries, flood control, seaport construction, water conservancy, irrigation and land reclamation."[52]

These proposed undertakings would contribute to China's overall economic development and indirectly to national defense. Still, national defense was conspicuous by its absence in the rationale for economic reconstruction; what motivated the Nationalist Party was widespread poverty and suffering. The Nationalist Central Executive Committee adopted a resolution in March 1930 stating that "a revolution aims not only at destruction; more importantly, it aims at reconstruction after destruction. . . . Everywhere one looks, one sees mass impoverishment and famished refugees swarming over the land. The only solution to the bankrupted economy and the extreme misery is economic reconstruction."[53] This emphasis on people's livelihood embodied itself in a 1931 resolution adopted by the fourth Nationalist Party congress, which stated that "Sun Yatsen begins his *Jianguo Dagang* by declaring the improvement of people's livelihood the first priority of nation-building. Therefore, it goes without saying that the first important task for the period of political tutelage is economic reconstruction aimed at improving people's livelihood."[54]

The first indication of a major shift from the preoccupation with people's livelihood to a focus on national defense—hence the revision of existing mental model—was a resolution the fourth Nationalist Party congress adopted four days later. Drafted in response to the Japanese invasion of Manchuria, the resolution asserted that "today every nation is building its strength for the purpose of either creating dangerous situations or meeting dangerous situations. In other words, every country focuses on building strength in national reconstruction. Once the time is ripe for action, a second world war will break out, and China will certainly become one of the battlefields. How is it possible for our nation to prevent itself from the catastrophe of helplessly waiting for destruction when confronted with such a situation? It is absolutely essential for the whole country to be of one mind and to make every effort in order to save our nation."

Recognizing the increasingly dangerous international situation, the Nationalist Party congress drafted "a four-year plan as a first step in national reconstruction" and was "determined to implement it to ensure the continued existence of the Chinese nation." What is more, the plan "focuses on national defense, uses a hypothetical enemy as the target of reconstruction, and defines the scope of reconstruction according to necessity and viability."[55]

It was in the context of a drastically changing international situation and a mental model revision that the Nationalist government created the National Defense Planning Commission in 1932 and within a few months drafted plans for developing national defense industries. By early 1936, the National Resources Commission had integrated these plans into a comprehensive plan. As explained in Chapter 1, this plan called for creating an industrial region for national defense and developing the ordnance and heavy industries.

In response to the imminent danger of war, the Nationalist government began to reformulate its priority of economic development. A resolution of the Fifth Central Executive Committee adopted in February 1937 declared, "Chinese economic reconstruction has two objectives: To meet the needs of national defense and to improve people's welfare. The first objective is designed to bring to fruition the Doctrine of Nationalism; the second objective is meant to implement the Doctrine of People's Livelihood."[56] The outbreak of war greatly strengthened this national defense orientation. In a 1938 essay, Qian Changzhao stated that "all economic reconstruction should of course focus on national defense. We should gradually build up our national defense, but we must also take immediate steps to create a center for national defense in the interior."[57]

Weng Wenhao shared with Qian his belief in the primary importance of national defense. In a national radio address delivered in July 1941, Weng elaborated on the meaning of economic reconstruction that focused on national defense. "Generally speaking, there are two basic approaches to economic reconstruction. We could either pay exclusive attention to the well-being of the people without any regard to the security of the state or focus entirely on national defense and security without much regard to short-term well-being of the people. It would be ideal if we could give equal consideration to the well-being of the people and national defense and security. In reality, however, it often proves difficult to give equal consideration to both. Consequently, we must prioritize various tasks in economic reconstruction and determine our priority on the basis of changing configurations of international situation. When there is international peace, economic reconstruction should aim at improving the well-being of the people. However, when the international situation becomes unstable, when powerful countries use their strength for aggressive action, economic reconstruction in a country that faces an imminent danger of being conquered or destroyed must concentrate on increasing the strength of national defense as its objective." As for China and given the international reality, "it goes without saying that one has to make the consolidation of national defense the first priority of modern economic reconstruction."[58]

In another speech delivered in March 1942, Weng further explained the need to concentrate on building up national strength. After describing how the Soviet Union and Germany undertook large-scale heavy industrial reconstruction by using five-year and four-year plans, he pointed out that "both the Soviet Union and Germany believed that economic reconstruction is the only solution to national rejuvenation. In other words, the sole meaning of economic reconstruction is to increase national strength. As long as economic reconstruction is designed to increase national strength, it is absolutely essential and appropriate for the whole nation to work hard and endure hardships. . . . The bottom line is that we either increase our national strength without living a comfortable life or living a comfortable life without increasing our national strength. We can choose either national strength or a comfortable life; we cannot have both at the same time. . . . In order to build our nation, we have to be prepared to work hard and endure hardships; otherwise we will never succeed in building our nation."[59]

There is little doubt that leading members of the scholarly community agreed with Nationalist leaders on the primary importance of national strength or national defense. As early as 1936, Luo Dunwei advocated the creation of a central region for national defense. In his view, China had entered an "extremely dangerous extraordinary period. Moreover, this extraordinary situation required extraordinary methods to deal with it." Consequently Luo proposed the creation of a "central region for national defense" that included Sichuan, Yunnan, Guizhou, Shanxi, Gansu, Henan, Hubei, and Hunan provinces. He believed that China should concentrate its limited resources and apply the model of the so-called planned and controlled economy in this region's economic reconstruction. For Luo, this was *"the only effective strategy for national survival under the difficult circumstances."*[60]

The industrial relocation and development in China's southwest after 1937 seemed to have validated Luo's recommendation for creating a central region for national defense. In a 1940 essay he stated that economic reconstruction in China's southwest was in keeping with "his suggestion of regional concentration." Luo argued that "today, economic reconstruction in the southwest is not simply a wartime reconstruction; nor is it simply a regional reconstruction. Rather, economic reconstruction in the southwest involves the creation of the foundation for an independent national economy."[61]

Luo was only one of many scholars who believed in the primary importance of national defense in economic reconstruction. Less than two years after the war broke out, Fang Xianting considered the development of national defense industries to be the first priority. He pointed out that until the eruption of war, not only did Chinese industry experience limited development; in terms of the priority of industrial development, conventional wisdom had stressed *minsheng* industries (literally, "industries directly related to people's livelihood") at the expense of national defense industries. The all-out Japanese aggression, the destruction of existing Chinese industries, and the need for continued industrial production during the war combined to convince the nation of the critical importance of developing industry, especially national defense industries. This analysis of China's past experience led Fang to argue that China had to "make the creation of national defense industries its first priority, followed by the development of *minsheng* industries."[62]

The need to concentrate on national defense industries is a major theme of another important essay. Writing in January 1942, Su Jicang offered a compelling rationale for making national defense industries China's number-one priority. Su began by explaining why China was poor and weak. For him, the answer lay in the fact that "Chinese industry is backward. Until now, our economy has by and large remained in the stage of agricultural production. Although industrial reconstruction has a history of several dozen years, not only do we not have a foundation for heavy industry; even our light industry is lagging far behind nations of Europe and America. The condition of being weak and being lagged behind in such a big agricultural nation as ours is completely exposed once the country is invaded by an industrial nation. China's defeat in several wars with foreign countries and its former colonial status can all be explained by the backwardness of Chinese industry. Today China suffers so much from Japanese military domination and suppression, the fundamental reason of which also has to be explained by economic backwardness." In other words, "China's poverty and weakness stem from its industrial backwardness. If China desires to be 'rich' and 'strong,' the most urgent task is to industrialize." For Su Jicang, "becoming 'rich' and 'strong' are two major objectives of China's industrial reconstruction." In order to be strong, "China must develop national defense industries; in order to be rich, China must develop *minsheng* industries. In other words, both national defense and people's livelihood are objectives of industrial reconstruction."

All the same, in the context of existing international relations where the law of the jungle prevailed and given the necessity of military resistance against Japan, Su believed that national defense industries should be given first priority because "national defense industries are the major source of military strength during the war." In addition, "the core of national defense industries is heavy industry" and "heavy industry is the basis of light industry." Finally, "national defense industries provide security for *minsheng* industries." For Su, "in order to be 'rich,' we must first make our nation 'strong;' to seek the development of *minsheng* industries, we must first establish national defense industries."[63]

In short, although the debate on the priority of economic reconstruction continued during the war, by the early 1940s a majority of government officials and scholars had determined to focus on national defense.[64] Moreover, the wartime debate on national defense and people's livelihood held profound implications for China's postwar economic reconstruction.

Wu Jingchao, another leading economist and part-time commissioner of the Central Planning Board,[65] noted in a 1942 essay that he had advocated the development of national defense industries as the first priority as early as 1938. For Wu, the critical question in 1942 was "whether we should continue to place becoming strong ahead of becoming rich for postwar economic reconstruction. My own view is that until we establish a solid foundation for national defense, we must keep 'national defense first' in mind for the next few decades."[66]

Planning versus Laissez Faire

Another integral part of the Nationalist ideology of the developmental state was the determination to create a planned socialist economic system. If China's objective was to become a modern industrial nation, how could it do so? Should the Chinese government follow the earlier policy of the first-industrialized nations by keeping its hands off economic activities, or was the goal of a modern industrial nation to be achieved through economic planning and eventually through a planned socialist economic system? The Nationalist elite chose the second path as they transformed the idea of economic planning into a coherent theory of a planned economic system.

Available evidence suggests that the idea of planning came from Sun Yatsen. Speaking to a British reporter in 1911, Sun mentioned the idea of planning in overthrowing the Manchu dynasty. He stated that "a new, enlightened and progressive government must replace the old government.

. . . We developed a comprehensive and carefully thought-out plan a long time ago in order to replace the old monarchy of China with a republic."[67]

Within months, Sun Yatsen applied the idea of planning to China's economic development. Several times from June to October 1912, he discussed the need for a railroad development plan. In August, he declared that his intention was to "develop industry, but in order to do so, we have to start with railroad construction. We ought to have a comprehensive national plan for railroad construction."[68] By October, Sun became so fascinated with the idea of planned railroad construction that he wrote an essay entitled "China's Railroad Plan and the People's Livelihood" to commemorate the 1911 Revolution, in which he explained the plan's content and significance. For Sun, this plan would "promote commercial prosperity and increase national wealth." More importantly, the creation of a network of national railroads would "guarantee a true unification, for China can survive only if she is unified. Once China is unified and prosperous, she will enter the family of nations as a world power, and she will no longer be subject to humiliation and exploitation inflicted by other nations."[69] Not surprisingly, Sun's railroad plan found expression in the 1912 *Manifesto of the Political Platform* of the Nationalist Party, which included the planned "development of state-owned transportation and communications industry."[70]

Thus more than five years before the Russian Revolution, Sun Yatsen had conceived the idea of economic planning, especially that for planning railroad development. By the time his *International Development of China* appeared in 1922, Sun had developed a comprehensive plan for economic development. His desire to use plans as a mechanism for economic development is attributable to at least three factors. First, Sun believed that, because of the backwardness of the Chinese economy, China would of necessity need foreign capital and technology for national development. His *International Development of China* was designed in part to solicit foreign assistance in this development. In order to obtain such assistance, however, he must present a plan to the "capital-supplying powers."[71]

Second, wartime economic planning in Europe and America also played a role in the formation of Sun Yatsen's idea of economic planning. In the introduction to his *International Development of China,* he pointed out that in order to carry out his plan successfully, "the various governments of the capital-supplying powers must agree to joint action and unified policy to form an international organization with their war worker organizers, administrators and experts of various lines to formulate plans and to standardize materials in order to prevent waste and to facilitate work." Again, "if war work methods, that is, gigantic planning and efficient organization, were applied to the construction of the harbor and the city, then an Oriental New York City would spring up in a very short time."[72]

Finally, a comprehensive plan was necessary for developing Chinese industry. After pointing out that "China must develop her industries by all means," Sun asked himself rhetorically: "shall we follow the old path of Western civilization?" For him "the path of Western civilization was an unknown one and those who went before groped in the dark as Columbus did on his first voyage to America. As a late comer, China can greatly profit in covering the space by following the direction already charted by Western pioneers."[73]

In Sun's view, the "unification and nationalization of all industries" was a "Second Industrial Revolution," a revolution more "far-reaching than that of the first one in which manual labor was displaced by machinery." For Sun then, this revolution pointed to the very direction China should follow. In the period immediately following World War I, China, he said, was the land "that still employs manual labor for production and has not yet entered the first stage of industrial evolution, while in Europe and America the second stage is already reached. So China has to begin the two stages of industrial evolution at once by adopting the machinery as well as the nationalization of production."[74]

In order to develop Chinese industry and realize both stages of the industrial evolution, according to Sun, China must develop a "comprehensive plan to take advantage of the propitious opportunity of the post war period and to make use of new capital and experienced personnel of the belligerent nations for the purpose of developing our large-scale industries." And he added that he had drawn up a special project called "Plan for Industrial Development" as part of his *Jianguo Fanglüe*.[75]

After 1928, the Nationalist government tried to put Sun's ideas of economic planning into practice.[76] At the same time, government officials and leading scholars criticized the problems in drafting plans and pointed out the need for practical and comprehensive planning. Commenting on the lessons learned from economic reconstruction, Weng Wenhao wrote in 1932 that "the necessity of planning has been widely accepted in China today, thus we hear about plans almost daily, although we have not made much progress in reconstruction in the last few years. On the other hand, the content of these plans are often far from based on facts, thus we end up in failure once these plans are carried out. [Therefore], it follows that reconstruction is not something to be easily accomplished. Reconstruction must be preceded by plan, and plan in turn must be based on hard facts."[77]

One year later, Weng stepped up his criticism of the "lack of planning and efficient organizational control." He underlined the need for a "comprehensive plan for economic reconstruction" by posing a rhetorical question: "if the government cannot control itself, how can it expect to control the national economy?"[78] As secretary-general of the National Defense Planning Commission and later director of the National Resources Commission, Weng was actively involved in drafting and implementing economic plans. During his tenure as head of the Ministry of Economic Affairs (1938–1946), he continued to stress the importance of planning. For example, he declared in 1939, "Industrialization must be carefully planned if desirable goals are to be reached within a reasonable time." "Since each country has its special needs and ideals, the goals may be different in different countries. But a comprehensive and well co-coordinated plan is always essential for effectively meeting needs and achieving goals."[79]

Weng's insistence on practical and comprehensive planning was shared by leading scholars such as Fang Xianting. Writing on the issue of controlled economic system in 1936, Fang severely criticized government economic planning. In his view, a major problem in establishing a controlled economic system in China was the "lack of practical and coordinated planning. Planning is the mother of control, for without planning control would at best be piecemeal reform. Economic planning in China has thus far been unpractical and ill-coordinated." Another problem was the lack of "coordination of organs for economic control." Until the end of 1935, according to Fang, there were "four national agencies in charge of national economic planning and control, not to mention the various ministries which also participated one way or the other in tasks of similar character." On the other hand, Fang noted that the government took steps to reorganize agencies with overlapping functions. Fang believed that the reorganization "represents a forward step in the rationalization of national economic administration."[80]

Other scholars concurred. Writing after the outbreak of the Sino-Japanese War, Chen Daisun asserted that "needless to say, in order to strengthen the economy in the rear-area, we must adopt an economic policy of planning and control. For unless this is done, we cannot fully mobilize domestic economic strength, cannot make effective use of our productive capacity on the most important undertakings, cannot improve the material life of the people in the rear area, and cannot replenish the needs of the front in large quantities and in a speedy manner. Consequently, even in countries with a laissez faire economic system the government has to make comprehensive plans and even temporarily nationalize private manufacturing enterprises during the time of war."[81]

The second major development in the planning theory during the latter part of the 1930s was the transition from the consensus on the necessity of economic planning to an explicit government policy of adopting a planned economic system. The continued Communist threat after the extermination campaigns, the tremendous economic burden the Nationalist government bore after the flood of the Yangzi and Huai rivers in 1931, and the nationwide economic crisis after 1931, all contributed to producing a radical change of government policy and a metamorphosis of planning theory. The fundamental cause of change, however, was the increasing Japanese threat to China's national security after Japan invaded Manchuria in 1931.[82] Japan's continued encroachment on China's sovereignty after 1931 forced Nationalist leaders to revise their existing mental model of domestic and international environment and reorganize national economic organizations for the purpose of creating a planned economic system. This development is reflected in a resolution the fifth Nationalist Party congress adopted in November 1935. According to this resolution: "It is the consensus of the entire nation that we urgently need to undertake a complete reorganization of national economic organizations under the extraordinary circumstance of foreign invasion and domestic trouble . . . Sun Yatsen's Doctrine of People's Livelihood has already laid out the basic principle of economic reform for us . . . However, in order to apply this principle to the situation of this extraordinary period and to come up with concrete methods to carry out economic reform, we must conduct in-depth research and draw carefully thought-out plans by utilizing the collective wisdom of party comrades and economic experts."

The resolution pointed out that, "today, nations such as the United States, Germany, the Soviet Union and Italy have all established organizations such as brain trusts or national economic planning agencies to make new economic policies and industrial plans and to supervise their implementation. The effectiveness of these organizations is well known among nations. We must make thorough preparations if our country desires to adopt a planned economic system. We have already created a National Economic Commission and a National Resources Commission, but their functions are different: the former is designed to undertake reconstruction with the additional objective of achieving international cooperation, whereas the latter is intended to prepare for national defense with an emphasis on the military aspect. In other words, we have yet to create an organization with the responsibility of making comprehensive economic policy and industrial plan for the entire nation. In view of the precedents in various countries and our own needs, we suggest that a National Economic Planning Commission be created under the Central Executive Committee for the purpose of creating a planned economic system and of implementing our party's Doctrine of the People's Livelihood."[83]

An outline of economic reconstruction that Chiang Kaishek and others submitted in early 1937 further defined the nature of the proposed planned economic system: "The policy of China's economic reconstruction should be the creation of a planned economic system. The government will make a comprehensive and carefully thought-out plan on the basis of domestic situation and needs. The plan will not only cover every aspect of the national economy, such as production, distribution, exchange and consumption, but serve as the guiding policy for all activities of economic reconstruction. To utilize resources effectively, the government will optimally allocate human and material resources of the entire nation without regard to regional boundaries. In addition, the government will ensure a fair distribution of the products of labor among all members of society for the purpose of improving people's welfare."[84]

With the outbreak of the Sino-Japanese War, the Nationalist Party became even more determined to create a planned economic system. In April 1938, the provisional Nationalist Party congress adopted a *Program for the War of Resistance and Nation Building*, which set forth the fundamental objectives in diplomacy, military, politics, economy, and education. With regard to the national economy, the program declared that "economic reconstruction should focus on military [needs] while paying due attention to the improvement of people's lives. In order to accomplish these objectives, we must create a planned economic system, encourage domestic and foreign investment, and expand wartime production."[85] The *Manifesto of Provisional Nationalist Party Congress* also asserted that "the government must create a planned economic system according to the Doctrine of People's Livelihood."[86]

The shift from recognizing the necessity of economic planning to calling for the creation of a planned economic system represented an important leap forward in the formation of a coherent theory of a planned economic system.[87] Again, leading government officials, theorists, and economists all contributed to this leap by developing a shared mental model through deliberation and communication, a model that underscored the need to establish a planned economic system. For example, Sun Ke stated in early 1940 that "by adopting a system of planned economy which is an adjunct of the Doctrine of People's Livelihood, we shall be able to quicken industrialization by diverting the greater part of the surplus national income from private enterprise in the form of income and profit taxes to state-owned industry."[88] About one month later, Sun further elaborated on the issue of planned economic system. After pointing out that free competition held indisputable sway under laissez-faire capitalism, he went on to describe the planned economic system. In Sun Ke's view, the Doctrine of People's Livelihood "proposes . . . to institute a planned economy." Moreover, under the planned economic system "all large-scale enterprises are to be operated and managed by the state."[89]

Weng Wenhao reached a similar conclusion. Writing in 1941, he distinguished between three different types of economic system:

> (1) Planned economic system based on complete state ownership as in the Soviet Union. The planned economic system calls for the concentration of all sovereign powers in the hands of the central government, and all activities in production and exchange are carried out by organizations established by the government according to government policies and concrete plans. (2) Total economic system completely controlled by the government as in Germany, Italy and Japan. Its fundamental principle is the preservation of private enterprise, but organizationally and operationally all private enterprises are subject to complete government control. (3) Partially controlled economic system in which free competition is predominant as in Great Britain and the United States.

Weng concluded that "expanding the power and function of government control has become a principle of [organizing] a modern economy." Although Weng recognized the merits of all three types of economic system, he believed that none of them was entirely consistent with China's needs. Consequently he proposed that China adopt these systems "eclectically." As he put it, China ought to create a "planned and controlled economic system," under which the "government shall take major responsibility by making national defense its top priority, by promoting state-owned enterprise to ensure the creation of a solid foundation, and by controlling private enterprise to ensure its healthy development."[90] Under this planned and controlled economic system, "the government will manage state-owned enterprise as well as guide and supervise private enterprise. One could argue that assuming the role of overall management and supervision would make it easy for the government to make comprehensive—without distinguishing state-owned from private enterprise—plans for economic reconstruction and to gradually implement these plans."[91]

The need to create a planned economic system also found expression in Chiang Kaishek's *China's Destiny and Chinese Economic Theory*, first published in March 1943. In Chiang's view, China "must adopt a planned economy and social legislation to secure the livelihood and survival of every citizen, and it is imperative that we eventually accomplish the objective of 'transforming [all] capital into state capital [nationalization of capital], and transforming [all] enjoyment into enjoyment by the masses.' " Again, "economic development must therefore be planned, and that planning must rest on a basic theory. The basic theory of the Doctrine of People's Livelihood is to develop state-owned enterprises and aid the people in order to improve their livelihood, while at the same time controlling private capital and equalizing land ownership in order to prevent the capitalistic control of the people's livelihood. Chinese economic principles are neither those of laissez-faire, nor those of promoting class struggle. They call for economic plans to 'nationalize capital for popular enjoyment'—to realize the ideal of [government] 'for the people,' whereby China may become a wealthy, healthy, and happy state."[92]

At the same time government leaders called for the creation of a planned economic system, leading scholars and economists also advocated the establishment of an economic system under comprehensive and national planning. As early as 1936 Luo Dunwei had promoted the idea of a controlled or planned economic system: "I believe by definition a controlled economic system refers to the procedure of economic reconstruction opposed to laissez faire economic system and under the control of the central government administration. It is a procedure of economic reconstruction aimed to achieve a balance between production and consumption. . . . In form, both the controlled economic system and planned economic system aim to achieve a balance between production and consumption. There is no quantitative difference between the two. In substantive terms, however, there is a marked difference between the controlled economic system and planned economic system (italics omitted). For example, the planned economic system of the Soviet Union is different from the controlled economic system of other countries in that the latter aims to achieve a balance between production and consumption from the perspective of state capitalism, whereas the former aims to expand production and develop material conditions of society from the perspective of state socialism. The ultimate goal of the latter is to seek profits, whereas the goal of the former is to consolidate material conditions of socialism."[93]

After the war began, Luo continued to push for the creation of a planned economic system. In a 1940 essay, he expressed the hope that the proposed "Central Planning Board" would serve as a "general staff" to guide and supervise the creation of a planned economic system.[94] By July 1942, Luo had reached the conclusion that "a controlled economic system or a planned economic system is the only way toward the creation of a national defense economy."[95]

Other scholars agreed. In a 1939 essay, Huang Zuo explained the rationale for creating a planned economic system: "The reason we advocate the creation of a planned economic system is because we believe a free enterprise system is completely incapable of meeting the needs of our country in the near future. The war of resistance against Japan has demonstrated that to ensure national survival, we must within a short period of time establish the foundation for basic national industries and gradually develop our country into a self-sufficient industrialized country. The war of resistance against Japan has also shown that unless we could create a powerful navy or air force within a short period of time, we should no longer concentrate our economic reconstruction in the major cities in the coastal regions or the lower Yangzi River valley. . . . Frankly speaking, one purpose of creating a planned economic system is to control our economic resources and use political power to achieve regional redistribution of these resources."[96]

By August 1941, Hu Yuanmin could state with confidence that "the urgent need to create a planned economic system has almost become a consensus both within and outside the government. It has also been written into the *Program for the War of Resistance and Nation Building* as article seventeen. Recently the government established a Central Planning Board, which shows the government's determination to create a planned economic system in a speedy manner. Theoretically speaking, then, the merit of the planned economic system is understood by all and requires no elaboration.

We have already seen the astonishing result the three five-year plans of the Soviet Union produced and how Germany's four-year plan transformed Germany from a weak country into a strong power. If we are determined to catch up with the advanced countries and to rank among the wealthy and powerful, the only shortcut is to create a planned economic system."

In order to create a planned economic system, Hu offered the following recommendations. All economic reconstruction "must revolve around national defense." The function and responsibility of state-owned and private enterprise should be defined. "Unlike the socialist Soviet Union where all enterprises are owned and managed by the state, private enterprise should be allowed to exist under the Three Doctrines of the People provided that private enterprise will not be harmful to the interest of the state. . . . Basic heavy industries related to national defense and those which require large investment capital ought to be managed by the state, whereas public utilities related to people's daily activities should be jointly managed by state-owned and private enterprise." Furthermore, there should be a redefinition of different regions for economic reconstruction. "Before the onset of the resistance war against Japan, various industries tended to concentrate in coastal regions, especially in the city of Shanghai, in violation of the principle of national defense. Consequently these industries suffered heavy losses early during the war. To correct this mistake and to ensure a balanced development of regional economies, we should divide the country into a number of economic regions and undertake economic reconstruction according to the distribution of material resources, products and population within these regions."[97]

In a 1939 essay, Song Zexing, a young economist, painted a clear picture of what people could expect under a planned economic system. In his view, "since the beginning of the resistance war against Japan, the changes in the economic organizations of our country have paved the way for creating a planned economic system. Still, these changes are far from adequate for creating a completely planned economic system in the near future." For Song, the creation of such a system would require satisfying the following conditions: the expansion of state-owned enterprise so as to control production in the entire country; the control and regulation of private enterprise; the control and manipulation of the consumer market; the transition from partial to complete state ownership and state management of foreign trade; the continuation and strengthening of the regulation of foreign exchange; and the control of national finance.[98]

The planned economic system would be a socialist economic system. In a 1943 essay, Chen Bozhuang stated that in the drive toward industrialization, China needed to create an economic system based on the Doctrine of People's Livelihood. He quoted Sun Yatsen as saying that "the Doctrine of People's Livelihood is socialism brought to fruition." Chen also stated that Sun pointed to "three paths" toward socialism: equalization of land ownership; regulation of capital; and development of state capital. In addition, he believed that Chiang Kaishek had made his contribution by pointing to the need to create a planned economic system and to make social legislation in his *China's Destiny and Chinese Economic Theory.* Chen considered the creation of a planned economic system and the making of social legislation as the "means" that complemented Sun's "three paths" toward socialism.[99] Chen Bozhuang was not alone in defining the planned economic system as a socialist one. In a 1944 essay, Xu Deheng asserted that "the essence of the planned economic system is socialism. Only a socialist society could establish a truly planned economic system, whereas a capitalistic society could at best create a controlled economic system under private capitalism or a policy of partial social relief."[100]

Many scholars believed the Doctrine of People's Livelihood to be equivalent to socialism. For example, Zhang Youjiang asserted in 1941 that "the Doctrine of People's Livelihood will lead our country toward a noncapitalist path of development—a path of peacefully building socialism or communism. . . . In short, the Doctrine of People's Livelihood is the only policy and only system by which an industrially backward country could peacefully build socialism or communism."[101] Leading officials of the Nationalist government also identified the Doctrine of People's Livelihood with socialism. Weng Wenhao, for instance, believed that "Sun Yatsen aimed at utilizing capitalism to create socialism" with his *Plan of Industrial Development.*[102] In a lecture delivered in January 1943, Weng again quoted Sun as saying that "on the one hand we seek to make our country rich and strong. On the other hand, we intend to prevent abuses of monopolistic capitalism, and the only effective policy to prevent these abuses is socialism. That explains why we have adopted the policy of state socialism in our platform."[103]

The National Resources Commission defined socialism as a central component of its mission in heavy industrial reconstruction. According to Qian Changzhao, the commission's mission consisted of three components: *economically* to bring about Chinese industrialization; *politically* to build national defense; and *socially* to create state capital and help the Chinese nation move towards socialism. With regard to the last component, Qian asserted that "the teachings of Sun Yatsen places special emphasis on the control of private capital. In Europe and North America, private capitalism has caused enough harm already. Consequently their postwar economic policy will certainly move toward socialization. Nonetheless, it will not be easy to change their well-established institutions and practices. One could argue that to destroy private capitalism will necessarily entail a struggle, and a very violent one at that. In contrast to conditions in Europe and North America, private capitalism has not taken roots in China. China is like a piece of blank paper, we can write whatever we want on it. Seen from the perspective of the Doctrine of People's Livelihood, no one may oppose the creation of state capital and the control of private capital; nor will our nation allow anyone to oppose them. We always hope to put an end to the unequal distribution of wealth. We always hope to eliminate privileged social classes in economic activities. Obviously this project is of vital and lasting importance with significant consequences for social stability. As the organization in charge of undertaking the reconstruction of state-owned heavy industry, the National Resources Commission undoubtedly has the mission to create state capital and help our nation move toward socialism."[104]

Toward the end of the Sino-Japanese War, more and more scholars pushed for the creation of a planned economic system. Among them, Shi Fuliang presented the most powerful argument. Writing in 1944, Shi asserted that "China is a backward country; economically it lags behind the advanced countries for at least several decades. In terms of timing and [international] environment, we no longer have the option of adopting a laissez faire policy, allowing free competition among entrepreneurs. What our country needs at present is to call upon the whole nation to do our utmost to catch up with the advanced countries, and to transform China into a modern industrialized country within the shortest possible time. To accomplish this we must create a planned economic system, make national economic plans according to the need for national defense and people's livelihood, and undertake economic reconstruction according to these plans."[105]

Six months later, Shi again called for the creation of a planned economic system. In his view, "just as socialism as an economic system is superior to capitalism, the planned economic system as a form of economic organization is superior to the laissez faire economic system. The experience of the Soviet Union is the best proof of this argument: by successfully imple-

menting three five-year plans and undertaking planned economic reconstruction, the Soviet Union has caught up with the advanced capitalist
countries within a period of a little more than a decade, whereas it has
taken several decades or more than a century for the capitalist countries to
get to where they are. Our country has a backward economy, and if we
want to catch up with the advanced countries, we should certainly follow
the example of the Soviet Union by creating a planned economic system."[106]

In late 1944, Qi Zhilu, secretary in the Ministry of Economic Affairs,
conducted a survey of all of the 574 essays in the 120 issues of *New Economy*,
the leading journal of political economy published during the Sino-
Japanese War. According to Qi, there was a "unanimous agreement" on
the necessity of creating a planned economic system in China.[107]

In addition to drawing a blueprint for creating a planned socialist economic system, scholarly discussion on economic planning increasingly focused on China's industrialization in general and the procedure of economic
planning in particular. In other words, the early 1940s witnessed not only
the establishment of a foundation of the ideological edifice of planned economic system but the actual construction of the edifice itself.

A major work on the subject of China's industrialization—*Industrialization
and Social Reconstruction* published in 1944—offers some insight into the
ideas of contemporary Chinese regarding the proper procedure for drawing
up comprehensive economic plans. In this book, Jian Guansan first discussed the meaning and necessity of industrialization, the difficulties, conditions, and ways of Chinese industrialization, and the relationship between
industrial reconstruction and planned society. Jian proceeded to address the
question of a planned economic system. In his view, a planned economic
system was central to a planned society and was a logical outcome of the
development of a modern economy from "a free economic system to a
controlled economic system, and from a controlled economic system to a
planned economic system." For Jian, a planned economic system was the
"end-result of social evolution." Nevertheless, in order to make plans viable
under the planned economic system, planning agencies had to follow certain procedures, which included gathering statistics, determining objectives;
drawing up departmental plans, and drafting the final plan. The planning
agencies would then submit the final plan to the highest authority for approval.[108]

The issue of planning procedure was also the focus of Gu Chunfan's *Planning and China's industrialization*. Gu believed that economic planning con-

sisted of three phases. In phase one the highest decision-making organization would set forth fundamental goals and policies and issue instructions. In phase two experts would draw up a production plan on the basis of available natural, human, and financial resources and input from related ministries. In the final phase, productive units would have an opportunity to review the agenda and provide feedback for revision. For Gu, the first phase was political, the second economic, and the third technical.[109]

To summarize, even though Sun Yatsen and the Nationalist elite saw the need for economic planning during the 1920s and early 1930s, major developments in the theory of economic planning took place during 1935–1945. In response to the growing Japanese threat to China's national security after the mid-1930s and the crisis triggered by the Sino-Japanese War, the Nationalist elite revised their mental model by transforming the idea of economic planning into a coherent theory of a planned economic system.

The Nationalist ideology of the developmental state took shape in a complex historical context. As a result of his experience before and during World War I, Sun Yatsen saw the huge gap in wealth between China and countries in Europe and North America, and hence the need to catch up with these countries. Sun believed that China should follow the Western example by using comprehensive economic planning and developing state-owned heavy industry but avoid the adverse consequences of laissez-faire capitalism. As a program of late development, Sun's Doctrine of People's Livelihood laid the theoretical foundation for the Nationalist ideology of the developmental state.

More important for the making of this ideology was China's changing domestic and international situation during the 1930s. The increasing Japanese threat to China's national security and the sustained systemic crisis triggered by the Sino-Japanese War forced the Nationalist elite to revise their mental model and collectively develop a coherent ideology of the developmental state. Central to this ideology were the emphasis on state-owned enterprise, heavy industry, and national defense, and the determination to create a planned socialist economic system. Although this ideology neither denied the need to develop light industry using private capital nor explicitly advocated the creation of a Soviet-style planned economic system, within the conceptual structure of the national economy private capitalism was subject to state control and regulation and was clearly placed in a subordinate position. Finally, the Nationalist ideology of the developmental state pointed to the creation of not simply a planned economic system but a planned socialist economic system.

The Nationalist elite obviously drew from different national experiences in developing the ideology of the developmental state. The world of the 1930s and 1940s made available a variety of resources in terms of models: the planned economic system of the Soviet Union; the total economic system of Germany, Italy, and Japan; and the partially controlled economic system of Great Britain and the United States. The Nationalist elite borrowed elements from each model and succeeded in developing a system they believed best suited China.

Conclusion

The basic institutional arrangement of China's state-owned enterprise—the bureaucratic governance structure, the distinctive management and incentive mechanisms, and the provision of social services and welfare—took shape in China during the Sino-Japanese War and was not derived from the Soviet model as is conventionally believed. In addition, the war saw the use of the term *danwei* to designate state-owned enterprise as well as other political, economic, and administrative organizations. Finally, the Nationalist ideology of the developmental state took its final form during the war, an ideology that served as the underpinnings for the state enterprise system. From the perspective of this study, institutional and ideological evolution, not revolution, explains the basic structure of state-owned enterprise and its ideology in post-1949 China.

The Formation of China's State Enterprise System

The sustained systemic crisis precipitated by Japan's occupation of Manchuria and its subsequent large-scale invasion of China proper explains why the basic institutional arrangement took shape during 1935–1945. The crisis forced the Nationalist elite to respond by recognizing the inadequacy of China's institutional environment and by developing shared new mental models, including the ideology of the developmental state. Their newly developed mental models, in turn, led them to reorder and restructure their institutional environment. This study demonstrates that each defining characteristic of the state-owned enterprise can be attributed to the sustained systemic crisis and the human response to it. The war of resistance led directly to the expansion of the ordnance and heavy industries and to the extension and expansion of the bureaucratic governance structure within

213

state-owned enterprises. Virtually all state-owned enterprises applied the organizational model of the formal administrative bureaucracy to their governance structure during the Sino-Japanese War.

The need for effective management led to important innovations in accounting practices. In response to the wartime need for efficiency and increased production, state-owned enterprises in the ordnance and heavy industries introduced a new system of cost accounting. By mid-1945, many state-owned enterprises had adopted the calculation of profits and losses as a standard procedure and used it as a major management mechanism. The same national crisis also called for the adoption of the Work Emulation Campaign to increase productivity. In addition to inventing a new institutional tradition of campaigns, the campaign method served to define the incentive mechanism in state-owned enterprises.

The crisis of national social and economic life necessitated the development of social service and welfare institutions. The evidence not only points to the formation of factory-run communities during the war, but also demonstrates how the war-triggered crisis, which manifested itself in the conditions of a new social environment, high labor turnover, and rising inflation, led directly to the revision of the mental model of factory officials and managers and indirectly to the development of social service and welfare institutions. By the end of 1945, these institutions had become a defining characteristic of China's state-owned enterprises.

The war-triggered crisis also shaped the Nationalist institutional rationalization. In response to wartime conditions, the Nationalists engaged in an extraordinary struggle to rationalize state institutions by implementing the three-in-one administrative system in the central administrative bureaucracy and in state-owned enterprises. As an unintended consequence, the wartime Nationalist institutional rationalization resulted in the *danwei* designation of political, economic, and administrative organizations, including state-owned enterprises.

Finally, the same sustained systemic crisis gave rise to the Nationalist ideology of the developmental state. As a radically altered mental model, the Nationalist ideology of the developmental state provided an interpretation of China's institutional environment as well as a prescription of how to reorder that environment. This ideology formed the ideational underpinnings of the new state enterprise system and led directly to its formation.

A recent study of the Japanese economic system and its historical origins further bolsters the argument that crisis shapes radical institutional change and determines its timing and magnitude as well. "The most significant feature of Japan's economic system lies in the fact that many of its important components came into being during the 1930s and the first half of the 1940s, in the process of building up the heavy and chemical industries and adapting the economy for war. Prior to this Japan had an orthodox capitalist, market-oriented system, which, though backward in some respects, differed little from those of the USA and European countries. . . . But over the course of the eight years from the start of the Sino-Japanese War in July 1937 until the end of the Pacific War in August 1945, it was completely transformed."[1] Although the nature of change varies in different national and institutional contexts, most scholars agree that World War II produced far-reaching consequences for the economic systems of belligerent nations.[2]

All the same, the sustained systemic crisis did not define the new institutional arrangement of state-owned enterprises. Why did the state-owned enterprise create a bureaucratic governance structure? Why did it adopt the system of cost accounting? Why did it resort to the campaign method? To answer these questions, one must examine China's institutional and ideological endowments.

As in the case of other civilizations, traditional Chinese civilization developed several distinctive characteristics that set it apart. These characteristics included the absolute monarchy, a bureaucratic system of government, a governing elite of scholar-officials, a civil service examination system, and Neo-Confucianism. These characteristics also define the limits of traditional Chinese institutional, ideological, and intellectual resources.

These characteristics of traditional Chinese civilization exerted a profound impact on China's modern transformation. For example, a pervasive institutional endowment, the organizational model of the formal administrative bureaucracy, served as China's only institutional resource when it began establishing ordnance factories in the 1860s. Consequently, most ordnance factories established between the 1860s and 1890s bore the name of "manufacturing bureaus," and traditional bureaucrats ran them as they would any other government bureau.

Despite the creation of a Chinese Republic in 1912 and corresponding political changes, government organizations largely followed the organizational model of the imperial bureaucracy. Even after the Nationalist Party established its regime in 1927, the Nationalist government continued to use an official ranking system. This system classified all government officials into four ranks for the purpose of determining prestige and compensation, with each rank bearing a different designation: *special appointment* for first rank, *selected appointment* for the second, *recommended appointment* for the third, and *delegated appointment* for the fourth.

Because of the limited institutional resources available, virtually all state-owned enterprises established during the Sino-Japanese War adopted the organizational model of the formal administrative bureaucracy. Through this model, they developed a governance structure characterized by administrative units made up of divisions and departments ranked according to their size and importance within the administrative hierarchy. All division and department heads had official ranks, as well as classes within ranks with corresponding privileges.

If the time-honored organizational model of the formal administrative bureaucracy served as the only institutional resource, then Sun Yatsen's Three Doctrines of the People functioned as the only ideological framework from which the Nationalists drew in creating the developmental state's ideology. In explaining the need to create a planned socialist economic system, the Nationalist elite frequently referred to Sun's teachings, especially his Doctrine of People's Livelihood. To be sure, Sun Yatsen never focused on the issue of national defense or used the phrase "planned economic system," but nonetheless the educated elite used his theory as an ideological resource.

When needed institutional, ideological, and intellectual resources were unavailable within China's resource endowments, the Nationalist elite appropriated them from the industrial nations. The transfer of the management "technology" of cost accounting to China's state-owned enterprise is a case in point. Studies have shown that "modern costing procedures" dated from the 1880s as a result of "nonmarket coordination of economic activity."[3] During the next three decades, the demand for new management information gave rise to the development of "a host of new cost measurement techniques" by "engineer-managers in American metal-working firms."[4]

In part because of the activities of these "pioneers in cost accounting," American colleges and universities began offering courses in financial and cost accounting. In 1900, only twelve institutions of higher learning taught accounting courses. By 1910, fifty-two colleges and universities listed accounting courses, and by 1916, the number had risen to 116. By then, these courses included auditing, public accounting, and cost accounting.[5] By the mid-1920s "virtually all management accounting practices used today had been developed: cost accounts for labor, material, and overhead; budgets for cash, income, and capital; flexible budgets, sales forecasts, standard costs, variance analysis, transfer prices, and divisional performance measures."[6]

In other words, when the Bureau of Ordnance started modernizing the ordnance industry during the early 1930s, and when the National Resources Commission began establishing heavy industrial enterprises in 1936, a new institutional resource of cost accounting was readily available for appropriation by the expanding state-owned enterprise in China.[7] The evidence shows that enterprise officials and managers appropriated this resource and established a new system of cost accounting during the Sino-Japanese War.

Another case of resource transfer was the appropriation of American theories of public administration. After the Nationalists came to power, they were immediately confronted with the challenge of how to make an essentially traditional bureaucratic system function smoothly and effectively. The lack of indigenous resources meant that the Nationalists needed to find them elsewhere. The evidence demonstrates that the Nationalist elite endeavored to build a new state by adopting and adapting American theories of public administration as key components of wartime Nationalist institutional rationalization—pursuit of administrative efficiency, emphasis on a system of delegating responsibility, and designation of administrative organizations as unit and work unit—all appear to have come from American theories of public administration.

The net effect of endogenous resource utilization and exogenous resource appropriation was the formation of the distinctive institutional arrangement of China's state-owned enterprise. The formation of the state enterprise system elucidates the indigenous roots of China's economic system and also represents a case of radical institutional change. A new state enterprise system had now replaced an economic system dominated by private enterprise toward the end of the Sino-Japanese War.[8]

Implications

The present study corroborates recent scholarship demonstrating a continuity between the Nationalist and Communist eras.[9] As these studies suggest, the elements of post-1949 institutional arrangements indeed developed well before 1949. Therefore, the critical issue is no longer that of establishing institutional and ideological continuity between the Nationalist and Communist eras; instead, it rests in understanding why and how the Chinese Communists kept intact, built on, and expanded existing institutions—including existing Communist institutions—in certain key areas of political, economic, and administrative life.

Questions such as these require considerable research in many areas of political, economic, and administrative life at the level of central policy making as well as that of individual enterprises. We will not have complete answers until more concrete research is presented. One possible answer has already emerged from the fact that before taking over state-owned and private enterprises in urban areas, the Communist Party decided in January 1949 not to make major changes in existing enterprises. "Facing the problems of heavy unemployment, economic disruption, and lack of management skills and experiences, the Communist authorities at first protected and encouraged private industry and commerce, and also avoided challenging existing management authorities in the newly nationalized industries. The original personnel, wage systems, labor insurance, bonus, and organizations in those confiscated enterprises remained unchanged under this prudent policy."[10]

The experience of the Kunming Machine Works—the immediate successor to the Central Machine Works—confirms the policy of the Communist Party. According to an internal survey, the Central Machine Works was renamed the Kunming Machine Works in October 1946 and at the same time it was reorganized to comprise a secretary office and the departments of general affairs, work affairs, business affairs, and accounting. The Communists took over the Kunming Machine Works in March 1950, but they made no major changes in the organizational and management structure until the end of 1952, when the existing four departments were reorganized into eleven departments, including those of planning, production, technology, examination, finance, supply, personnel and security.[11] In short, no major changes took place in the enterprise's organization and management between 1946 and 1952. When change did arrive, it only brought about further expansion of factory administration.

With regard to the origins of the *danwei* system, designating political, economic, and administrative organizations as *danwei* and developing their characteristics accordingly constituted only the initial steps in *danwei*-ization—a process by which political, economic, and administrative organizations became part of an all-encompassing administrative system and acquired the defining characteristics of Chinese *danwei*. Other steps were required before these organizations could be integrated into this system. Discovering the steps taken during the postwar decade (1945–1955) is essential for establishing the critical empirical links between these earlier developments and the *danwei* system, but further research is needed before we can determine their role in the *danwei*-ization of urban Chinese society.

Finally, this study contributes to the development of theories of institutional change. The theory presented in this study distinguishes between gradual or incremental institutional change and radical or revolutionary institutional change. The normal alteration of human conditions, the modification of mental models, and the partial reordering of institutional environments explain the dynamics of gradual or incremental institutional change. By contrast, the drastic alteration of human conditions, the transformation or replacement of existing mental models, and the complete reordering of institutional environments illuminate the logic of radical or revolutionary institutional change. Moreover, path dependence characterizes gradual or incremental institutional change because of the constraints of limited institutional endowments, whereas path independence describes radical or revolutionary institutional change due to the necessity of creating new resources to overcome the constraints of institutional endowments. Because it uses concepts that are not specific to any culture or polity, this theory can be applied to the study of institutional change in different historical and national contexts.

The formation of China's state enterprise system illustrates the path-dependent character of institutional change. Although this system took shape during the Sino-Japanese War, certain of its elements, such as the bureaucratic governance structure, the campaign mechanism, and the social service and welfare institutions, had roots in the period before the war. Nevertheless, institutional change is path-dependent not simply because of the powerful influence of the past on the present and future, but, more precisely, because of the constraints of limited institutional endowments.

More importantly, the formation of China's state enterprise system has implications for understanding radical institutional change. The development of the system represents a case of radical change because, within the short period of one decade, a new state enterprise system replaced an economic system dominated by private enterprise. The evidence demonstrates that sustained systemic crisis explains the radical nature of change. Crisis shapes radical institutional change by exposing the inadequacy of existing institutions or the absence of needed institutions and consequently forcing human actors to transform their mental models. In the case under scrutiny, the transformation of mental models manifested itself in the rationale for introducing cost accounting, launching the Work Emulation Campaign, expanding social service and welfare institutions, and developing the ideology of the developmental state. The transformed mental models, then, led the Nationalist elite to reorder their institutional environment, an endeavor that ultimately gave rise to the formation of a new state enterprise system. In other words, institutional change is not only path-dependent but path-independent because new resources must be created to overcome the constraints of institutional endowments.

APPENDIX: TABLES

ABBREVIATIONS

NOTES

INDEX

Appendix: Tables

Table 1.1. Name, location, relocation process, and the original name of sixteen ordnance factories and units, April 1941

Name of arsenal	Location	Relocation process	Original name
First Arsenal	Chongqing, Sichuan	Hanyang—Chenxi—Chongqing	Hanyang Arsenal
Second Arsenal	Chongqing, Sichuan	Hanyang—Chenxi—Chongqing	Hanyang Powder Plant
Tenth Arsenal	Chongqing, Sichuan	Zhuzhou—Chongqing	Research Division of Artillery Technology
Eleventh Arsenal	Chongqing, Sichuan	Gongxian—Changsha—Chongqing	Gongxian Arsenal
Twentieth Arsenal	Chongqing, Sichuan	Existing Chongqing Arsenal	Sichuan First Arsenal
Twenty-first Arsenal	Chongqing, Sichuan	Nanjing—Chongqing	Jinling Arsenal
Twenty-second Arsenal	Kunming, Yunnan	Nanjing—Kunming	Military Optical Instrument Plant
Twenty-third Arsenal	Luxian, Sichuan	Gongxian—Luxian	Gongxian Branch Arsenal
Twenty-fourth Arsenal	Chongqing, Sichuan	Existing Chongqing Arsenal	Chongqing Steel Plant
Twenty-fifth Arsenal	Chongqing, Sichuan	Zhuzhou—Chongqing	Cartridge Plant of the Research Division of Artillery Technology
Thirtieth Arsenal	Chongqing, Sichuan	Jinan—Chongqing	Jinan Arsenal
Fortieth Arsenal	Chongqing, Sichuan	Liuzhou—Chongqing	Guangxi First Arsenal
Forty-first Arsenal	Tongzi, Guizhou	Guangzhou—Rongxian—Tongzi	Guangdong First Arsenal
Forty-second Arsenal	Zunyi, Guizhou	Guangzhou—Liuzhou—Zunyi	Guangzhou Mask Arsenal
Forty-fourth Arsenal	Guiyang, Guizhou	Nanjing—Hengyang—Guiyang	Central Weapon Repair Shop[a]
Fiftieth Arsenal	Chongqing, Sichuan	Qingyuan—Chongqing	Guangdong Second Arsenal

Source: ZJBGDS, vol. 3, 245; Lu Dayue and Tang Runming, *Kangzhan shiqi chongqing de bingqi gongye* (The ordnance industry in Chongqing during the Sino-Japanese War) (Chongqing: Chongqing Chubanshe, 1995), 55–56.

a. The Central Weapon Repair Shop became the Central Weapon Repair Factory in the spring of 1940. The Bureau of Ordnance redesignated it as the Forty-fourth Arsenal only in July 1943. See ZJBGDS, vol. 3, 1253–1254.

Table 1.2. Comparison of increase in output of the Twenty-first Arsenal, 1927–1945

Name of product	Output		Absolute increase	Percentage increase
	1927–1937	1938–1945		
Light machine gun	—	9,833	9,833	—
Hand grenade	—	311,500	311,500	—
79mm rifle	—	206,864	206,864	—
Zhongzheng rifle	—	86,500	86,500	—
Heavy machine gun	3,904	18,068	14,164	363
82mm mortar	1,100	7,011	5,911	537
82mm mortar shell	516,080	3,212,252	2,596,172	421

Source: "Diershiyi gongchang changshi" (History of the Twenty-first Arsenal), in ZJBGDS, vol. 3, 1199–1207.

Table 1.3. Annual appropriations for the National Resources Commission (NRC) and its share in the state budget, 1936–1945 (in Ch$ thousands)

Year	Annual state budget	Appropriations for NRC	Share by NRC (%)	Multiple of 1936 price each year	NRC expenditure in 1936 prices
1936	1,334,873	5,493	0.4	1.0	5,493
1937	1,511,293	18,682	1.2	1.1	16,984
1938	963,329[a]	9,998[a]	1.0	1.5	6,665
1939	1,892,269	23,615	1.2	3.0	7,872[b]
1940	2,600,000	74,058	2.8	8.0	9,257
1941	10,732,584	232,300	2.2	21.0	11,062
1942	28,283,312	454,060	1.6	64.0	7,095
1943	57,400,000	508,300	0.9	249.0	2,041
1944	149,300,000	1,344,339	0.9	773.0	1,739
1945	1,363,600,000	9,251,073	0.7	2,565.0	3,607

Source: FYZWGS, 1948, 38–39; ZMDZH, part v, vol. 3, caizheng jingji, no. 5, 98.
a. Budget figure for half a fiscal year.
b. Original error in addition corrected.

Table 1.4. Output of selected ordnance products, 1940–1945

Name of product	1940	1941	1942	1943	1944	1945
Rifle	54,510	39,000	59,200	66,831	76,800	130,000
Machine gun	4,306	4,820	8,290	12,331	14,340	20,400
82mm mortar	900	500	760	1,381	1,680	2,400
7.9mm cartridge	113,878,000	120,584,580	140,010,340	144,050,000	175,200,000	252,000,000
75mm artillery shell	61,614	23,072	62,956	119,638	144,000	144,000
82mm mortar shell	641,900	413,661	545,192	715,979	780,000	1,300,000
Hand grenade	3,700,000	5,759,000	4,697,000	2,733,000	3,840,000	4,800,000

Source: The figures for the period between 1940 and 1943 are from the table of output figures compiled by the Bureau of Ordnance in 1944 (ZJBGDS, vol. 3, 426). The figures for 1944 are estimates based on the actual output for September 1944 (see ibid., 427–428). The figures for 1945 are mostly from the output figures compiled by the War Production Bureau in 1945 (see ibic., 435). Figures for the output of 75mm artillery shells for 1945 are estimates based on the monthly output on the eve of victory in 1945 (see ibid., 131–133).

Table 1.5. Output of government arsenals and proportion of increase, 1936–1945

Name of product	1936	1945	Increase
Rifle	98,948	130,000	1.3
Machine gun	1,006	20,400	20.3
82mm mortar	565	2,400	4.3
7.9mm cartridge	127,764,000	252,000,000	2.0
75mm artillery shell	91,126	144,000	1.6
82mm mortar shell	247,840	1,300,000	5.3
Hand grenade	1,976,900	4,800,000	2.4

Source: For 1936 figures, see output statistics compiled by the Bureau of Ordnance in April 1937, in ZJBGDS, vol. 3, 425. Figures for 1945 are from Table 1.4.

Table 1.6. Monthly average of the number of weapons and ammunition lost or damaged, produced, and replaced, 1937–1945

Name of product	Number lost or damaged	Number produced	Percentage of produced vs. lost	Actual number replaced
Rifle	8,368	5,675	68	10,450
Light machine gun	515	444	86	890
Heavy machine gun	119	195	164	247
Mortar	59	144	244	182
Mortar shell	62,997	62,411	99	77,150
Cartridge	17,811,666	11,151,648	63	24,579,150
Grenade launcher	267	877	328	911
Hand and other grenades	245,821	352,579	143	349,725

Source: Huang Liren, "Kangri zhanzheng shiqi zhongguo bingqi gongye neiqian chulun" (The relocation of China's ordnance industry during the Sino-Japanese War), in Huang Liren, *Kangzhan shiqi dahoufang jingjishi yanjiu, 1937–1945* [*A study of the economic history of the interior provinces during the Sino-Japanese War, 1937–1945*] (Beijing: Zhongguo dangan chubanshe, 1998), 142.

Note: "Replaced" indicates the number produced plus the number purchased from abroad.

Table 2.1. Annual appropriations for National Resources Commission and distribution by industry, 1938–1940 (in Ch$ thousands)

Year	Energy	Iron-steel	Fuel	Electric	Chemical	Machine	Reserve fund	Grand total	In 1936 prices
1938	1,170	3,692	783	1,129	160	1,060	6	8,000	5,333
1939	4,100	5,200	1,450	2,000	1,530	1,600	120	16,000	5,333
1940	6,050	2,350	3,450	1,430	2,850	1,540	330	18,000	2,250
Total	11,320	11,242	5,683	4,559	4,540	4,200	456	42,000	12,916
Percentage of grand total	26.95%	26.77%	13.53%	10.85%	10.81%	10.00%	1.09%	100%	

Source: Figures for 1938 and 1939 are from "Ziyuan weiyuanhui ershiba niandu gaisuanshu" (Budgetary estimates of the National Resources Commission for 1939 fiscal year) and "Xiuzheng ershiba niandu zhonggongye shiyefei gaisuan shuomingshu" (Explanation of revised expenditure figures of heavy industry budgetary estimates for 1939 fiscal year), SHA 4/17888. Figures for 1940 are from "Ziyuan weiyuanhui ershijiu niandu zhonggongye jingfei juban geshiye jihua gaiyao" (Outline of the revised plan for various undertakings by the National Resources Commission for 1940 fiscal year), SHA 4/15262.

Table 2.2. Allocations to the National Resources Commission's Special Fund for Heavy Industrial Reconstruction (SFHIR) as a percentage of Special Fund for Reconstruction Projects (SFRP), 1937–1944 (in Ch$ thousands)

Year	National budget	Allocations to SFRP	Share of SFRP in national budget (percent)	Allocations to SFHIR	Share of SFHIR in SFRP (percent)
1937	1,511,293	442,000	29.25	9,976	2.2
1938	963,329[a]	258,000	26.78	8,603[a]	3.33
1939	1,892,269	772,000	40.80	12,968	1.68
1940	2,600,000	1,309,124	50.35	84,691	6.47
1941	10,732,584	2,221,162	20.70	221,086	9.95
1942	28,283,312	5,736,778	20.28	438,291	7.64
1943	57,400,000	15,141,713	26.38	362,610	2.39
1944	149,300,000	18,653,104	12.49	918,790	4.93
1945	1,252,900,000	176,500,000	4.09	—	—

Source: Figures for the Special Fund for Reconstruction Projects for 1937 through 1939, are from Kong Xiangxi, "Zuijin caizheng shikuang" (Recent financial conditions), June 1939, and marked as "extremely secret," in ZMDZH, part v, vol. 2, caizheng jingji, no. 1, 342–375; the figure for 1940 is from "Guomin zhengfu shenjibu yijiusiling niandu zhongyang zhengfu suiru suichu juesuan shencha baogao" (Report by the Auditing Ministry on the general national budget of revenue and expenditure for 1940 fiscal year), in ibid., 251–256; figures for 1941 and 1942 are from a tabulation of the general national budget from 1937 to 1944, in ibid., 312–315; the figure for 1943 is from "Guoming zhengfu yijiusisan niandu guojia zongjuesuan zongshuomingshu (A general explanation of the general national budget for 1943 fiscal year), in ibid., 273–276; the figure for 1944 is from Kong Xiangxi's report on general national budget for 1944 fiscal year, in ibid., 277–286; the figure for 1945 is from the oral report by the minister of the Ministry of Financial Affairs dated February 2, 1946, in ZMDZH, part v, vol. 3, caizheng jingji, no. 1, 315–320. Figures for the Special Fund for Heavy Industrial Reconstruction for 1936 through 1943 are from "Ziyuan weiyuanhui touzi shumubiao" (Tabulation of investment capital by the National Resources Commission), SHA 282(2)/415; the figure for 1944 is extracted from National Resources Commission's budget tabulation from 1936 through 1946, SHA 28/2361.

a. Budget figure for half of the fiscal year (July 1–December 30, 1938).

231

Table 2.3. Capital distribution and investment priority by industry, 1936–1944 (in Ch$ thousands)

Year	Petroleum	Energy	Iron-steel	Electric	Coal	Machine	Metal	Chemical	Other	Cement	Grand total
1936	233	148	640	2,285	344	1,002	674	45	126	—	5,497[a]
1937	431	2,344	4,400	2,820	2,348	3,500	1,320	596	928	—	18,687[a]
1938	458	1,621	961	1,169	695	1,060	3,793	235	6	—	9,998
1939	2,556	6,946	1,474	2,250	1,441	1,600	5,463	1,680	205	—	23,615
1940	11,949	16,298	10,490	7,926	4,421	8,119	5,707	5,920	1,678	1,100	73,608[b]
1941	87,664	36,433	46,879	14,471	6,915	14,835	8,970	13,241	2,043	700	232,151[c]
1942	193,350	59,315	106,820	21,350	13,490	17,800	14,500	18,350	7,335	1,750	454,060
1943	220,200	87,640	72,700	36,900	11,150	40,260	19,450	17,500	2,500	—	508,300
1944	573,500	223,923	89,620	131,555	149,720	43,994	65,786	30,373	34,267	1,600	1,344,339
Total	1,090,341	434,668	333,984	220,726	190,524	132,170	125,663	87,940	49,088	5,150	2,670,254
Percentage of grand total	40.83%	16.28%	12.51%	8.27%	7.14%	4.95%	4.71%	3.29%	1.84%	0.19%	100%

Source: FYZWGS, 1948, 40; ZMDZH, part v, vol. 3, caizheng jingji, no. 5, 99.

a. Original error in addition connected.

b. The sum of Ch$450,000 for the sugar industry for the 1940 fiscal year appears in the original table but is not included in the total figures here.

c. The sum of Ch$150,000 for the sugar industry for the 1941 fiscal year appears in the original table but is not included in the total figures here, and the total investment figure for the ten-year period does not include the Ch$150,000 invested in sugar industry. Other than this Ch$600,000 investment, the National Resources Commission did not make significant investment in light industry during the war.

Table 2.4. Comparison of output between the Dadukou Iron and Steel Works (DISW) and total output of other enterprises of the National Resources Commission (NRC), 1940–1945 (in metric tons)

Year	Pig iron			Steel ingots and other steel products		
	NRC output	DISW output	Percentage by DISW	NRC output	DISW output	Percentage by DISW
1940	2,494	2,932	118.10	—	—	—
1941	4,437	4,441	100.09	116	113	97.41
1942	13,469	12,170	90.36	1,506	2,201	146.15
1943	20,853	11,699	56.10	4,646	5,313	114.36
1944	12,523	2,255	18.01	7,603	9,201	121.02
1945	22,556	524	2.32	10,206	8,323	81.55
Total	76,332	34,021	44.57%	24,077	25,151	104.46%

Source: Wang Ziyou, "Kangzhan banianlai zhi woguo gangtie gongye" (China's iron and steel industry during the Sino-Japanese War), ZWY 6, no. 1/2 (June 1946): 86–106; ZJGZ-C, vol. 3, part 2. 885.

233

Table 2.5. Number of factories, workers, and amount of capital in different industrial sectors, 1937

Industry	Number of factories	Percentage	Capital (Ch$ thousands)	Percentage	Number of workers	Percentage
Hydro-electric	119	3.06	59,808	15.83	5,377	1.18
Metallurgical	60	1.55	2,619	0.70	4,671	1.02
Machine	340	8.75	3,677	0.97	10,196	2.23
Electric	58	1.49	2,678	0.71	4,534	0.99
Ordnance	3	0.08	423	0.11	316	0.07
Chemical	708	18.22	47,998	12.70	47,131	10.31
Food processing	920	23.68	48,373	12.80	23,398	5.12
Textile	833	21.44	135,877	35.96	259,686	56.80
Other	844	21.73	76,395	20.22	101,834	22.28
Total	3,885	100.00%	377,848	100.00%	457,143	100.00%

Source: Weng Wenhao, "Zhongguo gongshang jingji de huigu yu qianzhan" (The retrospect and prospect of Chinese industrial and commercial economy), ZWG 5, no. 2 (August 16, 1943): 59–68; Huang Bingwei, "Wushi nianlai zhi zhongguo gongkuangye" (Chinese economy in the last fifty years), WNZZI, 173.

Table 2.6. Number of factories and workers, amount of capital, and horsepower of public enterprises in heavy industries and the transportation industry, 1935

Industry	Number of factories	Capital (Ch$)	Number of workers	Power (horsepower)	Output value
Metallurgical	4	860,106	5,050	464	1,547,542
Metal	1	4,961,082	948	—	49,180,647
Machine	4	340,000	856	191	470,212
Energy	8	6,159,804	1,404	22,721	2,167,322
Railroad machinery	27	—	15,432	9,201	4,797,434
Transportation equipment	7	5,754,987	3,276	592	3,707,674
Total	51	18,075,979	26,966	33,169	61,870,831

Source: ZMTT, table 50, p. 85.

Table 2.7. Comparison of public and private enterprise in heavy industries in the mid-1930s

Nature of enterprise	Number of factories	Percentage	Amount of capital	Percentage	Number of workers	Percentage
Public enterprise	17	2.9	12,320,992	17.81	8,258	32.9
Private enterprise	563	97.1	56,884,008	82.2	16,836	67.1
Total	580	100%	69,205,000	100%	25,094	100%

Source: Figures for public enterprises are adapted from data contained in Table 2.6. Figures for private enterprises are derived through calculations based on data contained in Tables 2.5 and 2.6. It is reasonable to assume that the 17 heavy industrial enterprises contained in Table 2.6 were among the 580 heavy industrial enterprises described in Table 2.5.

Table 2.8. Comparison of public and private enterprise in heavy industries in 1942

Industry	Number of factories			Amount of capital			Number of workers			Power equipment (horsepower)		
	Total	Public	Private	Total	Public	Private	Total	Public	Private	Total	Public	Private
Hydro-electric	123	60	63	143,414,236	127,601,056	15,813,180	4,618	2,519	2,099	51,213	20,738	30,475
Metal-lurgical	155	44	111	302,319,526	274,891,732	27,427,794	17,404	6,657	10,747	9,659	8,351	1,308
Metal	160	7	153	23,304,200	700,000	22,604,200	8,291	1,791	6,500	2,064	1,107	957
Machine	682	50	632	337,597,611	246,555,588	91,042,023	31,541	9,991	21,550	16,077	7,534	8,543
Electric	98	23	75	93,044,850	81,547,650	11,497,200	7,197	4,985	2,212	8,561	7,158	1,403
Total	1,218	184	1,034	899,680,423	731,296,026	168,384,397	69,051	25,943	43,108	87,574	44,888	42,686

Source: HGGT, 11.

Table 2.9. Comparison of public and private enterprise in average capital, number of workers, and power equipment in heavy industries, 1942

Industry	Amount of capital		Number of workers		Power equipment (horsepower)	
	Public	Private	Public	Private	Public	Private
Hydro-electric	2,126,684	251,003	42	33	346	484
Metallurgical	6,247,539	247,097	151	97	190	12
Metal	100,000	147,740	256	42	158	6
Machine	4,931,111	144,025	200	34	151	14
Electric	3,545,550	153,296	217	29	311	19
Average	3,390,177	188,632	173	47	231	107

Note: Calculation is based on figures contained in Table 2.8.

Table 2.10a. Increase of output of major products in heavy industries and the share of public enterprise in the increase, 1938–1941 (calculation of value of output based on 1933 constant prices)

Products	Units	1938 Output	1938 Public percentage	1939 Output	1939 Public percentage	1940 Output	1940 Public percentage	1941 Output	1941 Public percentage
Coal	Thousand tons	4,700	15.0	5,500	8.0	5,700	9.40	6,000	15.60
Pig iron	Tons	52,900	5.8	62,730	7.8	45,000	11.5	63,637	15.2
Steel	Tons	900	20.0	1,200	30.0	1,500	41.0	2,011	54.2
Petroleum	Tons	75	100.0	559	100.0	1,662	100.0	12,984	100.0
Electricity	Kilowatt-hours	73,622	5.5	91,494	10.5	11,931	10.0	127,302	13.80
Gas	Thousand gallons	—	—	4.2	100.0	73.5	100.0	209.3	100.0
Alcohol	Thousand gallons	304	25.0	812	36.0	4,590	30.0	6,157	27.0
Tin	Tons	15,440	40.0	14,244	50.0	17,416	50.0	16,589	60.0
Mercury	Tons	72	100.0	170	100.0	215	100.0	216	100.0
Copper	Tons	580	100.0	582	100.0	1,415	100.0	779	100.0
Lead	Tons	1,680	100.0	288	100.0	1,800	100.0	1,266	100.0
Zinc	Tons	600	100.0	122	100.0	250	100.0	214	100.0
Average			55.6		61.9		62.7		65.5

Source: Wu Taichang, "Kangzhan shiqi guomindang guojia ziben zai gongkuangye de longduan diwei jiqi yu minying ziben bijiao" (The monopolistic position of the Nationalist state capital in industry and mining and its comparison with private capital during the Sino-Japanese War), *Zhongguo jingjishi yanjiu* (Study in Chinese economic history) 3 (September 1987): 133–150.

Table 2.10b. Increase of output of major products in heavy industries and the share of public enterprise in the increase, 1942–1945 (value of output based on 1933 constant prices)

Products	Units	1942		1943		1944		1945	
		Output	Public percentage	Output	Public percentage	Output	Public percentage	Output	Public percentage
Coal	Thousand tons	6,314	18.7	6,617	23.7	5,502	25.0	5,238	25.0
Pig iron	Tons	96,000	25.7	70,000	51.0	40,134	56.0	48,495	64.8
Steel	Tons	3,000	81.0	6,800	91.7	13,361	92.0	18,234	96.4
Petroleum	Tons	60,888	100.0	67,035	100.0	75,723	100.0	72,336	100.0
Electricity	Kilowatt-hours	136,850	18.0	146,437	24.0	154,220	33.8	196,695	36.0
Gas	Thousand gallons	1,896	100.0	3,220	100.0	4,048	100.0	4,305	100.0
Alcohol	Thousand gallons	9,352	37.6	10,715	45.0	10,731	43.0	16,222	42.0
Tin	Tons	14,003	65.0	10,800	70.0	5,102	85.0	2,704	95.0
Mercury	Tons	311	100.0	226	100.0	224	100.0	125	100.0
Copper	Tons	693	100.0	613	100.0	898	100.0	623	100.0
Lead	Tons	1,134	100.0	1,200	100.0	646	100.0	567	100.0
Zinc	Tons	396	100.0	500	100.0	331	100.0	328	100.0
Average			70.5		75.4		77.9		79.9

Source: Same as Table 2.10a.

Table 3.1. Rank, class within a given rank, and salary in the Five Yuan (branches of government) and various ministries and commissions, 1936

Rank	Class	Monthly salary (Ch$ yuan)	Examples
1st rank, *teren* (special appointment)		800	Head of ministries (*buzhang*) Chairman of commissions (*weiyuanzhang*)
2nd rank, *jianren* (selected appointment)	1	680	Deputy minister (*cizhang*)
	2	640	Vice chairman of commissions (*fu weiyuanzhang*)
	3	600	
	4	560	Secretary-general (*mushuzhang*)
	5	520	
	6	490	Bureau chief (*shuzhang*)
	7	460	Department head (*sizhang, tingzhang*)
	8	430	
3rd rank, *jianren* (recommended appointment)	1	400	Secretary (*mishu*)
	2	380	Department head (*kezhang*)
	3	360	
	4	340	Chief engineer (*jizheng*)
	5	320	
	6	300	Department staff (*jianren keyuan*)
	7	280	

241

Table 3.1 (*continued*)

Rank	Class	Monthly salary (Ch$ yuan)	Examples
	8	260	
	9	240	
	10	220	
	11	200	
	12	180	
4th rank, *weiren*	1	200	Associate engineer (*jishi*)
(delegated appointment)	2	180	Assistant engineer (*jizuo*)
	3	160	
	4	140	Clerk (*Shujiyuan*)
	5	130	
	6	120	Office worker (*banshiyuan*)
	7	110	
	8	100	
	9	90	
	10	85	
	11	80	
	12	75	
	13	70	
	14	65	
	15	60	
	16	55	

Source: Adapted from "Zhanxing wenguan guandeng guanfengbiao" (Illustration of official rank and salary at all levels of government) promulgated on September 23, 1933; revised on September 23, 1936, in GZZZDSZ, vol. 2, 54–55.

Table 3.2. Expansion of bureaucratic organization in an ordance factory by 1943

Factory Director	
	Welfare Division
	School for Employees' Children
	Farm
General Office	Hospital
Security Guard Unit	Training Department
Security Inspection Team	Supply Department
Warehouse of Finished Product	
Transportation Department	
Maintenance Department	Technology Division
Accounts Receivable and Payable	Experiment Workshop
Purchasing Department	Laboratory
General Affairs Department	Inspection Department
Personnel Department	Planning Office
Correspondence Department	
	Work Affairs Division
	Vocational School
Accounting Division	Material Warehouse
Auditing Department	Work Allocation Department
Payroll Department	Work Preparation Department
Cost Calculation Department	Manufacturing Plants (a total of 10)
Bookkeeping Department	

Source: "Binggongshu binggongchang zuzhi xitongbiao" (Illustration of the organizational structure for ordnance factories of the Bureau of Ordnance), April 6, 1943, in ZJBGDS, vol. 3, 246–248.

Table 3.3. Organizational structure of the Twenty-first Arsenal as of February 1948

Factory Director

General Office
Correspondence Department
Personnel Department
General Affairs Department
Purchasing Department
Maintenance Department
Accounts Receivable and Payable
Night School
Warehouse for Finished Product
Ninghe Middle School
Transportation Team
First Primary School
Security Inspection Team
Branches of First Primary School
Security Guard Unit
Eleventh Vocational School

Accounting Division
Auditing Department
Payroll Department
Cost Calculation Department
Bookkeeping Department

Welfare Division
Training Department
Supply Department
Hospital
Accounting Office
Farm
Grain Mill
Consumer Cooperative

Work Affairs Division
Inspection Department
Material Department
Business Department
Operation Department
Power Plant
Machine Plant
Heavy Machine Gun Plant
Other Manufacturing Plants (a total of 14)

Source: "Binggongshu di ershiyi gongchang zuzhi xitongbiao" (Illustration of the organizational structure of the Twenty-first Arsenal), February 1948, in ZJBGDS, vol. 3, 1199–1210.

Table 3.4. Rank, class within a given rank, and salary for selected employees of the National Resources Commission n.d.

Rank	Class	Monthly salary (Ch$ yuan)	Examples
1st rank, *teren* (special appointment)		800	
2nd rank, *jianren* (selected appointment)	1	680	Director (*zhuren weiyuan*)
	2	640	Deputy director (*fu zhuren weiyuan*)
	3	600	
	4	560	Chief secretary (*zhuren mishu*)
	5	520	
	6	490	
	7	460	
	8	430	
3rd rank, *jianren* (recommended appointment)	1	400	Department head (*kezhang*)
	2	380	
	3	360	Chief engineer (*jizheng*)
	4	340	
	5	320	
	6	300	
	7	280	
	8	260	
	9	240	
	10	220	

Table 3.4 (*continued*)

Rank	Class	Monthly salary (Ch$ yuan)	Examples
	11	200	
	12	180	
4th rank, *weiren* (delegated appointment)	1	200	Department staff (*keyuan*)
	2	180	Associate engineer (*jishi*)
	3	160	
	4	140	Assistant engineer (*jizuo*)
	5	130	
	6	120	Office worker (*banshiyuan*)
	7	110	
	8	100	
	9	90	
	10	85	
	11	80	
	12	75	
	13	70	
	14	65	
	15	60	
	16	55	

Source: Adapted from ZWFH, vol. 2, 1–3.

Table 3.5. Organizational structure of Dadukou Iron and Steel Works, 1942

Accounting Division	Welfare Division
Auditing Department	Farm
Payroll Department	Hospital
Coast Calculation Department	School for Employees' Children
Bookkeeping Department	Library
	Real Estate Department
Secretariat	Hygiene Department
Accounts Receivable and Payable	Training Department
Personnel Department	Supply Department
Statistics Department	
Correspondence Department	Purchasing Division
	Transportation Team
Work Affairs Division	Quarry
Work Allocation Department	Printing Shop
Work Preparation Department	Investigation Department
Materials Warehouse	Purchasing Department
	Business Affairs Department
Office of Chief Engineer	
Research Department	Construction Engineering Division
Planning Department	Planning Department
Physical Laboratory	Construction Department
Chemical Laboratory	Maintenance Department

Source: CMA, 0105/2777; KHYGS. 81.

Table 3.6. Organizational structure of Gansu Petroleum Administration, September 1941

Office of Accounting
Examination Department
Payroll Department
Cost Calculation Department

Secretariat
Business Department
Personnel Department
Correspondence Department

Work Affairs Division
Work Station
Work Affairs Department
Materials Department
Purchasing Department
Correspondence Department

Transportation Division
Transportation Station
Inspection Department
Supply Department
Maintenance Department
Transportation Department
Correspondence Department

Finance Division
Accounts Payable
Receivable and
Management Department

General Affairs Division
Security Unit
General Affairs Department
Transportation Department
Welfare Department
School for Employees' Children
Hospital and Clinics
Correspondence Department

Electric Machinery Division
Electric Machinery Plants
Planning Department
Materials Department
Correspondence Department

Construction Engineering Division
Construction Workshops
Survey and Drawing Department
Materials Department
Correspondence Department

Source: "Gansu youkuangju zhanxing zuzhi zhangcheng" (Provisional organizational regulations of Gansu Petroleum Administration), September 28, 1941, ZWG 1, no. 4 (October 16, 1941): 51–52.

Table 3.7. Rank, class within a given rank, and salary of all DISW *zhiyuan* in December 1940

Rank	Number in each rank	Class	Number in each class	Monthly salary (Ch$ yuan)	Number in salary rank
1st rank, *teren* (special appointment)	0		0	800	0
2nd rank, *jianren* (selected appointment)	9	1	0	680	0
		2	0	640	0
		3	1	600	1
		4	0	560	0
		5	0	520	0
		6	2	490	2
		7	1	460	1
		8	5	430	5
3rd rank, *jianren* (recommended appointment)	47	1	3	400	3
		2	3	380	3
		3	4	360	4
		4	3	340	3
		5	4	320	4
		6	0	300	0
		7	4	280	4
		8	2	260	2
		9	7	240	7
		10	12	220	12
		11	5	200	5
		12	0	180	—

249

Table 3.7 (*continued*)

Rank	Number in each rank	Class	Number in each class	Monthly salary (Ch$ yuan)	Number in salary rank
4th rank, *weiren* (delegated appointment)	329	1	4	200	4
		2	16	180	16
		3	9	160	9
		4	13	140	13
		5	6	130	6
		6	21	120	21
		7	19	110	19
		8	44	100	44
		9	23	90	23
		10	7	85	7
		11	46	80	46
		12	13	75	13
		13	29	70	29
		14	18	65	18
		15	47	60	47
		16	14	55	14
Below rank	136	No class	136	20–50	136

Source: "Ziyuan weiyuanhui zhiyuan xinfeng biaozhun" (Salary standard for *zhiyuan* of the National Resources Commission), November 1941, in KHYGS, 699; "Gangqianhui kaoji zhanxing guize" (DISW's provisional regulations for assessing job performance), December 28, 1941, in ibid., 684–685; "Gangtiechang qianjian weiyuanhui ershijiunian di zaizhi renyuan xingeibiao" (Complete payroll list of all *zhiyuan* of the DISW at the end of 1940), CMA 0201/104.

Note: The DISW director and a few others were not listed on the payroll. Consequently I have not been able to determine their ranks. The figures for the number of people in each class are the same as the ones for the number of people in salary rank, because a *zhiyuan*'s class determines his or her salary.

Table 3.8. Comparison of educational level of all *zhiyuan* in the DISW and its subsidiary factories and collieries, 1943–1944

Units	Year	Percentage of college graduates	Percentage of high school graduates	Percentage of junior high school graduates
Central Administration	1943	29.02	46.69	24.28
	1944	34.00	26.16	39.84
Nantong Colliery	1943	28.00	6.76	64.25
	1944	30.67	6.13	63.20
Jijiang Iron Mine	1943	31.01	13.18	55.81
	1944	38.71	17.21	44.08
Division of Jijiang Waterway	1943	15.00	25.00	60.00
	1944	21.00	28.00	51.00
Dajian Branch Plant	1943	26.74	45.34	27.90
	1944	29.10	40.70	30.20
Division of Railroad Construction	1943	26.22	29.50	44.26
	1944	30.00	30.00	40.00
Manganese Mine	1943	21.21	36.36	42.43
	1944	20.83	33.34	45.80
Total	1943	27.35	33.76	38.87
	1944	31.70	26.20	42.10

Source: "Sanshi sanniandu mishuchu gongzuo baogao" (Work report by the secretariat for the 1944 fiscal year), *Taosheng* (Crashing waves), special new-year issue, January 1, 1945, 10–13, CMA 0202/552.

Table 3.9. Name, official title, and educational background of fifteen cadres of the DISW as of September 1945

Name	Official title	Educational background
Yang Jizeng	DISW's Director	University of Berlin, Germany, mechanical engineering
Lu Xunran	DISW's Associate Director	German university, mining
Liang Qiang	Chief Secretary	Imperial University, Japan, civil engineering
Tong Zhicheng	Head, Welfare Division	French university, chemical engineering
Yang Junya	Head, Accounting Division	Fudan University, China, accounting
Li Zhongqiang	Head, Purchasing Division	Beijing University, China, mining and metallurgy
Meng Xianting	Head, Work Affairs Division	Tongji University, China, mechanical engineering
Weng Dexin	DISW's Chief Engineer	University of Glasgow, Scotland, mechanical engineering
Chen Dong	Director, 1st Manufacturing Plant	Nanyang University, China, electrical engineering
Chen Qia	Director, 2nd Manufacturing Plant	Japanese university, industrial engineering
Zhou Ziding	Director, 3rd Manufacturing Plant	Tangshan Engineering Institute, China, mining
Xu Jize	Director, 4th Manufacturing Plant	Communications University, China, electrical engineering
Sun Xiangpeng	Director, 5th Manufacturing Plant	Berlin Industrial University, mechanical engineering
Lu Futang	Director, 7th Manufacturing Plant	Communications University, China, electrical engineering
Han Zhaoqi	Director, Transportation Plant	Tangshan Communications University, mechanical engineering

Source: "Gangqianhui zhuguan renyuan minglu" (A roster of chief officials of the DISW), in KHYGS, 85.

Table 4.1. DISW earnings (+) and deficits (−), January–December 1945 (in Ch$)

Month	Production units	Service units	Management units	Income statement
January	Monthly −17,950,263 Cumulative N/A	Monthly −4,378,764 Cumulative N/A	Monthly −5,612,313	Monthly −27,941,340
February	Monthly +33,403,607 Cumulative +15,453,394	Monthly −420,284 Cumulative −3,948,467	Monthly −8,315,086	Monthly +25,508,808
March	Monthly +37,683,903 Cumulative +40,773,793	Monthly +1,588,702 Cumulative −2,409,765	Monthly −10,526,055	Monthly +28,696,550
April	Monthly −46,456,467 Cumulative −5,682,674	Monthly −8,747,860 Cumulative −11,157,625	Monthly −17,224,102	Monthly −72,428,431
May	Monthly −28,912,372 Cumulative −40,646,905	Monthly +5,079,405 Cumulative −6,663,000	Monthly −33,491,865 Cumulative −75,169,426	Monthly −57,324,832
June	Monthly −183,382,006 Cumulative −225,944,112	Monthly +1,033,130 Cumulative −5,045,094	Monthly −21,310,068 Cumulative −127,537,420	Monthly −203,658,944
July	Monthly +438,245,603 Cumulative +214,291,491	Monthly +11,846,456 Cumulative +6,801,362	Monthly −28,448,845 Cumulative −155,355,266	Monthly +421,643,214

Table 4.1 (*continued*)

Month	Production units	Service units	Management units	Income statement
August	Monthly −82,474,881 Cumulative +132,016,610	Monthly +6,969,899 Cumulative +13,798,261	Monthly −31,299,005 Cumulative −187,281,271	Monthly −105,776,987
September	Monthly +2,361,433 Cumulative +134,378,024	Monthly −3,011,156 Cumulative +10,757,104	Monthly −41,645,141 Cumulative −227,418,278	Monthly −42,322,864
October	Monthly −23,711,335 Cumulative +110,666,688	Monthly +4,129,476 Cumulative +14,886,581	Monthly −36,957,034 Cumulative −265,884,447	Monthly −56,538,893
November	Monthly −11,777,714 Cumulative +98,888,974	Monthly −3,971,940 Cumulative +10,914,640	Monthly −40,525,086 Cumulative −306,409,533	Monthly −56,274,741
December	Monthly −15,163,954 Cumulative +83,725,019	Monthly −25,348,592 Cumulative −14,433,952	Monthly −43,881,648 Cumulative −350,291,181	Monthly −84,394,195

Source: Mishuchu tongbao (Bulletin of the secretariat): no. 476, March 15, 1945, CMA 0105/376; no. 493, April 5, 1945, CMA 0105/376; no. 516, May 2, 1945, CMA 0105/377; no. 540, May 28, 1945, CMA 0105/377; no. 572, July 3, 1945, CMA 0105/377; no. 602, August 7, 1945, CMA 0105/378; no. 646, September 29, 1945, CMA 0105/378; no. 667, October 25, 1945, CMA 0105/378; no. 698, December 1, 1945, CMA 0105/378; no. 713, December 19, 1945, CMA 0105/379; no. 741, January 21, 1946, CMA 0105/379; no. 777, March 7, 1946, CMA 0105/379. Original figures in all categories are used as they appear in the archives, despite certain obvious errors in calculation.

Table 5.1. Index for retail market price, cost of living, and wages for industrial workers in Chongqing, 1937–1945

Year	Month	Retail market price	Cost of living	Workers' real wages
1937	July	1.01	1.03	1.02
	December	1.14	1.10	1.02
1938	July	1.23	1.21	1.55
	December	1.57	1.41	1.55
1939	July	1.91	1.87	1.18
	December	2.82	2.82	1.18
1940	July	5.33	4.92	0.80
	December	11.12	12.70	0.80
1941	July	14.97	22.10	0.55
	December	26.79	31.80	0.55
1942	July	48.30	46.00	0.50
	December	69.50	68.20	0.50
1943	July	105.00	119.00	0.42
	December	199.00	205.00	0.42
1944	July	422.00	505.00	0.43
	December	651.00	588.00	0.43
1945	July	1763.00	1679.00	0.37
	December	2415.00	2033.00	0.37

Source: The index for retail market price and cost of living is from Arthur N. Young, *China's Wartime Finance and Inflation, 1937–1945* (Cambridge, Mass.: Harvard University Press, 1965), appe. B. tables 51 and 52. The index for workers' real wages is adapted from "Zhanshi Chongqing gongren shenghuofei zhishu ji gongzi zhishu" (The cost of living and wage indexes for workers in wartime Chongqing), in ZMDZH, part v, vol. 3, caizheng jingji, no. 4, 205. (The base is January–June = 1 for all three indexes.)

Abbreviations

CMA   Chongqing Municipal Archives, Chongqing, China.

CN   Chonggang nianjian (The 1994 yearbook of Chongqing Iron and Steel Corporation). Chengdu: Sichuan kexue jishu chubanshe, 1995.

CWZ   Chongqing wenshi ziliao (Collection of Chongqing historical materials), 1978–? Chongqingshi zhengzhi xieshang huiyi wenshi ziliao weiyuanhui. Xinan shifan daxue chubanshe.

DP   Duli pinglun (Independent review), 1932–1937. Beiping: Duli pinglunshe.

DT   Diangong tongxun (Correspondence for electric industry), 1938–1943. Published by Central Electric Works.

DYSY   Dangan yu shiliao yanjiu. 1989–2003. Chongqing Municipal Archives.

DZ   Dongfang zazhi (The oriental journal), 1904–1948. Shanghai: Shangwu yinshuguan.

DZLN   Diyici zhongguo laodong nianjian (First China labor yearbook). Beiping shehui yanjiubu, 1928.

ENZLN   Ershier nian zhongguo laodong nianjian (China labor yearbook for 1933). Shiyebu: Zhongguo laodong nianjian bianzuan weiyuanhui, 1934.

FYZWGS   Fuyuan yilai ziyuan weiyuanhui gongzuo shuyao (A survey of the achievements of the National Resources Commission since 1945). Ziyuan weiyuanhui, 1948.

GJC   Gongzuo jingsai chuyi (Preliminary proposal for work emulation). Zhongyang xunlian weiyuanhui. Chongqing, 1940.

GJJY   Guomin jingji jianshe yundong (National economic reconstruction campaign). Shagnhai: Zhongguo wenti yanjiuhui bian, 1936.

GJS   Guangdong jungong shiliao, 1840–1949 (Historical materials of military industry in Guangdong province, 1840–1949), ed. Cao Wenli and others. Guangzhou: Guangdong sheng guofang keji gongye bangongshi. N.d.

GJY   Gongzuo jingsai yuebao (Work emulation monthly), November 1943–? Chongqing: Gongzuo jingsai yuebaoshe.

GJZJ   Gongzuo jingsai zuotianhui jiyao (A summary of panel discussion on work emulation). Chongqing: Gongzuo jingsai tuixing weiyuanhui bian, 1942.

GZJZS   Guomin zhengfu junzheng zuzhi shiliao (Historical materials on the organization of military administration of the Nationalist government), ed. Zhou Meihua. 4 vols. Taibei: Guoshiguan, 1996.

GZZZDSX   Guomindang zhengfu zhengzhi zhidu dangan shiliao xuanbian (Selections of archival materials on the political system of the Nationalist government). Zhongguo dier lishi danganguan bian. 2 vols. Hefei: Anhui jiaoyu chubanshe, 1994.

HGGT   Houfang gongye gaikuang tongji (A statistical survey of Chinese industry). Jingjibu tongjichu bian. Chongqing, 1943.

HGZZW   Huiyi guomindang zhengfu ziyuan weiyuanhui (Recollections of the National Resources Commission under the Nationalist government). Beijing: Zhongguo wenshi chubanshe, 1988.

JG   Jingjibu gongbao (Bulletin of the Ministry of Economic Affairs), 1938–1947.

JJJ   Jingji jianshe jikan (Economic reconstruction quarterly). Chongqing, 1942–1945.

JZ   Jindaishi ziliao (Source materials in modern Chinese history). Beijing: Zhongguo shehui kexue chubanshe. Multiple volumes. N.d.

KHYGS   Kangzhan houfang yejin gongye shiliao (Archival materials for metallurgical industry in China's interior provinces during the Sino-Japanese War). Chongqing danganguan bian. Chongqing, 1987.

KJSSJ   Kangzhan jianguo shiliao—shehui jianshe (Historical materials for the war of resistance against Japan and nation building—social reconstruction), ed. Qin Xiaoyi. 5 vols. Taibei: Zhongyang wenwu gongyingshe, 1984.

KSNXGQ   Kangzhan shiqi neiqian xinan de gongshang qiye (The industrial enterprises relocated to the southwest during the Sino-Japanese War), ed. Guo Zongying. Kunming: Yunnan renmin chubanshe, 1988.

MESQXY   Minguo ershi sinian quanguo xinshenghuo yundong (Collection of materials for the New Life Campaign for 1935). 2 vols. Xinshenghuo yundong chujin zonghui bianyin. Reprint ed. Taibei: Wenhai chubanshe. n.d.

MESXYZ   Minguo ershi sannian xinshenghuo yundong zongbaogao (A Complete report of the New Life Campaign for 1934). Xinshenghuo yundong chujin zonghui bianyin. Reprint ed. Taibei: Wenhai chubanshe. n.d.

MZN Minguo zhiguan nianbiao (Chronological table of government posts in Republican China), ed. Liu Shoulin and others. Beijing: Zhonghua shuju, 1995.

SHA Second Historical Archives of China, Nanjing, China.

SJJ Sichuan jingji jikan (Sichuan economy quarterly). Chengdu, 1943–?

SKW Sun Ke wenji (Collection of writings by Sun Ke). Taibei: Taiwan shangwu yinshuguan, 1970.

SY Shiyebu yuekan (Monthly of the Ministry of Industries), 1936–?

SYW Sun Yueqi wenxuan (A selection of writings by Sun Yueqi). Beijing: Tuanjie chubanshe, 1992.

SZQ Sun Zhongshan quanji (Complete works of Sun Yatsen). Beijing: Zhonghua shuju chuban, 1981–?

SZS Silian zongchu shiliao (Historical materials on the Joint Administrative Agency of the Central Bank of China, the Bank of China, the Bank of Communications, and the Farmers' Bank). 3 vols. Chongqingshi danganguan, chongqingshi renmin yinhang jinrong yanjiusuo hebian. Beijing: dangan chubanshe, 1993.

SZZJ Shinianlai zhi zhongguo jingji (The Chinese economy during the last decade), ed. Tan Xihong. Taibei: Wenhai chubanshe. Reprint ed. Originally published in 1948.

WNZZJ Wushi nianlai zhi zhongguo jingji (The Chinese economy during the last fifty years, 1896–1947). Zhongguo tongshang yinhang bian. Shanghai, 1947. Reprint ed. Taibei: Wenhai chubanshe. n.d.

WWLJJ Weng Wenhao lun jingji jianshe (Weng Wenhao on economic reconstruction), Beijing, Tuanjie chubanshe, 1989.

WZX Wenshi ziliao xuanji (Selections of historical materials). Beijing: Zhongguo wenshi chubanshe, 1986–?

XJ Xin jingji (The new economy). Xinjingji banyuekan she. Chongqing, 1938–1945.

XJSYZ Xianzongtong jianggong sixiang yanlun zongji (The complete works of late president Chiang Kaishek), ed. Qin Xiaoyi. Taibei: Zhongguo guomindang zhongyang weiyuanhui dangshi weiyuanhui, 1984.

XST Xinan shiye tongxun (Correspondence of southwestern industry). Chongqing, 1940–?

XYXYHD Xinshenghuo yundong: xinshenghuo yundong huibian diyiji (Collection of materials for the New Life Campaign). Xinshenghuo yundong chujin zonghui bianyin. N.d.

YPA Yunnan Provincial Archives, Kunming, China.

ZDG Zhongyang dangwu gongbao (Bulletin of central party affairs). Guomindang zhongyang zhixing weiyuanhui mushuchu. 12 vols. Chongqing, July 1939–December 1947.

ZGDB   Zhongguo gongye diaocha baogao (Report on conditions of Chinese industry), ed. Liu Dajun. Shanghai: Jingji tongji yanjiusuo, 1937.

ZGX   Zhongguo guomindang xuanyanji (Collection of manifestos of the Chinese Nationalist Party), ed. Xiao Jizong. Taibei: Zhongguo guomindang zhongyang weiyuanhui dangshi weiyuanhui, 1976.

ZJBG   Zhongguo jindai bingqi gongye—qingmo zhi minguo de bingqi gongye (A history of modern Chinese ordnance industry: from late Qing to Republican China), ed. Wang Zhiguang and others. Beijing: Guofang gongye chubanshe, 1998.

ZJBGDS   Zhongguo jindai bingqi gongye dangan shiliao (Archival materials on the history of ordnance industry in modern China). 4 vols. Beijing: Bingqi gongye chubanshe, 1993.

ZJGZ-C   Zhongguo jindai gongyeshi ziliao (Source materials on the history of industry in modern China), ed. Chen Zhen. 4 vols. Beijing: Sanlian shudian, 1957–1961.

ZJGZ-S   Zhongguo jindaishi gongyeshi ziliao (Source materials on the history of industry in modern China), ed. Sun Yutang. 2. vols. Taibei: Wenhai chubanshe, 1979.

ZJJL   Zhongguo jingji jianshe luncong (Collection of essays on Chinese economic reconstruction by Weng Wenhao). Published by the secretariat of the National Resources Commission, 1943.

ZJJYZ   Zhongguo jindai jingjishi yanjiu ziliao (Research materials in modern Chinese economic history). Shanghai: Shanghai shehui kexueyuan chubanshe, 1984–?

ZJY   Zhongguo jingji yanjiu (Studies in Chinese economy), ed. Fang Xianting. 3 vols. Changsha: Shangwu yinshuguan, 1938.

ZMDZH   Zhonghua minguoshi dangan ziliao huibian (Collection of archival materials in the history of Republican China). 90 vols. Nanjing: Jiangsu guji chubanshe, 1991–1999.

ZMTT   Zhonghua minguo tongji tiyao (Statistical abstract of Republican China). Guomin zhengfu zhujichu tongjiju bian, Chongqing, 1940.

ZMZSC   Zhonghua minguo zhongyao shiliao chubian—duiri kangzhan shiqi (Preliminary selection of important historical materials of Republican China for the period of the Sino-Japanese War), ed. Qin Xiaoyi. Multiple vols. Taibei: Zhongguo guomindang zhongyang weiyuanhui dangshi weiyuanhui.

ZWDSC   Ziyuan weiyuanhui dangan shiliao chubian (Preliminary selection of archival materials of National Resources Commission). 2 vols. Taibei: Guoshiguan, 1984.

ZWFH   Ziyuan weiyuanhui fagui huibian (Statutes of the National Resources Commission). 2 vols. Ziyuan weiyuanhui canshishi bian, 1947.

ZWG   Ziyuan weiyuanhui gongbao (Bulletin of the National Resources Commission), 1941–1948.

ZWJ   Ziyuan weiyuanhui jikan (National Resources Commission quarterly), 1941–1946.

ZWJRFSS   Ziyuan weiyuanhui jishu renyuan fumei shixi shiliao—minguo sanshiyinian huipai (Archival Materials on the Thirty-One Technical Personnel Sent to the United States for Practical Training in 1942), ed. Zhu Huishen. 3 vols. Taibei: Guoshiguan, 1988.

ZWY   Ziyuan weiyuanhui yuekan (National Resources Commission monthly), 1939–1941.

ZZJWY   Zhongguo zhanhou jingji wenti yanjiu (Studies in economic problems in postwar China by Fang Xianting). Chongqing: Shangwu yinshuguan, 1945.

Notes

Introduction

1. This definition does not address changes in the institutional arrangement of state-owned enterprise since the 1980s.
2. CN, 47. For lack of an appropriate symbol, "Ch$" is used to refer to the Chinese currency unit "yuan."
3. CN, 54.
4. Ibid., 105.
5. Ibid., 157–158.
6. Ibid., 183, 187.
7. Ibid., 193–195.
8. Ibid., 144–146.
9. Ibid., 197–200.
10. A. Doak Barnett, *Communist Economic Strategy: The Rise of Mainland China* (Washington, D.C.: National Planning Association, 1959), 7.
11. K. C. Yeh, "Soviet and Communist Chinese Industrialization Strategies," in *Soviet and Chinese Communism: Similarities and Differences,* ed. Donald W. Treadgold (Seattle: University of Washington Press, 1967), 327–363.
12. Chu-yuan Cheng, *The Economy of Communist China* (Ann Arbor: University of Michigan Center for Chinese Studies, 1971), 2.
13. Chu-yuan Cheng, *China's Economic Development: Growth and Structural Change* (Boulder, Colo.: Westview Press, 1982), 261.
14. Dwight H. Perkins, "China's Economic Policy and Performance," in *Cambridge History of China,* ed. R. MacFarquhar and John Fairbank (Cambridge, UK: Cambridge University Press, 1991), vol. 15, 475.
15. Robert F. Dernberger, "The People's Republic of China at 50: The Economy," *China Quarterly* 159 (September 1999): 607–615.
16. Louis Putterman and Xiao-yuan Dong, "China's State-Owned Enterprises: Their Role, Job Creation, and Efficiency in Long-Term Perspective," *Modern China* 26, no. 4 (October 2000): 403–447.
17. A notable exception is *Germany and Republican China* (Stanford, Calif.: Stanford

University Press, 1984) by William C. Kirby. See also his "Continuity and Change in Modern China: Economic Planning on the Mainland and on Taiwan, 1943–1958," *Australian Journal of Chinese Affairs* 24 (1990): 121–141.

18. Defined broadly, the term *danwei system* refers to the prevailing administrative system encompassing virtually all government, business, and educational institutions in urban China during the post–1949 period.

19. Gail E. Henderson and Myron S. Cohen, *The Chinese Hospital: A Socialist Work Unit* (New Haven, Conn.: Yale University Press, 1984), 139.

20. Martin K. Whyte and William L. Parish, *Urban Life in Contemporary China* (Chicago: University of Chicago Press, 1984), 358–359.

21. Elizabeth J. Perry, "From Native Place to Workplace: Labor Origins and Outcomes of China's *Danwei* System," in *Danwei: The Changing Chinese Workplace in Historical and Comparative Perspective,* ed. Xiaobo Lü and Elizabeth J. Perry (Armonk, N.Y.: M. E. Sharpe, 1997), 42–59.

22. Zhou Yihu and Yang Xiaomin, *Zhongguo* danwei *zhidu* (The Chinese *danwei* system) (Beijing: Zhongguo jingji chubanshe, 1999), 3, 103.

23. Lu Feng, "Danwei: yizhong teshu de shehui zhuzhi xingshi" (*Danwei*: a special form of social organization), *Zhongguo shehui kexue* (Chinese social science), no. 1 (1989): 71–88.

24. Lu Feng, "Zhongguo danwei zhidu de qiyuan he xingcheng" (The origins and formation of China's *danwei* system), *Zhongguo shehui kexue jikan* (Chinese social science quarterly) 11 (1993): 66–87. The article is translated (almost in its entirety) and published as "The Origins and Formation of the Unit *(Danwei)* System," *Chinese Sociology and Anthropology* 25, no. 3 (spring 1993): 1–91.

25. Lü Xiaobo, "Minor Public Economy: The Revolutionary Origins of the *Danwei*," in *Danwei: The Changing Chinese Workplace in Historical and Comparative Perspective,* ed. Xiaobo Lü and Elizabeth J. Perry, 21–41.

26. Yeh Wen-Hsin, "Corporate Space, Communal Time: Everyday Life in Shanghai's Bank of China," *American Historical Review* 100, no. 1 (February 1995): 97–122. See also her "Republican Origins of the *Danwei*: The Case of Shanghai's Bank of China," in *Danwei: The Changing Chinese Workplace in Historical and Comparative Perspective,* ed. Xiaobo Lü and Elizabeth J. Perry, 60–88.

27. Mark W. Frazier, *The Making of the Chinese Industrial Workplace: State, Revolution, and Labor Management* (Cambridge, UK: Cambridge University Press, 2002), xiv, 234.

28. According to Peter A. Hall and Rosemary C. R. Taylor, these schools of thought include historical institutionalism, rational choice institutionalism, and sociological institutionalism. See their "Political Science and the Three New Institutionalisms," *Political Studies* 44, no. 5 (December 1996): 936–957. For recent surveys of historical institutionalism, see Kathleen Thelen, "Historical Institutionalism in Comparative Politics," *Annual Review of Political Science* 2 (1999): 369–404; Paul Pierson and Theda Skocpol, "Historical Institutionalism

in Contemporary Political Science," in *Political Science: The State of the Discipline,* ed. Ira Katznelson and Helen Milner (New York: W. W. Norton, 2002), 693–721.

29. Douglass C. North, "Economic Performance through Time," in *Empirical Studies in Institutional Change,* ed. Lee J. Alston and others (Cambridge, UK: Cambridge University Press, 1996), 342–355. For North, "the study of institutions and institutional change necessitates as a first requirement the conceptual separation of institutions from organizations." See his "Five Propositions about Institutional Change," in *Explaining Social Institutions,* ed. Jack Knight and Itai Sened (Ann Arbor: University of Michigan Press, 1995), 15–26.

30. Douglass North also identifies organizations and entrepreneurs as agents of institutional change. See his *Institutions, Institutional Change and Economic Performance* (Cambridge, UK: Cambridge University Press, 1990), 5, 84, 89, 98–100; and "Five Propositions about Institutional Change," in *Explaining Social Institutions,* 15–26.

31. North, "Economic Performance through Time," in *Empirical Studies in Institutional Change,* 342–355.

32. North, *Institutions, Institutional Change and Economic Performance,* 98, 99.

33. Recently, Anil Hira and Ron Hira suggest that "the new institutionalism is unable to provide a satisfactory explanation of change." See "The New Institutionalism: Contradictory Notions of Change," *American Journal of Economics and Sociology* 59, no. 2 (April 2000): 267–282.

34. Elias L. Khalil, "Organizations versus Institutions," *Journal of Institutional and Theoretical Economics* 151, no. 3 (1995): 445–466.

35. Eirik G. Furubotn and Rudolf Richter, *Institutions and Economic Theory: The Contribution of the New Institutional Economics* (Ann Arbor: University of Michigan Press, 1997), 6–7.

36. Alfred D. Chandler Jr., "Decision Making and Modern Institutional Change," *Journal of Economic History* 33, no. 1 (March 1973): 1–15.

37. Alan Booth, Joseph Melling, and Christoph Dartmann, "Institutions and Economic Growth: The Politics of Productivity in West Germany, Sweden, and the United Kingdom, 1945–1955," *Journal of Economic History* 57, no. 2 (June 1997): 416–444.

38. Philip N. Johnson-Laird, *Mental Models: Towards a Cognitive Science of Language, Inference, and Consciousness* (Cambridge, Mass.: Harvard University Press, 1983), 10.

39. Philip N. Johnson-Laird, "Formal Rules versus Mental Models in Reasoning," in *The Nature of Cognition,* ed. Robert J. Sternberg (Cambridge, Mass.: MIT Press, 1999), 587–624. Other leading scholars seem to agree with his definition. For example, Anthony J. Sanford and Linda M. Moxey wrote, "Perhaps everyone would accept that a mental model is a representation which is assumed to correspond to some aspect of the world or the narrative world. Even more than that, most researchers would almost certainly accept the idea

that a mental model is a representation which captures the essence or essentials of that aspect of the world. In other words, it is made of selected material which bears a systematic relation to an aspect of the world." See their "What Are Mental Models Made of?" in *Mental Models in Discourse Processing and Reasoning*, ed. Gert Rickheit and Christopher Habel (Amsterdam: Elsevier, 1999), 57–76.

40. Johnson-Laird, *Mental Models*, 419. Two leading authorities believed that this structural analogy "may turn out to be the defining characteristic of mental models." See Gert Rickheit and Lorenz Sichelschmidt, "Mental Models: Some Answers, Some Questions, Some Suggestions," in *Mental Models in Discourse Processing and Reasoning*, 9–40.

41. Arthur T. Denzau and Douglass C. North, "Shared Mental Models: Ideologies and Institutions," *Kyklos: International Review for Social Sciences* 47, no. 1 (1994): 3–30.

42. Joel Mokyr believes that there are two types of knowledge: "what" or propositional knowledge, and "how" or prescriptive knowledge. Although the two types of knowledge are analytically distinguishable, they are not always separable in empirical reality. For Mokyr's explanation, see his *The Gifts of Athena: Historical Origins of the Knowledge Economy* (Princeton, N.J.: Princeton University Press, 2002): 4–15.

43. Douglass North, "Economic Performance through Time," in *Empirical Studies in Institutional Change*, 342–355. For recent efforts to apply theories of cognitive science to studying institutional change, see Jack Knight and Douglass North, "Explaining Economic Change: The Interplay between Cognition and Institutions," *Legal Theory* 3 (1997): 211–226; Jack Knight, "Social Institutions and Human Cognition: Thinking about Old Questions in New Ways," *Journal of Institutional and Theoretical Economics* 153 (1997): 693–699.

44. In this study, the meaning of ideology is restricted to the set of doctrines and beliefs that form the basis of a social, economic, and political system. For an elaborate definition of political ideology, see Terence Ball and Richard Dagger, *Political Ideologies and Democratic Ideal* (New York: Longman, 2002), 5–7.

45. Arthur T. Denzau and Douglass C. North, "Shared Mental Models: Ideologies and Institutions," *Kyklos: International Review for Social Sciences* 47, no. 1 (1994): 3–30.

46. I use the term *normal* in Thomas S. Kuhn's sense. The term *normal alteration* has a connotation parallel to that of "normal science." See Kuhn's *The Structure of Scientific Revolutions* (Chicago: University of Chicago Press, 1996), 3rd ed. See also his "What Are Scientific Revolutions?" in *The Road since Structure*, ed. James Conant and John Haugeland (Chicago: University of Chicago Press, 2000), 13–32.

47. The modification of mental models has a close parallel to "normal change" in the development of science. As Thomas Kuhn points out, normal change is the sort that "results in growth, accretion, cumulative addition, to what was known before." See *The Road since Structure*, 14.

48. The parallel to "perceptual transformations" in the development of science is striking. According to Thomas Kuhn, "in normal change, one simply revises or adds a single generalization; all others remaining the same. In revolutionary change one must either live with incoherence or else revise a number of interrelated generalizations together." "What characterizes revolutions is, thus, change in several of the taxonomic categories prerequisite to scientific descriptions and generalizations. That change, furthermore, is an adjustment not only of criteria relevant to categorization, but also of the way in which given objects and situations are distributed among preexisting categories." The transformation of mental models also finds support in the recent literature on mental models. For example, in addressing the question of "how to conceive 'qualitative" changes in a mental model," Gert Rickheit and Lorenz Sichelschmidt wrote, "it is generally believed that under certain circumstances a particular mental model can be replaced by an alternative one. While mental model maintenance means that the current representation is updated or extended, 'qualitative' change implies that the current representation is discarded in favor of a new one." See James Conant and John Haugeland, eds., *The Road since Structure*, 29–30; Thomas Kuhn, *The Structure of Scientific Revolutions*, 112; Gert Rickheit and Lorenz Sichelschmidt, "Mental Models: Some Answers, Some Questions, Some Suggestions," in *Mental Models in Discourse Processing and Reasoning*, 9–40.

49. Joseph A. McCartin, "The New Deal Era," in *The Oxford Companion to United States History*, ed. Paul S. Boyer (Oxford: Oxford University Press, 2001), 546–549.

50. Kuhn, *The Structure of Scientific Revolutions*, 74–75.

51. As Marc A. Eisner pointed out, "There is nothing inherent in a crisis that determines the precise features of the political-institutional response." See his *From Warfare State to Welfare State. World War I, Compensatory State Building, and the Limits of the Modern Order* (University Park: Pennsylvania State University Press, 2000), 3.

52. According to Harold Demsetz, "initial endowments include weather, terrain, plants, animals and minerals. . . . Initial endowments owe nothing to past human behavior and cannot be constructed as institutional arrangements." See his "Dogs and Tails in the Economic Development Story," in *Institutions, Contracts and Organizations: Perspectives from New Institutional Economics*, ed. Claude Menard (Cheltenham, UK: Edward Elgar, 2000), 80.

53. Ibid., 84. It appears that Harold Demsetz uses the term *institutions* as new institutional economists define it, but that does not make his argument about institutional endowments invalid.

54. William Sewell, "Three Temporalities: Toward an Eventful Sociology," in *The Historic Turn in Human Sciences*, ed. Terrance J. McDonald (Ann Arbor: University of Michigan Press, 1996), 245–280.

55. James Mahoney, "Path Dependence in Historical Sociology," *Theory and Society* 29, no. 4 (August 2000): 507–548.

56. Paul Pierson, "Increasing Returns, Path Dependence, and the Study of Politics," *American Political Science Review*, 94, no. 2 (June 2000): 251–267.
57. James Mahoney, "Path Dependence in Historical Sociology," *Theory and Society* 29, no. 4 (August 2000): 507–548.
58. Ibid.
59. I first sketched this argument in "The Sino-Japanese War and the Formation of the State Enterprise System in China: A Case Study of the Dadukou Iron and Steel Works, 1938–1945," *Enterprise & Society* 3, no. 1 (March 2002): 80–123.
60. Again, the parallel to paradigm shift in the development of science is striking. According to Thomas Kuhn, "the transition from a paradigm in crisis to a new one from which a new tradition of normal science can emerge is far from a cumulative process, one achieved by an articulation or extension of the old paradigm. Rather it is a reconstruction of the field from new fundamentals, a reconstruction that changes some of the field's most elementary theoretical generalizations as well as many of its paradigm methods and applications." In other words, scientific revolutions refer to "those non-cumulative developmental episodes in which an older paradigm is replaced in whole or in part by an incompatible new one." More recently, cognitive scientists have reached a similar conclusion with regard to the relationship between "prior knowledge" and "new knowledge" in learning. "On the one hand, prior knowledge is a prerequisite for the acquisition of new knowledge. On the other hand, however, prior knowledge can also impede comprehension and learning, because it is frequently incompatible with the new knowledge to be acquired. Therefore, learning requires not only the acquisition of new knowledge, but frequently also the reorganization of existing knowledge, a process that is usually referred to as conceptual change." See *The Structure of Scientific Revolutions*, 84–85, 92; Wolfgang Schnotz and Achim Preub, "Task-Dependent Construction of Mental Models as a Basis for Conceptual Change," in *Mental Models in Discourse Processing and Reasoning*, 131–167.
61. The distinction between gradual or incremental change and radical or revolutionary change should help erase the "sharp dichotomy between periods of institutional innovation and institutional stasis." See Kathleen Thelen, "How Institutions Evolve: Insights from Comparative Historical Analysis," in *Comparative Historical Analysis in the Social Sciences*, ed. James Mahoney and Dietrich Rueschemeyer (Cambridge, UK: Cambridge University Press, 2003), 208–240.
62. It was a "sustained" crisis because the crisis not only lasted for almost a decade but also affected the entire organism of the Chinese body politic. The crisis was unprecedented in modern Chinese history in part because it threatened the very existence of the Chinese body politic. At the same time, the crisis was a "systemic" one because of the inability of existing institutional arrangements to overcome the crisis—hence the necessity of undertaking radical institutional changes.

1. Development of the Ordnance Industry

1. Thomas L. Kennedy, *The Arms of Kiangnan: Modernization in the Chinese Ordnance Industry, 1860–1895* (Boulder, Colo.: Westview Press, 1978), 27–29, 34–57. Although published a quarter of a century ago, this remains the only English-language study of Chinese ordnance industry available.

2. ZJBG, 216–239. According to Wang Ermin, twenty-four ordnance bureaus and factories were established. Thomas Kennedy suggested, however, that a total of thirty ordnance bureaus and factories came into existence during the same time period. See Wang Ermin, *Qingji binggongye de xingqi* (The rise of the ordnance industry during the late Qing dynasty) (Taibei: Zhongyang yanjiuyuan jindaishi yanjiusuo, 1963), 125–127; Kennedy, *The Arms of Kiangnan*, 175–176.

3. Kennedy, *The Arms of Kiangnan*, 156.

4. Susan Naquin and Evelyn S. Rawski, *Chinese Society in the Eighteenth Century* (New Haven, Conn.: Yale University Press, 1987), 26–27.

5. Memorials by Zhu Yixin, October 25, 1884, by Hu Rufen, July 1895, and by Xu Yu, December 31, 1903, in ZJBGDS, vol. 1, 41, 46.

6. Imperial edict, August 11, 1895, ibid., 42.

7. Memorial by Zhejiang governor Liao Shoufeng, January 22, 1896, ibid., 42–43.

8. Kennedy, *The Arms of Kiangnan*, 155–156.

9. Cited from Kennedy, *The Arms of Kiangnan*, 97.

10. Memorial by Wang Wenshao, February 1, 1877, in ZJBGDS, vol. 1, 128–129.

11. Memorial by Zhu Yixin, October 25, 1884, ibid., 27.

12. Memorial by Bian Baodi, October 1884, in ZJGZ-S, vol. 1, 508–509.

13. Official correspondence, early 1890, in ZJBGDS, vol. 1, 213–217.

14. Memorial by Lin Shu, April 11, 1895, ibid., vol. 1, 38–39.

15. Memorial by Zhang Zhidong, July 19, 1895, ibid., 40–41.

16. Memorial by Rong Lu, November 1897, ibid., 44.

17. Edict by Emperor Guangxu, December 15, 1897, ibid., 44.

18. ZJBG, 216–239.

19. Liu Kunyi's letter and memorial, January 25 and July 14, 1898, in ZJBGDS, vol. 1, 59, 61–62.

20. Zhang Zhidong's memorial, March 17, 1903, ibid., 286–290.

21. The Bureau of Government Affairs was established in 1901 in order to examine reports and memorials dealing with reforms. The bureau would submit a written opinion to the emperor for approval upon completing deliberations. In 1906 the bureau became the Deliberation Bureau of Government Affairs *(huiyi zhengwuchu)*. It was abolished in 1911. See *Zhongguo lishi dacidian—Qingshi* (A dictionary of Chinese history: Qing dynasty) (Shanghai: Shanghai cishu chubanshe, 1992), vol. 2, 505.

22. Memorial by the Bureau of Government Affairs, July 9, 1903, in ZJBGDS, vol. 1, 290–291.

23. Zhang Zhidong's memorial, June 1, 1904, ibid., 293–298.
24. The Bureau of Military Reorganization was established in 1903 for the purpose of reorganizing the Chinese military. It was a high-level adjunct of the Grand Council, which reported directly to the Empress Dowager on military reform. The organization was abolished in 1906, and its functions were absorbed by a new Ministry of War *(lujunbu)*. See Stephen R. Mackinnon, *Power and Politics in Late Imperial China: Yuan Shi-kai in Beijing and Tianjin, 1901–1908* (Berkeley: University of California Press, 1980), 72, 108–110, 114.
25. Memorial by the Bureau of Military Reorganization, June 15, 1904, in ZJBGDS, vol. 1, 299–300.
26. Tie Liang's report, February 21, 1905, in ZJBGDS, vol. 1, 304–306. Tie Liang's "comprehensive solution" may have resulted from the politics of compromise. See Zhang Zhidong's telegram to Duan Fang, September 16, 1904, ibid., 301; Thomas L. Kennedy, "The Kiangnan Arsenal 1895–1911: The Decentralized Bureaucracy Responds to Imperialism," *Qingshi wenti* 1, no. 1 (October 1969): 17–37.
27. Report by the Bureau of Military Reorganization, June 15, 1905 in ZJBGDS, vol. 1, 307–309.
28. Yi Kuang (Prince Qing)'s memorial on July 15, 1909, ibid., 337–338.
29. Joint memorial by Yi Kuang, Yuan Shikai, and Tie Liang, December 24, 1903. The memorial stated, "As the sole provider of military supplies, the manufacturing bureaus and factories of ordnance in the various provinces are the lifeblood of the army. Consequently we should place them under the direct supervision of the Bureau of Military Reorganization," in ZJBGDS, vol. 1, 327.
30. *Cambridge History of China* (Cambridge: Cambridge University Press, 1980), vol. 11, Late Qing, 1800–1911, part 2, 385.
31. Memorial by the Ministry of War, late 1906, in ZJBGDS, vol. 1, 330–332.
32. Regulations of organizational establishment, February 1909, ibid., 336.
33. Regulations of organizational establishment, March 1911, ibid., 360–362.
34. Revised official system of the Ministry of War, July 10, 1914, in ZJBGDS, vol. 2. 18–19.
35. Ibid., 47–49.
36. Plan for the consolidation of ordnance factories, ibid., 50–51.
37. Report by the Ministry of War, January 8, 1919, ibid., 234.
38. Report by the Ministry of War, June 26, 1919, ibid., 236.
39. Internal Report by the Ministry of War, May 24, 1921, ibid., 254.
40. Letter of the Department of Weaponry, September 9, 1925, ibid., 217.
41. For example, Dexian Arsenal dismissed all of its employees in 1926, February 26, 1926, ibid., 246.
42. Organizational regulations, November 21, 1928, in ZJBGDS, vol. 3, 1–3.
43. The term *ke* is generally translated as "department," but since the term *si* also appears in this context, and is also generally translated as "department," I have reserved the term "department" for the term *si* while translating the

term *ke* as "section." See the organizational regulations of the Bureau of Ordnance, December 11, 1928, ibid., 12–13.

44. "Junzhengbu chengli jingguo yu zhuzhi gaiyao" (A brief survey of the establishment and organization of the Ministry of Military Administration), April 1935, in ZMDZH, part v, vol. 1, junshi, no. 1, 50–51.

45. ZMDZH, part v, vol. 1, junshi, no. 1, 52–59; ZJBGDS, vol. 3, 4–9.

46. ZJBGDS, vol. 3, 51.

47. Ibid., vol. 3, 57.

48. Li Yuanping, *Yu Dawei zhuan* (A biography of Yu Dawei) (Taiwan: Taiwan ribaoshe, 1993), 15–24, 26–36; William Kirby, *Germany and Republican China*, 55–56; Theodore H. White and Annalee Jacoby, *Thunder Out of China* (New York: William Sloane Associates, 1946), 116–117.

49. Li Yuanping, *Yu Dawei zhuan*, 36.

50. Record of the planning meeting. The meeting was held on July 12, 1932, in ZJBGDS, vol. 3, 90.

51. Excerpt of Chiang Kaishek's letter to the head of the Ministry of Military Administration, ibid., 91.

52. Budget of the Bureau of Ordnance, August 1932, ibid., 92–93. It should be noted that the Nationalist fiscal year ended June 30 until mid-1938. Thereafter they were calendar years, and the second half of 1938 was treated as a separate fiscal period. See Arthur N. Young, *China's Wartime Finance & Inflation, 1937–1945* (Cambridge, Mass.: Harvard University Press, 1965), 11.

53. Correspondence of the General Staff, August 29, 1932, in ZJBGDS, vol. 3, 94–95.

54. "Binggongchang zhengli jihua caoan" (Draft plan for consolidating ordnance factories), ibid., 95–100. The term *pacification* apparently refers to extermination campaigns against the Communists.

55. Ibid., 95–100.

56. Secret telegrams between Chiang Kaishek and Kong Xiangxi, in ZMDZH, part v, vol. 1, caizheng jingji, no. 1, 392–400.

57. Calculations are based on the expenditure of the five arsenals in March 1935, in ZJBGDS, vol. 3, 774–778.

58. Budget estimate by the Bureau of Ordnance, ibid., 773.

59. Wang Guoqiang, *Zhongguo binggong zhizaoye fazhanshi* (History of the development of Chinese ordnance industry) (Taibei: Liming wenhua shiyu gongsi, 1987), 95–96.

60. "Gongxian binggong dierchang choujian jinkuang baogao" (Progress report on the construction of gongxian second arsenal), in ZJBGDS, vol. 3, 310–312.

61. "Di ershisanchang changshi" (History of the Twenty-third Arsenal), 1948, ibid., 1210–1216.

62. Chen Xiuhe, "Youguan shanghai binggongchang de huiyi" (My recollection of Shanghai Arsenal), 1961, in WZX, no. 19, 69–94.

63. ZJBGDS, vol. 3, 234–237.

64. "Guomin zhengfu zhengzhi zongbaogao" (General political report of the national government), November 1931, in ZMZSC, vol. 3, 216.

65. Chiang Kaishek's telegram, September 22, 1932, ibid., 292.

66. Yang Jizeng's report to He Yingqin, August 28, 1936, in ZJBGDS, vol. 3, 394–395.

67. Correspondence between Chen Yi and Chiang Kaishek, in ZMZSC, vol. 3, 291.

68. Guofangbu shizheng bianyiju, ed., *Junzheng shiwunian* (Fifteen years in military administration) (Taibei: 1984), 177.

69. "Guofang sheji weiyuanhui niju binggong shengchan kuocong jihuashu" (Program for expanding ordnance production), 1932, in ZJBGDS, vol. 3, 101–108.

70. "Binggongshu zhizaosi jishusi junxiesi ershisan niandu gongzuo baogao zaiyao" (Summary of work report for 1934 fiscal year by the departments of manufacturing, technology, and military weaponry of the Bureau of Ordnance), 1935, ibid., 141–146.

71. "Binggongchang zhengli jihua caoan" (Draft plan for consolidating ordnance factories), ibid., 95–100.

72. "Minguo ershier niandu junshi weiyuanhui junshi jinxing gangyao" (Military program drafted by the Military Affairs Commission for 1933 fiscal year), in ZMZSC, vol. 3, 318–324.

73. ZJBGDS, vol. 3, 676–678.

74. Proposal by Wang Qi, Li Zonghuang, Wang Luyi, Fu Rushen, June 17, 1935, in ZMDZH, part v, vol. 1, caizheng jingji, no. 5, 919–920.

75. Ibid., 920–931. The National Resources Commission was established in 1935 to develop heavy industries. Its predecessor was the National Defense Planning Commission created in 1932. See Chapter 2 for a systematic analysis of these two organizations.

76. "Guofang gongye jianshe huiyi jilu" (Records of meetings on reconstructing national defense industries). The meetings were held on February 18 and 25, 1936. See ibid., 931–934.

77. Chiang wrote the letter in his capacity as president of the National Resources Commission, ibid., 934–935.

78. "Zhonggongye jianshe taolunhui huiyi jilu" (Discussion records of the meeting on heavy industrial reconstruction). The meeting was held on February 25, 1936, ibid., 948–951.

79. Report by the Special Commission of National Defense, March 30, 1936, ibid., 953–959.

80. The Central Political Commission approved the revised plan in its fourteenth meeting, which appears to have taken place in May 1936. See ibid., 952–953.

81. Zhuang Quan's report to the Bureau of Ordnance, July 13, 1936, in ZJBGDS, vol. 3, 281.

82. "Dishichang yange" (The evolution of the Tenth Arsenal), July 1949, ibid., 1182–1187.

83. Output statistics compiled by the Bureau of Ordnance, April 1937, ibid., 425.

84. "Junxiesi ershisan niandu gongzuo baogao zaiyao" (Summary of work report for fiscal year 1934 by the department of weaponry), summer 1935, ibid., 148–152.

85. "Shanghai liangangchang jianshi baogao" (Inspection report of Shanghai Steel Plant), March 1935, ibid., 1180–1182.

86. Bureau of Ordnance's telegram, August 28, 1937. Cited from Huang Liren, "Kangri zhanzheng shiqi zhongguo bingqi gongye neiqian chulun" (The relocation of China's ordnance industry during the Sino-Japanese War), in Huang Liren, *Kangzhan shiqi dahoufang jingjishi yanjiu, 1937–1945* (A study of the economic history of the interior provinces during the Sino-Japanese War, 1937–1945) (Beijing: Zhongguo dangan chubanshe, 1998), 128.

87. Lu Dayue and Tang Runming, *Kangzhan shiqi chongqing de bingqi gongye* (The ordnance industry in Chongqing during the Sino-Japanese War) (Chongqing: Chongqing chubanshe, 1995), 41, 45.

88. For changes in the military situation, see Zhang Xianwen, ed., *Zhongguo kangri zhanzhengshi, 1931–1945* (History of the Sino-Japanese War, 1931–1945) (Nanjing: Nanjing daxue chubanshe, 2001), 506–532.

89. Lu Dayue and Tang Runming, *Kangzhan shiqi chongqing de bingqi gongye*, 45.

90. For the Changsha campaign, see Zhang Xianwen, ed., *Zhongguo kangri zhanzhengshi*, 608–628.

91. Lu Dayue and Tang Runming, *Kangzhan shiqi chongqing de bingqi gongye*, 46.

92. ZJBGDS, vol. 3, 240.

93. They were the Jinling Arsenal, Gongxian Arsenal, Jinan Arsenal, Hanyang Arsenal, Hanyang Powder Plant, Shanghai Steel Plant, and Gongxian Branch Arsenal. See ZJBGDS, vol. 3, 421.

94. ZJBG, 142–144.

95. "Quanguo binggongchang yilanbiao" (Tabulation of ordnance factories), March 1931, in ZJBGDS, vol. 3, 234–237.

96. Program of reform drafted by Li Chenggan, September 1934, in ibid., vol. 3, 770–771; "Zhizaosi ershisan niandu gongzuo baogao zaiyao" (Summary of work report for fiscal year 1934 by the department of manufacturing), ibid., 141–152; Li Chenggan's farewell address, March 10, 1947, ibid., 301–303.

97. "Diershiyi gongchang changshi" (History of the Twenty-first Arsenal), ibid., 1199–1207.

98. Zhang Xianwen, ed., *Zhongguo kangri zhanzhengshi*, 259–287.

99. Zheng Hongquan, "Aiguo binggong zuanjia lichenggan" (Li Chenggan: The weapons expert who devoted his life to his country), in CWZ, no. 35, 116–136.

100. ZJBGDS, vol. 3, 297.

101. "Diershiyi gongchang changshi" (History of the Twenty-first Arsenal), ibid., 1199–1207.

102. ZJBG, 142–148.

103. "Diershiyi gongchang changshi" (History of the Twenty-first Arsenal), in ZJBGDS, vol. 3, 1199–1207.

104. Ibid.
105. Zheng Hongquan, "Aiguo binggong zuanjia lichenggan" (Li Chenggan: The weapons expert who devoted his life to his country), in CWZ, no. 35, 116–136.
106. For an explanation of Hapro, see William Kirby, *Germany and Republican China*, 120–122.
107. ZJBG, 194–196; Lun Han, "Guangdong pajiang paochang jianchang shimo" (Chronological account of the establishment of the Pajiang Artillery Factory in Guangdong province), in GJS, 481–489; for the text of the contract signed in July 1933, see ibid., 185–196.
108. Lun Han, "Guangdong pajiang paochang jianchang shimo" (Chronological account of the establishment of the Pajiang Artillery Factory in Guangdong province), in ibid., 481–489.
109. Deng Yancun, "Pajiang binggongchang shimo" (Chronological account of the Pajiang Arsenal), ibid., 177–184.
110. ZJBG, 194–196; Lun Han, "Guangdong pajiang paochang jianchang shimo" (Chronological account of the establishment of the Pajiang Artillery Factory in Guangdong province), in GJS, 481–488.
111. "Diwushi gongchang changshi" (History of the Fiftieth Arsenal), March 1948, in ZJBGDS, vol. 3, 1255–1265.
112. Ibid., "Diwushi gongchang qianyi jingguo ji xianzai sheshi baogaoshu" (Report on relocation and existing facilities by the Fiftieth Arsenal), March 1939, CMA, 0101/3889.
113. "Diwushi gongchang changshi" (History of the Fiftieth Arsenal), March 1948, in ZJBGDS, vol. 3, 1255–1265. Minsheng Corporation was a major Chinese-owned shipping company.
114. Ibid., vol. 3, 1255–1265.
115. Report by Guangdong Second Arsenal, July 10, 1937, CMA 0103/368–369; Lun Han, "Guangdong pajiang paochang jianchang shimo" (Chronological account of the establishment of the Pajiang Artillery Factory in Guangdong province), in GJS, 481–489.
116. "Diwushi gongchang changshi" (History of the Fiftieth Arsenal), March 1948, in ZJBGDS, vol. 3, 1255–1265.
117. "Binggongshu ershiba niandu gaisuanshu" (The budget estimate for the 1939 fiscal year by the Bureau of Ordnance), in ZJBGDS, vol. 3, 784–788.
118. In this study, all calculations of 1936 constant price are based on price information contained in Appendix Table 1.3.
119. "Yijiu sanjiu niandu guojia putong suiru suichu zongyusuan (General national budget of revenue and expenditure for the 1939 fiscal year), in ZMDZH, part v, vol. 2, caizheng jingji, no. 1, 189–191.
120. "Junzhengbu zhuguan guofang jianshefei yusuan fenpeibiao (Tabulation of distribution of national defense expenditure among units under the jurisdiction of the Ministry of Military Administration), February 1942, SHA 171/833. The Ch$3,302,980,582 budget figure for national defense is different from the one given in the general national budget for 1942, which was

Ch$3,773,185,534. See "Zhonghua minguo sanshiyi niandu guojia suichu zongyusuan" (General national budget for the 1942 fiscal year), in ZMDZH, part v, vol. 2, caizheng jingji, no. 1, 224–232.

121. "Zhonghua minguo sanshiyi niandu guojia suichu zongyusuan" (General national budget for the 1942 fiscal year), in ZMDZH, part v, vol. 2, caizheng jingji, no. 1, 224–232.

122. In the second half of the twentieth century, China would, under a different regime, again implement a program for the massive establishment and relocation of the ordnance industry in the interior provinces—the so-called Third Front—because of the perceived new threat to China's national security. For a recent examination of the "Third Front" in the English language, see Barry Naughton, "The Third Front: Defense Industrialization in the Chinese Interior," *China Quarterly*, no. 115 (September 1988), 351–386. At the time Barry Naughton did the research for his article, most of the primary sources used in this book were simply unavailable. That may explain his conclusion that "there simply is no real precedent for the Third front. Never before has such a large portion of a nation's industrial development effort been directed into a program with ultimately military justification."

2. Expansion of Heavy Industries

1. See Chapter 8 for a systematic discussion of Sun Yatsen's idea of economic planning.

2. For a brief description of the National Reconstruction Commission and the National Economic Commission, see Kirby, *Germany and Republican China*, 82–85. For a description of the organizational structure of the National Economic Commission, see Li Junping, "Quanguo jingji weiyuanhui zuzhi jigou jieshao" (A description of the organizational structure of the National Economic Commission), *Minguo dangan* (Republican archives), no. 1 (February 1990): 124–127.

3. Gideon Chen, *Chinese Government Economic Planning and Reconstruction since 1927* (China Institute of Pacific Relations, 1933, printed in Tianjin, China), 7–9.

4. The term *sanmin zhuyi* is generally translated as "Three Principles of the People." However, the concept of "principle" does not adequately convey the substance of any of the three *zhuyi*, hence my rendering of it as "Three Doctrines of the People."

5. "Dui zhengzhi baogao zhi jueyi an" (Resolution on political affairs), March 27, 1929, in ZMDZH, part v, vol. 1, zhengzhi, no. 2, 75–86.

6. "Xunzheng shiqi jingji jianshe shishi gangyao fangzhen an" (Outline program for implementing economic reconstruction during the period of political tutelage), April 22, 1929, ibid., 118–119.

7. "Shiye jianshe chengxu an" (Resolution on the procedure for industrial reconstruction), May 2, 1931, ibid., 289–293.

8. Xu Youcun and others, eds., *Minguo renwu da cidian* (Dictionary of figures in

Republican China) (Shijiazhuang: Hebei renmin chubanshe, 1991), 731–732; Wu Zhaohong, "Wosuo zhidao de ziyuan weiyuanhui" (The National Resources Commission I know), in HGZZW, 63–141; Li Xuetong, *Shusheng congzheng: Weng Wenhao* (From scholar to statesman: A biography of Weng Wenhao) (Lanzhou: Lanzhou daxue chubanshe, 1996).

9. Weng Wenhao, "Jianshe yu jihua" (Reconstruction and planning), DP, no. 5 (June 19, 1932): 9–12.

10. Chiang Kaishek, "Jiaoyu yu jingji wei liguo jiuguo liang yaosu" (Education and economic reconstruction as two means of saving China), October 31, 1932, in XJSYZ, vol. 10, 655–665.

11. Xu Youcun and others, eds., *Minguo renwu da cidian* (Dictionary of figures in Republican China), 1528; Wu Zhaohong, "Wosuo zhidao de ziyuan weiyuanhui" (The National Resources Commission I know), in HGZZW, 65–66; Zheng Youkui and others, *Jiuzhongguo de ziyuan weiyuanhui: Shishi yu pingjia* (The National Resources Commission, 1932–1949: Historical facts and assessment) (Shanghai: Shanghai shehui kexueyuan chubanshe, 1991), 2–3.

12. Qian Changzhao, "Guomindang ziyuan weiyuanhui shimo" (Survey of the National Resources Commission), in HGZZW, 1.

13. According to Qian's recollection, his motives for suggesting the creation of a national defense planning commission were as follows: First, he believed that eventually Japan would launch a large-scale invasion of China. Second, he had consistently advocated the cause of China's industrialization, and he believed such a cause could get twice the result with half the effort if he could find support from as powerful a person as Chiang Kaishek. Finally, he had political ambitions, and he wanted to accumulate political capital through the creation of such an organization with a constellation of bankers, industrialists, and distinguished scholars. According to Wu Zhaohong's account, however, the original idea of creating a national defense planning agency came from Huang Fu, who was not only Chiang's close ally but a relative of Qian by marriage. According to Wu, Huang Fu knew that China's prominent scholars had called for resistance against Japan, and he also knew that Chiang needed to strengthen his still shaky position within the Nationalist government. Consequently, he asked Qian to present the idea of creating a national defense planning agency to Chiang, which Qian did. Jiang immediately accepted the idea. See ibid., 1–2; Wu Zhaohong, "Wosuo zhidao de ziyuan weiyuanhui" (The National Resources Commission I know), in HGZZW, 66–67.

14. Weng Wenhao, "Huigu wangshi" (Recollections of my experience), WZX, no. 80, 1–2.

15. Wu Zhaohong, "Wosuo zhidao de ziyuan weiyuanhui" (The National Resources Commission I know), in HGZZW, 67–68.

16. "Guofang sheji weiyuanhui zuzhi tiaoli" (Organizational regulations of the National Defense Planning Commission), in ZWDSC, vol. 1, 18–20.

17. They were Weng Wenhao, Qian Changzhao, Huang Musong, Yang Jie, Chen

Yi, Zhou Yaheng, Lin Wei, Ding Wenjiang, Chen Lifu, Wang Chongyou, Liu Hongsheng, Mu Ouchu, Zeng Zhaolun, Zhao Shimin, Tao Menghe, Liu Dajun, Wu Dingchang, Xu Xinliu, Tang Youren, Yang Duanliu, Wan Guoding, Shen Zonghan, Hu shiqing, Chen Bozhuang, Gu Zhen, Shen Yi, Yan Renguang, Qian Changzuo, Zhou Gengsheng, Qian Tai, Xu Shuxi, Yu Dawei, Xie Guansheng, Pei Fuzhi, Wang Shijie, Jiang Menglin, Hu Shi, Yang Zhensheng, Zhou Binglin. See "Qian Changzhao zhi Jiang Jieshi han" (A letter from Qian Changzhao to Chiang Kaishek), cited from Wang Weixing, "Guofang sheji weiyuanhui huodong pingshu" (An assessment of the activities of the National Defense Planning Commission), *Xuehai* (Sea of learning) 5 (1994): 78–83.

18. "Guofang sheji weiyuanhui gongzuo dagang" (Outline work program of the National Defense Planning Commission), SHA 28(2)/3739; "Guofang sheji weiyuanhui tian" (Proposals of the National Defense Planning Commission), SHA 28 (2) /3730.

19. "Guofang sheji weiyuanhui gongzuo dagang" (Outline work program of the National Defense Planning Commission), SHA 28(2)/3739.

20. "Guofang sheji weiyuanhui gongzuo gaikuang" (Survey of the National Defense Planning Commission), *Minguo dangan* (Republican archives), no. 2 (May 1990): 28–37; Shen Xiaoyun, "Liuxue guiguo renyuan yu guofang sheji weiyuanhui de chuangshe" (Returned talents and the creation of National Defense Planning Commission), *Jindaishi yanjiu* (Studies of modern history) 3 (May 1996): 241–258.

21. "Canmo benbu guofang sheji weiyuanhui mishuting gongzuo baogao" (Work report of the secretariat of the National Defense Planning Commission), 1934, SHA 28(2)/3749.

22. "Guofang sheji weiyuanhui renshi wenjian" (Personnel documents of National Defense Planning Commission), 1934, SHA 47/115.

23. The term *technocracy* is generally defined as "a government or social system controlled by technicians, especially scientists and technical experts." In this study, technocracy is defined as a government organization controlled by technical and professional experts and designed to develop and manage state-owned enterprises. Correspondingly, a technocrat refers to a technical or professional expert in an administrative or a managerial position. For a different definition of technocracy, see Walter A. McDougall, *The Heavens and the Earth: A Political History of the Space Age* (New York: Basic Books, 1985), 5.

24. ZWDSC, vol. 1, 26–27; Sun Cheng, "Ziyuan weiyuanhui jingguo shulue" (Brief survey of the National Resources Commission), ZWY 1, no. 1 (April 1939): 3–10.

25. Qian Changzhao, "Guomindang ziyuan weiyuanhui shimo" (Survey of the National Resources Commission), in HGZZW, 3; Wu Zhaohong, "Wosuo zhidao de ziyuan weiyuanhui" (The National Resources Commission I know), ibid., 75–76; Sun Cheng, "Ziyuan weiyuanhui jingguo shulue" (Brief

survey of the National Resources Commission), ZWY 1, no. 1 (April 1939): 3–10.

26. For an examination of the *Three-Year Heavy Industrial Reconstruction Plan* and its implementation, see Kirby, *Germany and Republican China,* 206–217.

27. ZWDSC, vol. 1, 104.

28. Qian Changzhao, "Liangnianban chuangban zhonggongye zhi jingguo ji ganxiang" (The experience of and reflection on creating heavy industry for the past two and a half years), XJ 2, no. 1 (June 16, 1939): 2–6.

29. Cheng Linsun, "Lun kangri zhanzheng shiqi ziyuan weiyuanhui qiye huodong jiqi lishi zuoyong" (Enterprise activities of the National Resources Commission and their historical role), in ZJJYZ, 1–26.

30. "Jingjibu ziyuan weiyuanhui zuzhi tiaoli" (Organizational regulations of the National Resources Commission), August 1, 1938, ZWY 1, no. 1 (April 1939): 63–64.

31. ZWDSC, vol. 1, 28–30.

32. "Jingjibu ziyuan weiyuanhui zuzhifa" (Organizational law of the National Resources Commission), May 13, 1942, ZWY 1, no. 1 (April 1939): 51–52.

33. "Guofang zhuanmen weiyuanhui baogao shencha guofang zhonggongye jianshe jihua ji ge binggongchang jianshe jihua" (Opinion by the Special Commission of National Defense on the plans for heavy industrial reconstruction and the reconstruction of ordnance factories), March 30, 1933, in ZMDZH, part v, vol. 1, caizheng jingji, no. 5, 953–954.

34. "Ziyuan weiyuanhui guanyu zhonggongye fangmian zhi gongzuo baogao" (Report of National Resources Commission on its work in heavy industrial reconstruction), June 1935, in ibid., part v, vol. 1, caizheng jingji, no. 5, 922–925.

35. "Xiuzheng jianshe yiban zhonggonye jihua yilanbiao" (Tabulation of the revised reconstruction plan for general heavy industries), in ZMDZH, part v, vol. 1, caizheng jingji, no. 5, 954–957.

36. "Ziyuan weiyuanhui yange" (Evolution of the National Resources Commission), 1947, in ZJGZ-C, vol. 3, part 2, 839; FYZWGS, 1948, 38. The document also appears in ZMDZH part v, vol. 3, caizheng jingji, no. 5, 48–108.

37. "Xinan gesheng sannian guofang jianshe jihua" (Three-year reconstruction plan for national defense in southwestern provinces), 1939, SHA 28(2)/37. The document also appears in ZMDZH, part v, vol. 2, caizheng jingji, no. 6, 82–103.

38. FYZWGS, 38–9; ZMDZH, part v, vol. 3, caizheng jingji, no. 5, 98.

39. The term *energy* refers only to electric energy in this book.

40. "Guofang gongye zhanshi sannian jihua gangyao" (Outline of three-year plan for national defense industries), in ZMDZH, part v, vol. 2, caizheng jingji, no. 6, 120–128.

41. "Guofang gongye sannian jihua dagang" (Outline of three-year plan for national defense industries), in ZJBGDS, vol. 3, 109–122.

42. For a survey of the four banks, see Zhu tongjiu, "Woguo sida guojia yinhang

de yanjin" (The evolution of China's four state-run banks), XJ 6, no. 6 (December 1941): 124–126.

43. Xu Kan, "Zongzong jiaonong siyinhang lianhe banshi zongchu zhi zhuzhi jiqi gongzuo" (The organization and work of the Joint Administrative Agency of the Four Banks), December 1939, in *Jingji huibao* (Economic report) 1, no. 5/ 6 (January 1940). Cited from SZS, vol. 1, 53–56.

44. "Zhanshi jianquan zhongyang jinrong jigou banfa" (Measures to strengthen wartime central financial institutions), September 8, 1939, ibid., 67–68.

45. For an excellent study, see Huang Liren, "Silian zongchu de chansheng, fazhan he shuaiwang" (The rise, development, and decline of the Joint Administrative Agency of the Four Banks), *Zhongguo jingjishi yanjiu* (Study in Chinese economic history), no. 2 (June 1991): 46–67.

46. "Jiang Jieshi jiu silian zongchu gongzuo shoulinggao" (Chiang Kaishek's handwritten instructions to the Joint Administrative Agency of the Four Banks), March 28, 1940, in SZS, vol. 1, 154–155.

47. "Lishihui guanyu sannian jingji jinrong jihua de jueyi" (Resolutions on the three-year economic and financial plans by the board of directors), March 30, 1940, ibid., 165–166.

48. "Jingji sannian jihua shishi banfa an" (Methods for implementing three-year economic plan), April 6–7, 1940, CMA 0101/221; SZS, vol. 1, 166–174.

49. Wu Zhaohong's finance report, ZWG 13, no. 2 (August 1947): 68–71.

50. "Ziweihui chengwen" (Report by the National Resources Commission), March 9, 1944, SHA 4/16636.

51. Ibid., February 12, 1944; "Zhongyang yinhang cheng jingjibu wen" (Report by the Central Bank to the Ministry of Economic Affairs), September 1, 1945, SHA 4/16579; "Zhongguo jiaotong erhang chengfang ziyuan weiyuanhui suoshu ge danwei daikuan fenlei tongji" (Statistics on the loans to the various *danwei* of the National Resources Commission by the Bank of China and the Bank of Communications for 1944 fiscal year), CMA 0101/1677. However, according to Wu Zhaohong, the National Resources Commission actually received only Ch$9 billion for the 1944 fiscal year (Ch$1.23 million in 1936 constant price) because it had to pay back outstanding loans. See "Ziweihui sanshisan niandu gongdai wenti tanhua jilu" (Record of the meeting on the National Resources Commission's industrial loans for the 1944 fiscal year). The meeting was held on June 22, 1944, CMA 0101/1677.

52. Wu Zhaohong's finance report, August 4, 1947, ZWG 13, no. 2 (August 1947): 68–71; Lin Lanfang, *Ziyuan weiyuanhui de tezhong kuangchan tongzhi, 1936–49* (The National Resources Commission's control over special mining products, 1936–49) (Taibei, Taiwan: Guoli zhengzhi daxue chubanshe, 1998), 121.

53. The agency was abolished in 1943.

54. "Ziyuan weiyuanhui wuti zhuankuan linian yingyu yongtu yilanbiao" (Tabulation of the use of the special fund from tungsten and antimony trade), 1945, SHA 4/8630.

55. "Ziyuan weiyuanhui touzi shumubiao" (Tabulation of investment capital by the National Resources Commission), SHA 282(2)/415; Lin Lanfang, *Ziyuan weiyuanhui de tezhong kuangchan tongzhi, 1936–1949*, 212.

56. "Shenjibu shencha minguo ershijiu niandu zhongyang zhengfu suiru suichu zongjuesuanshu jianyi gaijin shixiang" (Suggestions for improving the drafting of general national budget of revenue and expenditure by Ministry of Auditing), in ZMDZH, part v, vol. 2, caizheng jingji, no. 1, 256–259.

57. FYZWGS, 1948, 40; ZMDZH, part v, vol. 3, caizheng jingji, no. 5, 99.

58. Calculation is based on "Ziyuan weiyuanhui jingban shiye yilanbiao" (Tabulation of enterprises and organizations of the National Resources Commission), ZWG 9, no. 2 (August 16, 1945): 43–51.

59. "Ziyuan weiyuanhui jingban shiye yilanbiao" (Tabulation of enterprises and organizations of the National Resources Commission), ZWG 10, no. 3/4 (April 16, 1946): 68–75.

60. Chen Zhongxi, "Ziyuan weiyuanhui de dianli shiye" (Energy enterprises of the National Resources Commission), ZWG 13, no. 5 (November 16, 1947): 69–73.

61. "Ziyuan weiyuanhui ershijiu niandu zhonggongye jingfei juban geshiye jihua gaiyao" (Outline of the revised plan for various undertakings by the National Resources Commission for 1940 fiscal year), SHA 4/15262. Available evidence indicates the plant was unable to get the new generator transported to Guiyang due to the huge cost of transportation and the fact that the Vietnamese government prohibited this German-made generator from leaving Vietnam after the outbreak of war in Europe. Subsequently, the Guiyang plant purchased and installed two used generators with a capacity of generating 520 kilowatts of electricity. See "Guiyang dianchang gaikuang" (Survey of Guiyang power plant), 1940, SHA 28(2)/1787; Sun Yusheng, "Kangzhan banianlai zhi dianqi shiye" (Energy enterprises during the Sino-Japanese War), ZWJ 6, no. 1/2 (June 1, 1946): 141–149.

62. "Kunhu dianchang ershiba niandu shiye baogao" (Work report by Kunhu power plant for 1939 fiscal year), YPA 88(1)/537; Yang Shucun, "Ji kunming dianye xianqu—kunhu dianchang" (The pioneer of energy industry in Kunming—Kunhu power plant), in KSNXGQ, 195–201.

63. "Kunhu dianchang shiye baogao" (Work report by Kunhu power plant), 1940, YPA 88(1)/537.

64. "Ziyuan weiyuanhui ershijiu niandu zhonggongye jingfei juban geshiye jihua gaiyao" (Outline of the revised plan for the undertakings of the National Resources Commission for 1940 fiscal year), SHA 4/15262.

65. "Wanxian suidianchang shiye gaikuang" (Survey of the wanxian hydropower plant), ZWY 1, no. 3 (June 1939): 188–193.

66. "Ziyuan weiyuanhui yijiusisan niandu shizheng jihua" (Program of implementation for the 1943 fiscal year), October 1942, SHA 4/15289.

67. Chen Zhongxi, "Ziyuan weiyuanhui de dianli shiye" (Energy enterprises of the National Resources Commission), ZWG 13, no. 5 (November 16, 1947): 69–73.

68. Zheng Youkui and others, *Jiuzhongguo de ziyuan weiyuanhui*, 83.

69. Ibid., 84.

70. Weng Wenhao, "benhui qian zhuren weiyuan weng fuyuanzhang xunci" (Speech by Weng Wenhao), June 10, 1946, ZWG 11, no. 1 (July 16, 1946): 65–68.

71. Song Honggang and others, *Sun Yueqi zhuan* (Biography of Sun Yueqi) (Beijing: Shiyou gongye chubanshe, 1994), 147.

72. "Ziyuan weiyuanhui ji gefushu jigou linian yusuan zongbiao" (Tabulation of annual budget of the National Resources Commission and its subordinate enterprises, 1936–1945), SHA 28/2361.

73. Sun Yueqi, "Ji gansu yumen youkuang de chuangjian he jiefang" (My recollection of the creation and liberation of the Yumen oil field in Gansu province), in SYW, 37–38; Song Honggang and others, *Sun Yueqi zhuan*, 147–148.

74. "Weng Wenhao ziding nianpu chugao" (Weng Wenhao's own chronological account of his life), 1949, in JZ, no. 88 (May 1996): 47–104.

75. A geological report completed two months later asserted that the oil reservoir extended to an area covering thirty-nine square miles. See Zheng Youkui and others, *Jiuzhongguo de ziyuan weiyuanhui*, 89–90.

76. Song Honggang and others, *Sun Yueqi zhuan*, 149.

77. "Ziyuan weiyuanhui ershijiu niandu zhonggongye jingfei juban geshiye jihua gaiyao" (Outline of the revised plan for the undertakings of the National Resources Commission for the 1940 fiscal year), SHA 4/15262; "Ziyuan weiyuanhui ji gefushu jigou linian yusuan zongbiao" (Tabulation of annual budget of the National Resources Commission and its subordinate enterprises, 1936–45), SHA 28/2361.

78. "Sun Yueqi zhuan" (A biography of Sun Yueqi), in *Zhongguo ge minzhu dangpaishi renwuzhuan* (Biographies of prominent figures in the history of Chinese democratic parties) (Beijing: Huaxia chubanshe, 1993), ed. Yan Qi, vol. 4, 284–285; Song Honggang and others, *Sun Yueqi zhuan*, 148–150; "Gansu youkuangju gongzuo gaikuang" (Survey of Gansu Petroleum Administration), December 1944, SHA 28/17243.

79. The amount of gas extracted from crude oil would be significantly higher had U.S.-made equipment been used. As it was, China-made equipment extracted only about 20 percent gas from crude oil, whereas U.S.-made equipment would have extracted 64 percent gas. See Zhang Limen and He Baoshan, "Shinianlai zhi zhongguo shiyou shiye" (Chinese petroleum industry during the last decade) in SZZJ, 0329–0330; "Gansu youkuang shiye gaikuang" (Survey of Gansu oil enterprise), 1944, SHA 28(2)/2910.

80. "Gansu youkuang shiye gaikuang" (Survey of Gansu oil enterprise), 1944, SHA 28(2)/2910; "Jingjibu ziyuan weiyuanhui gongzuo baogao" (Work report by the National Resources Commission), 1941, SHA 28/17582.

81. The Highway Bureau for the Northwest received 20,000 gallons of gas out of the 20,550 gallons distributed among reconstruction enterprises. See "Jingjibu ziyuan weiyuanhui gongzuo baogao" (Work report by the National Resources Commission), 1942, SHA 28(2)/44.

82. Despite its contributions, the Gansu Petroleum Administration sustained a net loss of Ch$20.14 million between January 1941 and June 1943 due to the enormous transportation cost, the dramatic increase of price for raw materials, the lack of liquid capital, and an inability to raise product price. See "Gansu youkuang shiye gaikuang" (Survey of Gansu oil enterprise), 1944, SHA 28(2)/2910.

83. Cheng Yifa, "Zhongyang gangtiechang choubei gaikuang" (Survey of the preparation for the Central Iron and Steel Works), ZWY 1, no. 3 (June 1939): 163–193.

84. "Ziyuan weiyuanhui jingban shiye yilanbiao" (Tabulation of enterprises of the National Resources Commission), ZWG 10, no. 3/4 (April 16, 1946): 68–75.

85. Wang Ziyou, "Kangzhan banianlai zhi woguo gangtie gongye" (China's iron and steel industry during the Sino-Japanese War), ZWJ 6, no. 1/2 (June 1946): 86–106.

86. "Benhui qianjian gaikuang" (Survey of the relocation and reconstruction of the DISW), March 1943, CMA, gongyelei, file no. 30.

87. "Gangtiechang qianjian weiyuanhui ershiba niandu shiye baogao" (Work report by the DISW for 1939 fiscal year), and "Gangtiechang qianjian weiyuanhui ershijiu niandu shiye baogao" (Work report by the DISW for 1940 fiscal year), CMA 0201/104.

88. The National Resources Commission was not directly involved in the DISW's management, nor did it provide the DISW any funding as part of its budget. Consequently, the iron and steel output of the National Resources Commission's enterprises does not include that of the DISW.

89. "Benhui qianjian gaikuang" (Survey of the DISW), March 1943, CMA, gongyelei, file no. 30; Wang Ziyou, "Kangzhan banianlai zhi woguo gangtie gongye."

90. "Nantong meikuang choubeichu shiye gaikuang" (Survey of conditions of the preparatory division of Nantong coal mine) and "Jijiang tiekuang choubeichu shiye gaikuang" (Survey of conditions of the preparatory division of Jijiang iron mine), ZWY 3, no. 2/3 (March 1941): 1–20.

91. "Benhui qianjian gaikuang" (Survey of the DISW), March 1943, CMA, gongyelei, file no. 30.

92. Wang Ziyou, "Kangzhan banianlai zhi woguo gangtie gongye."

93. "Ziyuan weiyuanhui jingban shiye yilanbiao" (Tabulation of the enterprises of the National Resources Commission), ZWG 10, no. 3/4 (April 16, 1946): 68–75.

94. Ma Wenhe, "Kangzhan shiqi neiqian kunming de zhongyang jiqichang" (The Central Machine Works relocated to Kunming during the Sino-Japanese War), in KSNXGQ, 80–90; Du Tieying, "Kangzhan banianlai zhi jixie gongye" (Machine industry during the Sino-Japanese War), ZWJ 6, no. 1/2 (June 1946): 107–123.

95. Ma Wenhe, "Kangzhan shiqi neiqian kunming de zhongyang jiqichang."

96. Du Tieying, "Kangzhan banianlai zhi jixie gongye."

97. "Jingjibu ziyuan weiyuanhui min ershibanian ji ershijiunian shangbannian jianshe zhuankuan zhonggongye shiyefei kuaiji baogao" (Accounting report concerning the allocation of the special fund for heavy industrial reconstruction), SHA 28/1995.

98. "Ziyuan weiyuanhui ge danwei linian kubo zijin mingxibiao" (Tabulation of annual government appropriations for various *danwei* of the National Resources Commission, 1936–1948), SHA 28(2)/415.

99. Ma Wenhe, "Kangzhan shiqi neiqian kunming de zhongyang jiqichang;" "Ziyuan weiyuanhui ershiba niandu juesuan" (Final accounts of the National Resources Commission for 1939 fiscal year), SHA 4/17888.

100. "Ziyuan weiyuanhui gongchang gongzuo yuebao" (Monthly factory work report by the National Resources Commission), for September 1939, YPA 48(1)/238.

101. Ibid., for September 1941 YPA 48(1)/243.

102. Ibid., for September 1943 YPA 48(1)/245.

103. Ma Wenhe, "Kangzhan shiqi neiqian kunming de zhongyang jiqichang."

104. "Liunianlai zhuyao shengchan xiaoshou tongji" (Key statistics of production and distribution for the last six years), SHA 28(2)/1162.

105. "Benchang chanpin xiaoshou duixiang baifenbi" (Percentage of product distribution, July 1944–June 1945), SHA 28(2)/1162.

106. "Guofang huaxue gongye chubu jianshe an" (Preliminary plan for developing national defense chemical industry), SHA 28/8; Zheng Youkui and others, *Jiuzhongguo de ziyuan weiyuanhui*, 99.

107. Wei Yanshou, "Sichuan jiujingchang choubei jingguo ji xiankuang" (The preparation for Sichuan alcohol factory and its present conditions), ZWY 1, no. 5 (August 1939): 309–312.

108. Cao Liying and Zhao Shiqi, "Zhongguo zhanshi jiujing gongye yanjiu" (Study of the alcohol industry during the Sino-Japanese War), ZWJ 5, no. 1 (March 1945): 14–120; Jin Guitao, "Kangzhan banianlai zhi jiujing gongye" (The alcohol industry during the Sino-Japanese War), ZWJ 6, no. 1/2 (June 1946): 132–140; "Ziyuan weiyuanhui jingban shiye yilanbiao" (Tabulation of enterprises of the National Resources Commission), ZWG 10, no. 3/4 (April 16, 1946): 68–75.

109. Jin Guitao, "Kangzhan banianlai zhi jiujing gongye."

110. "Ziyuan weiyuanhui jingban shiye yilanbiao" (Tabulation of enterprises of the National Resources Commission), ZWG 10, no. 3/4 (April 16, 1946): 68–75.

111. Yun Zhen, "Diangong qicaichang zhi choubei jingguo ji xiankuang" (The preparation for the Central Electric Works and its present conditions), ZWY 1, no. 1 (April 1939): 23–29.

112. Guo Dewen and Sun Keming, "Kangzhan banianlai zhi dianqi gongye" (The electric industry during the Sino-Japanese War), ZWJ 6, no. 1/2 (June 1946): 124–131.

113. "Ziyuan weiyuanhui zhongyang diangong qicaichang" (Survey of the Central Electric Works), September 1941, SHA 28(2)/1230.

114. "Ziyuan weiyuanhui ji gefushu jigou linian yusuan zongbiao" (Tabulation of annual budget of the National Resources Commission and its enterprises, 1936–1945), SHA 28/2361.

115. "Ziyuan weiyuanhui ershiba niandu zhonggongye jingfei juban geshiye xiuzheng jihua gaiyao" (Outline of the revised plan for various undertakings by the National Resources Commission for 1939 fiscal year), SHA 4/15389; "Ziyuan weiyuanhui ershijiu niandu zhonggongye jingfei juban geshiye jihua gaiyao" (Outline of the revised plan for various undertakings by the National Resources Commission for 1940 fiscal year), SHA 4/15262; "Ziyuan weiyuanhui ji gefushu jigou linian yusuan zongbiao" (Tabulation of annual budget of the National Resources Commission and its enterprises, 1936–1945), SHA 28/2361; Yun Zhen, "Zhongyang diangong qicaichang ershiba niandu shiye baogao" (Work report by the Central Electric Works for 1939 fiscal year), ZWY 2, no. 4/5 (May 1940): 10–22.

116. "Zhongyang diangong qicaichang gaikuang" (Survey of the Central Electric Works), July 1944, SHA 28/15461.

117. Guo Dewen and Sun Keming, "Kangzhan banianlai zhi dianqi gongye" (The electric industry during the Sino-Japanese War), ZWJ 6, no. 1/2 (June 1946): 124–131; "Zhongyang diangong qicaichang gaikuang" (Survey of the Central Electric Works), July 1944, SHA 28/15461.

118. DT, no. 24 (April 1943): 19, SHA 28/7103.

119. "Zhongyang diangong qicaichang gaikuang" (Survey of the Central Electric Works), July 1944, SHA 28/15461; Lai Tao, "Kangzhan qianhou de zhongyang diangong qicaichang" (The Central Electric Works during the Sino-Japanese War), in KSNXGQ, 91–99.

120. Public enterprise included both state-owned and province-run enterprise. I assume that the state-owned enterprise held a dominant position among public enterprises.

121. ZGDB, vol. 1, 1–5.

122. Ibid., vol. 2, 33–64.

123. Thomas G. Rawski, *Economic Growth in Prewar China* (Berkeley: University of California Press, 1989), 3.

124. Ibid., 360–361.

125. ZGDB, vol. 2, 33–64.

126. ZMTT, table 50, p. 85.

127. The ascendancy of public enterprise is obvious even when one includes all industrial enterprises. The same statistical survey listed 656 public enterprises out of a total of 3,758 enterprises. On average, however, the amount of capital of a public enterprise was 12.6 times that of a private enterprise, the number of workers 1.9 times that of a private enterprise, and the power equipment 2.2 times that of a private enterprise. See Wu Taichang, "Kangzhan shiqi guomindang guojia ziben zai gongkuangye de longduan diwei jiqi

yu minying ziben bijiao" (The monopolistic position of the Nationalist state capital in industry and mining and its comparison with private capital during the Sino-Japanese War), *Zhongguo jingjishi yanjiu* (Study in Chinese economic history) 3 (September 1987): 133–150.

128. The seventeen products used in their estimates are: coal, pig iron, steel, non-ferrous metal, petroleum, electricity, alcohol, gas substitute, acid, alkali, cement, machinery and electric products, cotton yarn, cotton cloth, flour, match, and paper. See Xu Dixin and Wu Chengming, eds., *Xinminzhu zhuyi geming shiqi de zhongguo ziben zhuyi* (Chinese capitalism during the period of new democratic revolution, 1921–1949) (Beijing: Renmin chubanshe, 1993), 521, 541–545.

3. Enterprise Governance Structure

1. Li Hongzhang's memorial, September 20, 1865, in ZJBGDS, vol. 1, 53–56. Until the end of the Qing dynasty, the Jiangnan Arsenal actually used the name Jiangnan Manufacturing Bureau *(jiangnan zhizaoju)*, not Jiangnan General Manufacturing Bureau *(Jiangnan zhizao zhongju)*.

2. The first volume of ZJBGDS contains archival materials on thirty-eight ordnance factories established between 1864 and 1908. Among these factories the term *bureau (ju)* was used as part of the name for thirty-one factories.

3. Beginning with the Three Kingdom period and until the end of the Qing dynasty in 1911, all government officials and the posts they occupied were divided into nine ranks for the purpose of determining prestige, compensation, and priority in court audience. Ranks were commonly subdivided into two classes. Thus the normal number of gradations was 18, but 30 was not unusual. See ZJBGDS, vol. 1, 1151–1153; Charles O. Hucker, *A Dictionary of Official Titles in Imperial China* (Stanford, Calif.: Stanford University Press, 1985), 177.

4. Zhu Enba's recommendations, 1910, ZJBGDS, vol. 1, 345–346.

5. Report by Jilin Machinery Manufacturing Bureau, August 13, 1884, ibid., 1161.

6. Report by Jinling Manufacturing Bureau, November 1906, ibid., 1183–1184.

7. Tabulation of officials and their ranks of Sichuan New Machine Factory, June 1908, ibid., 1189.

8. Kennedy, *Arms of Kiangnan*, 158.

9. Telegram to Zhang Zhidong, January 3, 1896, in ZJBGDS, vol. 1, 1120.

10. Zhu Enba's telegram to the Ministry of War, December 20, 1909, ibid., 340–341.

11. "Lujunbu chouni gesheng zhizao junxie juchang jieshou hou banfa dagang" (Program for ordnance bureaus and factories in the provinces after takeover by the Ministry of War), 1910, ibid., 359–360.

12. Zhu Enba's report, November 1910, ibid., 353–535.

13. Shanghai Manufacturing Bureau's telegram, December 17, 1912, in ZJBGDS, vol. 2, 80.

14. Order by the Ministry of War, August 27, 1913, ibid., 83–84.

15. "Gebu guanzhi tongze xiuzheng caoan" (Draft of revised general regulations on the official system of various ministries), May 23, 1912, in ZMDZH, part iii, vol. 1, zhengzhi, no. 1, 6–9; "Beiyang zhengfu gongshangbu guanzhi" (Official system of the Ministry of Industry and Commerce of Beiyang government), August 8, 1912, in ZMDZH, part iii, gongkuangye, 1–2. The pinyin spelling of the character "jian" is the same for the second and the third rank, but the character "jian" for the third rank is written and pronounced differently. I distinguish the two characters by adding an *n* in the spelling for the third rank. Thus the spelling for "jian" for the second rank remains "jian," whereas the spelling for "jian" for the third rank is changed to "jiann."

16. "Wenguan renyongfa caoan" (Draft administrative law governing civil service appointment), in ZMDZH, part iii, vol. 1, zhengzhi, no. 1, 292–294.

17. "Lujunbu niding binggongchang guanzhi caoan" (A draft of the official system for ordnance factories under the Ministry of War), 1917, in ZJBGDS, vol. 2, 20–22.

18. Strauss, *Strong Institutions in Weak Polities: State Building in Republican China, 1927–1940* (Oxford, UK: Clarendon Press), 32.

19. GZJZS, vol. 3, 5–29.

20. ZJBGDS, vol. 3, 12–13; GZJZS, vol. 3, 58–61.

21. ZJBGDS, vol. 3, 15–16.

22. GZJZS, vol. 3, 68, 81–84.

23. Ibid., vol. 3, 75–94; ZJBGDS, vol. 3, 4–8.

24. "Junyong wenguan renyong zhanxing tiaoli" (Provisional regulations concerning civilian officials employed by the military) and "Junyong jishu renyong zhanxing tiaoli" (Provisional regulations concerning technical personnel employed by the military) promulgated on July 22, 1937 and transmitted by the Bureau of Ordnance on January 25, 1938, in ZJBGDS, vol. 3, 831–835.

25. "Binggongchang zuzhifa" (Organizational law of ordnance factories), October 31, 1929, in ZJBGDS, vol. 3, 231–233.

26. "Xiuzheng binggongchang zuzhifa" (Revised Organizational law of ordnance factories), July 15, 1931, ibid., 238–240.

27. Report of Jinling Arsenal, September 4, 1936, ibid., 296–297.

28. ZWDSC, vol. 1, 26–27; Sun Cheng, "Ziyuan weiyuanhui jingguo shulüe" (Brief survey of the National Resources Commission), ZWY 1, no. 1 (April 1939): 3–10.

29. ZWDSC, vol. 1, 28–30.

30. "Jingjibu ziyuan weiyuanhui zuzhifa" (Organizational law of the National Resources Commission), May 13, 1942, ZWY 1, no. 1 (April 1939): 51–52.

31. Wu Fuyuan, "Ziyuan weiyuanhui de renshi guanli zhidu" (The system of personnel management of the National Resources Commission), in HGZZW, 201.

32. "Jingjibu ziyuan weiyuanhui zhuzhi tiaoli" (Organizational regulations of the

National Resources Commission) promulgated on February 28, 1938 and amended on August 1, 1938, JG 1, no. 3 (March 1938): 96–97; 1, no. 13 (August 1938): 608–609; ZWY 1, no. 1 (April 1939): 63–64.

33. ZWFH, vol. 2, 1–3.

34. Zhanxing wenguan guandeng guanfengbiao" (Illustration of official rank and salary of the Nationalist government) first promulgated on September 23, 1933; revised on September 23, 1936, in GZZZDSX, vol. 2, 54–55.

35. ZWFH, vol. 2, 1–3; Wu Fuyuan, "Ziyuan weiyuanhui de renshi guanli zhidu" (The system of personnel management of the National Resources Commission), in HGZZW, 201.

36. "Ziyuan weiyuanhui fushu shiye zuzhi zhanxing tongze" (Provisional organizational regulations for subordinate organizations of the National Resources Commission), November 28, 1938, ZWY 1, no. 1 (April 1939): 66–70.

37. "Xiuzheng ziyuan weiyuanhui fushu shiye zuzhi zhanxing tongze" (Revised provisional organizational regulations for subordinate organizations of the National Resources Commission), September 23, 1941, ZWG 1, no. 4 (October 16, 1941): 35–41.

38. KHYGS, 80.

39. "Gangtiechang qianjian weiyuanhui zanxing zuzhi tiaoli" (Provisional organizational regulations of the DISW), December 21, 1939, CMA 0201/76.

40. "Gangtiechang qianjian weiyuanhui banshi guize" (Regulations on conducting business at the DISW), March 30, 1940, CMA 0201/76.

41. "Bangongting tongzhi" (Notice by the general office), December 30, 1941, CMA 0105/780.

42. "Gangtiechang qianjian weiyuanhui zanxing zuzhi tiaoli" (Provisional organizational regulations of the DISW), March 16, 1943, CMA 0204/16.

43. "Gangtiechang qianjian weiyuanhui di erbai sishierci huibao jilu" (Record of the 242nd meeting of the DISW), October 21, 1944, CMA 0105/762.

44. Qi Zhilu, "Shinianlai zhi jingji jianshe" (Economic reconstruction during the past decade), in SZZJ, 1262.

45. This phenomenon also manifested itself in private enterprises in other national contexts. In Germany, for example, "bureaucratization preceded industrialization, and bureaucratic structures, processes, and values therefore profoundly shaped the process and character of industrialization in Germany." As a result, technicians, supervisory personnel, salespersons, clerks, or office employees at the Siemens & Halske electrical manufacturing firm conceived of themselves as "private civil servants." As late as 1921, the Siemens Company reintroduced a ranking system (beamter) that "led to an internal differentiation" among white collar workers. See Jürgen Kocka, "Capitalism and Bureaucracy in German Industrialization before 1914," *Economic History Review* 34 (August 1981): 453–468; "Family and Bureaucracy in German Industrial Management, 1850–1914: Siemens in Comparative Perspective," in his *Industrial Culture and Bourgeois Society: Business, Labor, and Bureaucracy in Modern Germany* (New York: Berghahn Books, 1999), 27–50; Heidrun Hom-

burg, "Scientific Management and Personnel Policy in the Modern Germany Enterprise, 1918–1939: The Case of Siemens," in *Managerial Strategies and Industrial Relations: An Historical and Comparative Study*, eds. Howard F. Gospel and Graig R. Littler (Aldershot, Hampshire: Gower Publishing Company Limited, reprint ed., 1986), 137–156.

46. "Ziyuan weiyuanhui gongchang gongzuo yuebao" (Monthly work report of factories under the jurisdiction of the National Resources Commission), YPA 48(1)/243, 48(1)/245.

47. The calculation of the ratio between *zhiyuan* and workers is based on a number of archival sources. They include statistics on the turnover of *zhiyuan* and workers between June and September 1943, CMA 0105/1327; "Gangqianhui benbu renshi baogao" (Personnel report of the DISW), 1944, CMA 0201/105.

48. Contracts between the Bureau of Ordnance and Max Kanner, in ZJBGDS, vol. 3, 1134–1136.

49. "Meiguo kenna xiansheng canguan woguo gongchang zhi piping—zhi jingjibu weng buzhang zhi baogao" (The criticism of Chinese factories by Mr. Kannar of the United States—a report submitted to Weng Wenhao), *Taosheng* (Crashing waves) 1, no. 8 (October 15, 1944): 6–7, CMA 0202/552.

50. "Dangqian gongkuangye yiban wenti" (General problems in industry and mining), n.d., SHA 28/5245.

51. "Gangtiechang qianjian weiyuanhui renshi renyong" (Provisions for DISW personnel appointment), 1942, in KHYGS, 679–682.

52. "Gangtiechang qianjian weiyuanhui ershijiunian di zaizhi renyuan xingeibiao" (Complete payroll list of all *zhiyuan* of the DISW at the end of 1940), CMA 0201/104.

53. Yun Zhen, "Lun banli guoying gongkuang shiye" (On managing state-owned enterprise in industry and mining), XJ 8, no. 10 (March 16, 1943): 178–182.

54. "Jiang Jieshi guanyu queli zhanhou jingji shiye zhidu ji maoyi zhidu de daidian" (Document concerning the establishment of postwar economic enterprise system and trade system approved by Chiang Kaishek), November 26, 1945, in ZMDZH, part v, vol. 3, caizheng jingji, no. 1, 6–10; SHA 28/1360.

55. For example, Alfred D. Chandler Jr. refers to modern business enterprises as "new bureaucratic enterprises" due to the existence of a managerial hierarchy. See Chandler, *The Visible Hand: The Managerial Revolution in American Business* (Cambridge, Mass.: Harvard University Press, 1977), 7–11.

56. Alfred D. Chandler Jr., *Scale and Scope: The Dynamics of Industrial Capitalism* (Cambridge, Mass.: Harvard University Press, 1990), 17.

57. Chandler, *The Visible Hand*, 376, 497. Business historians have criticized Chandler for his neglect of the political dimension of economic development. See Richard R. John, "Elaborations, Revisions, Dissents: Alfred D. Chandler, Jr.'s, *The Visible Hand* after Twenty Years," *Business History Review* 71 (Summer 1997): 151–200; Daniel Nelson, "Western Business History: Experience and Comparative Perspectives," in *Chinese Business History: Interpretive Trends and*

Priorities for the Future, ed. Robert Gardella, Jane K. Leonard, and Andrea McElderry (Armonk, N.Y.: M. E. Sharpe, 1998), 151–165.

58. "Jingjibu ziyuan weiyuanhui xunling" (Instruction of the National Resources Commission), December 16, 1938, CMA 0105/582. This document later appeared as "Gao benhui fushu jiguan zhuchi renyuan shu" (Letter to officials of the subordinate organizations of the National Resources Commission), ZWY 1, no. 1 (April 1, 1939): 1–2.

59. Wellington K. K. Chan, *Merchants, Mandarins, and Modern Enterprise in Late Qing China* (Cambridge, Mass.: Harvard University Press, 1977), 161–165, 177.

60. William C. Kirby, "China Unincorporated: Company Law and Business Enterprise in Twentieth Century China," *Journal of Asian Studies* 54, no. 1 (May 1998): 43–63.

61. "Jianshe weiyuanhui zuzhifa" (Organizational law of the National Reconstruction Commission) promulgated on December 8, 1928. Revised on February 19, 1930. Revised again on February 17, 1931 and on November 4, 1936, in GZZZDSX, vol. 1, 128–130.

62. "Quanguo jingji weiyuanhui zuzhi tiaoli" (Organizational regulations of the National Economic Commission), June 15, 1931; "Xiuzheng quanguo jingji weiyuanhui zuzhi tiaoli" (Revised regulations of the National Economic Commission), September 27, 1933, in ibid., 182–186.

63. "Shiyebu zuzhifa" (Organizational law of the Ministry of Industries) first promulgated on January 17, 1931. Revised three times on the following dates: February 21, 1931, June 1, 1935, and November 2, 1936, in GZZZDSX, vol. 1, 238–242.

64. "Jianshe weiyuanhui zuzhifa" (Organizational law of the National Reconstruction Commission) promulgated on December 8, 1928. Revised on February 19, 1930. Revised again on February 17, 1931 and on November 4, 1936; "Quanguo jingji weiyuanhui zuzhi tiaoli" (Organizational regulations of the National Economic Commission), June 15, 1931; "Xiuzheng quanguo jingji weiyuanhui zuzhi tiaoli" (Revised organizational regulations of the National Economic Commission), September 27, 1933, in ibid., 128–130, 182–186.

65. Chiang Kaishek, "Geming chengbai de jishi he jianshe gongzuo de fangfa" (The opportunity for the success of our revolution and the method of reconstruction work), November 14, 1933, in XJSYZ, vol. 11, 601–615.

66. Da, "Xingzheng jiguan gaige de biyao" (The necessity for reforming administrative organizations), DP, no. 25 (November 6, 1932): 10–16.

67. Ibid.

68. Ibid.

69. Ibid.

70. The author expressed his belief in the importance of this question in these words: "This kind of question is of great significance, since we are in the stage of a final struggle for the life and death of China. Undertaking large-

scale reconstruction enterprises in an era of absolute poverty among the people is like attempting to prolong life with the last drop of blood. If we keep repeating the failure of the China Merchants' Steamship Navigation Company, Hanyeping Coal and Iron Company, and a number of state-run railways, I am afraid not only will our enterprise have much less hope in the future; the Chinese nation will be doomed to fail." Ibid.

71. Through careful reading I was able to establish the author's identity using the pen name "Da." More than two years after this essay appeared in the twenty-fifth issue of the *Independent Review,* a scholar named Ren Shuyong published an essay in the sixty-eighth issue of the same journal. In that essay Ren summarized the central argument of the essay by "Da." Ren also stated that "on the 25th issue of this journal Mr. Junda had discussed the necessity of reforming government administrations." It was well known then that "Junda" was the pen name of Weng Wenhao, meaning "Mr. Doctor"— referring to the doctoral degree he earned in Belgium. See Ren Shuyong, "jishu hezuo yingcong hechu zuoqi" (What should we do to prepare for technological cooperation with the League of Nations?), DP, no. 68 (September 17, 1933): 5–8.

72. Wu Zhaohong, "Wosuo zhidao de ziyuan weiyuanhui" (The National Resources Commission I know), in HGZZW, 67–68.

73. Ren Shuyong, "Jishu hezuo yingcong hechu zuoqi."

74. As noted in note 23 of Chapter 2, I choose to define technocracy as a government organization controlled by technical and professional experts and designed to develop and manage state-owned enterprises. Correspondingly, a technocrat refers to a technical or professional expert in an administrative or managerial position.

75. Zhu Enba's report, November 1910, in ZJBGDS, vol. 1, 353–355.

76. Memorial by the Ministry of War, May 8, 1911, ibid., 355.

77. Correspondence, June 23, 1914, in ZJBGDS, vol. 2, 451–452.

78. Letter, February 4, 1915, ibid., 452–453.

79. "Binggong xuexiao shiliao" (Historical materials on ordnance school), 1948, in ZJBGDS, vol. 3, 1296–1298.

80. Record of cases (1913–1923), in ZJBGDS, vol. 2, 449–460.

81. A senior *zhiyuan* who had worked in the Shanghai Arsenal from the late 1920s wrote, "The Jiangnan Manufacturing Bureau only employed foreign engineers and technicians during its formative period. Later when foreign engineers and technicians left China, their management and technical positions were filled by former interpreters and Chinese foremen. It was not until the Nationalists came to power that senior intellectuals and technical personnel began to enter ordnance factories and occupy management and technical positions." See Chen Xiuhe, "Youguan shanghai binggongchang de huiyi" (My recollection of Shanghai Arsenal), 1961, WZX, no. 19, 69–94.

82. "Binggong xuexiao shiliao" (Historical materials on ordnance school), 1948, in ZJBGDS, vol. 3, 1296–1298.

83. Constitution of the Hanyang Special School of Ordnance Manufacturing, May 29, 1929, ibid., 981–984.

84. Ibid., 1002–1004.

85. *Minguo renwu dacidian*, 893.

86. Chen Xiuhe, "Youguan shanghai binggongchang de huiyi" (My recollection of Shanghai Arsenal), 1961, WZX, no. 19, 69–94.

87. I say "roughly" because the nature of a few schools cannot be determined with certainty from the description given in the archival material.

88. "Binggongshu zhiyuanlu" (*Zhiyuan* roster of the Bureau of Ordnance), April 1, 1929, in ZJBGDS, vol. 3, 53–56.

89. Ibid., vol. 3, 249–252.

90. Wu Zhaohong, "Wosuo zhidao de ziyuan weiyuanhui."

91. Qian Changzhao, "Liangnianban chuangban zhonggongye zhi jingguo ji ganxiang" (The experience of and reflection on creating heavy industry in the past two and a half years), XJ 2, no. 1 (May 16, 1939): 2–6.

92. Ibid.

93. "Jingjibu ziyuan weiyuanhui xunling" (Instruction by the National Resources Commission), December 16, 1938, CMA 0105/582. This document later appeared as "Gao benhui fushu jiguan zhuchi renyuan shu" (Letter to officials of the subordinate organizations of the National Resources Commission), ZWY 1, no. 1 (April 1, 1939): 1–2.

94. "Qian fuzhuren weiyuan xunci" (Speech by Qian Changzhao), January 21, 1942, ZWG 2, no. 1 (January 16, 1942): 83–91.

95. Qian Changzhao's petition to Chiang Kaishek, June 1943, SHA 28(2)/940.

96. Qian Changzhao, "Guanyu gongye jianshe de jige wenti" (Issues concerning industrial reconstruction), DGB, December 30, 1945; ZWG 10, no. 1/2 (February 16, 1946): 66–68.

97. "Ziyuan weiyuanhui jiangzhu jiaoyu ji yanjiu jiguan gongkuangye jishu zhanxing banfa" (Provisional regulations on assisting educational and research institutions in the area of industrial and mining technology), June 24, 1941, in KHYGS, 763–764.

98. "Ziyuan weiyuanhui shezhi daxue jiangxuejin zhanxing banfa" (Provisional regulations on establishing financial assistance in colleges and universities), July 8, 1942, ZWG 3, no. 1 (July 16, 1942): 17.

99. "Ziyuan weiyuanhui yu gedaxue hezuo jiangzhu gongkuang jishu zhanxing banfa" (Provisional regulations on assisting the development of technology in industry and mining in cooperation with universities), September 8, 1942, ZWG 3, no. 4 (October 16, 1942): 17.

100. ZWG 11, no. 6 (December 16, 1946): 69.

101. ZWJRFSS, vol. 1, 31.

102. William C. Kirby, "The Chinese War Economy," in *China's Bitter Victory: The War with Japan, 1937–1945*, ed. James C. Hsiung and Steven I. Levine (Armonk, N.Y.: M. E. Sharpe, 1992), 201.

103. ZWJRFSS, vol. 1, 5.

104. Wu Zhaohong, "Wosuo zhidao de ziyuan weiyuanhui."

105. Zheng Youkui and others, *Jiuzhongguo de ziyuan weiyuanhui*, 313.

106. ZWG 1, no. 4 (October 16, 1941): 73; 3, no. 4 (October 16, 1942): 41; 5, no. 4 (October 16, 1943): 27; 7, no. 5 (November 16, 1944): 29.

107. *Guancha* (Observations) 1, no. 2 (September 7, 1946): 19–20.

108. For an excellent discussion of technocratic organization and technological development, see William C. Kirby, "Technocratic organization and Technological Development in China: The Nationalist Experience and Legacy, 1928–1953," in *Science and Technology in Post-Mao China*, ed. Denis F. Simon and Merle Goldman (Cambridge, Mass.: Harvard University Press, 1989), 23–43.

4. Enterprise Management and Incentive Mechanisms

1. According to Robert Gardella, the basis of the old government accounting was the so-called four columns system, which established four categories for recording official receipts and disbursements: balance forwarded, new receipts, outlays, and present balance. This was a single-entry system based on a simple principle: the balance forwarded plus new receipts must equal outlays plus present balance. See Gardella's "Squaring Accounts: Commercial Bookkeeping Methods and Capitalist Rationalization in Late Qing and Republican China," *Journal of Asian Studies* 51, no. 2 (May 1992): 317–339.

2. "Binggong kuaiji shixing guize caoan" (Draft trial regulations on ordnance accounting), September 2, 1933, in ZJBGDS, vol. 3, 741–742.

3. "Binggong kuaiji shixing guize" (Trial regulations on ordnance accounting), May 1934, ibid., 744–745.

4. Ge Jingkang's report, April 18, 1934, ibid., 742–743.

5. Report by the Bureau of Ordnance, July 10, 1934, ibid., 745–746.

6. "Zhizaosi ershisannian du gongzuo baogao zhaiyao" (Summary of the work report by the department of manufacturing for the 1934 fiscal year), July 1935, ibid., 141–143.

7. "Junzhengbu binggongshu shanghai liangangchang jianshi baogao" (Inspection report by the Shanghai Steel Plant), March 1935, CMA 0105/679.

8. "Di sanshi gongchang changshi" (History of the Thirtieth Arsenal), 1947, in ZJBGDS, vol. 3, 1235–1245.

9. "Gangtiechang qianjian weiyuanhui qianyuhou dierci weiyuanhui huiyilu" (Record of the second DISW meeting after relocation to Chongqing). The meeting was held on October 22, 1938. CMA 0105/770.

10. "Gangtiechang qianjian weiyuanhui sheshi ji gongzuo qingxing baogaoshu" (Report on the installation and conditions of the DISW), April 1941, CMA 0201/8.

11. "Gangtiechang qianjian weiyuanhui banshi guize" (Regulations on conducting business at the DISW), March 30, 1940, CMA 0201/76.

12. "Gangtiechang qianjian weiyuanhui kuaijichu chuli wenshu zhanxing banfa" (Provisional regulations for dealing with documents in the accounting division), May 24, 1940, CMA 0105/954.

13. "Chengben kuaiji diyici taolunhui jilu" (Record of the first cost accounting meeting). The meeting was held on December 14, 1940, CMA 0105/779.

14. "Kuaijichu gongzuo baogao" (Work report of the accounting division, January–April 1943), CMA 0201/95. The DISW fiscal year was from January to December.

15. Ibid.; Ray H. Garrison and Eric W. Noreen, *Managerial Accounting,* 7th ed. (Homewood, Ill.: Richard D. Irwin, 1994), 34–36.

16. Chandler, *The Visible Hand,* 267–268. See also Robert S. Kaplan, "The Evolution of Management Accounting," *Accounting Review* 59 (July 1984): 390–418.

17. "Benhui shiban fenbu yingkui jisuan de mudi ji xiwang" (The objectives and expectations of calculating profits and losses among the constituent parts on a trial basis), *Taosheng* (Crashing waves) 1, no. 7 (September 30, 1944): 7–8, CMA 0202/552.

18. Ibid.

19. Ibid.

20. Ibid.

21. "Kuaijichu gongzuo baogao" (Work report of the accounting division, January–April 1943), CMA 0201/95.

22. *Mishuchu tongbao* (Bulletin of the secretariat), no. 85, March 24, 1943, CMA 0204/16.

23. Yang Jizeng's instruction at the 189th meeting of the DISW held on July 15, 1943, CMA 0105/763.

24. "Kuaijichu gongzuo baogao" (Work report of the accounting division, May–September 1943) CMA 0201/95.

25. *Mishuchu tongbao* (Bulletin of the secretariat), no. 171, December 28, 1943, CMA 0105/373.

26. Ibid., no. 172, December 31, 1943, CMA 0105/373.

27. Ibid., no. 218, May 12, 1944, CMA 0105/374.

28. "Kuaijichu gongzuo baogao" (Work report of the accounting division, March–April 1944), CMA 0201/95.

29. *Mishuchu tongbao* (Bulletin of the secretariat), no. 232, May 29, 1944, CMA 0105/374.

30. "Kuaijichu gongzuo baogao" (Work report of the accounting division, May–July 1944), CMA 0201/95.

31. Ibid., June–September 1944, CMA 0201/95.

32. Instruction by Yang Jizeng at the 243rd meeting of the DISW held on October 28, 1944, CMA 0105/762.

33. Ibid., no. 444, February 2, 1945, CMA 0105/376.

34. Ibid., no. 602, August 7, 1945, CMA 0105/378.

35. Ibid., no. 609, August 15, 1945, CMA 0105/378.

36. Yang Jizeng's instruction, July 29, 1943, *Mishuchu tongbao* (Bulletin of the secretariat): no. 119, CMA 0105/373; "Benhui shiban fenbu yingkui jisuan de mudi ji xiwang" (The objectives and expectations of calculating profits and losses among the constituent parts on a trial basis), *Taosheng* (Crashing waves) 1, no. 7 (September 30, 1944): 7–8, CMA 0202/552.

37. A contemporary study of the management policies and practices of thirty-one leading industrial corporations in the United States reveals that, although the number of divisions varied widely, in one well-organized company practically all activities headed up to "four divisional vice-presidents in charge of manufacturing, marketing, financial, and purchasing activities." See Paul E. Holden and others, *Top-Management Organization and Control* (Stanford, Calif.: Stanford University Press, 1941), 28.

38. "Gangtiechang qianjian weiyuanhui kuaiji zhidu" (The accounting system of the DISW), CMA, gongyelei, file no. 30.

39. "Kuaijichu gongzuo baogao" (Work report of the accounting division, March–April 1944), CMA 0201/95.

40. "Benhui shiban fenbu yingkui jisuan de mudi ji xiwang" (The objectives and expectations of calculating profits and losses among the constituent parts on a trial basis), *Taosheng* (Crashing waves) 1, no. 7 (September 30, 1944): 7–8, CMA 0202/552.

41. In 1944 the DISW codified its new accounting system in "Gangtiechang qianjian weiyuanhui kuaiji zhidu" (The accounting system of the DISW), CMA, gongyelei, file no. 30. It should be noted that, as the DISW manufactured materials essential for ordnance production, it adopted an accounting system obtained in the ordnance industry.

42. "Ziyuan weiyuanhui fushu jiguan kuaiji guicheng" (Accounting regulations for subordinate organizations of the National Resources Commission), November 1936, SHA 28/1834.

43. "Ziyuan weiyuanhui kuaiji baogao" (Accounting report of the National Resources Commission), 1940, SHA 28/1995.

44. "Jingjibu ziyuan weiyuanhui xunling" (Instruction of the National Resources Commission), December 16, 1938, CMA 0105/582; "Gao benhui fushu jiguan zhuchi renyuan shu" (Letter to officials of subordinate organizations of the National Resources Commission), ZWY 1, no. 1 (April 1, 1939): 1–2.

45. Qian Zuling, "Kuaiji zhidu duiyu benhui shiye fazhan zhi qieyao" (The urgent necessity of establishing an accounting system for enterprise development of the National Resources Commission), n.d., although it appears to have been written in 1939, SHA 28/2030.

46. Zhang Jun's report, April 1940, SHA 28/1967.

47. Zhang Jun, "Benhui zonggongye jianshe jijin suoshu jiguan kuaiji zhidu sheji jingguo gailüe" (Survey of the history of drafting the accounting system for subordinate organizations of the National Resources Commission using the heavy industrial reconstruction fund), summer 1942, SHA 28/1876. Zhang Jun received college education in the United States. Upon returning to China, he taught at Communications University in Shanghai and Wuhan University. Later he worked as head of the auditing division of the Nationalist Military Affairs Commission before joining the National Resources Commission as head of its accounting office. When the National Resources Commission reorganized its accounting office in January 1943, it appointed

Zhang to head the accounting division. Zhang was the principal architect of the cost accounting system of the National Resources Commission. He also appointed many of his former students to leading accounting positions in the commission's subordinate organizations. See Zheng Youkui and others, *Jiuzhongguo de ziyuan weiyuanhui,* 328; *Mishuchu tongbao* (Bulletin of the secretariat), no. 58, January 18, 1943, CMA 0204/16.

48. Zhang Jun's telegrams to Weng Wenhao and Qian Changzhao, September 1939. SHA 28–2080.
49. Zhang Jun, "Benhui zonggongye jianshe jijin suoshu jiguan kuaiji zhidu sheji jingguo gailüe."
50. "Jingjibu ziyuan weiyuanhui zonggongye jianshe jijin suoshu jiguan kuaiji zhidu" (The accounting system of subordinate organizations of the National Resources Commission using the heavy industrial reconstruction fund), August 1940, CMA, jingjilei, file no. 622–1.
51. Zhang Jun's report to Weng Wenhao and Qian Changzhao after 1945, SHA 28–1876.
52. "Gangtiechang qianjian weiyuanhui kuaiji zhidu" (The accounting system of the DISW), CMA, gongyelei, file no. 30
53. "Ziyuan weiyuanhui sanshier niandu gongzuo jihua" (Work plan of the National Resources Commission for the 1943 fiscal year), early 1943, SHA 28(2)/34.
54. Zhang Jun's report to Qian Changzhao, September 5, 1944, SHA 28/2001.
55. Yun Zhen, "minguo sanshiernian zhi jihua yu mubiao" (Our plan and objectives for the 1943 fiscal year), DT, no. 21 (January 1943): 1–2, SHA 28/7103.
56. "Zhongyang diangong qicaichang dierchang zhizao chengben tongjibiao" (Statistical table of manufacturing cost for the second plant of the Central Electric Works for 1943 fiscal year), CMA 0101/245.
57. "Gechang chanpin danwei chengben guji huizongbiao" (Tabulation of estimated unit cost of products made by subordinate enterprises of the National Resources Commission for January 1945), SHA 28/6105.
58. I prefer to render the term *yundong* as "campaign" instead of "movement." Although both terms mean a series of actions advancing a principle or tending toward a particular end, a movement often lasts longer and has broader socioeconomic and political objectives than a campaign.
59. Lloyd E. Eastman, *The Abortive Revolution: China under Nationalist Rule, 1927–1937* (Cambridge, Mass.: Harvard University Press, 1974), 66–74; Arif Dirlik, "The Ideological Foundations of the New Life Movement: A Study in Counterrevolution," *Journal of Asian Studies* 34, no. 4 (1975): 945–980; Kirby, *German and Republican China,* 176–185.
60. The term *Gnomindang* refers to the Nationalist Party. See Eastman, *Abortive Revolution,* 67, 13.
61. Dirlik, "Ideological Foundations."
62. Kirby, *Germany and Republican China,* 176.
63. Chiang Kaishek, "Geming chengbai de jishi he jianshe gongzuo de fangfa,"

(The chance for the success of the revolution and the method for economic reconstruction), speech delivered at Nanchang field headquarters, November 14, 1933, in XJSYZ, vol. 11, 601–615.

64. Summary of speech by Deng Wenyi, February 26, 1934, in XYXYHD, 84.

65. Dirlik, "Ideological Foundations."

66. Chiang Kaishek, "Xinshenghuo yundong fafan" (The launching of the New Life Campaign); "Xinshenghuo yundong zhi yaoyi" (The meaning of the New Life Campaign), February 17 and 19, 1934, respectively, in XJSYZ, vol. 12, 69; 70–80.

67. Chiang Kaishek, "Xinshenghuo yundong zhi zhenyi" (The true meaning of the New Life Campaign), March 26, 1934, ibid., 176–182. For the rest of 1934, Chiang Kaishek continued to deliver speeches reiterating and elaborating the basic themes of the New Life Campaign. See ibid., 87–94; 111–115; 137–147; 176–182; 583–587.

68. Chiang Kaishek, "Sichuan ying zuowei fuxing minzu zhi genjudi" (Sichuan should serve as a base for national rejuvenation), March 4, 1935, in XJSYZ, vol. 13, 113–119.

69. Dirlik, "Ideological Foundations."

70. Cao Yi, "Xinshenghuo yundong he guomin jingshen zongdongyuan lunxi" (Examination of the New Life Campaign and the general national spiritual mobilization), Minguo dangan (Republican archives) 56, no. 2 (1999): 97–104.

71. MESXYZ, 139–144.

72. Chiang Kaishek, "Xinshenghuo yundong erzhounian jinian ganxiang" (My reflection on the New Life Campaign on its second anniversary), in SQXY, vol. 2, 815–818.

73. XYXYHD, 5.

74. Chiang Kaishek made the statement in an interview with reporters in Guiyang on April 1, 1935, in GJJY, 2–3.

75. Chiang Kaishek, "Guomin jingji jianshi yundong zhi yiyi jiqi shishi" (The meaning and implementation of the National Economic Reconstruction Campaign), October 1, 1935, in GJJY, 17–26. See also his "Guomin zijiu jiuguo zhi yaodao: xinshenghuo yundong yu guomin jingji jianshe yundong" (The key for saving oneself and saving the nation: the New Life Campaign and the National Economic Reconstruction Campaign), January 1, 1936, in MESQXY, vol. 1, 46–53.

76. According to Parks M. Coble, Chiang did not explicitly emphasize national defense issues in the public address because of the effort to satisfy commitments made to Japan in peace talks. Japan was supposed to be the "friendly neighbor" at this point. See Coble's Facing Japan: Chinese Politics and Japanese Imperialism, 1927–1937 (Cambridge, Mass.: Council on East Asian Studies, Harvard University, 1991), 182–194.

77. Chiang Kaishek, "Xiandai guojia de shengmingli" (The vitality of a modern state), September 8, 1935, in XJSYZ, vol. 13, 404–418.

78. Gao Shukang, "Shinianlai zhi jingji zhengce" (The economic policy during the past decade), in SZZJ, 21–72.

79. ZMDZH, part v, vol. 1, zhengzhi, no. 2, 574–582.
80. "Guomin jingji jianshe yundong weiyuanhui zhangcheng" (Regulations of the Commission for the National Economic Reconstruction Campaign), June 1936, in GJJY, 1–16.
81. For a recent Chinese study of the National Economic Reconstruction Campaign, see Ye Cunfeng, "Shixi kangzhanqian de guomin jingji jianshe yundong" (Examination of the National Economic Reconstruction Campaign before 1937), *Shixue yuekan* (Historical studies monthly), no 2 (1987): 112–118.
82. Although direct evidence linking the three campaigns is lacking, the comments by a senior party leader in the context of discussing the Work Emulation Campaign revealed as much: "I have been a party member for many years. Based on my observation over these years, I can tell you that our Supreme Leader would launch a campaign, such as the New Life Campaign and the National Economic Reconstruction Campaign, in response to a certain turn of events during certain time period," in GJZJ, 9.
83. Chiang Kaishek, "Gaijin dangwu zhengzhi jingji zhi yaodian" (Key elements for improving party work, politics and economy), November 15, 1939, in XJSYZ, vol. 16, 453–457.
84. Chiang Kaishek, "Jingji kangzhan zhi jingshen he yaowu" (The spirit and task of the economic war of resistance against Japan), May 12, 1940, ibid., vol. 17, 332–338.
85. Chiang Kaishek, "Gaijin dangwu zhengzhi jingji zhi yaodian."
86. Gan Naiguang, "Gongzuo jingsai de yuanli" (The rationale for work emulation), originally published in the Nationalist *Central Daily News* on March 18, 1940, in GJC, 37–40; Wang Shixian, "Gongzuo jingsai yu gongyehua" (Work emulation and industrialization), GJY 1, no. 1 (November 15, 1943): 8–13.
87. "Gongzuo jingsai zhidu dagang" (Program for the work emulation system), CMA 0201/80.
88. Gan Naiguang, "Gongzuo jingsai yundong" (The Work Emulation Campaign), in his *Zhongguo xingzheng xinlun* (A New approach to government administration in China) (Chongqing, Shangwu yinshuguan: 1943), 110–111.
89. GJC, 1.
90. Chiang Kaishek, "Tichang gongzuo jingsai wancheng shengchan jianshe" (Promoting work emulation and bringing to fruition the task of economic reconstruction), March 12, 1940, in GJC, 2.
91. Gan Naiguang, "Gongzuo jingsai de yuanli."
92. GJZJ, 12.
93. Li Zhongxiang, "Liangnianlai de gongzuo jingsai tuixing weiyuanhui" (A survey of the Commission for Promoting Work Emulation for the past two years), GJY 1, no. 1 (November 15, 1943): 8–13.
94. GJZJ, 4.
95. Gu Zhenggang, "Zhankai gongzuo jingsai yundong" (Let's implement the Work Emulation Campaign), ZDG 4, no. 8 (April 16, 1942): 3–5.
96. Gu Zhenggang, "Tuixing gongzuo jingsai zhi jingguo ji jianglai zhi zhanwang" (The experience of promoting work emulation and the prospect for the fu-

ture), in *Quanguo gongzuo jingsai geijiang dianli jinian tekan* (Special Issue in commemorating the national awards ceremony for work emulation), July 1943, 41–44.

97. Wang Longhui, "Tuijin gongzuo jingsai wancheng jianguo daye" (Promoting work emulation and bringing to fruition the task of nation-building), ibid., 49.

98. "Sannianlai tuixing gongzuo jingsai gaikuang" (Survey of the Work Emulation Campaign for the past three years), originally published in March 1945, DYSY 41, no. 1 (1999): 21–27.

99. CMA 0105/388.

100. Xiong Shiping, "Benhui shixing gongzuo jingsai zhi zhunbei gongzuo" (The preparation for implementing work emulation at the DISW), *Taosheng* (Crashing waves), 1, no. 5 (April 1944): 6–8 and 1, no. 6 (July 1944): 15–18, CMA 0202/555 and 0202/552. The best evidence comes from the DISW's daily *Mishuchu tongbao* (Bulletin of the secretariat). There was no mention of the Work Emulation Campaign between October 1942, when the Bulletin was launched, and April 8, 1944, when the DISW announced the methods to be used for the Work Emulation Campaign.

101. Xiong Shiping, "Benhui shixing gongzuo jingsai zhi zhunbei gongzuo."

102. *Mishuchu tongbao* (Bulletin of the secretariat), no. 197, April 8, 1944, CMA 0105/373.

103. Meeting record of the Committee for Promoting Work Emulation held in September 1944, CMA 0105/767.

104. *Mishuchu tongbao* (Bulletin of the secretariat), no. 307, August 24, 1944, CMA 0105/375.

105. The draft version is contained in the meeting record of the Committee for Promoting Work Emulation, CMA 0105/767. For the final version, see *Taosheng* (Crashing waves) 1, no. 10 (November 4, 1944): 14–15, CMA 0202/532.

106. *Taosheng fukan* (Supplement to crashing waves) 1, no. 1 (November 1944): 2, CMA 0202/553.

107. "Sangeyuelai de gongzuo jingsai" (The Work Emulation Campaign for the past three months), *Taosheng* (Crashing waves), (Special New Year's issue, January 1, 1945): 2–3, CMA 0202/552.

108. "Jiguan guanli gongzuo jingsai tongze" (Regulations for work emulation in managing administrative organizations), *Taosheng* (Crashing waves), 2, no. 4 (March 1945): 14–15, CMA 0202/538.

109. *Taosheng fukan* (Supplement to crashing waves), no. 17–22 (February–March 1945), CMA 0105/2834.

110. "Benhui gongzuo jingsai qingkuang huibao" (Report on the Work Emulation Campaign at the DISW), *Taosheng* (Crashing waves), 2, no. 8 (June 1, 1945): 21–24, CMA 0202/543. The use of campaigns was not a Nationalist monopoly. In addition to the Rectification Campaign in 1942 and the Production Campaign in 1943, the Communist Party conducted other campaigns

such as the Zhao Zhankui Campaign in ordnance production in the Communist base areas in 1944. See Mark Selden, *China in Revolution: The Yenan Way Revisited* (Armonk, N.Y.: M. E. Sharpe, 1995), 152–165, 196–199; ZJBGDS, vol. 4, 100–106, 140–146.

5. Enterprise Provision of Social Services and Welfare

1. DZLN, 1–13, 73–93.
2. ENZLN. 270–278.
3. Li Zhancai, ed., *Zhongguo tielu shi, 1876–1949* (A history of the Chinese railroad, 1876–1949) (Shantou: Shantou daxue chubanshe, 1994), 540.
4. DZLN, 83–85, 90–93.
5. Wu Zhixin, *Zhongguo huigong shiye* (A survey of social services and welfare in China) (Shanghai: Shijie shuju, 1940), introduction.
6. Ibid., 1–3, 27.
7. Elisabeth Köll, *From Cotton Mill to Business Empire: The Emergence of Regional Enterprises in Modern China* (Cambridge, Mass.: Harvard University Asia Center, 2003), 82–92.
8. *Rongjia qiye shiliao* (Historical materials of Rongs' family enterprise) (Shanghai: Shanghai renmin chubanshe, 1980), vol. 1, 580.
9. Lin Songhe, *Factory Workers in Tangku* (Beiping: Social Research Department, 1928), 14–25, 30–39.
10. ZMDZH, part v, vol. 1, caizheng jingji, no. 6, 165–166, 171–172.
11. Chen Da, *Zhongguo laogong wenti* (Labor problems in China) (Shanghai: Shangwu yinshuguan, 1933), 495–498; Zhuang Yu, "Sanshiwu nianlai zhi shangwu yinshuguan" (A survey of the Commercial Press for the last thirty-five years), in Wang Yunwu, *Shangwu yinshuguan yu xinjiaoyu nianpu* (The Commercial Press and the chronicle of new education) (Taibei: Taiwan shangwu yinshuguan, 1973), 305–329, and in *Shangwu yinshuguan jiushiwu nian, 1897–1992* (Reminiscences of the Commercial Press, 1897–1992) (Beijing: Shangwu yinshuguan, 1992), 721–763.
12. Gail Hershatter, *The Workers of Tianjin, 1900–1949* (Stanford, Calif.: Stanford University Press, 1986), 165.
13. "Junzhengbu binggongshu shanghai liangangchang jianshi baogao" (Inspection report prepared by the Shanghai Steel Plant), March 1935, CMA 0105/679.
14. ZJBGDS, vol. 3, 296–297.
15. "Xiuzheng junzhengbu binggongshu zhixia gechang gongren daiyu zhanxing guize" (Revised regulations on the treatment of workers employed by ordnance factories under the direct jurisdiction of the Bureau of Ordnance), ZJBGDS, vol. 3, 893–897.
16. "Xiuzheng binggongchang zhigong zidi xuexiao jianzhang" (Regulations on school for employees' children in ordnance factories), May 31, 1937, ibid., vol. 3, 1042–1043.

17. Lun Han, "Guangdong pajiang paochang jianchang shimo" (A chronological account of the establishment of the Pajiang Artillery Factory in Guangdong province), in GJS, 481–489; "Junzhengbu guangdong dier binggongchang zuzhi zongze" (General organizational regulations of Guangdong Second Arsenal), November 1937, CMA 0101/1.

18. "Zhigong fulichu zuzhi guicheng" (Organizational regulations of welfare division), November 1937, CMA 0101/1.

19. Untitled report drafted by the head of welfare division, June 14 1939. CMA 0103/197–200.

20. "Di wushichang changshi" (History of the Fiftieth Arsenal), CMA 0101/264; ZJBGDS, vol. 3, 1255.

21. Draft report by the Fiftieth Arsenal, July 9, 1937, CMA 0103/368–369.

22. Wu Zhixin, *Zhongguo huigong shiye*, preface by Cheng Haifeng.

23. Lu Dayue and Tang Runming, *Kangzhan shiqi Chongqing de bingqi gongye*, 55–56.

24. "Gangtiechang qianjian weiyuanhui gailüe" (Survey of the DISW), November 1941, in ZJBGDS, vol. 3, 1232.

25. Statistics on service and welfare facilities, July–December 1943, CMA 0201/340.

26. "Di ershichang changshi" (History of the Twentieth Arsenal), 1948, in ZJBGDS, vol. 3, 1197.

27. Zheng Hongquan, "Aiguo binggong zhuanjia lichenggan" (Li Chenggan: The weapons expert who devoted his life to his country), CWZ, no. 35 (1991): 116–136.

28. ZJBGDS, vol. 3, 1208.

29. Ibid., 1219, 1222.

30. KSNXGQ, 142–143, 150, 153.

31. Li Chenggan, "Kangzhan zhong fuwu binggong huiyilu" (Memoirs of service in the ordnance industry during the Sino-Japanese War), February 1947, CMA 0104/6–9.

32. "Di ershiyi gongchang changshi" (History of the Twenty-first Arsenal), 1948, in ZJBGDS, vol. 3, 962, 1199–1202.

33. "Junzhengbu binggongshu di shisan zidi xuexiao gaikuang" (Survey of the thirteenth school for employees' children), July 1941, CMA 0105/972.

34. Documents concerning the establishment of a middle school, CMA 0201/438.

35. ZJBGDS, vol. 3, 1044.

36. Ibid., 1045–1046; CMA 0101/329.

37. "Binggongshu gechang sheli zidi zongxue banfa" (Regulations concerning the establishment of employee children's middle schools in ordnance factories), January 1944, in ZJBGDS, vol. 3, 1047; CMA 0101/329.

38. Zheng Hongquan, "Aiguo binggong zhuanjia lichenggan" (Li Chenggan: The weapons expert who devoted his life to his country), CWZ, no. 35 (1991): 116–136.

39. "Di wushichang changshi" (History of the Fiftieth Arsenal), 1948, in ZJBGDS, vol. 3, 1261.

40. "Gangtiechang qianjian weiyuanhui sheshi ji gongzuo qingxing baogaoshu" (DISW report on installation and work progress), April 1941, CMA 0201/8.

41. The estimate is based on figures in "Yiyuan gongzuo baogao" (work report by the hospital, May–September 1943), CMA 0201/342.

42. "Zhigong fulichu gongzuo baogao" (Work report by the welfare division, May–August 1943), CMA 0201/342.

43. "Di shichang yange" (The evolution of the Tenth Arsenal), 1949, in ZJBGDS, vol. 3, 1185.

44. "Di ershichang changshi" (History of the Twentieth Arsenal), 1948, ibid., 1197.

45. "Di ershiyichang changshi" (History of the Twenty-first Arsenal), 1948, ibid., 1200–1202.

46. "Di ershiwuchang changshi" (History of the Twenty-fifth Arsenal), 1948, ibid., 1219, 1222.

47. "Di sanshi gongchang changshi" (History of the Thirtieth Arsenal), 1947, ibid.,1241.

48. "Benchang qianyi jingguo ji xianzai sheshi baogaoshu" (Report on the relocation and existing facilities of the Fiftieth Arsenal) and "Di wushichang yewu baogao" (Work report by the Fiftieth Arsenal), March 1939, CMA 0101/3889.

49. "Di wushichang changshi" (History of the Fiftieth Arsenal), 1948, in ZJBGDS, vol. 3, 1261.

50. "Neiqian guizhou de di sishiyi he sishier binggongchang" (A survey of the Forty-first and Forty-second Arsenals that relocated to Guizhou province), in KSNXGQ, 152–154.

51. "Gangtiechang qianjian weiyuanhui xiaofei hezuoshe diyici sheyuan daibiao dahui huiyilu" (Record of the DISW's first meeting of member representatives of the consumer cooperative). The meeting was held on February 5, 1940, CMA 0201/408.

52. "Gangtiechang qianjian weiyuanhui sanshiyinian chunji jianshi baogao" (Inspection report by the DISW for spring 1942), CMA 0201/1.

53. "Di ershichang changshi" (History of the Twentieth Arsenal), 1948, in ZJBGDS, vol. 3, 1198.

54. "Di ershiyi gongchang changshi" (History of the Twenty-first Arsenal), 1948, ibid., 1201–1202.

55. "Di wushichang changshi" (History of the Fiftieth Arsenal), 1948, ibid., 1261.

56. KSNXGQ, 143, 150, 153.

57. "Zhigong fulichu gongzuo baogao" (Work report by the welfare division, May–August 1943), CMA 0201/342.

58. "Di ershichang changshi" (History of the Twentieth Arsenal), 1948, in ZJBGDS, vol. 3, 1198.

59. "Di wushichang changshi" (History of the Fiftieth Arsenal), ibid., 1261.

60. "Di ershiyi gongchang changshi" (History of the Twenty-first Arsenal), 1948, ibid., 1201–1202.

61. Li Chenggan, "Kangzhan zhong fuwu binggong huiyilu" (Memoirs of service

in the ordnance industry during the Sino-Japanese War), February 1947, CMA 0104/6–9.

62. "Di ershiyi gongchang changshi" (History of the Twenty-first Arsenal), 1948, in ZJBGDS, vol. 3, 1202; Li Chenggan, "Kangzhan zhong fuwu binggong huiyilu."

63. "Gangtiechang qianjian weiyuanhui sheshi ji gongzuo qingxing baogaoshu" (DISW report on installation and work progress), April 1941, CMA 0201/8.

64. Xie Shicheng and others, "Minguo shiqi gongmuzhi de chuangjian yu yan-bian" (The creation and evolution of the institution of the public cemetery during Republican China), *Minguo dangan* (Republican archives), no. 2 (1995): 119–125.

65. Here lie the origins of what Andrew G. Walder describes as "employee de-pendence on the enterprise." See his "Organized Dependency and Cultures of Authority in Chinese Industry," *Journal of Asian Studies* 43, no. 1 (No-vember 1983): 51–76.

66. "Di shichang yange" (The evolution of the Tenth Arsenal), July 1949, in ZJBGDS, vol. 3, 1184–1185.

67. "Di ershichang changshi" (History of the Twentieth Arsenal), 1948, ibid., 1197–1198.

68. Chart of the organizational structure of Jinling Arsenal, September 1936, ibid., 296–297.

69. Chart of the organizational structure of the Twenty-first Arsenal, August 1939, CMA 0201/1.

70. "Di ershiyi gongchang changshi" (History of the Twenty-first Arsenal), 1948, in ZJBGDS, vol. 3, 1200, 1205.

71. DISW chart of organizational structure, June 1938, CMA 0201/1.

72. "Benhui qianjian gaikuang" (Survey of the relocation and construction of the DISW), March 1943, CMA gongyelei, file no. 30; "Gangtiechang qianjian weiyuanhui zuzhi tiaoli" (Organizational regulations of the DISW), February 1940, in ZJBGDS, vol. 3, 329–332.

73. DISW chart of organizational structure 1942, CMA 0201/18.

74. "Di sanshi gongchang changshi" (History of the Thirtieth Arsenal), 1947, in ZJBGDS, vol. 3, 1241.

75. Song Degong and Liang Zongze, "Kangzhan fenghuozhong dansheng de di-wushiyi binggongchang" (Survey of the Fifty-first Arsenal born during the Sino-Japanese War); Yang Cihong and Tao Zhimin, "Neiqian guizhou de disi-shiyi he disishier binggongchang" (Survey of the Forty-first and Forty-second Arsenals relocated to Guizhou province during the Sino-Japanese War), both in KSNXGQ, 149–151, 152–153.

76. "Di wushichang changshi" (History of the Fiftieth Arsenal), in ZJBGDS, vol. 3, 1261–1262.

77. Letter to the DISW by the Bureau of Ordnance, August 1939, CMA 0201/1.

78. Early in 1940 the Bureau of Ordnance decided that "large factories should establish welfare divisions whereas small factories should establish welfare

departments," in "Diyici gechang zhigong fuli shiye huiyi jilu" (Records of the first meeting concerning employee welfare). The meeting was held on February 16, 1940, CMA 0201/338.

79. "Di wushichang changshi" (History of the Fiftieth Arsenal), in ZJBGDS, vol. 3, 1259.

80. "Di ershisan gongchang changshi" (History of the Twenty-third Arsenal), 1948, ibid., 1211.

81. "Di ershiwu gongchang changshi" (History of the Twenty-fifth Arsenal), 1948, ibid., 1219.

82. "Di ershiyi gongchang changshi" (History of the Twenty-first Arsenal), 1948, ibid., 1208.

83. Zhou Younglin and Zhou Young, "Zailun jindai Chongqing jingji zhongxin de xingcheng jiqi yanjin" (Elaborations on the formation and evolution of Chongqing as a regional economic center), in *Yige shiji de licheng: Chongqing kaibi yibai zhounian* (The course in the last 100 years: the centennial anniversary of Chongqing as a port for foreign trade) (Chongqing: Chongqing chubanshe, 1992), 164–194.

84. Report by the Division of Industry and Mining Regulations, June 1941, in ZMDZH, part v, vol. 2, caizheng jingji, no. 6, 451. In a survey published in 1942, Lin Jiyong, Nationalist official in charge of industrial relocation, placed the number at 452. See Lin Jiyong, *Minying changkuang neiqian jilüe: woguo gongye zongdongyuan zhi xumu* (A Survey of the relocation of private enterprises: the prelude to China's industrial mobilization) (Chongqing, 1942), 67.

85. Lu Chuanxu, ed., *Chongqing kangzhan dashiji* (Chronicle of events in Chongqing during the Sino-Japanese War) (Chongqing: Chongqing chubanshe, 1995), 75–76.

86. Report by the Division of Industry and Mining Regulations, October 1938, in ZMDZH, part v, vol. 2, caizheng jingji, no. 6, 444.

87. "Jingjibu gongkuang tiaozhengchu gongzuo baogao" (Work report of the Division of Industry and Mining Regulations, August to December of 1938), CMA 0101/1.

88. Lin Jiyong, *Minying changkuang neiqian jilüe*, 36.

89. Report by the Division of Industry and Mining Regulations, June 1941, in ZMDZH, part v, vol. 2, caizheng jingji, no. 6, 453.

90. Order by the Bureau of Ordnance, July 1938, in ZJBGDS, vol. 3, 816.

91. Order by the Bureau of Ordnance and attached notice, April 18, 1939, CMA 0103/92–93.

92. Order by the Bureau of Ordnance, October 23, 1939, in ZJBGDS, vol. 3, 947.

93. "Gechang zhigong fuli shiye choushi huiyi jilu" (Record of meeting of ordnance factories for planning employee welfare enterprise). The meeting was held on June 7, 1939. See also the order of the Bureau of Ordnance on July 10, 1939, in ZJBGDS, vol. 3, 1993, 960–963, 1051–1053.

94. Order by the Bureau of Ordnance, September 14, 1939, CMA 0104/197–200; 0201/337.

95. As defined by the statistics division of the Ministry of Social Affairs, the term *industrial workers* referred to those who worked in machine, printing, flour-making, and textile industries, in "Chongqingshi gongzi zhishu" (Wage index for Chongqing), July 1942, CMA 0101/114.

96. For a brief discussion of the effect of inflation on different segments of the population, see Young, *China's Wartime Finance and Inflation,* 316–328.

97. "Di ershi gongchang changshi" (History of the Twentieth Arsenal), 1948, in ZJBGDS, vol. 3, 1196–1197.

98. "Di sanshi gongchang changshi" (History of the Thirtieth Arsenal), 1947, ibid., 1237.

99. "Anding gongren shenghuo fangan ji shishi chengxu" (Program for stabilizing workers' lives and schedule for implementation), in ZJBGDS, vol. 3, 961–963.

100. Ibid.

101. "Gechang zhigong fuli shiye choushi huiyi jilu" (Record of meeting of ordnance factories for planning employee welfare enterprise). The meeting was held on June 7, 1939, in ZJBGDS, vol. 3, 1993, 960.

102. Order by the Bureau of Ordnance, July 10, 1939, ibid.

103. Order by the Bureau of Ordnance, September 14, 1939, CMA 0104/197–200; 0201/337.

104. Order by the Bureau of Ordnance, December 6, 1939, CMA 0103/94–97.

105. Order by the Bureau of Ordnance, June 8, 1942, CMA 0103/94–97.

106. Order by the Bureau of Ordnance, August 15, 1942, CMA 0103/94–97.

107. "Gaijin zhigong fuli shiye fangan" (Program for improving employee welfare), October 1942, CMA 0103/197–200.

108. "Gangtiechang qianjian weiyuanhui ershiba niandu shiye baogao" (DISW work report for the 1939 fiscal year), 1940, CMA 0201/104.

109. "Gangtiechang qianjian weiyuanhui ershijiu niandu shiye baogao" (DISW work report for the 1940 fiscal year), 1941, CMA 0201/104.

110. CMA 0105/1266.

111. CMA 0105/2324.

112. "Gangtiechang qianjian weiyuanhui di yibai wushiwuci huibao jilu" (Record of the 155th meeting of the DISW). The meeting was held on October 9, 1942, CMA 0201/26.

113. Tong Shude's reports, October 29 and 30, 1942, CMA 0105/1119.

114. "Gangtiechang qianjian weiyuanhui fuli fangan" (Welfare plan for the DISW), October 29, 1942, CMA 0201/344.

115. Ibid.

116. Tong Zhicheng's instruction to foreman, November 27, 1942, CMA 0103/34.

117. *Mishuchu tongbao* (Bulletin of the secretariat), no. 80, March 13, 1943, CMA 0204/16.

118. "Laogong yidong de toushi" (An analysis of labor turnover), *Taosheng fukan* (Supplement to crashing waves), no. 37 (June 23, 1945): 1, CMA 0105/2830.

119. "Diyici gechang zhigong fuli shiye huiyi jilu (Record of the first meeting con-

cerning employee welfare). The meeting was held on February 16, 1940, CMA 0201/338.

120. "Gongchang fuli shiye yu shiwu renyuan" (Factory welfare enterprise and the people who run it), *Taosheng* (Crashing waves), 3, no. 2 (December 1, 1945): 1–2, CMA 0202/548.

121. "Yiwushi" (Description of medical office), DT, no. 1 (August/September 1938): 6, SHA 28/7103.

122. "Yinianlai benchang zhigong fuli zhi sheshi" (Welfare facilities of the Central Electric Works since July 1939), DT, no. 6 (August 1940): 6; no. 7 (September 1940): 3–4, SHA 28/7103.

123. Shih Kuo-heng, *China Enters the Machine Age: A Study of Labor in Chinese Industry*. Ed. and trans. by Fei Hsiao-tung and Francis L. K. Hsu (Cambridge, Mass.: Harvard University Press, 1944), 94–110.

124. "Yinianlai banli tuoersuo zhi gaishu" (Survey of child-care facilities of the Central Electric Works), DT, no. 28 (September 1943): 5–6, SHA 28/7103.

125. "Zhongyang diangong qicaichang dierchang sanshi sanniandu shiye baogao" (Work report by the second factory of the Central Electric Works for 1944 fiscal year), CMA 0101/1689.

126. "Yu erzhichang sanshi sanniandu shiye baogao" (Work report by Chongqing branch factory for the 1944 fiscal year); "Zhongyang diangong qicaichang lanzhou dianchi zhichang sanshi sanniandu nianbao" (Annual report by Lanzhou battery factory of the Central Electric Works for the 1944 fiscal year), CMA, 0101/1689; 0101/2192.

127. Wang Ziyou, "Kangzhan banianlai zhi woguo gangtie gongye" (China's iron and steel industry during the Sino-Japanese War), ZWJ 6, no. 1/2 (June 1946): 86–106.

128. "A brief description of Yunnan Iron and Steel Works" (original document in English), November 30, 1944, SHA 28/6519.

129. "Jingji shiye diaochabiao" (Survey of economic enterprises), October 1943, YPA 124/114.

130. "Yunnan gangtiechang yuangong fuli shiye diaochabiao" (Survey of welfare enterprise of Yunnan Iron and Steel Works), December 1944, YPA 124/154.

131. "Gansu youkuangju shiye gaikuang" (Survey of Gansu Petroleum Administration), January 1944, SHA 28(2)/2910; "Gansu youkuangju shicha baogao" (Inspection report by Gansu Petroleum Administration), October 1943, SHA 28/17297; "Gansu youkuangju gongzuo gaikuang" (Work report by Gansu Petroleum Administration), December 1944, SHA 28/17243.

132. "Gansu youkuangju gongzuo gaikuang" (Work report by Gansu Petroleum Administration), December 1944, SHA 28/17243; Song Honggang and others, *Sun Yueqi zhuan*, 166–172; SYW, 68–70.

133. "Tanhua jiyao" (Conversation record), January 25, 1937, SHA 28(2)/928.

134. Wu Zhixin, *Zhongguo huigong shiye*, introduction.

135. "Ziyuan weiyuanhui xunling" (Directive by the National Resources Commission), November 19, 1938, CMA 0201/337.

136. Wu Fuyuan, "Ziyuan weiyuanhui de renshi guanli zhidu" (The system of

personnel management of the National Resources Commission), in HGZZW, 206; "Benhui gechangkuang banli yuangong jingshen zhidao ji fuli gongzuo dagang" (Outline of employee spiritual guidance and welfare work for subordinate enterprises of the National Resources Commission), February 23, 1940, CMA 0201/22.

137. "Ziyuan weiyuanhui xunling" (Directive by the National Resources Commission), November 29, 1940, YPA 124/148; CMA 0201/338.

138. "Ziyuan weiyuanhui guanli yuangong fuli shiye jijin banfa" (Measures for managing funds of employee welfare enterprises), February 19, 1941, ZWG 1, no. 1 (July 16, 1941): 22–23.

139. "Ziyuan weiyuanhui xunling" (Directive by the National Resources Commission) and "Ziyuan weiyuanhui fushu jiguan yuangong fuli gongzuo shishi biaozhun" (Standard for implementing welfare work in the subordinate organizations of the National Resources Commission), February 18, 1942, CMA 0201/338; ZWG 2, no. 3 (March 16, 1942): 17–18.

140. "Ziyuan weiyuanhui xunling" (Directive by the National Resources Commission), April 28, 1942, YPA 124/218.

141. Calculation of the number of enterprises is based on "Ziyuan weiyuanhui jingban shiye yilanbiao" (Tabulation of enterprises and organizations of the National Resources Commission), ZWG 2 (August 16, 1945): 43–51.

142. "Ziyuan weiyuanhui xunling" (Directive by the National Resources Commission), April 15, 1943, CMA 0201/340; YPA 88/45.

143. "Ziyuan weiyuanhui xunling" (Directive by the National Resources Commission), January 24, 1944, CMA 0201/340.

144. "Gongkuang shiye fuli gongzuo shuoming" (Explanation of welfare work in industrial and mining enterprises), n.d., but clearly written after 1944, SHA 28/17640.

145. "Shehui fuli tongji" (Statistics on social service and welfare facilities for 1944), CMA, zhengwulei, file no. 51, 48–50; KJSSJ, vol. 5, 497–507.

146. "Shehui fuli tongji" (Statistics on social service and welfare facilities for 1945), SHA 11(2)/33; "Quanguo laogong fuli jigou jiqi sheshi zhi fazhan" (The evolution of national labor welfare agencies and facilities), June 1948, in ZMDZH, part v, vol. 3, caizheng jingji, no. 4, 203.

147. "Quanguo laogong fuli jigou jiqi sheshi zhi fazhan" (The evolution of national labor welfare agencies and facilities), June 1948, in ZMDZH, part v, vol. 3, caizheng jingji, no. 4, 203.

148. KJSSJ, vol. 2, 82.

149. Xie Zhengfu served as head of the Department of Social Welfare from July 29, 1942 to November 3, 1945. See MZN, 599–600.

150. Xie Zhengfu, "Sanshi sannian du shehui fuli zhi zhongxin gongzuo" (The central task of social welfare work for the 1944 fiscal year), *Shehui gongzuo tongxun yuekan* (Monthly newsletter of social work) 1, no., 2 (February 15, 1944), in KJSSJ, vol. 5, 7.

6. *Danwei* Designation of State-Owned Enterprises

1. As David Waldner has pointed out, "state-building" has multiple meanings, ranging from the initial differentiation of governmental functions from social institutions to the centralization of power in absolutist states, to the proliferation and rationalization of state institutions. For the purposes of this study, the meaning of state building is restricted to rationalization of state institutions. See Waldner, *State Building and Late Development* (Ithaca, N.Y.: Cornell University Press, 1999), 21.

2. By rationalization I mean the adoption and employment of all means and mechanisms for the purpose of improving organizational efficiency and effectiveness.

3. Strictly speaking, both the Central Planning Board and the Party and Government Work Evaluation Commission were party organizations. However, since the Nationalist state was by definition a party state, this chapter treats all Nationalist organizations as state organizations.

4. Liu Jingquan and others, eds., *Zhongguo kangri zhanzheng renwu dacidian* (Biographical dictionary of China's war of resistance against Japan) (Tianjin: Tianjin daxue chubanshe, 1999), 84.

5. Zhang Xianwen and others, eds., *Zhonghua minguoshi dacidian* (Historical dictionary of Republican China) (Nanjing: Jiangsu guji chubanshe, 2001), 498.

6. Gan Naiguang, *Zhongguo xingzheng xinlun* (A new approach to government administration in China) (Chongqing: Shangwu yinshuguan, 1943), 7. Gan's transcript at the University of Chicago shows that he audited classes in municipal government and American political theories in 1928.

7. Frederick C. Mosher, ed., *Basic Literature of American Public Administration, 1787–1950* (New York: Holmes & Meier, 1981), 66–67, 125.

8. Leonard D. White, *Introduction to the Study of Public Administration* (New York: Macmillan Co., 1926), 2; *Introduction to the Study of Public Administration* (New York: Macmillan Co., 1939), 7.

9. Book review by H. N. B., in *Public Administration: The Journal of the Institute of Public Administration*, vol. 6, 1928: 192–195.

10. White, *Introduction*, (1926), 59; *Introduction* (1939), 45–46, 561–562.

11. White, *Introduction* (1926), 68, 77, 192–193; *Introduction* (1939), 40, 83, 187.

12. White, *Introduction* (1939), 40, 44

13. William Anderson, *American City Government* (New York: Henry Holt and Co., 1925), 11.

14. William Anderson, *The Units of Government in the United States: An Enumeration and Analysis* (Chicago, Ill.: Public Administration Service, 1934, publication no. 42), 2, 4, 5, 9.

15. Walter Rautenstrauch, "The Larger Aspects of Industrial Engineering," *The Society for the Advancement of Management Journal* 1, no. 1 (January 1936): 25–28.

16. *The Work Unit in Federal Administration* (Chicago, Ill.: Public Administration Service, 1937, publication no. 56), Foreword, 3, 7, 13–14.

17. Ibid., 43–44, 46.

18. Luther Gulick and L. Urwick, eds., *Papers on the Science of Administration* (Original edition 1937; reprinted by Augustus M. Kelley Publishers, 1973), 3, 15.

19. It appears that Gan had returned to China by 1931, for he was again elected to the Nationalist Central Executive Committee that year. See Zhang Xianwen and others, eds., *Zhonghua minguoshi dacidian*, 498.

20. Gan, *Zhongguo xingzheng xinlun*, 7, 36–37.

21. Although it is uncertain whether Gan had read the second edition of White's study or the studies of units and work units, Gan's writings show that he was familiar with the trend in the study of public administration in the United States. Ibid., 33–35.

22. Ibid., 13–14, 51.

23. Tien Hung-Mao, *Government and Politics in Kuomintang China, 1927–1937* (Stanford, Calif.: Stanford University Press, 1972), 24.

24. Gan, *Zhongguo xingzheng xinlun*, 46, 122.

25. Ibid., 44; William F. Willoughby, *Principles of Public Administration* (Baltimore, Md.: Johns Hopkins University Press, 1927), 7.

26. Gan, *Zhongguo xingzheng xinlun*, 40.

27. Julia C. Strauss, *Strong Institutions in Weak Polities: State Building in Republican China, 1927–1940* (Oxford: Clarendon Press, 1998), 42.

28. Gan, *Zhongguo xingzheng xinlun*, 121–127.

29. Ibid., 173, 181.

30. Chiang Kaishek, "Geming chengbai de jishi he jianshe gongzuo de fangfa" (The chance for the success of the revolution and the method for economic reconstruction), November 14, 1933, in XJSYZ, vol. 11, 601–615.

31. MZN, 511–512; ZMDZH, part v, vol. 1, zhengzhi no. 1, 73; Gan, *Zhongguo xingzheng xinlun*, 155, 158.

32. Gan, *Zhongguo xingzheng xinlun*, 54, 247–248.

33. ZMDZH, part v, vol. 2, zhengzhi no. 1, 18–31.

34. Chiang Kaishek's speech, March 29, 1938, in ZMDZH, part v, vol. 2, zhengzhi no. 1, 374.

35. "Zhongguo guomindang kangzhan jianguo gangling" (Program for the war of resistance and nation building of the Chinese Nationalist Party), July 1938, in ZMDZH, part v, vol. 2, zhengzhi no. 1, 149–153.

36. Chiang Kaishek, "Bannianlai gongzuo zhi jiantao yu zhongshu jigou zhi tiaozheng" (An examination of work for the past six months and the reorganization of central organizations), July 6, 1940, in XJSYZ, vol. 17, 386–391.

37. Chiang Kaishek, "Dangzheng kaohe zhi zeren yu gongzuo yaozhi" (The responsibility and objectives of party and government work evaluation), February 15, 1941, ZDG 3, no. 19 (September 1, 1941): 1–6.

38. ZMDZH, part v, vol. 2, zhengzhi, no. 1, 497–498.

39. Reports by the Central Planning Board and the Party and Government Work Evaluation Commission, SHA 171/29, 171/97.

40. Chiang Kaishek, "Jianshe jiben gongzuo—xingzheng sanlianzhi dagang" (Basic task of reconstruction—an outline of the three-in-one administrative system), December 1, 1940, in XJSYZ, vol. 17, 525–548.

41. Report by the Central Planning Board to Chiang Kaishek, July 26, 1941, SHA 171/50.

42. "Zhongyang shejiju gongzuo baogao" (Work report by the Central Planning Board), May 5, 1945, SHA 171/51(1).

43. "Guofang zuigao weiyuanhui gongzuo baogao" (Work report by the Supreme National Defense Council), December 1941, SHA 43/3.

44. "Zhongyang shejiju sheji weiyuanhui disanci tanhuahui jilu" (Record of the third deliberation conference of the planning commission of the Central Planning Board), June 10, 1942, SHA 171/78.

45. "Zhongyang shejiju gongzuo baogao" (Work report by the Central Planning Board), October 15, 1942, SHA 171/16.

46. "Zhanhou wunian guofang ji jingji jianshe yaodian" (Key aspects of postwar five-year national defense and economic reconstruction), January 20, 1943, SHA 171/1157.

47. "Zhongyang shejiju liuyuefen huiyi jilu" (Meeting record of the Central Planning Board for the month of June), July 6, 1943, SHA 171/82; "Zhongyang shejiju gongzuo baogao" (Work report by the Central Planning Board), May 5, 1945, SHA 171/51(1).

48. ZMDZH, part v, vol. 2, caizheng jingji no. 5, 34–35.

49. "Liunianlai zhi zhongyang shejiju" (The Central Planning Board for the past six years), December 1946, SHA 171/29.

50. ZMDZH, part v, vol. 2, zhengzhi no. 1, 53.

51. Chiang Kaishek, "Jianshe jiben gongzuo—xingzheng sanlianzhi dagang."

52. *Zhongyang ribao* (Central daily news), December 19, 1942.

53. Gan, *Zhongguo xingzheng xinlun*, 81–86.

54. "Geji jiguan niding fenceng fuze banshi xize zhi yuanze yu fangshi" (Principles and methods for drafting regulations for conducting business by delegating responsibility according to administrative levels), ZDG 3, no. 6 (March 10, 1941): 31–34.

55. Gan, *Zhongguo xingzheng xinlun*, 80.

56. "Sifayuan suoshu jiguan fenceng fuze banshi tongze" (General regulations for conducting business for subordinate organizations of the Judicial Yuan), March 21, 1941; "Zhongyang zhixing weiyuanhui gebuchuhui banshi tongze" (General regulations for conducting business for the ministries, departments, commissions of the Central Executive Committee), April 28, 1941, SHA 170/1088(1).

57. "Dangzheng gongzuo kaohe weiyuanhui banshi xize" (Detailed regulations for conducting business of the Party and Government Work Evaluation Commission), August 4, 1941, SHA 170/1088(1).

58. "Zhongyang zhixing weiyuanhui zuzhibu banshi xize" (Detailed regulations

for conducting business of the Organizational Department of the Central
Executive Committee), May 11, 1942, ZDG 4, no. 11 (June 1, 1942):
35–46.

59. "Junzhengbu fenceng fuze banshi xize" (Detailed regulations for conducting
business of the Ministry of Military Administration), March 1943, SHA 161/
13.

60. "Caizhengbu fenceng fuze banshi xize" (Detailed regulations for conducting
business of the Ministry of Financial Administration), April 1943, SHA 161/
1242.

61. "Zhongyang zhixing weiyuanhui mishuchu sheji kaohe weiyuanhui banshi
xize" (Detailed regulations for conducting business of the Planning and Assessment Committee of the Secretariat of the Central Executive Committee),
August 9, 1943, in ZDG 5, no. 17 (September 1, 1943): 22–27.

62. "Xingzhengyuan shishi xingzheng sanlianzhi baogao" (Report by the Executive Yuan concerning the implementation of the three-in-one administrative
system), May 1943, SHA 161–110.

63. Resolution adopted by the ninth plenary session of the fifth Nationalist Central Executive Committee, December 20, 1941, in ZMDZH, part v, vol. 2,
zhengzhi no. 1, 576.

64. "Dangzhengjun jiguan renshi jigou tongyi guanli gangyao" (Outline of unified management for personnel organs of party, government, and military organizations), December 27, 1941, SHA 171/45.

65. "Zhongyang dangbu renshi jigou tongyi guanli shishi banfa" (Measures for
implementing unified management among personnel organs of the Central
Party Headquarters), March 2, 1942, SHA 171/45. Also in ZDG 4, no. 6
(March 16, 1942): 25–26.

66. "Renshi guanli tiaoli" (Regulations of personnel management), September 2,
1942, in GZZZDSX, vol. 2, 64–66.

67. Political report of the sixth Nationalist Party congress, May 7, 1945, in
ZMDZH, part v, vol. 2, zhengzhi no. 1, 773.

68. "Dangzheng gongzuo kaohe banfa" (Methods for assessing party and government work), July 4, 1941, ZDG 3, no. 16 (July 16, 1941): 6, 22–23.

69. Chiang Kaishek, "Dangzhengjun gongzuo zhi jiantao yu jinhou zhi jiwu" (An
examination of party, government, and military work and the urgent task
ahead), January 5, 1942; ZDG 4, no. 3 (February 1, 1942): 1–6.

70. "Neizhengbu dangzheng gongzuo kaohe banfa shishi xize" (Detailed regulations on implementing methods of assessing party and government work in
the Ministry of Interior Administration), November 17, 1941, SHA 161/4.

71. "Shenjibu fengji kaohe shishi xize" (Detailed regulations on implementing
assessment according to organizational levels in the Ministry of Auditing),
May 23, 1942, SHA 161/4.

72. "Guofang zuigao weiyuanhui gongzuo baogao" (Work report by the Supreme
National Defense Council), November 1942, SHA 161/1253.

73. Chiang Kaishek's telegram and "dangzheng gejiguan sheji kaohe weiyuanhui

zuzhi tongze" (General regulations for party and government planning and assessment commissions), February 18, 1943, ZDG 5, no. 5 (March 1, 1943): 5–6.

74. "Dangzheng gongzuo kaohe weiyuanhui gongzuo zongbaogao" (General report by the Party and Government Work Evaluation Commission), March 1947, SHA 171–97.

75. Zhang Xianwen and others, eds., *Zhonghua minguoshi dacidian*, 498.

76. Report by the Central Planning Board to Chiang Kaishek, October 4, 1940, SHA 171/50.

77. Gan, *Zhongguo xingzheng xinlun*, 98–100.

78. Chiang Kaishek, "Jianshe jiben gongzuo—xingzheng sanlianzhi dagang."

79. Gan, *Zhongguo xingzheng xinlun*, 87–88.

80. Contemporary sources lend strong support to such an assessment. For example, Chen Zhimai, adviser of the Executive Yuan, wrote in 1943, "although Gan Naiguang is the Central Planning Board's deputy-secretary, he authored many of the regulations in creating the three-in-one administrative system." See XJ 9, no. 1 (May 1, 1943): 20–22.

81. For a comprehensive assessment of wartime Nationalist institutional rationalization, see Morris L. Bian, "Building State Structure: Guomindang Institutional Rationalization during the Sino-Japanese War, 1937–1945," *Modern China* 31, no. 1 (January 2005): 35–71.

82. Xiaobo Lü and Elizabeth J. Perry, "The Changing Chinese Workplace in Historical and Comparative Perspective," in *Danwei: The Changing Chinese Workplace in Historical and Comparative Perspective*, ed. Xiaobo Lü and Elizabeth J. Perry (Armonk, N.Y.: M. E. Sharpe, 1997) 3.

83. Yeh Wen-Hsin, "Republican Origins of the *Danwei:* The Case of Shanghai's Bank of China," ibid., 60–88.

84. See Lu Feng, "Danwei: yizhong teshu de shehui zhuzhi xingshi" (*Danwei:* a special form of social organization), *Zhongguo shehui kexue* (Chinese social science), no. 1 (1989): 71–88; "Zhongguo danwei zhidu de qiyuan he xingcheng" (The origins and formation of China's *danwei* system), *Zhongguo shehui kexue jikan* (Chinese social science quarterly) 11 (1993): 66–87; Lü Xiaobo, "Minor Public Economy: The Revolutionary Origins of the *Danwei*," in *Danwei: The Changing Chinese Workplace in Historical and Comparative Perspective*, 21–41; Elizabeth J. Perry, "From Native Place to Workplace: Labor Origins and Outcomes of China's *Danwei* System," ibid., 42–59; Yeh Wen-Hsin, "Republican Origins of the *Danwei:* The Case of Shanghai's Bank of China," ibid., 60–88; Mark W. Frazier, *The Making of the Chinese Industrial Workplace: State, Revolution, and Labor Management* (Cambridge, UK: Cambridge University Press, 2002), xiv, 234.

85. *Hanyu cidian* (Dictionary of Chinese language) (Shanghai: Shangwu yinshuguan, 1937. Reprint ed., 1957), 175.

86. "Geji jiguan niding fenceng fuze banshi xize zhi yuanze yu fangshi" (Principles and methods for drafting regulations for conducting business by dele-

gating responsibility according to administrative levels), ZDG 3, no. 6 (March 10, 1941): 31–34.

87. Gan, *Zhongguo xingzheng xinlun*, 244.

88. "Zhongyang zhixing weiyuanhui zuzhibu banshi xize" (Detailed regulations for conducting business of the Organizational Department of the Central Executive Committee), May 11, 1942, ZDG 4, no. 11 (June 1, 1942): 35–46.

89. "Zhongyang zhixing weiyuanhui mishuchu sheji kaohe weiyuanhui banshi xize" (Detailed regulations for conducting business of the Planning and Assessment Committee of the Secretariat of the Central Executive Committee), August 9, 1943, in ZDG 5, no. 17 (September 1, 1943): 22–27.

90. Zhongyang dangbu renshi jigou tongyi guanli shishi banfa" (Measures for implementing unified management among personnel organs of the Central Party Headquarters), March 2, 1942, SHA 171/45; ZDG 4, no. 6 (March 16, 1942): 25–26.

91. Chiang Kaishek, "Duiyu dangzheng gongzuo zongjiantao zhi zhishi" (Instructions for an overall examination of party and government work), November 21, 1942, in XJSYZ, vol. 19, 371–388.

92. "Qian fuzhuren xunci" (Speech by Qian Changzhao), January 21, 1942, SHA 28(2)/314.

93. "Jingjibu fushu jiguan tebie jianshe jihua" (Special reconstruction plan for subordinate organizations of the Ministry of Economic Affairs for the 1942 fiscal year), 1942, in ZMDZH, part v, vol. 2, caizheng jingji, no. 6, 25; "Zhongyang zhengfu suiru suichu zongjuesuan shencha baogao" (Report on the final budget of revenue and expenditure for 1940 fiscal year), 1943, in ibid., no. 1, 252; "Kong Xiangxi shencha yijiu sisi niandu guojia suiru suichu zongyusuanan baogao" (Kong Xiangxi's report on the total national budget estimate of revenue and expenditure for the 1944 fiscal year), 1944, in ibid., no. 1, 284.

94. *Zhongyang ribao* (Central daily news), May 20, 1942.

95. Ibid., May 23, 1942.

96. Ibid., April 17, 1943.

97. GJC, 20, 42–44.

98. Such a use of the term *work unit* suggests that Gan Naiguang was not the only one who was instrumental in the transfer of American "technology" of public administration and management, for many officials and managers of China's state-owned enterprises received education in Europe and America and undertook reforms in management administration according to Western practice. In addition, the National Resources Commission sent several groups of engineering and management personnel to receive advanced training in American business and government organizations between 1942 and 1945. The majority received technical training, but two members of the first group focused exclusively on business management and brought back hundreds of volumes of relevant books and journals. Although it is difficult to find all the empirical links between American theories and practices and their applica-

tion in the Chinese context, the evidence points to the American theories as the source of reform in management administration in China's state-owned enterprises. See GJZJ, 73–6; Kirby, "The Chinese war economy," in *China's Bitter Victory: The War with Japan, 1937–1945,* 185–212; ZWJRFSS, vol. 2, 1–115, 2097–2164.

99. *Tongji changshi* (General knowledge of statistics) (Nanjing: Ministry of Social Affairs, 1945), 7.

100. Record of the 51st meeting of the DISW, February 24, 1940, CMA 0201/29.

101. Yang Jizeng's written instructions, February 5, 1941, CMA 0105/783.

102. Record of the 87th meeting of the DISW, March 1, 1941, CMA 0201/29.

103. "Sanshiyinian chunji jianshi baogao" (Inspection report for the spring of 1942), June 1942, CMA 0201/1.

104. *Mishuchu tongbao* (Bulletin of the secretariat), no. 29, November 28, 1942, CMA 0204/16.

105. "Gangtiechang qianjian weiyuanhui di yibai bashierci huibao jilu" (Record of the 182nd meeting of the DISW). The meeting was held on May 10, 1943, CMA 0105/763.

106. *Mishuchu tongbao* (Bulletin of the secretariat), no. 112, 114, June 28 and July 3, 1943, CMA 0105/373.

107. Tong Zhicheng, "Ruhe zengjin women de gongzuo xiaolü," *Taosheng* (Crashing waves) 1, no. 3 (July 7, 1943): 3–4, CMA 0202/552.

108. Record of the 189th meeting of the DISW, July 15, 1943, CMA 0105/763.

109. I translate "Guanli *danwei*" and "gongzuo *danwei*," respectively, as "management unit" and "work unit" in this book, although I leave other uses of the word *danwei* untranslated.

110. *Mishuchu tongbao* (Bulletin of the secretariat), no. 125, August 16, 1943, CMA 0105/373.

111. Ibid., no. 194, March 21, 1944, CMA 0105/373.

112. "Benhui shixing fenceng fuze zhidu banfa" (Measures for implementing the system of delegating responsibility according to administrative levels at the DISW), March 1944, CMA 0105/679.

113. Ibid.

114. *Mishuchu tongbao* (Bulletin of the secretariat), no. 202, April 25, 1944, CMA 0105/374.

115. Ibid., no. 286, July 31, 1944, CMA 0105/374.

116. "Gangtiechang qianjian weiyuanhui di erbai sishiqici huibao jilu" (Record of the 247th meeting of the DISW). The meeting was held on December 9, 1944, CMA 0105/763.

117. *Taosheng fukan* (Supplement to crashing waves), no. 15, January 20, 1945, CMA 0202/553.

118. "Gangtiechang qianjian weiyuanhui di erbai wushiqici huibao jilu" (Record of the 257th meeting of the DISW). The meeting was held on March 15, 1944, CMA 0105/762.

119. *Taosheng* (Crashing waves) 2: 6 (April 1, 1945): 1, CMA 0202/540.

120. "Benhui tuixing gongzuo jingsai yundong chubu jihua" (Preliminary plan for promoting the Work Emulation Campaign), *Taosheng* (Crashing waves) 1, no. 10 (November 4, 1944): 14–15, CMA 0202/532; "Sanshi sanniandu mish-uchu gongzuo baogao" (The work report by the secretariat for the 1944 fiscal year), *Taosheng* (Crashing waves), special new-year issue, January 1, 1945, 10–13, CMA 0202/552; "Fenceng fuze de quanshi" (An explanation of delegating responsibility according to administrative levels), *Taosheng* (Crashing waves) 2, no. 6 (April 1, 1945): 1, CMA 0202/540.
121. *Mishuchu tongbao* (Bulletin of the secretariat), no. 262, July 3, 1944, CMA 0105/374.
122. Ibid., no. 601, August 6, 1945, CMA 0105/378. In its post-1949 usage the term *work unit* kept its meaning as workplace but no longer had the conno-tation of standard or criterion.
123. "Fenceng fuze de quanshi" (An explanation of delegating responsibility ac-cording to administrative levels), *Taosheng* (Crashing waves) 2, no. 6 (April 1, 1945): 1, CMA 0202/540.

7. Nationalist Ideology of the Developmental State

1. The concept of "developmental state" was first used by Chalmers Johnson in his study of Japanese industrial policy. According to Johnson, the Japanese developmental state is characterized by the existence of an elite bureaucracy with sufficient scope to take the initiative and operate effectively, the exis-tence of a pilot organization to lead economic development, and the perfec-tion of market-conforming methods of state intervention in the economy. Taking as their point of departure Johnson's account of the Japanese devel-opmental state, recently a number of scholars have examined the theory and practice of developmental state in the context of East Asia. The concept of developmental state has also been fruitfully appropriated by scholars of Re-publican China, although as this chapter shows, the nature of Chinese devel-opmental state is different from that of Japanese developmental state. See Chalmers Johnson, *MITI and the Japanese Miracle: The Growth of Industrial Policy, 1925–1975* (Stanford, Calif.: Stanford University Press, 1982); Meredith Woo-Cumings, ed., *The Developmental State* (Ithaca, N.Y.: Cornell University Press, 1999); Vivek Chibber, "Building a Developmental State: The Korean Case Reconsidered," *Politics & Society* 27, no. 3 (September 1999): 309–346; and William C. Kirby, "Engineering China: Birth of the Developmental State, 1928–1937," in *Becoming Chinese: Passages to Modernity and Beyond,* ed. Wen-hsin Yeh (Berkeley: University of California Press, 2000), 137–160.
2. In this chapter, the meaning of ideology is further restricted to the set of ideas, concepts, and principles that formed the basis of the emerging state enterprise system, which took its final form at the end of the Sino-Japanese War. As explained in the Introduction, ideologies are mental models shared by groups of individuals that provide both an interpretation of the environ-ment and a prescription of how that environment should be ordered.

3. The term *sanmin zhuyi* is generally translated as "Three Principles of the People." I believe a more accurate rendering to be "Three Doctrines of the People."

4. Sun Yatsen, *Jianguo Fanglüe* (Shanghai: Shangwu yinshu guan, 1927). The second part—"Material Reconstruction"—was translated into English in 1921 and published in 1922 as *International Development of China* by G. P. Putnam's Sons (New York and London: Knickerbocker Press, 2nd ed., 1929).

5. Sun Yatsen, *International Development of China,* 11, 237.

6. Speech by Sun Yatsen, April 1, 1912, in SZQ, vol. 2, 323.

7. Sun Yatsen, "Zhongguo zhi tielu jihua yu minsheng zhuyi" (China's railroad plan and the Doctrine of People's Livelihood), October 10, 1912, ibid., vol. 2, 493.

8. Speech by Sun Yatsen, October 1921, ibid., vol. 2, 521.

9. Ibid., vol. 2, 323, 521.

10. ZGX, vol. 69, 91.

11. L. T. Chef, ed., *San Min Chu I: The Three Principles of the People* (New York: Da Capo Press, 1975), 441–442.

12. One indication of the acceptance of Sun's vision of economic development is a 1924 article written by Wang Jingwei, who elaborated on Sun's position on state-owned enterprise. See ZGX, 84–86.

13. "Xunzheng shiqi jingji jianshe shishi gangyao fangzhen an" (Outline program for implementing economic reconstruction during the period of political tutelage), March 23, 1929, in ZMDZH, part v, vol. 1, zhengzhi, no. 2, 102–103, 118–119. Throughout this chapter, legislation, resolutions, and policy statements are taken as an expression and reflection of the evolving mental model of the Nationalist elite.

14. "Shiyie jianshe chengxu an" (Procedure for industrial development), May 2, 1931, ibid., part v, vol. 1, zhengzhi, no. 2, 209–293.

15. "Guanyu jianshe fangzhen an" (Proposal for reconstruction policy), March 3, 1930, ibid., part v, vol. 1, zhengzhi, no. 2, 162–164.

16. Kirby, *Germany and Republican China,* 97–98.

17. "Jingjibu jinshi gongzuo jiyao" (Work summary by the Ministry of Economic Affairs), XJ 1, no. 2 (December 1, 1938): 58–62.

18. Qian Changzhao, "Liangnianban chuangban zhonggongye zhi jingguo ji ganxiang" (The experience of and reflection on creating heavy industry for the past two and a half years), SHA 28(2)/939. See also XJ 2, no. 1 (June 16, 1939): 2–6.

19. Weng Wenhao, "Kaifa neidi" (Developing the interior), *Jingji dongyuan* (Economic mobilization) 2, no. 4 (January 31, 1939): 217–218.

20. Weng Wenhao, "Guoying zhonggongye de yiyi yu renshi tongren de zeren" (The meaning of state-owned heavy industry and the responsibility of fellow comrades), 1942, ZWG 3, no. 2 (August 16, 1942): 75–80.

21. Weng Wenhao, "Zhongguo jingji jianshe gailun" (Survey of Chinese economic reconstruction), in ZJJL, 81–82.

22. Weng's preference for state-owned enterprise is reflected in his inclination to

deny the existence of a well-defined boundary between state and private ownership. In explaining the meaning of the concept *state ownership* in January 1943, Weng quoted Sun Yatsen as saying that "the state belongs to the people, thus state ownership is no different from private ownership." See Weng Wenhao, "Weng buzhang dui guilin bushu jiguan renyuan xunci" (Weng Wenhao's speech to his subordinates in Guilin), November 2, 1933, ZWG 5, no. 5 (November 16, 1943): 49–52; "Zhongguo jingji jianshe gailun."

23. Sun Ke (Sun Fo), "China's War and Peace Aims, November 2, 1940, in *China Looks Forward* (New York: John Day Co., 1944), 42–43. I changed "Min-Sheng-Zhu-I" in the English translation to "The Doctrine of People's Livelihood."

24. The list of commodities to be marketed by state-owned enterprises was long, including foodstuff, rice, wheat, salt, clothing, linen, silk, and cigarette and liquor. See Sun Ke, "Jianguo bixu fada guoying shiye" (We must develop state-owned enterprise for nation building), December 16, 1940, in SKW, 654–677.

25. Sun Ke, "Zhongguo jingji jianshe zhi jiben wenti" (The fundamental problems of Chinese economic reconstruction), September 8, 1942, in ibid., 677–690.

26. Sun Ke, "Zhengzhi minzhuhua, jingji jihuahua" (Creating political democracy and a planned economic system), February 23, 1944, in ibid., 157–165.

27. Shi Weixin, "Guojia ziben jianshelun" (On developing state capital), *Jianshe* (Reconstruction), no. 16 (December 1934): 5–44.

28. Wu Bannong, "Zhanshi gongye jianshe wenti" (Problems of wartime industrial reconstruction), *Shishi leibian* (Current affairs), no. 20 (August 16, 1938): 10–14.

29. Wu Bannong, *Guoying shiye de fanwei wenti* (The Scope of state-owned enterprise) (Chongqing: Zhongguo wenhua fuwushe, 1941), 10.

30. Ibid., 29–33.

31. "Zhongyang shejiju xianzhi renyuan jianlice" (Personnel roster of Central Planning Board), February 1943, SHA 171/45.

32. Chen Bozhuang, *Jingjian wulun* (Five essays on economic reconstruction) (Chongqing: Zhongguo jingji jianshe xiehui, 1943), 5–6, 40–42.

33. Sun Yatsen, *International Development of China*, 197.

34. Chef, ed., *San Min Chu I: The Three Principles of the People*, 441.

35. Weng Wenhao, "Kangzhan yilai zhi jingji jianshe" (Economic reconstruction since the outbreak of resistance war against Japan), March 1940, CMA jingjilei, file no. 714, 1–14.

36. Weng Wenhao, "Three Years of Economic Reconstruction," *China Quarterly* 5, no. 4 (Autumn 1940): 566–569.

37. Weng Wenhao, "Zhanshi jingji jianshe" (Wartime economic reconstruction), 1941, CMA jingjilei, file no. 706, 1–21.

38. Qian Changzhao, "Zhonghua minguo zai guojijian yingyou de diwei" (The status Republican China deserves within the community of nations), January 21, 1942, ZWG 2, no. 1 (January 16, 1942): 83–91.

39. Weng Wenhao, "Guoying zhonggongye de yiyi yu renshi tongren de zeren" (The meaning of state-owned heavy industry and the responsibility of fellow comrades), 1942, ZWG 3, no. 2 (August 16, 1942): 75–80.

40. Sun Ke, "Zhongguo jingji jianshe zhi jiben wenti" (The fundamental problems of Chinese economic reconstruction), September 8, 1942, in SKW, 677–690.

41. Scholars often used the concepts of *controlled economic system* and *planned economic system* during the 1930s. Although they recognized the different meaning and emphasis of the phrases, they generally used them indiscriminately or as interchangeable concepts. See Fang Xianting, "Tongzhi jingji yu zhongguo" (Controlled economic system and China), in ZJY, 57; Luo Dunwei, *Zhongguo tongzhi jingijlun* (On controlled economic system in China) (Shanghai: Xin shengming shuju, 1934), 11–3; Ma Yinchu, *Zhongguo jingji gaizao* (China's economic transformation) (Shanghai: Shangwu yinshuguan, 1935), 191–192.

42. Luo Dunwei, *Zhongguo tongzhi jingjilun*, 138.

43. Wu Bannong, "Wuoguo jingji jianshe zhi mubiao wenti" (The goal of Chinese economic reconstruction), XJ 4, no. 1 (July 1, 1940): 19–23.

44. Fang Xianting (H. D. Fong), *Toward Economic Control in China* (Tientsin: Chihli Press, 1936), 66.

45. Fang Xianting, "Shinianlai zhi zhongguo jingji jianshe" (Chinese economic reconstruction during the last decade), in ZJY, vol. 1, 71–78.

46. Fang Xianting (H. D. Fong), *The Post-War Industrialization of China* (Washington, D.C.: National Planning Association, June 1942), 78–79.

47. Jian Guansan, *Gongyehua yu shehui jianshe* (Industrialization and social reconstruction) (Shanghai: Zhonghua shuju, 1945), 59.

48. Liu Dajun, *Gongyehua yu zhongguo gongye jianshe* (Industrialization and Chinese industrial reconstruction) (Chongqing: Shangwu yinshuguan, 1944), 72–76.

49. For example, Wu Daye argued that the "reconstruction of light industry and heavy industry is complementary"; see his "Zhanhou jianshe de jingji" (Postwar economic reconstruction), which first appeared in JJJ 1, no. 3 (January 1943); in ZZJWY, 90.

50. Chen Zhenhan, "Fangren zhengce ganshe zhengce haishi jihua jingji?" (Laissez-faire policy? Interventionist policy? Or planned economic system?), *Dongfang zazhi* (The oriental journal) 31, no. 11 (August 1943), in ZZJWY, 37.

51. "Dui zhengzhi baogao zhi jueyi an" (Resolution on political report), March 27, 1929, in ZMDZH, part v, vol. 1, zhengzhi, no. 2, 75–86.

52. "Xunzheng shiqi jingji jianshe shishi gangyao fangzhen an" (Outline program for implementing economic reconstruction during the period of political tutelage), April 22, 1929, in ZMDZH, part v, vol. 1, zhengzhi, no. 2, 118–119.

53. "Guanyu jianshe fangzhen an" (Resolution on reconstruction policy), March 3, 1930, ibid., part v, vol. 1, zhengzhi, no. 2, 162–164.

54. "Yiju xunzheng shiqi yuefa guanyu guomin shengji zhi guiding queding qi shishi fangzhen an" (Resolution on the policy of improving people's livelihood and its implementation), November 17, 1931, ibid., part v, vol. 1, zhengzhi, no. 2, 324–326.

55. "Guojia jianshe chuqi fangan an" (Resolution on national reconstruction in the near future), November 21, 1931, ibid., part v, vol. 1, zhengzhi, no. 2, 337.

56. "Zhongguo jingji jianshe fangan" (Resolution on Chinese economic reconstruction), February 19, 1937, in ZMDZH, part v, vol. 1, zhengzhi, no. 2, 618–625.

57. Qian Changzhao, "Liangnianban chuangban zhonggongye zhi jingguo ji ganxiang" (The experience of and reflection on creating heavy industry for the past two and a half years), SHA 28(2)/939. See also XJ 2, no. 1 (June 16, 1939): 2–6.

58. Weng Wenhao, "Guofang jingji jianshe zhi yaoyi" (The meaning of economic reconstruction for national defense), July 25, 1941, reprinted in ZWG 1, no. 2 (August 16, 1941): 69–72.

59. Weng Wenhao, "Zhongguo jingji jianshe zhi lunkuo" (Survey of Chinese economic reconstruction), March 1942, in ZJJL, 23–40. The speech was reprinted in ZWG 3, no. 5 (November 16, 1942): 55–62.

60. Luo Dunwei, "Zhongguo tongzhi jingji wenti" (Problems of controlled economic system in China), February 1, 1936, SY 1, no. 1 (April 1936): 11–28. Italics appear in the original.

61. Luo Dunwei, "Xinan jingji jianshe yu jihua jingji" (Economic reconstruction in the southwest and the planned economic system), XST 2, no. 3 (September 1940): 5–8.

62. Fang Xianting, "Kangzhan qijian zhongguo gongye zhi moluo jiqi fuxing tujing" (The decline of Chinese industry and the means toward recovery during the resistance war), XJ 1, no. 4 (January 1, 1939): 90–96.

63. Su Jicang, "Zhanshi zhongguo gongye jianshe de tujing" (The means of industrial reconstruction in wartime China), *Zhongguo gongye* (Chinese industry) 1, no. 1 (January 25, 1942): 9–13.

64. Wu Bannong noted that "the debate on national defense and people's livelihood arose after the outbreak of the Sino-Japanese War." In his opinion, no consensus existed as of 1940. See his "Wuoguo jingji jianshe zhi mubiao wenti" (The goal of Chinese economic reconstruction), XJ 4, no. 1 (July 1, 1940): 19–23.

65. "Zhongyang shejiju xianzhi renyuan jianlice" (Personnel roster of Central Planning Board), February 1943, SHA 171/45.

66. Wu Jingchao, "Zhongguo jingji jianshe zhilu" (The path toward economic reconstruction in China), JJJ 1, no. 1 (July 1942): 14–20.

67. SZQ, vol. 1, 556.

68. Ibid., vol. 2, 405.

69. Ibid., vol. 2, 487–493.

70. ZGX, 38.

71. Sun, *International Development of China*, 10.

72. Ibid., 9, 35.

73. Ibid., 236–237.

74. Ibid., 4–5.

75. Sun Yatsen, *Fundamentals of National Reconstruction* (Taipei: Sino-American Publishing Co., 1953), 189.

76. For the numerous plans drafted before 1937, see Gideon Chen, *Chinese Government Economic Planning and Reconstruction since 1927* (Tianjin, 1933), 7–18; Kirby, *Germany and Republican China*, 99–101, 192.

77. Weng Wenhao, "Jianshe yu jihua" (Reconstruction and planning), DP, no. 5 (June 19, 1932): 9–13.

78. Weng Wenhao, "Jingji jianshezhong de jige zhongyao wenti" (Important issues in economic reconstruction), DP, no. 69 (September 24, 1933): 2–5.

79. Weng Wenhao, "China's Industrial Development and the Necessity for Foreign Cooperation," *China Quarterly* 5, no. 1 (Winter 1939): 1–11.

80. Fang Xianting (H. D. Fong), *Toward Economic Control in China*, 76–79.

81. Chen Daisun, "Jihua houfang jingji jianshe fangzhen niyi" (Policy recommendations on planning economic reconstruction in the rear area), XJ 1, no. 1 (November 16, 1938): 6–9.

82. Fang Xianting (H. D. Fong), *Toward Economic Control in China*, 5–12.

83. "Guomin jingji jianshe jihua weiyuanhui an" (Resolution on creating a national economic reconstruction planning commission), November 22, 1935, in ZMDZH, part v, vol. 1, zhengzhi, no. 2, 504–510.

84. "Zhongguo jingji jianshe fangan" (Program of Chinese economic reconstruction), February 19, 1937, in ibid., part v, vol. 1, zhengzhi, no. 2, 618–625.

85. "Zhongguo guomindang kangzhan jianguo gangling" (Program for the war of resistance and nation building), April 1, 1938, in ZMDZH, part v, vol. 2, zhengzhi, no. 1, 386–389.

86. "Zhongguo guomindang linshi daibiao dahui xunyan" (Manifesto of provisional Nationalist Party congress), April 1, 1938, in ibid., part v, vol. 2, zhengzhi, no. 1, 403–416.

87. I use the term *theory* in the sense of a system of assumptions and accepted principles devised to analyze or predict the nature or behavior of a specified set of phenomena.

88. Sun Ke, "Sun Yatsen and Soviet Russia," originally appeared in *Free China*, March 12, 1940. Quoted from Sun Ke (Sun Fo), *China Looks Forward*, 1–11.

89. Sun Ke (Sun Fo), "China's War and Peace Aims," November 2, 1940, in *China Looks Forward*, 42–43.

90. Weng Wenhao, "Jingjian fangxiang yu gongtong zeren" (The direction of economic reconstruction and our shared responsibilities), SHA 28(2)/314; XJ 6, no. 7 (January 1, 1942): 136–139.

91. Weng Wenhao, "Zhongguo jingji jianshe de qianzhan" (The prospect for Chinese economic reconstruction), JJJ 1, no. 1 (July 1942): 1–6.

92. Chiang Kaishek, *China's Destiny and Chinese Economic Theory* (New York: Yoy

Publishers, 1947), 173, 277–278. I made changes in the translation to make the terms used consistent.

93. Luo Dunwei, "Zhongguo tongzhi jingji wenti" (Problems of controlled economic system in China), February 1, 1936, SY 1, no. 1 (April 1936): 11–28.

94. Luo Dunwei, "Xinan jingji jianshe yu jihua jingji" (Economic reconstruction in the southwest and the planned economic system), XST 2, no. 3 (September 1940): 5–8.

95. Luo Dunwei, "Guofang jingji jianshe de daolu" (The path toward the reconstruction of a national defense economy), JJJ 1, no. 1 (July 1942): 38–48.

96. Huang Zuo, "Women xuyao yige zhongyang jingji jihua jigou" (We need a central economic planning organization), XJ 1, no. 11 (April 16, 1939): 281–283.

97. Hu Yuanmin, "Zhanhou jingji jianshe zhi tujing" (The path toward postwar economic reconstruction), *Jingji huibao* (Economic report) 4, no. 3 (August 1, 1941): 31–35.

98. Song Zexing, "Jingji jigou yu jihua jingji" (Economic organization and planned economic system), XJ 2, no. 6 (September 16, 1939): 138–142.

99. Chen Bozhuang, "Minsheng zhuyi de jingji zhidu" (The economic system based on the Doctrine of People's Livelihood), XJ 10, no. 1 (November 1, 1943): 2–4.

100. Xu Deheng, "Jihua jingji yu zhongguo shehui" (Planned economic system and Chinese society), SJJ 1, no. 4 (September 15, 1944): 14–31.

101. Zhang Youjiang, "Lun minsheng zhuyi de jingji zhengce" (On the economic policy of the Doctrine of People's Livelihood), *Shishi leibian* (Current affairs), no. 60 (February 10, 1941): 18–23.

102. Weng Wenhao, "Zhanhou zhongguo gongyehua wenti" (Problems of postwar industrialization in China), January 943, in ZJJL, 41–47.

103. Weng Wenhao, "Zhongguo jingji jianshe gailun" (Survey of Chinese economic reconstruction), January 1943, in ibid., 49–88.

104. Qian Changzhao, "Zhonggongye jianshe de xianzai ji jianglai" (The present and future of heavy industrial reconstruction), XJ 7, no. 6 (June 16, 1942); reprinted in ZWG 3, no. 3 (September 16, 1942): 49–54.

105. Shi Fuliang, "Zhongguo jingji de qiantu yu zhongguo renmin de juewu" (The future of the Chinese economy and the awakening of the Chinese people), SJJ 1, no. 2 (March 15, 1944): 1–9.

106. Shi Fuliang, "Zhanhou zhongguo yingcaiqu de jingji zhengce" (The economic policy China should adopt during the postwar period), SJJ 1, no. 4 (September 15, 1944): 1–13.

107. Qi Zhilu, "Xinjingji yibaiershiqi zhongyao jingji lunwen neirong zongfenxi" (An analysis of the content of important economic essays published in the 120 issues of *New Economy*), XJ 10, no. 12 (October 1, 1944): 236–251.

108. These procedures were similar to the one actually used in drafting the First Five-Year Plan from 1944 to 1945. See Jian Guansan, *Gongyehua yu shehui jianshe* (Industrialization and social reconstruction) (Shanghai: Zhonghua

shuju, 1945), 89, 94, 102; Fang Xianting (H. D. Fong), *Reminiscences of a Chinese Economist at 70*, 70–72.

109. Gu Chunfan, *Zhongguo gongyehua jihualun* (Planning and China's industrialization) (Chongqing: Shehui jingji chubanshe, 1945), 41–42.

Conclusion

1. Tetsuji Okazaki and Masahiro Okuno-Fujiwara, eds., *The Japanese Economic System and Its Historical Origins* (New York: Oxford University Press, 1999), 2, 14.

2. Mark Harrison, ed., *The Economics of World War II: Six Great Powers in International Comparison* (Cambridge, UK: Cambridge University Press, 1998).

3. Paul S. Garner, *Evolution of Cost Accounting to 1925* (Birmingham: University of Alabama Press, 1954), 343; H. Thomas Johnson, "Toward a New Understanding of Nineteenth-Century Cost Accounting," *Accounting Review* 56, no. 3 (July 1981): 510–518.

4. H. Thomas Johnson and Robert S. Kaplan, *Relevance Lost: The Rise and Fall of Management Accounting* (Boston, Mass.: Harvard Business School Press, 1991), 47–48.

5. Chandler, *Visible Hand*, 464–465.

6. Johnson and Kaplan, *Relevance Lost*, 12.

7. Many technocrats in management positions received education and training in universities and factories in Europe and the United States. As a result, they were instrumental in the transfer of management technology such as cost accounting. As noted in Chapter 4, Zhang Jun, the principal architect of the cost accounting system of the National Resources Commission, received college education in the United States. For another example, the National Resources Commission sent a trainee to the Tennessee Valley Authority in 1943. Part of his responsibility was to study "the installation of both the general and cost accounting system." His report includes careful description and analysis of TVA's accounting system. See ZWJRFSS, vol. 2, 2097–2164.

8. While the Sino-Japanese War witnessed an unprecedented expansion of state-owned enterprise, private enterprise suffered a serious blow. In fact, "the war had greatly weakened the capitalists." See Parks M. Coble, *Chinese Capitalists in Japan's New Order: The Occupied Lower Yangzi, 1937–1945* (Berkeley: University of California Press, 2003), 212.

9. William C. Kirby, "Continuity and Change in Modern China: Economic Planning on the Mainland and on Taiwan, 1943–1958," *Australian Journal of Chinese Affairs* 24 (1990): 121–141; Kirby, "Engineering China: Birth of the Developmental State, 1928–1937," in *Becoming Chinese: Passages to Modernity and Beyond*, 137–160; Joseph W. Esherick, "Ten Theses on the Chinese Revolution," *Modern China* 21, no. 1 (January 1995): 45–76, "War and Revolution: Chinese Society during the 1940s," *Twentieth-Century China* 27, no. 1 (November 2001): 1–37.

10. Lu Feng, "The Origins and Formation of the Unit *(Danwei)* System," *Chinese Sociology and Anthropology* 25: 3 (spring 1993): 1–91. For details, see his Chinese article, "Zhongguo danwei zhidu de qiyuan he xingcheng" (The origins and formation of China's *danwei* system), *Zhongguo shehui kexue jikan* (Chinese social science quarterly), no. 11 (1993): 66–87.

11. *Kunming jichuangchang zhi* (Survey of Kunming Machine Works, 1936–1989) (Kunming: Yunnan guofang yinshuachang, n. d.), 7–15.

Index